D0129577

Hana-Kimi

For You in Full Blossom

story and art by
HISAYA NAKAJO

HANA-KIMI
For You in Full Blossom
VOLUME 17

STORY & ART BY HISAYA NAKAJO

Translation & English Adaptation/David Ury
Touch-Up Art & Lettering/Primary Graphix
Design/Izumi Evers
Editor/Jason Thompson

Managing Editor/Megan Bates
Editorial Director/Elizabeth Kawasaki
Editor in Chief/Alvin Lu
Sr. Director of Acquisitions/Rika Inouye
Sr. VP of Marketing/Liza Coppola
Exec. VP of Sales & Marketing/John Easum
Publisher/Hyoe Narita

Hanazakari no Kimitachi he by Hisaya Nakajo © Hisaya Nakajo 2001
All rights reserved. First published in Japan in 2002 by HAKUSENSHA, Inc., Tokyo.
English language translation rights in America and Canada arranged with
HAKUSENSHA, Inc., Tokyo. New and adapted artwork and text © 2007 VIZ Media, LLC.
The HANA-KIMI logo is a trademark of VIZ Media, LLC. The stories, characters and
incidents mentioned in this publication are entirely fictional.

No portion of this book may be reproduced or transmitted in any form or by any means
without written permission from the copyright holders.

Printed in the U.S.A.

Published by VIZ Media, LLC, P.O. Box 77010, San Francisco, CA 94107

Shôjo Edition
10 9 8 7 6 5 4 3 2 1

First printing, April 2007

www.viz.com
store.viz.com

RATED T+ FOR OLDER TEEN

PARENTAL ADVISORY
HANA-KIMI is rated T+ for Older Teen and is recom-
mended for ages 16 and up. Contains strong language, sexual themes and alcohol and tobacco usage.

CONTENTS

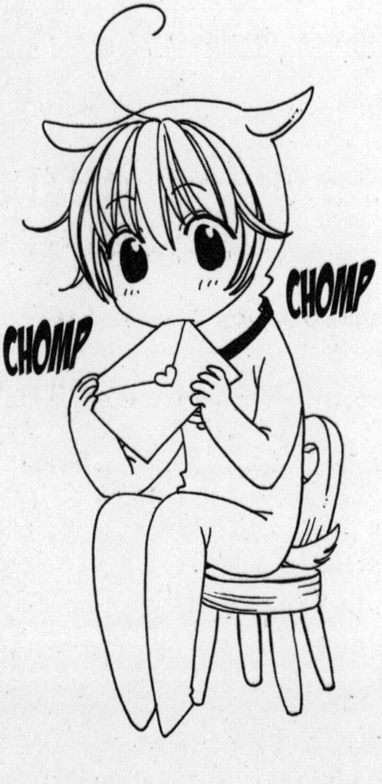
CHOMP
CHOMP

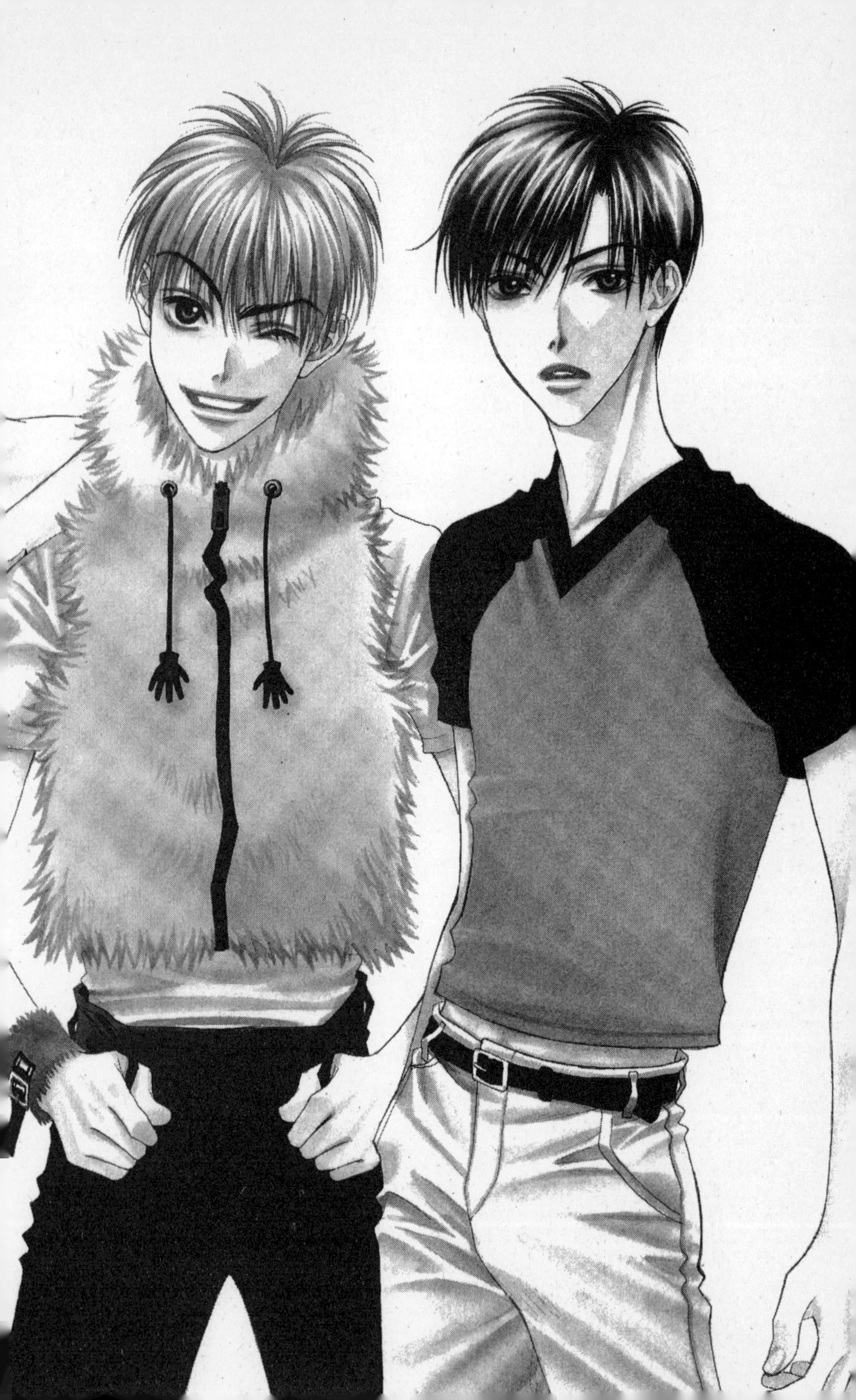

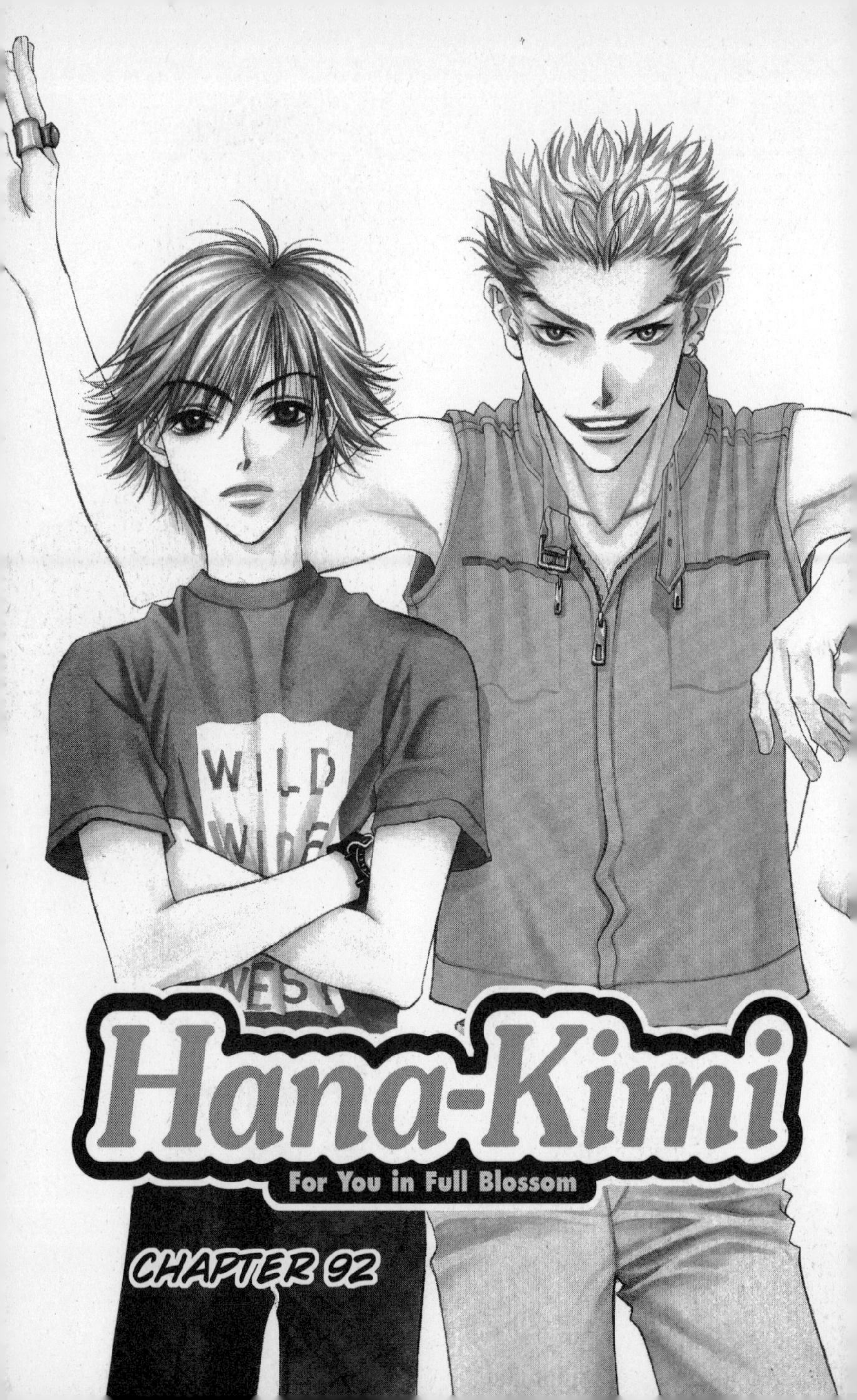
WILD
Hana-Kimi
For You in Full Blossom
CHAPTER 92

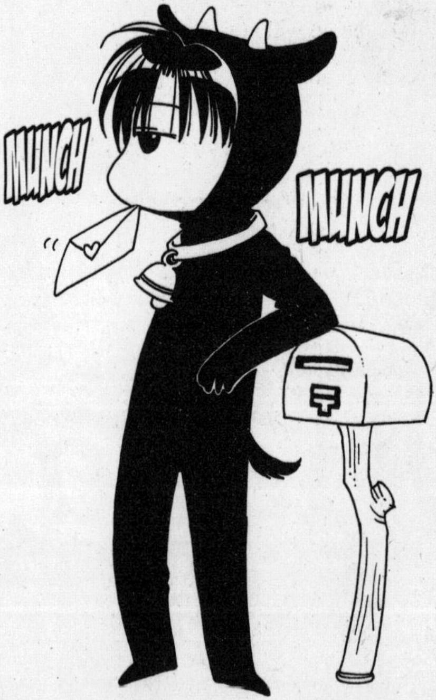
MUNCH
MUNCH

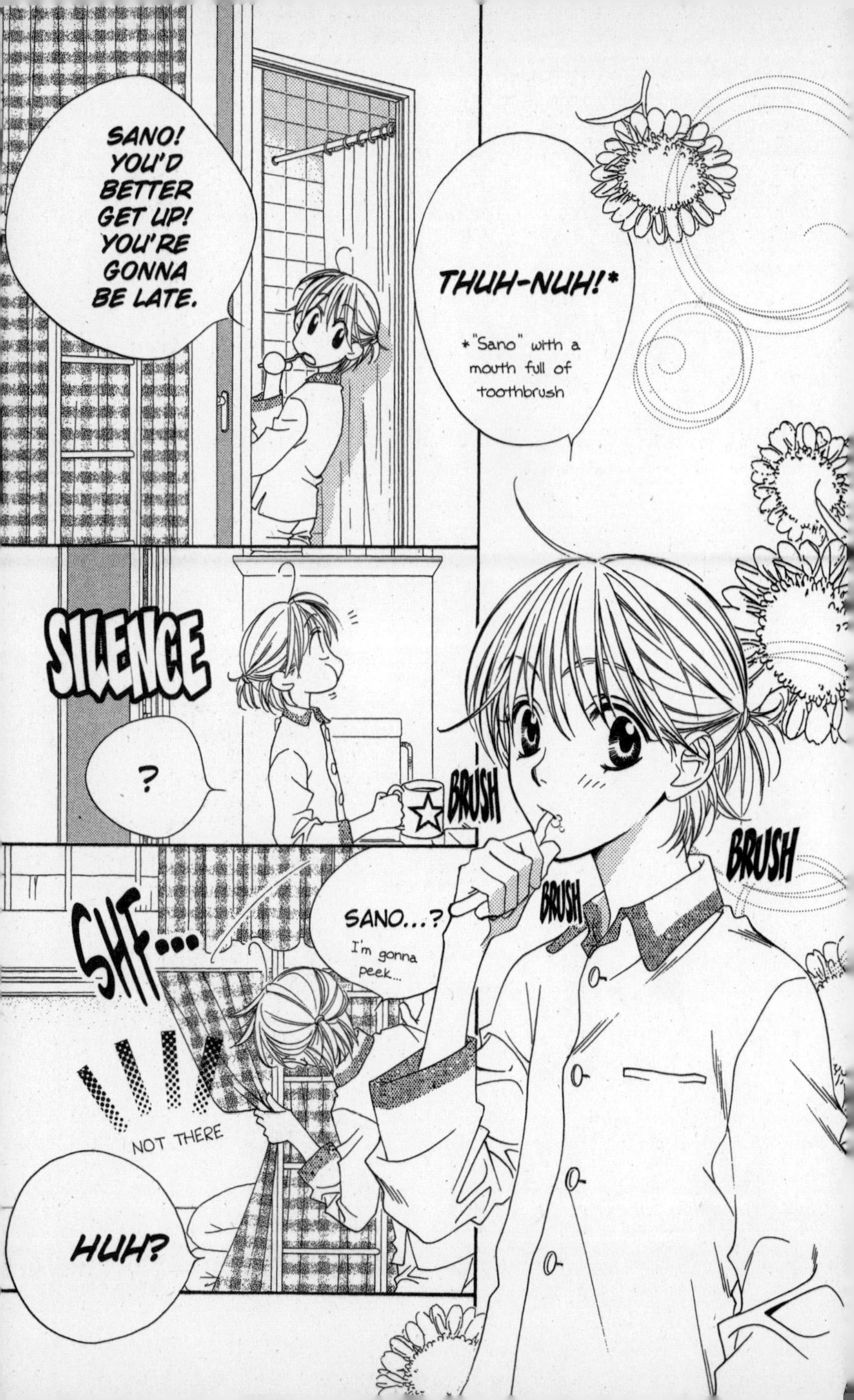
THUH-NUH!*
*"Sano" with a mouth full of toothbrush
BRUSH
BRUSH
BRUSH
SANO! YOU'D BETTER GET UP! YOU'RE GONNA BE LATE.
SILENCE
?
SANO...?
I'm gonna peek...
SHF...
NOT THERE
HUH?

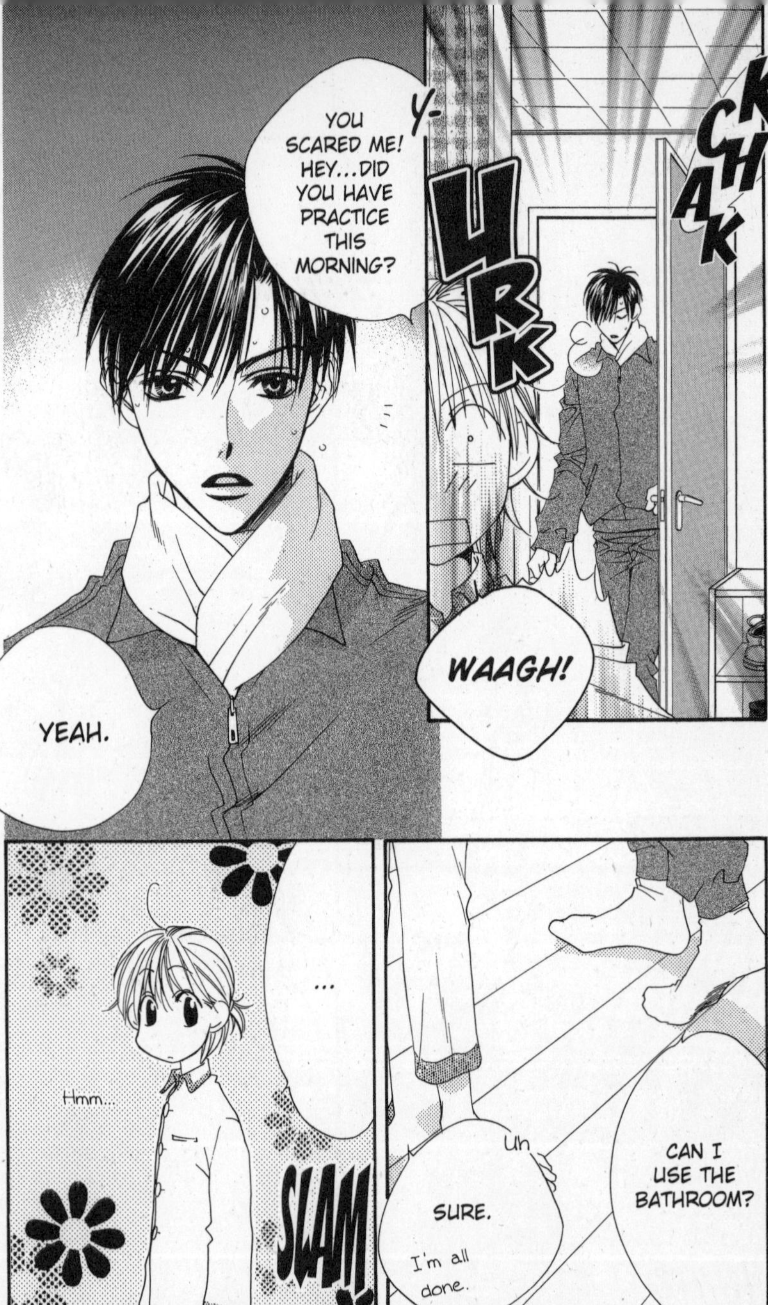
CKCHAK
HURK
WAAGH!
Y-
YOU SCARED ME! HEY...DID YOU HAVE PRACTICE THIS MORNING?
YEAH.
CAN I USE THE BATHROOM?
Uh
SURE.
I'm all done.
...
SLAM
Hmm...

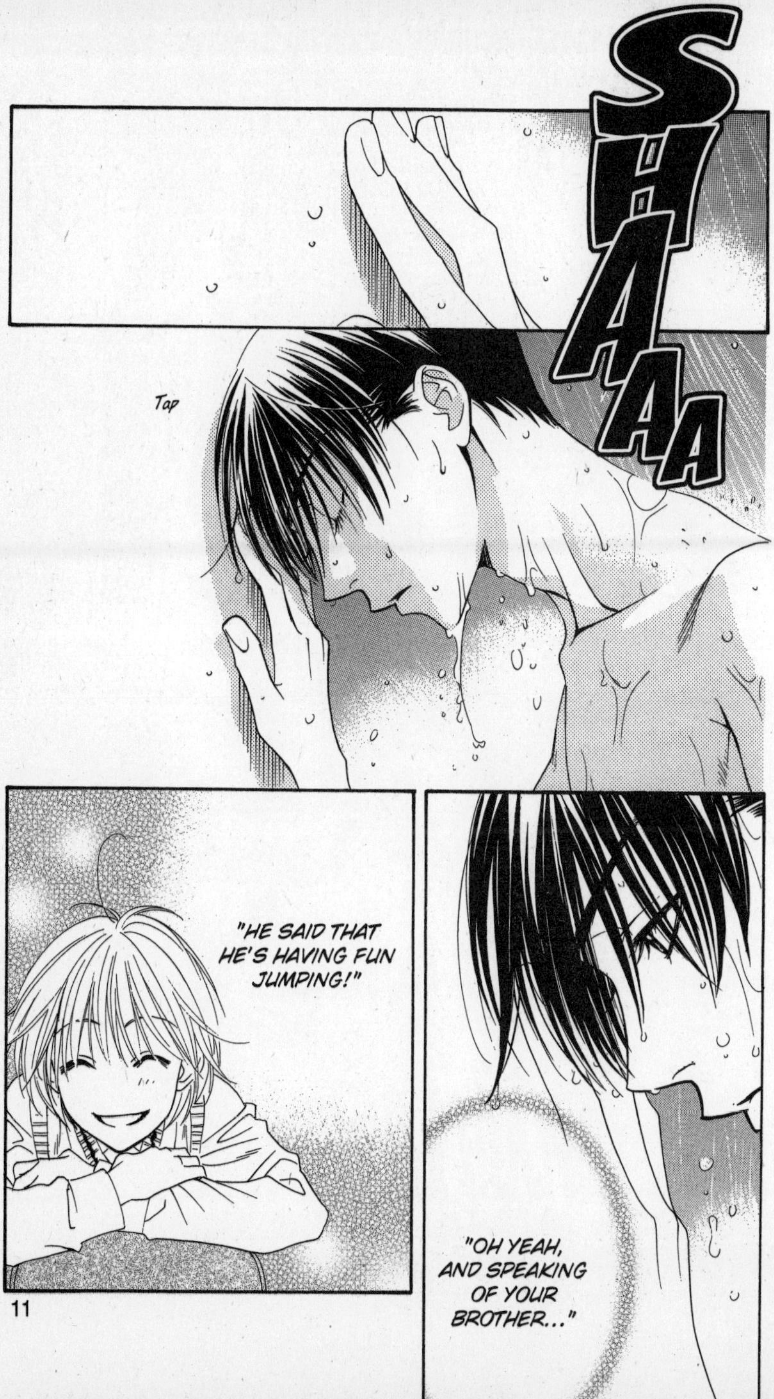
SHAAAA
Tap
"OH YEAH, AND SPEAKING OF YOUR BROTHER..."
"HE SAID THAT HE'S HAVING FUN JUMPING!"

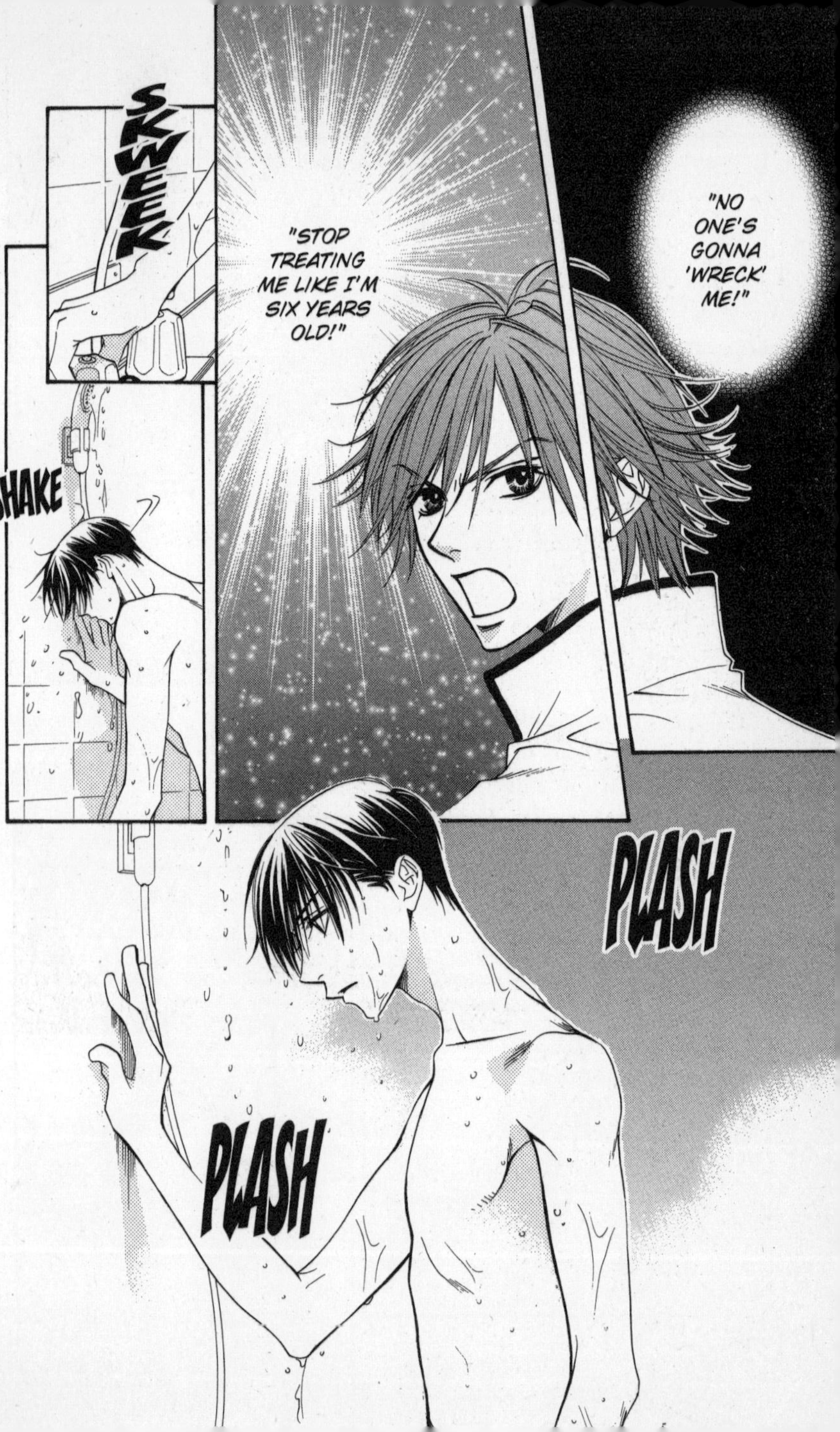
"NO ONE'S GONNA 'WRECK' ME!"
"STOP TREATING ME LIKE I'M SIX YEARS OLD!"
SKWEEK
SHAKE
PLASH
PLASH

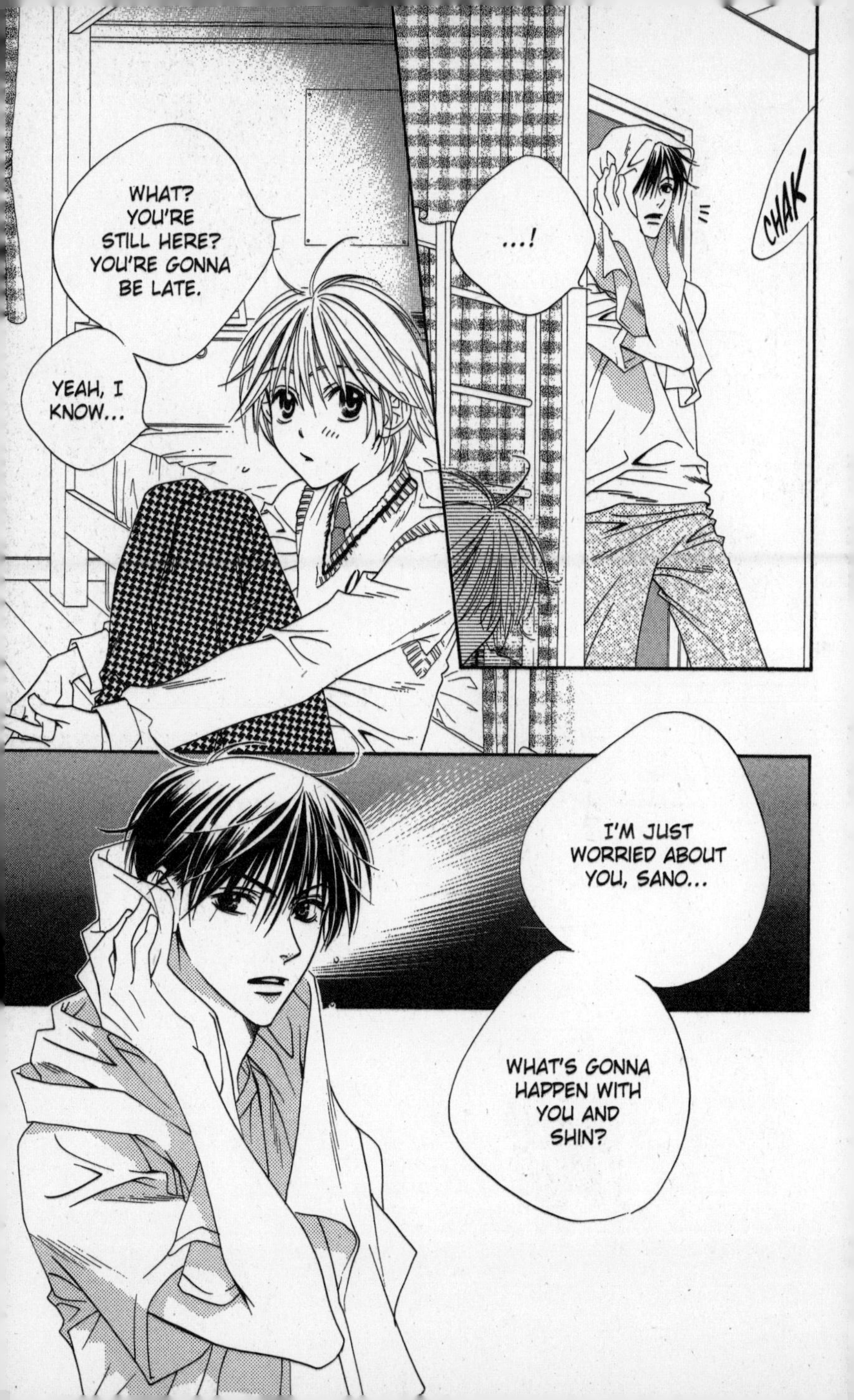
CHAK
...!
WHAT? YOU'RE STILL HERE? YOU'RE GONNA BE LATE.
YEAH, I KNOW...
I'M JUST WORRIED ABOUT YOU, SANO...
WHAT'S GONNA HAPPEN WITH YOU AND SHIN?

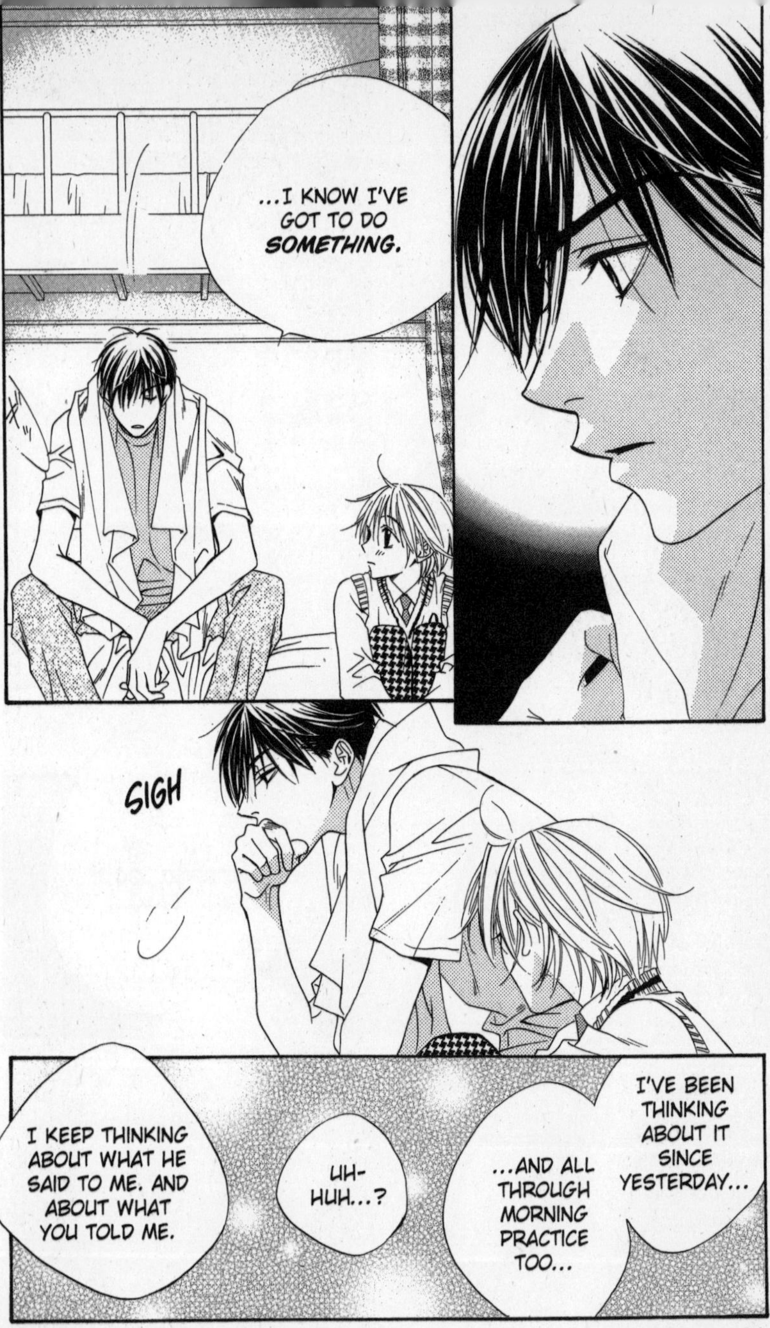
...I KNOW I'VE GOT TO DO SOMETHING.
SIGH
I'VE BEEN THINKING ABOUT IT SINCE YESTERDAY...
...AND ALL THROUGH MORNING PRACTICE TOO...
UH-HUH...?
I KEEP THINKING ABOUT WHAT HE SAID TO ME. AND ABOUT WHAT YOU TOLD ME.

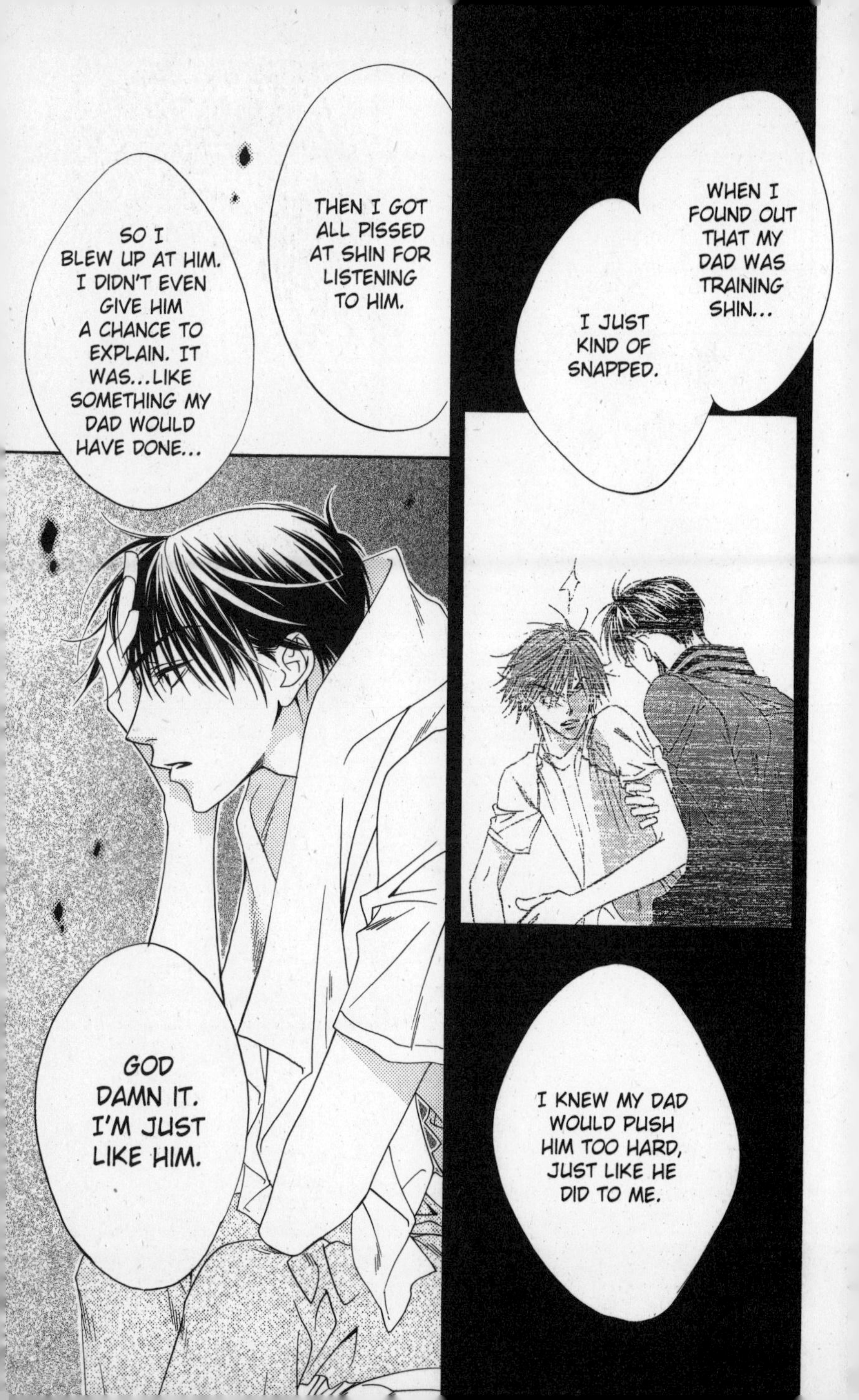
WHEN I FOUND OUT THAT MY DAD WAS TRAINING SHIN...
I JUST KIND OF SNAPPED.
I KNEW MY DAD WOULD PUSH HIM TOO HARD, JUST LIKE HE DID TO ME.
THEN I GOT ALL PISSED AT SHIN FOR LISTENING TO HIM.
SO I BLEW UP AT HIM. I DIDN'T EVEN GIVE HIM A CHANCE TO EXPLAIN. IT WAS...LIKE SOMETHING MY DAD WOULD HAVE DONE...
GOD DAMN IT. I'M JUST LIKE HIM.

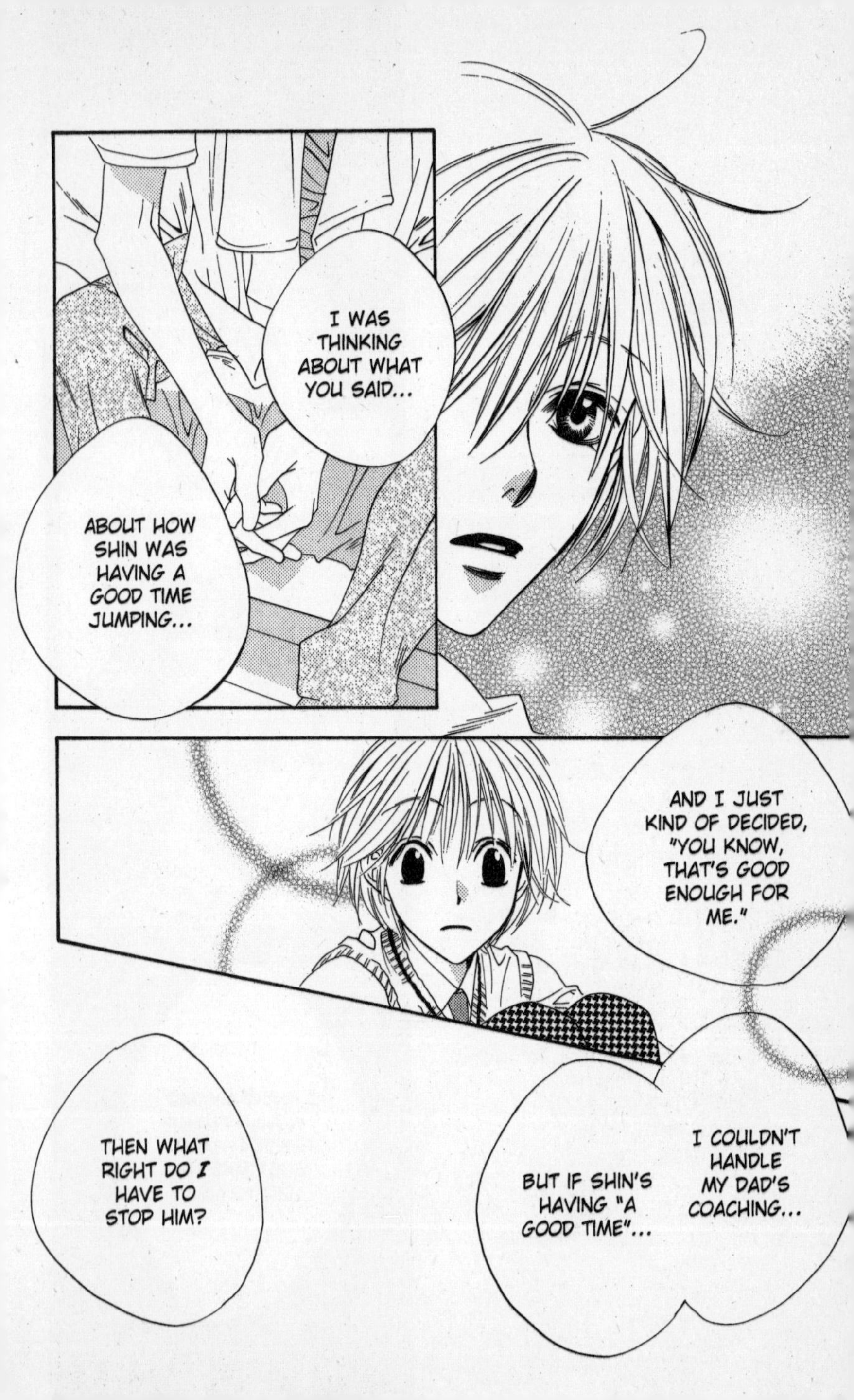
I WAS THINKING ABOUT WHAT YOU SAID...
ABOUT HOW SHIN WAS HAVING A GOOD TIME JUMPING...
AND I JUST KIND OF DECIDED, "YOU KNOW, THAT'S GOOD ENOUGH FOR ME."
I COULDN'T HANDLE MY DAD'S COACHING...
BUT IF SHIN'S HAVING "A GOOD TIME"...
THEN WHAT RIGHT DO *I* HAVE TO STOP HIM?

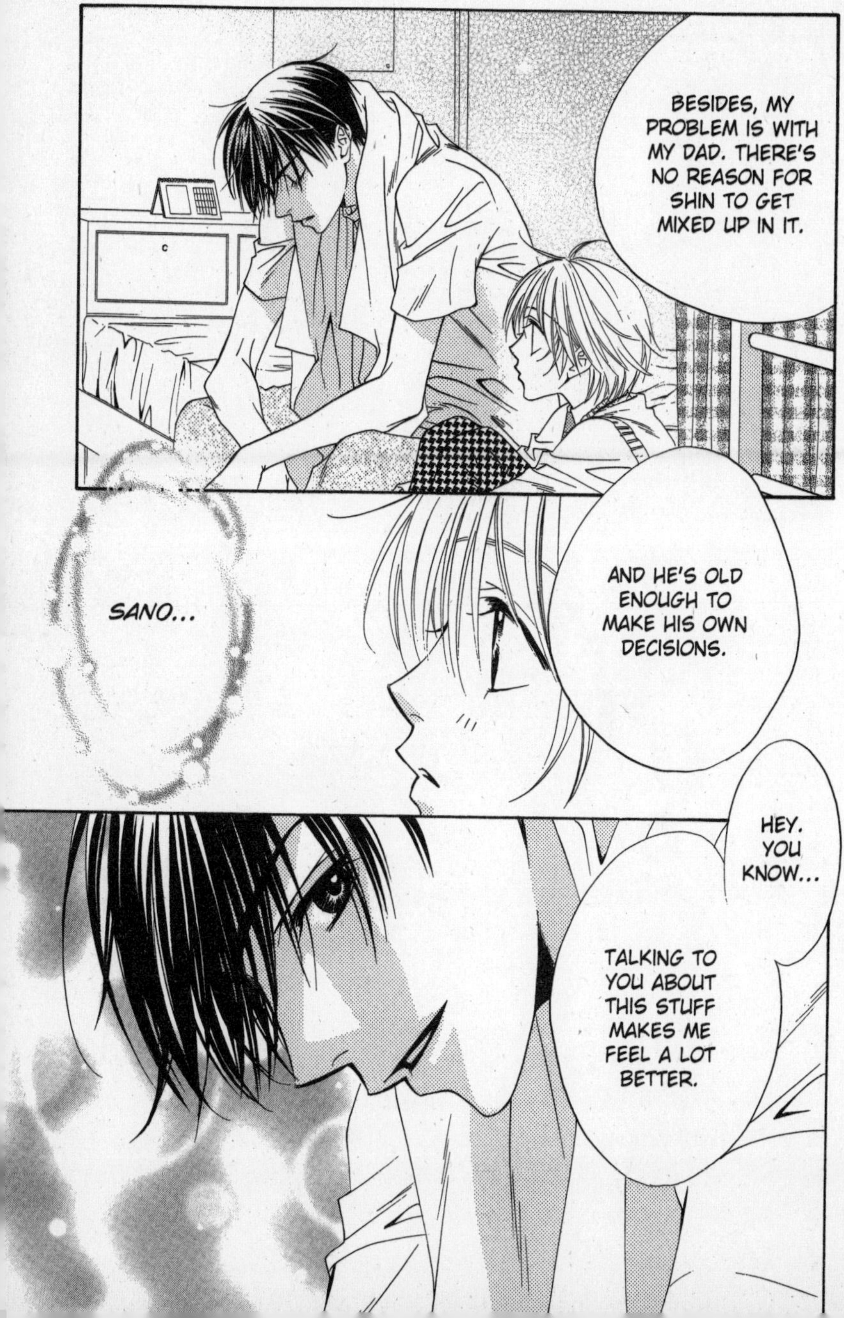
BESIDES, MY PROBLEM IS WITH MY DAD. THERE'S NO REASON FOR SHIN TO GET MIXED UP IN IT.
AND HE'S OLD ENOUGH TO MAKE HIS OWN DECISIONS.
SANO...
HEY. YOU KNOW...
TALKING TO YOU ABOUT THIS STUFF MAKES ME FEEL A LOT BETTER.

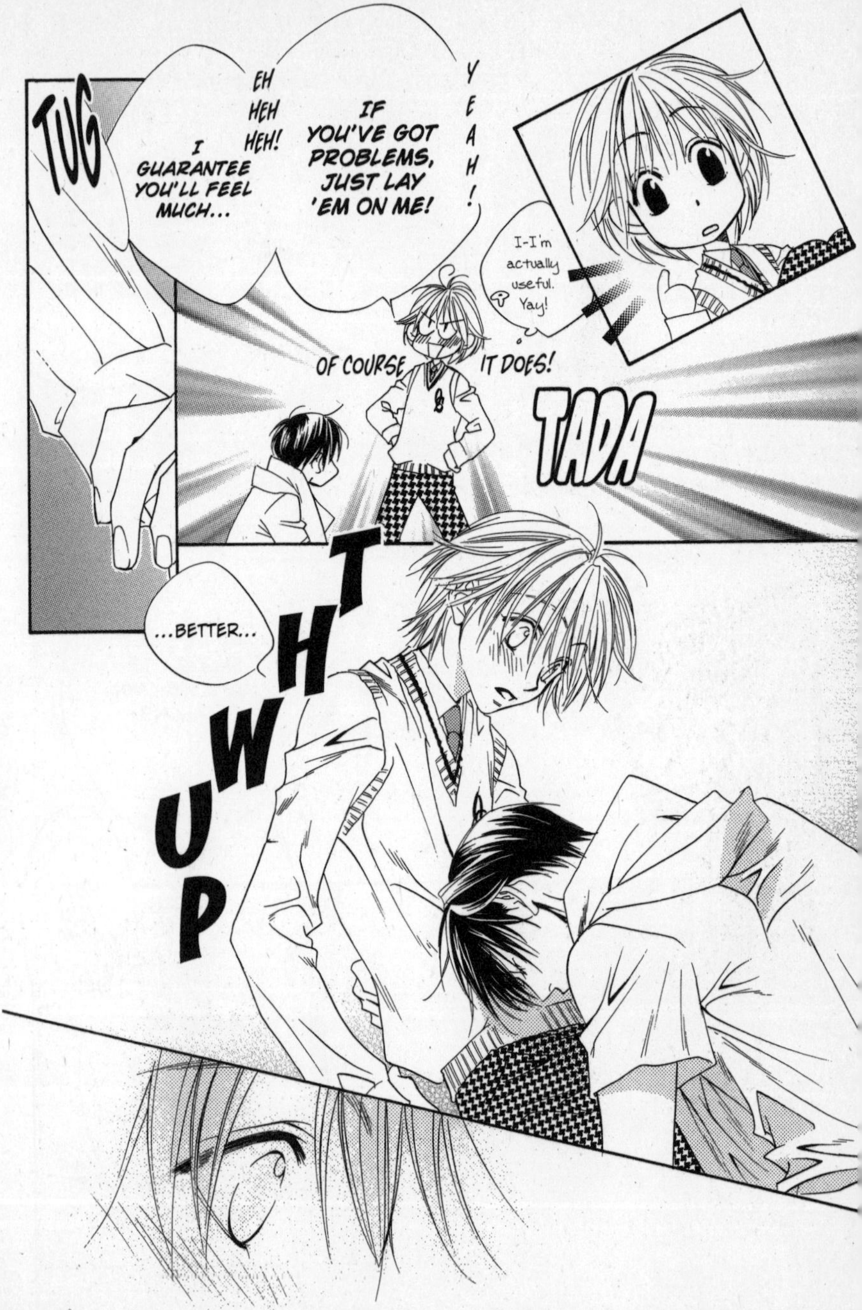
YEAH!
IF YOU'VE GOT PROBLEMS, JUST LAY 'EM ON ME!
EH HEH HEH!
OF COURSE IT DOES!
TADA
I-I'm actually useful. Yay!
TUG
I GUARANTEE YOU'LL FEEL MUCH...
...BETTER...
THWUP

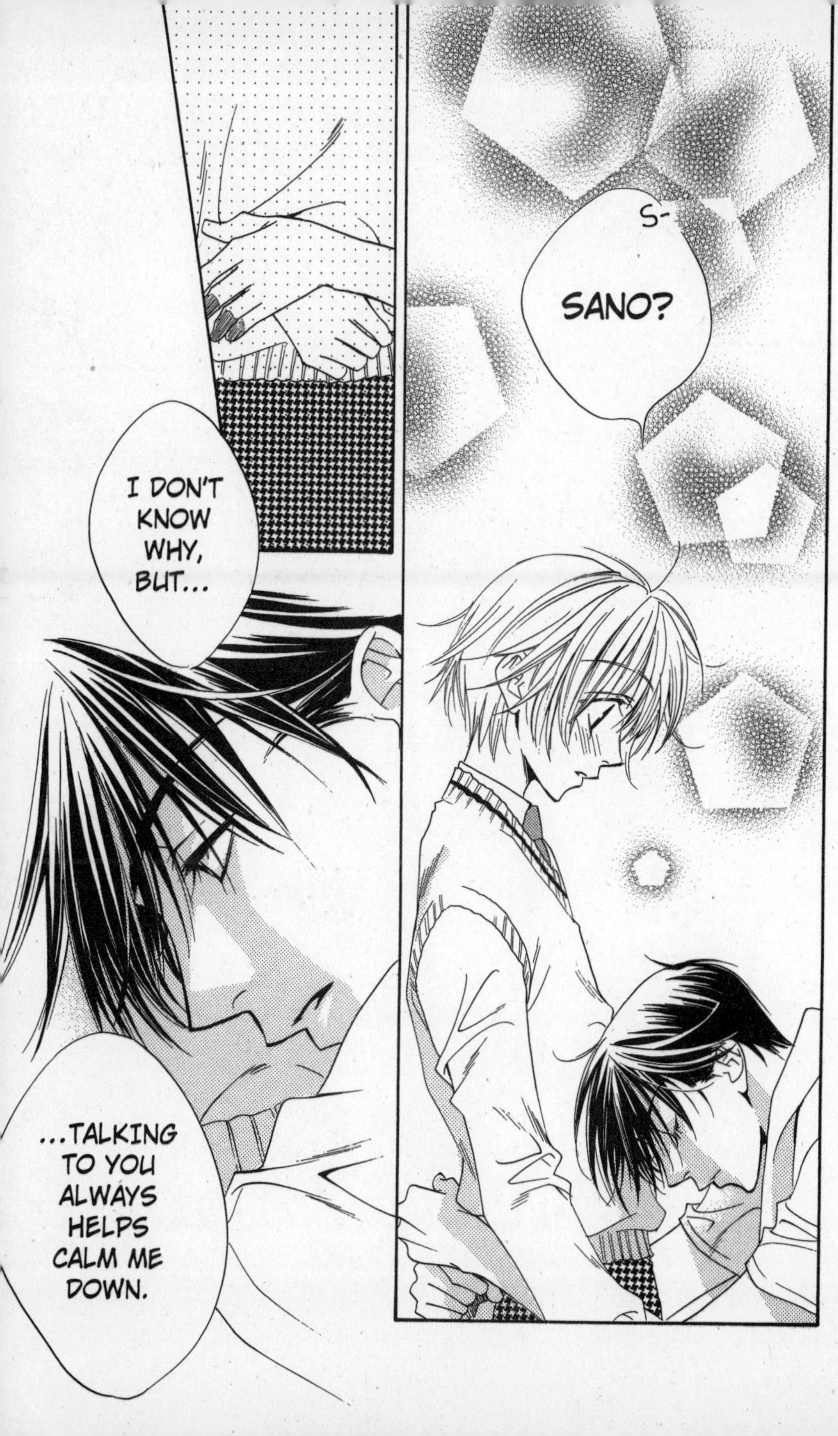
S-
SANO?
I DON'T KNOW WHY, BUT...
...TALKING TO YOU ALWAYS HELPS CALM ME DOWN.

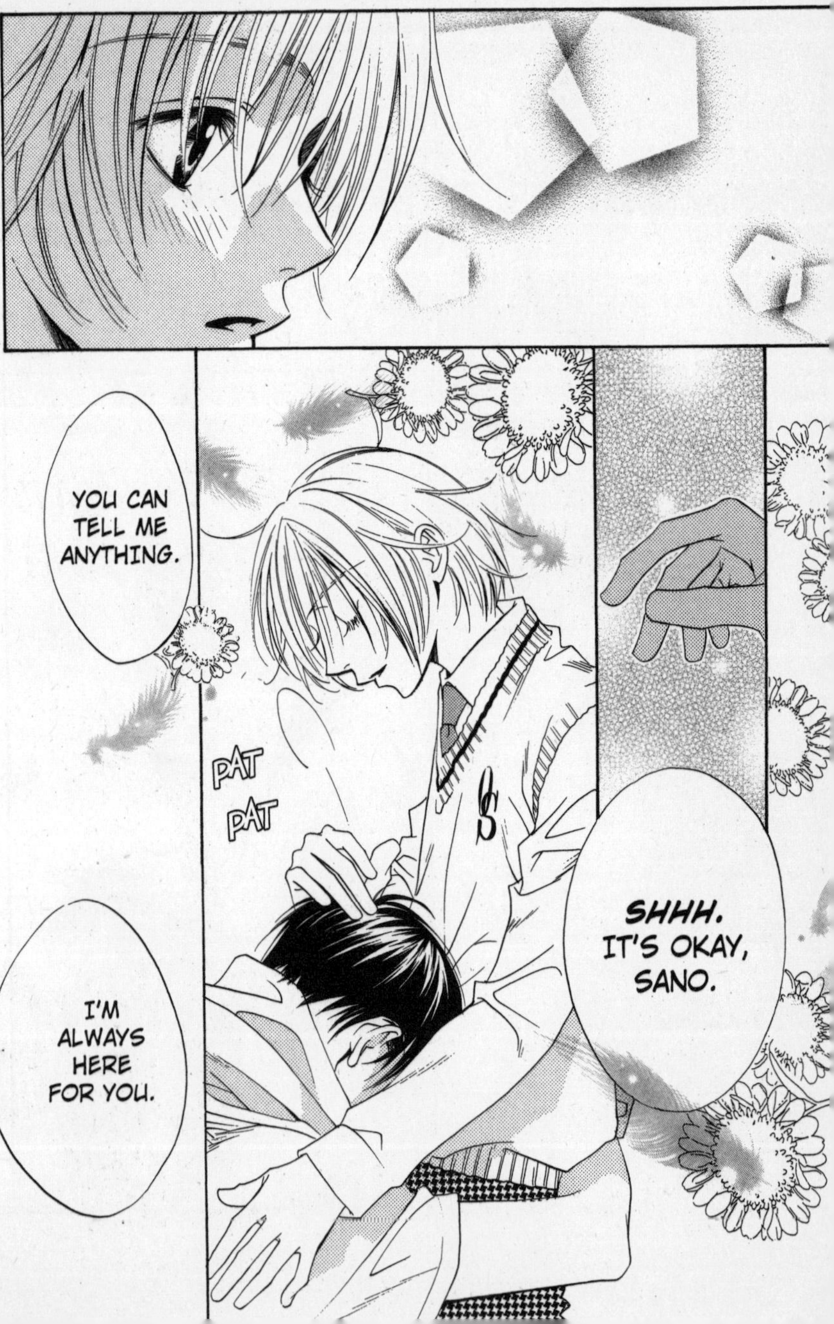
SHHH. IT'S OKAY, SANO.
PAT PAT
YOU CAN TELL ME ANYTHING.
I'M ALWAYS HERE FOR YOU.

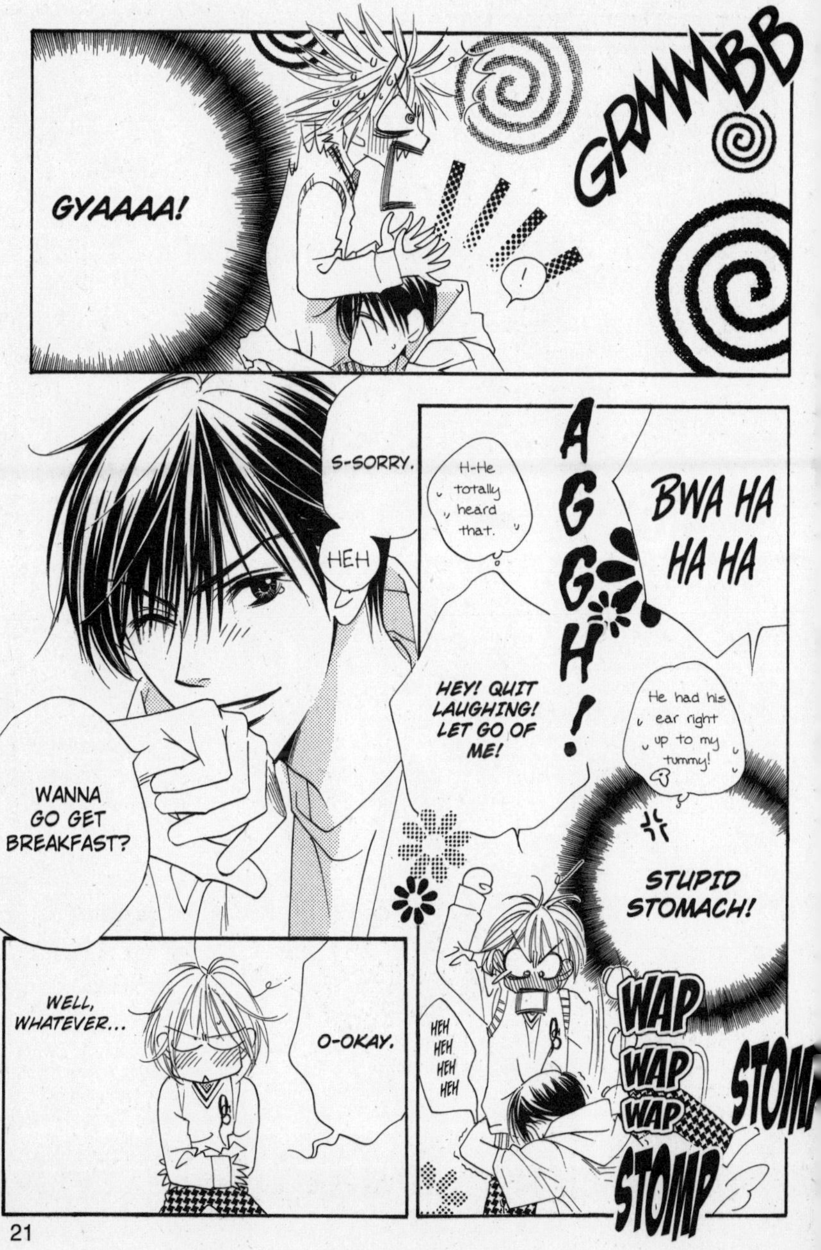

GRMMBB
GYAAAA!
!
AGGGH!
BWA HA HA HA
H-He totally heard that.
HEY! QUIT LAUGHING! LET GO OF ME!
He had his ear right up to my tummy!
STUPID STOMACH!
WAP WAP WAP
STOMP
STOMP
HEH HEH HEH HEH
S-SORRY.
HEH
WANNA GO GET BREAKFAST?
O-OKAY.
WELL, WHATEVER...

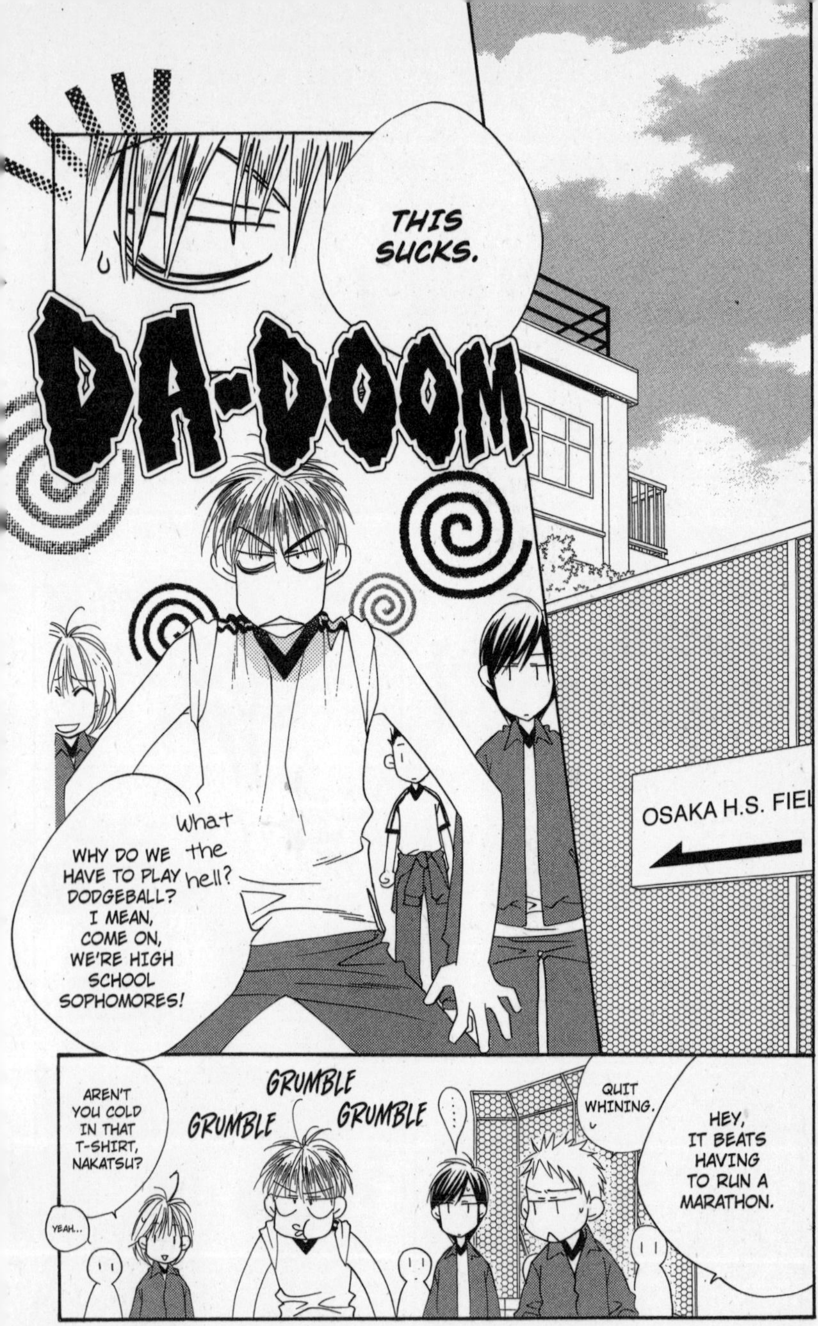
THIS SUCKS.
DA-DOOM
OSAKA H.S. FIEL
What the hell?
WHY DO WE HAVE TO PLAY DODGEBALL? I MEAN, COME ON, WE'RE HIGH SCHOOL SOPHOMORES!
HEY, IT BEATS HAVING TO RUN A MARATHON.
QUIT WHINING.
...
GRUMBLE
GRUMBLE
GRUMBLE
AREN'T YOU COLD IN THAT T-SHIRT, NAKATSU?
YEAH...

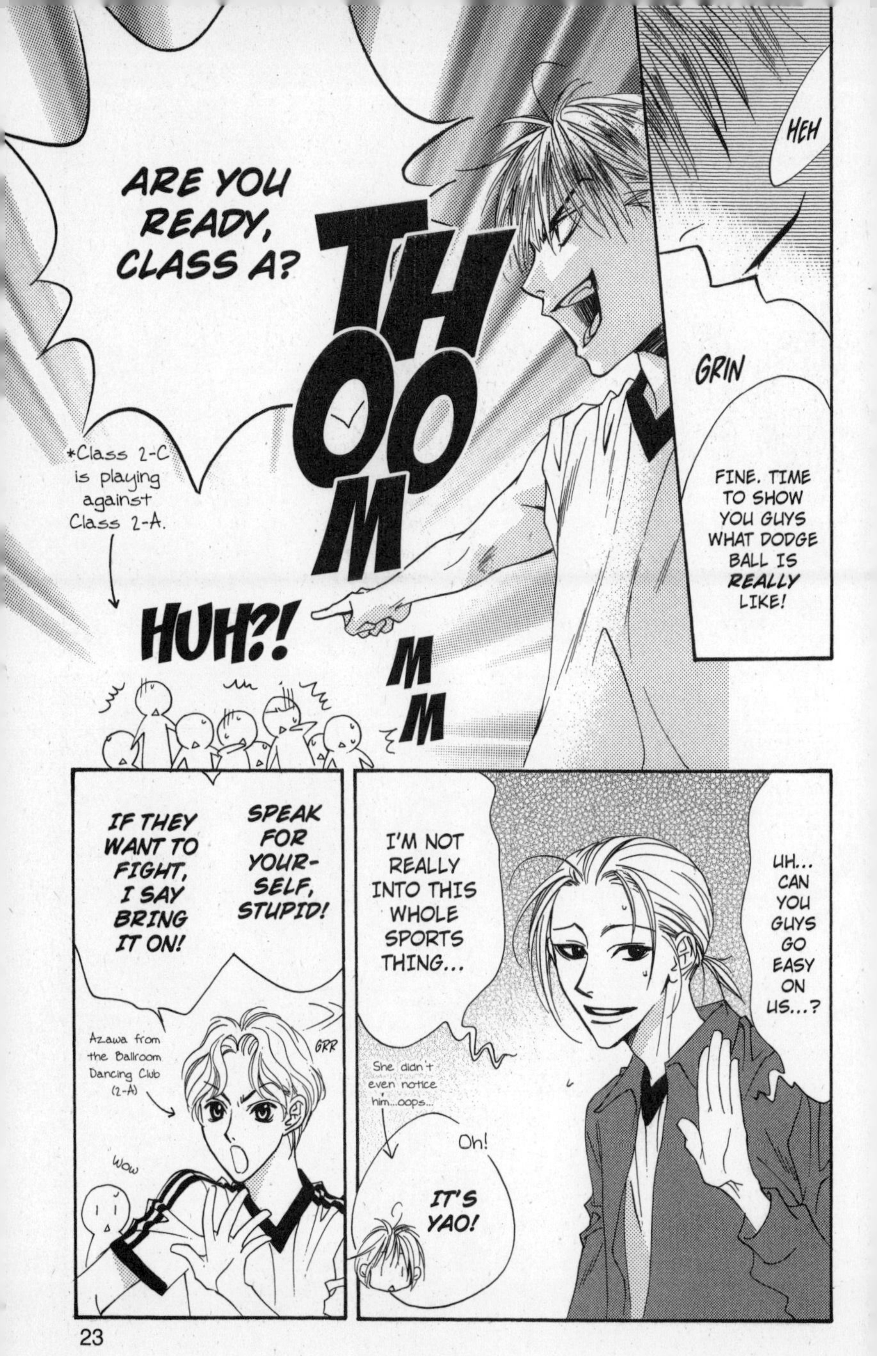
HEH
GRIN
FINE. TIME TO SHOW YOU GUYS WHAT DODGE BALL IS REALLY LIKE!
ARE YOU READY, CLASS A?
THOOM
*Class 2-C is playing against Class 2-A.
HUH?!
MMM
UH... CAN YOU GUYS GO EASY ON US...?
I'M NOT REALLY INTO THIS WHOLE SPORTS THING...
Oh!
IT'S YAO!
She didn't even notice him...oops...
SPEAK FOR YOURSELF, STUPID!
IF THEY WANT TO FIGHT, I SAY BRING IT ON!
GRR
Azawa from the Ballroom Dancing Club (2-A)
Wow

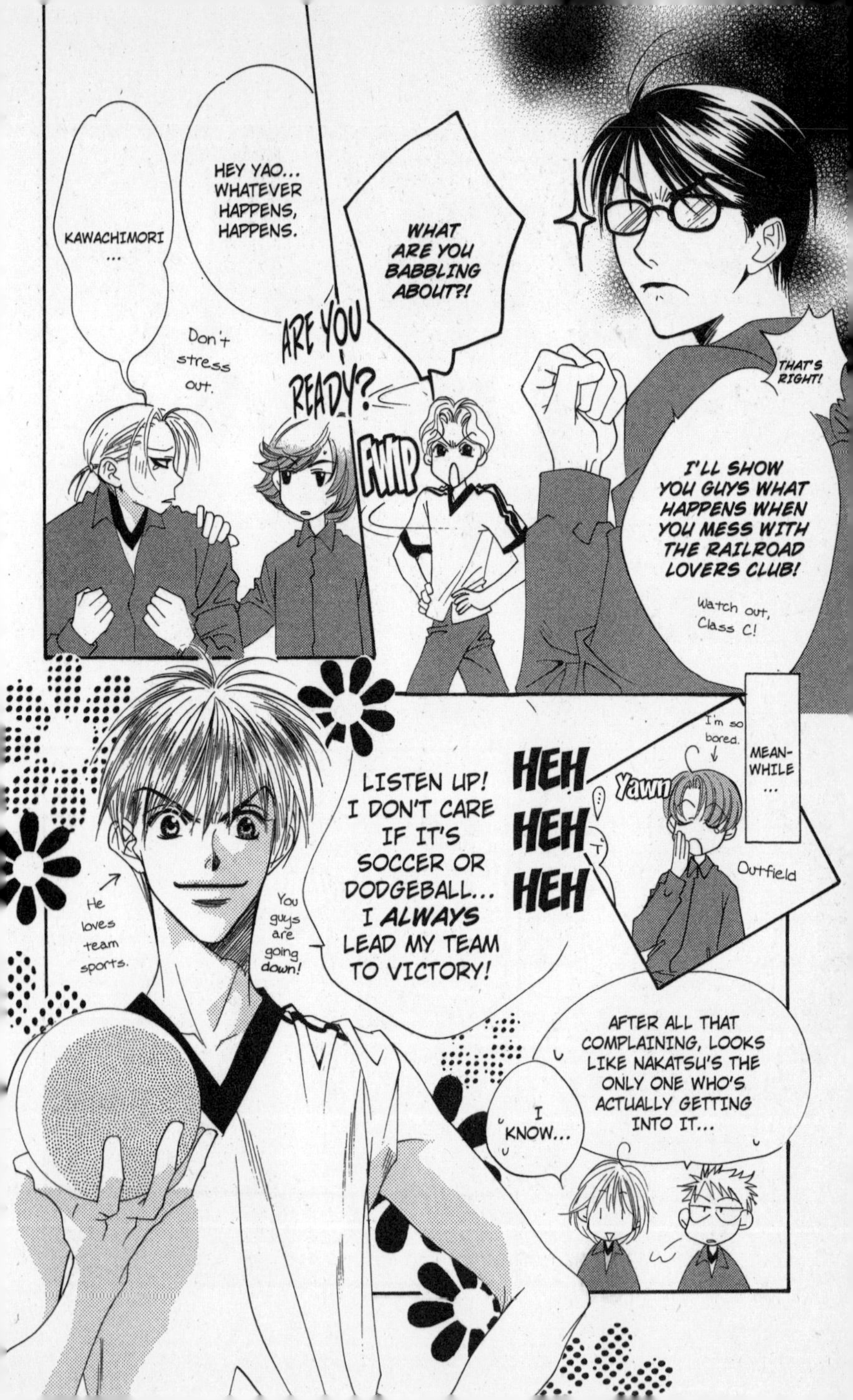
THAT'S RIGHT!
I'LL SHOW YOU GUYS WHAT HAPPENS WHEN YOU MESS WITH THE RAILROAD LOVERS CLUB!
Watch out, Class C!
WHAT ARE YOU BABBLING ABOUT?!
ARE YOU READY?
FWIP
HEY YAO... WHATEVER HAPPENS, HAPPENS.
KAWACHIMORI...
Don't stress out.
MEAN-WHILE...
I'm so bored.
Yawn
Outfield
AFTER ALL THAT COMPLAINING, LOOKS LIKE NAKATSU'S THE ONLY ONE WHO'S ACTUALLY GETTING INTO IT...
I KNOW...
HEH HEH HEH
LISTEN UP! I DON'T CARE IF IT'S SOCCER OR DODGEBALL... I ALWAYS LEAD MY TEAM TO VICTORY!
You guys are going down!
He loves team sports.

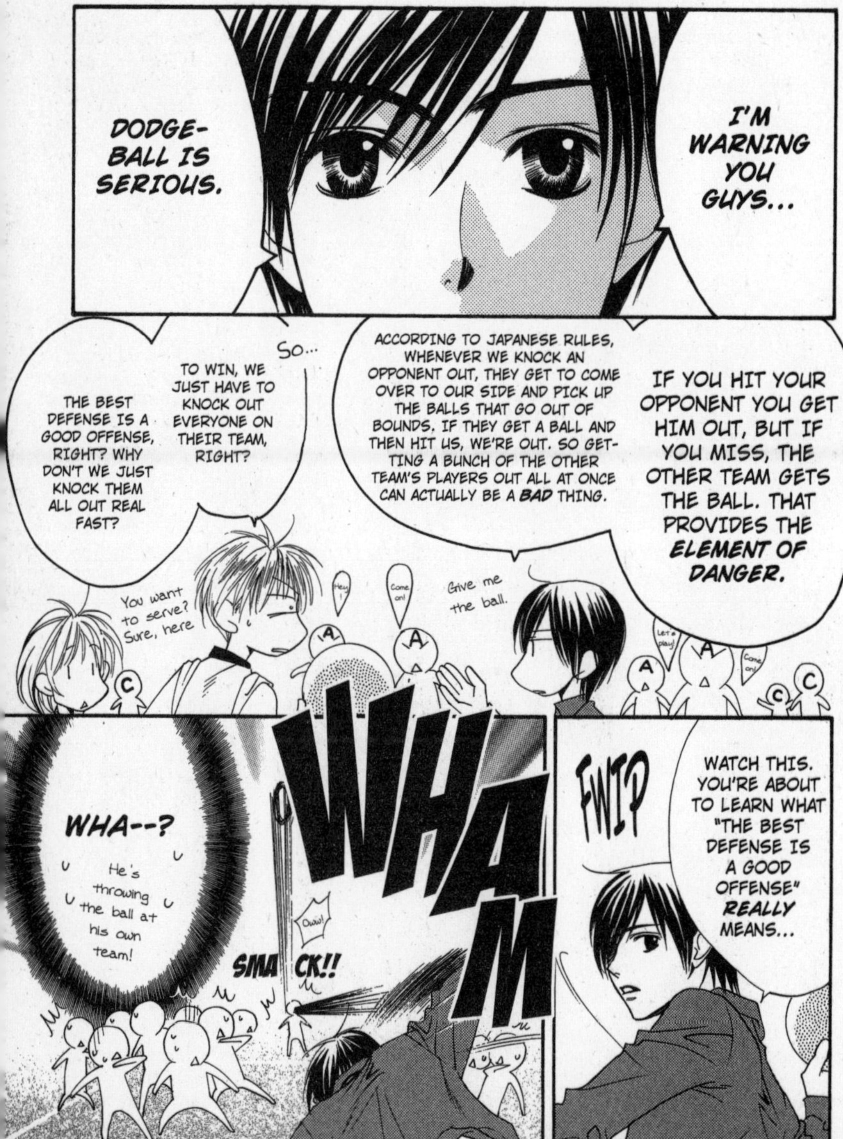
I'M WARNING YOU GUYS...
DODGE-BALL IS SERIOUS.
IF YOU HIT YOUR OPPONENT YOU GET HIM OUT, BUT IF YOU MISS, THE OTHER TEAM GETS THE BALL. THAT PROVIDES THE ELEMENT OF DANGER.
ACCORDING TO JAPANESE RULES, WHENEVER WE KNOCK AN OPPONENT OUT, THEY GET TO COME OVER TO OUR SIDE AND PICK UP THE BALLS THAT GO OUT OF BOUNDS. IF THEY GET A BALL AND THEN HIT US, WE'RE OUT. SO GETTING A BUNCH OF THE OTHER TEAM'S PLAYERS OUT ALL AT ONCE CAN ACTUALLY BE A BAD THING.
So...
TO WIN, WE JUST HAVE TO KNOCK OUT EVERYONE ON THEIR TEAM, RIGHT?
THE BEST DEFENSE IS A GOOD OFFENSE, RIGHT? WHY DON'T WE JUST KNOCK THEM ALL OUT REAL FAST?
Come on!
Let's play!
Give me the ball.
Come on!
Hey!
You want to serve? Sure, here
FWIP
WATCH THIS. YOU'RE ABOUT TO LEARN WHAT "THE BEST DEFENSE IS A GOOD OFFENSE" REALLY MEANS...
WHAM
Oww!
SMACK!!
WHA--?
He's throwing the ball at his own team!

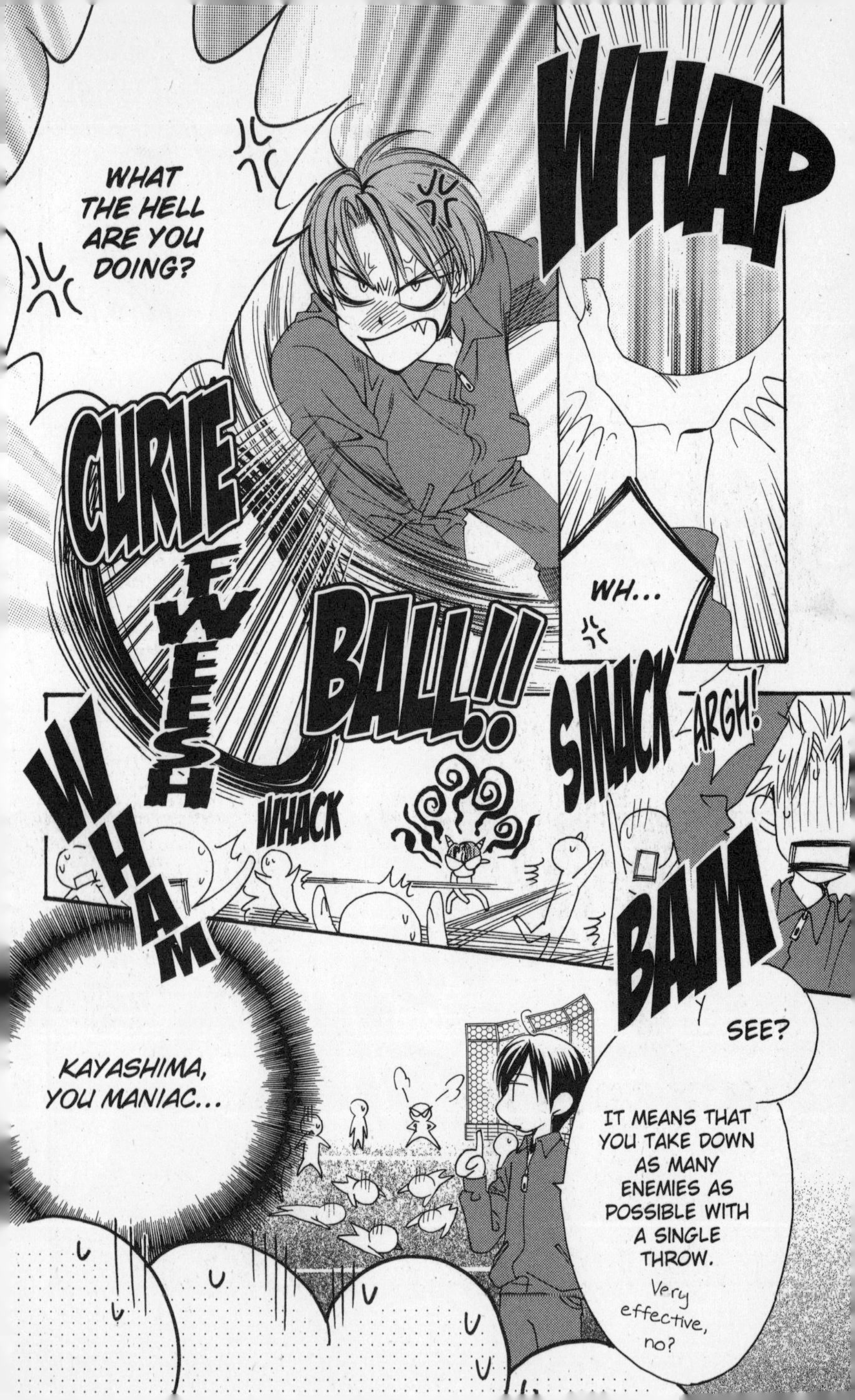
WHAP
WHAT THE HELL ARE YOU DOING?
CURVE
BALL!!
WH...
SMACK
ARGH!
SWEESH
WHACK
WHAM
BAM
SEE?
IT MEANS THAT YOU TAKE DOWN AS MANY ENEMIES AS POSSIBLE WITH A SINGLE THROW.
Very effective, no?
KAYASHIMA, YOU MANIAC...

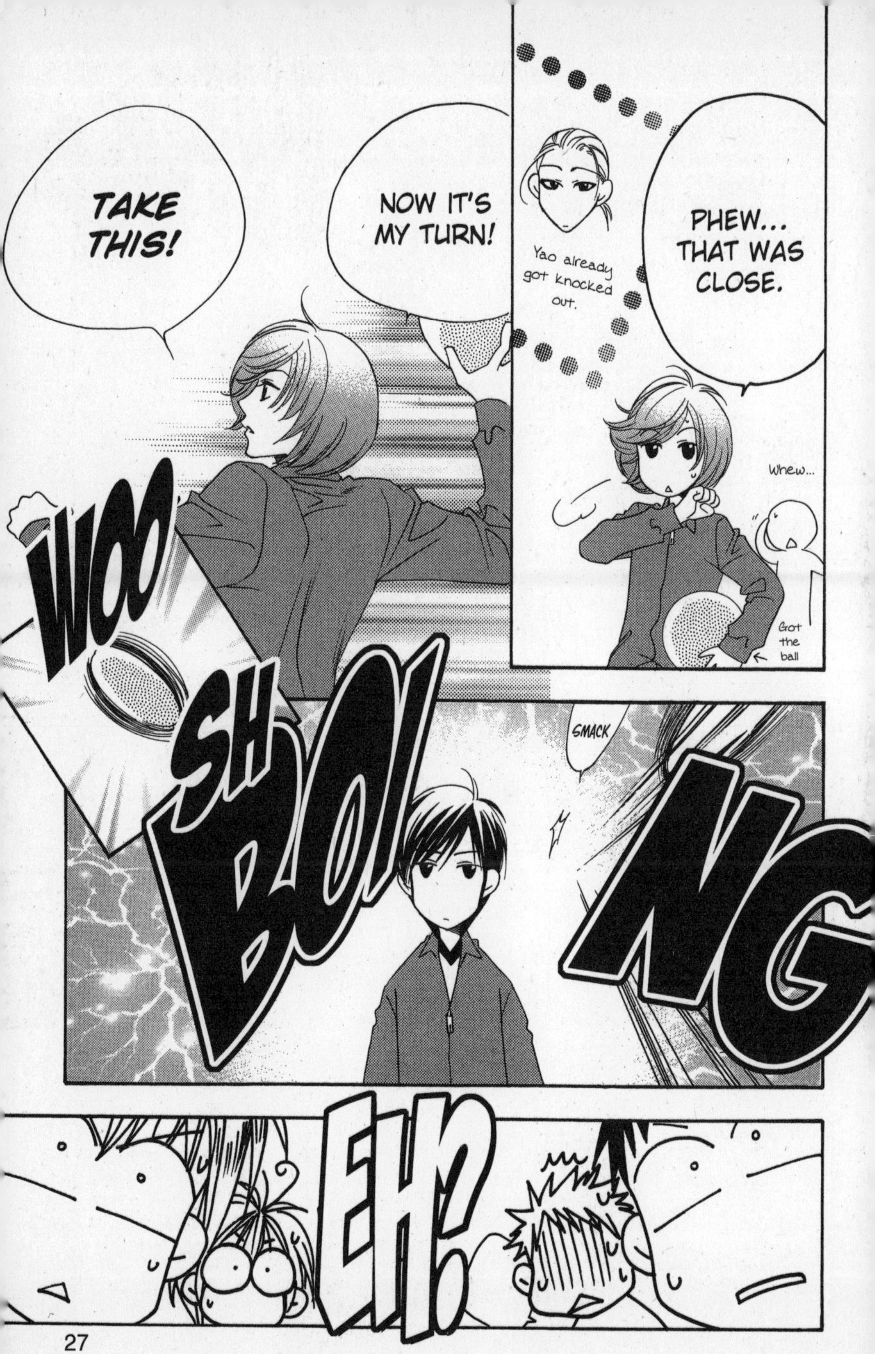
PHEW... THAT WAS CLOSE.
Yao already got knocked out.
Whew...
Got the ball
NOW IT'S MY TURN!
TAKE THIS!
WOOSH
SMACK
BOING
EH?

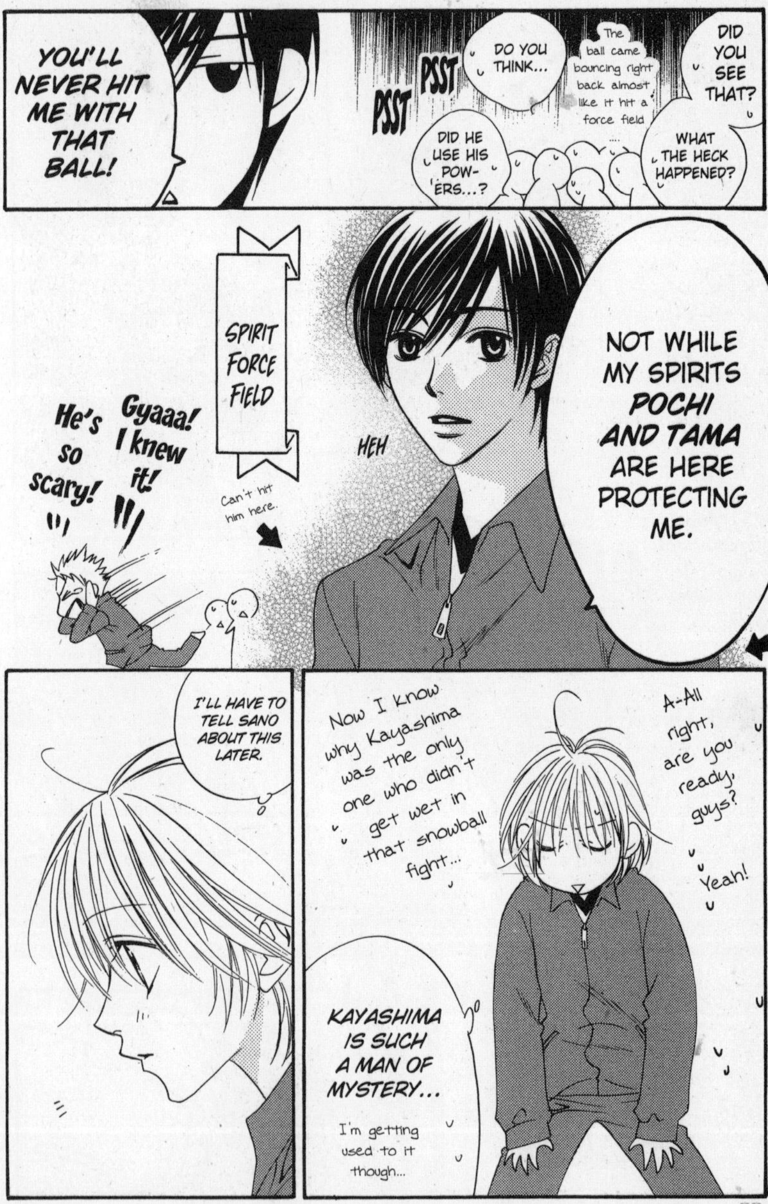
DID YOU SEE THAT?
WHAT THE HECK HAPPENED?
The ball came bouncing right back almost like it hit a force field ....
DO YOU THINK...
DID HE USE HIS POWERS...?
PSST PSST
YOU'LL NEVER HIT ME WITH THAT BALL!
NOT WHILE MY SPIRITS POCHI AND TAMA ARE HERE PROTECTING ME.
Or here either.
HEH
Can't hit him here.
SPIRIT FORCE FIELD
Gyaaa! I knew it!
He's so scary!
A-All right, are you ready, guys?
Yeah!
Now I know why Kayashima was the only one who didn't get wet in that snowball fight...
KAYASHIMA IS SUCH A MAN OF MYSTERY...
I'm getting used to it though...
I'LL HAVE TO TELL SANO ABOUT THIS LATER.

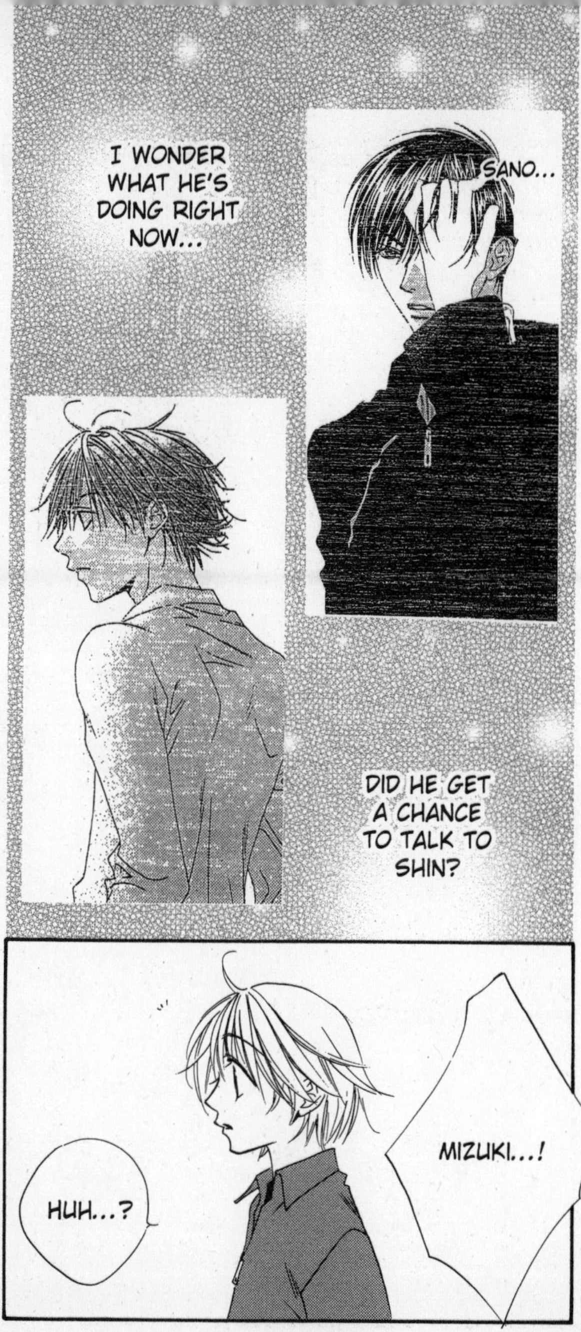
SANO...
I WONDER WHAT HE'S DOING RIGHT NOW...
DID HE GET A CHANCE TO TALK TO SHIN?
MIZUKI...!
HUH...?

17

Hello. It's Hana-Kimi book 17. Mizuki is on the cover, surrounded by cherries. She's in almost the exact same pose as Shin on the cover of book 16. Well okay, maybe not exactly...Okay, forget I said anything! ✧ There was another illustration that I considered using for the cover, but after thinking long and hard I decided to go with this one. I'm not bragging or anything, but I love all my illustrations, so I always have a hard time deciding which ones I'm gonna use. (By the way, the other illustration I was considering was one of Mizuki surrounded by chocolates!)

Regardless of their quality

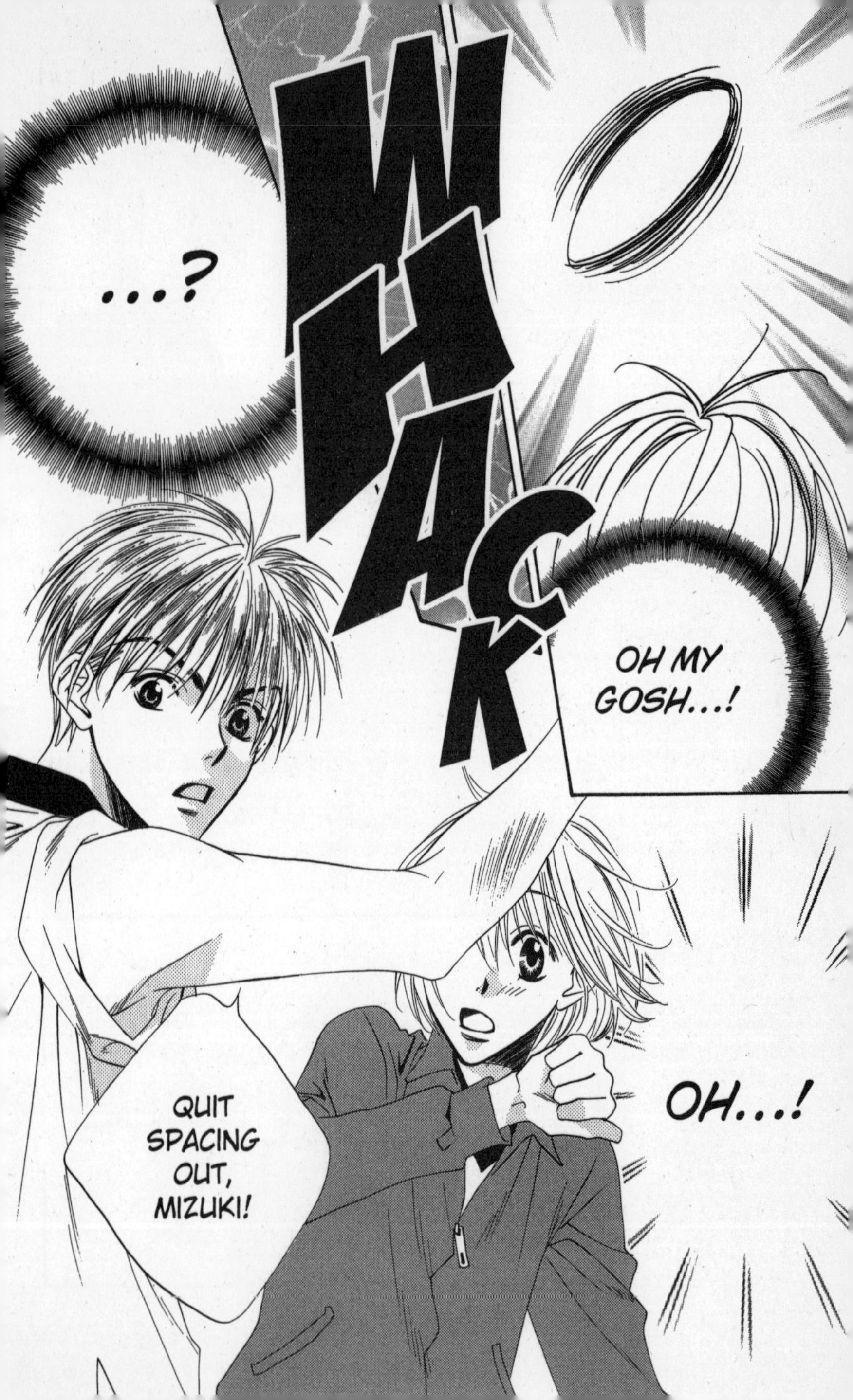
WHACK
...?
OH MY GOSH...!
OH...!
QUIT SPACING OUT, MIZUKI!

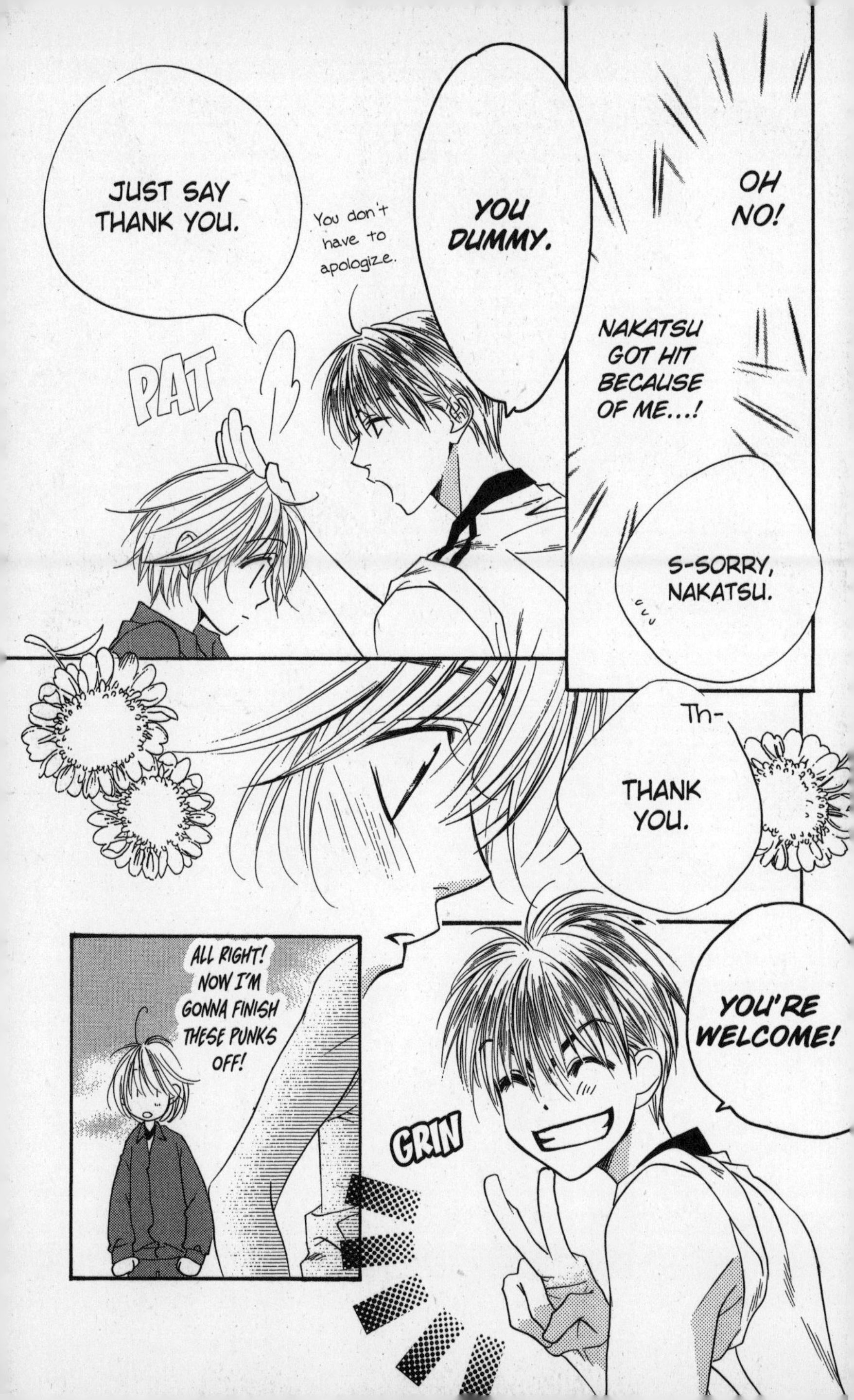
OH NO!
NAKATSU GOT HIT BECAUSE OF ME...!
S-SORRY, NAKATSU.
YOU DUMMY.
You don't have to apologize.
JUST SAY THANK YOU.
PAT
Th-
THANK YOU.
YOU'RE WELCOME!
GRIN
ALL RIGHT! NOW I'M GONNA FINISH THESE PUNKS OFF!

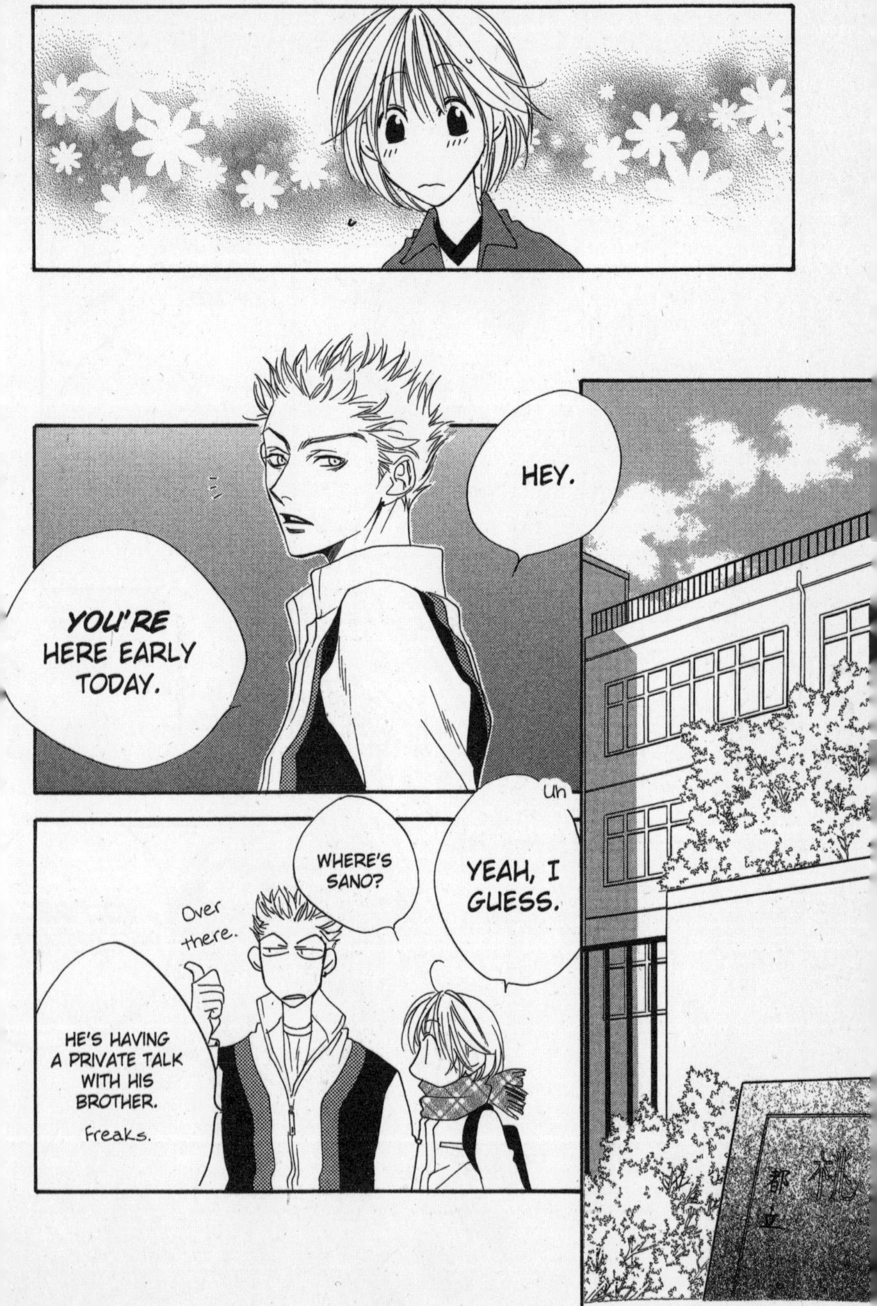
HEY.
YOU'RE HERE EARLY TODAY.
Uh
YEAH, I GUESS.
WHERE'S SANO?
Over there.
HE'S HAVING A PRIVATE TALK WITH HIS BROTHER.
Freaks.

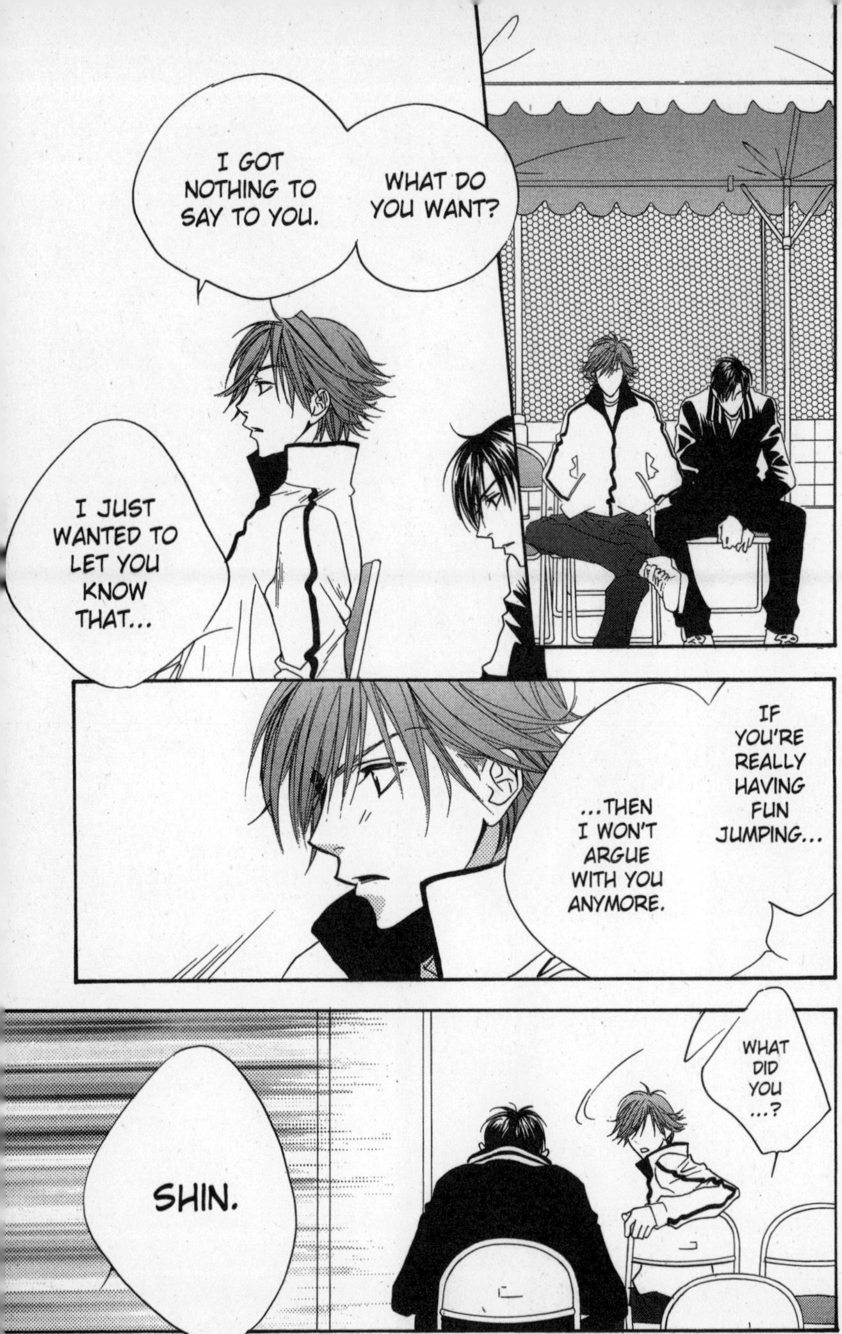
WHAT DO YOU WANT?
I GOT NOTHING TO SAY TO YOU.
I JUST WANTED TO LET YOU KNOW THAT...
IF YOU'RE REALLY HAVING FUN JUMPING...
...THEN I WON'T ARGUE WITH YOU ANYMORE.
WHAT DID YOU ...?
SHIN.

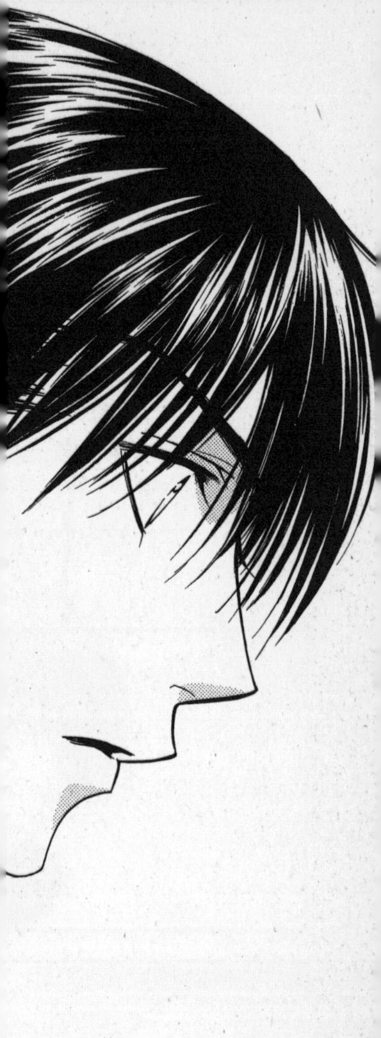

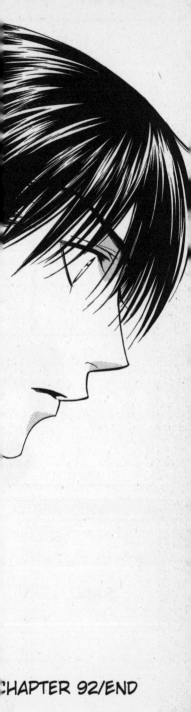

CHAPTER 92/END

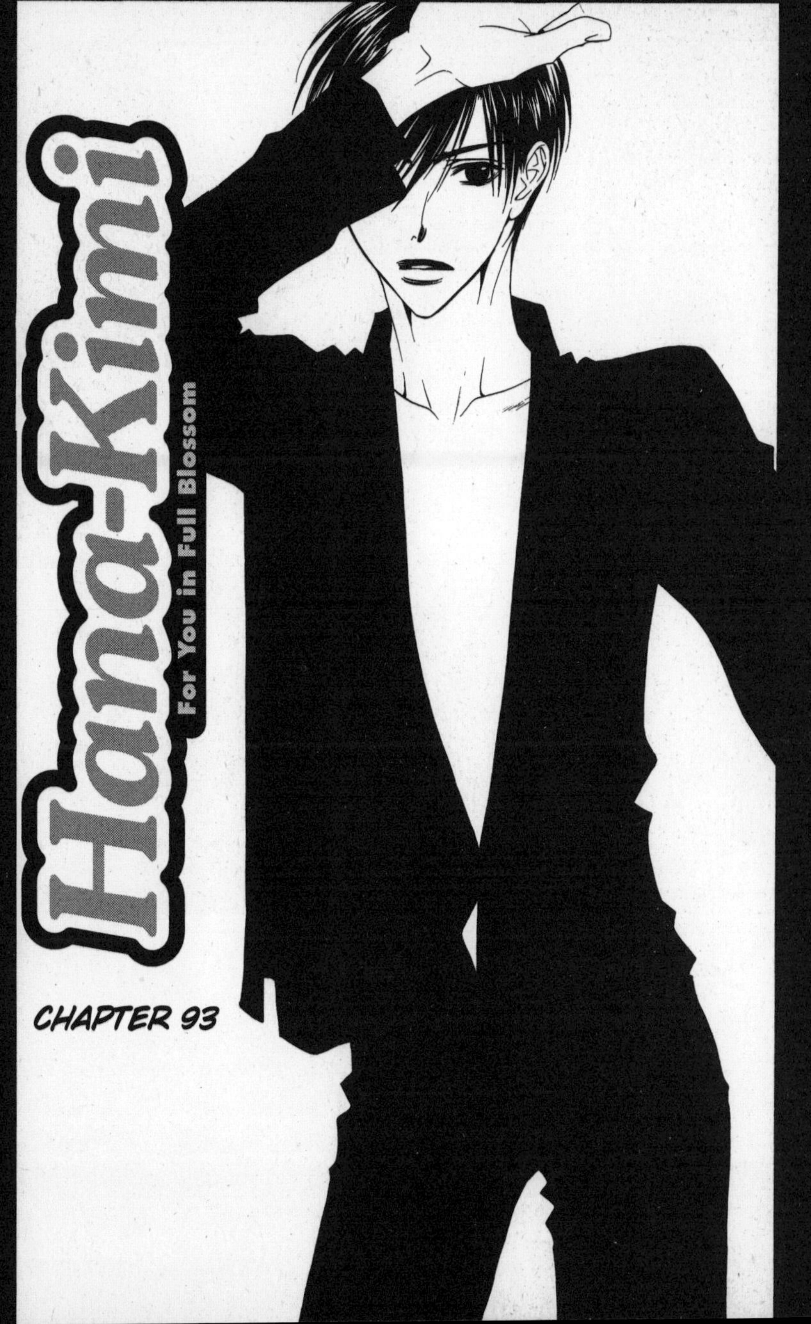
Hana-Kimi
For You in Full Blossom
CHAPTER 93

LONG TIME NO SEE, IZUMI.

CLANK

MOMOICHIGO (Peach Strawberries)

They're soooo good! I love them! I first found out about them when I was watching a cooking show on TV. As a closet strawberry lover (?), I really wanted to try them myself, so I had some delivered to my home! Only the very tips of regular strawberries are sweet and delicious (at least that's my opinion), but with Momoichigo strawberries, the whole thing is really sweet and tasty! And they're super juicy! They're so big that there's no way you could eat one in a single bite! Momoichigo are definitely the king of strawberries! They're pretty expensive, though...I love regular strawberries too.

They're only grown in Tokushima

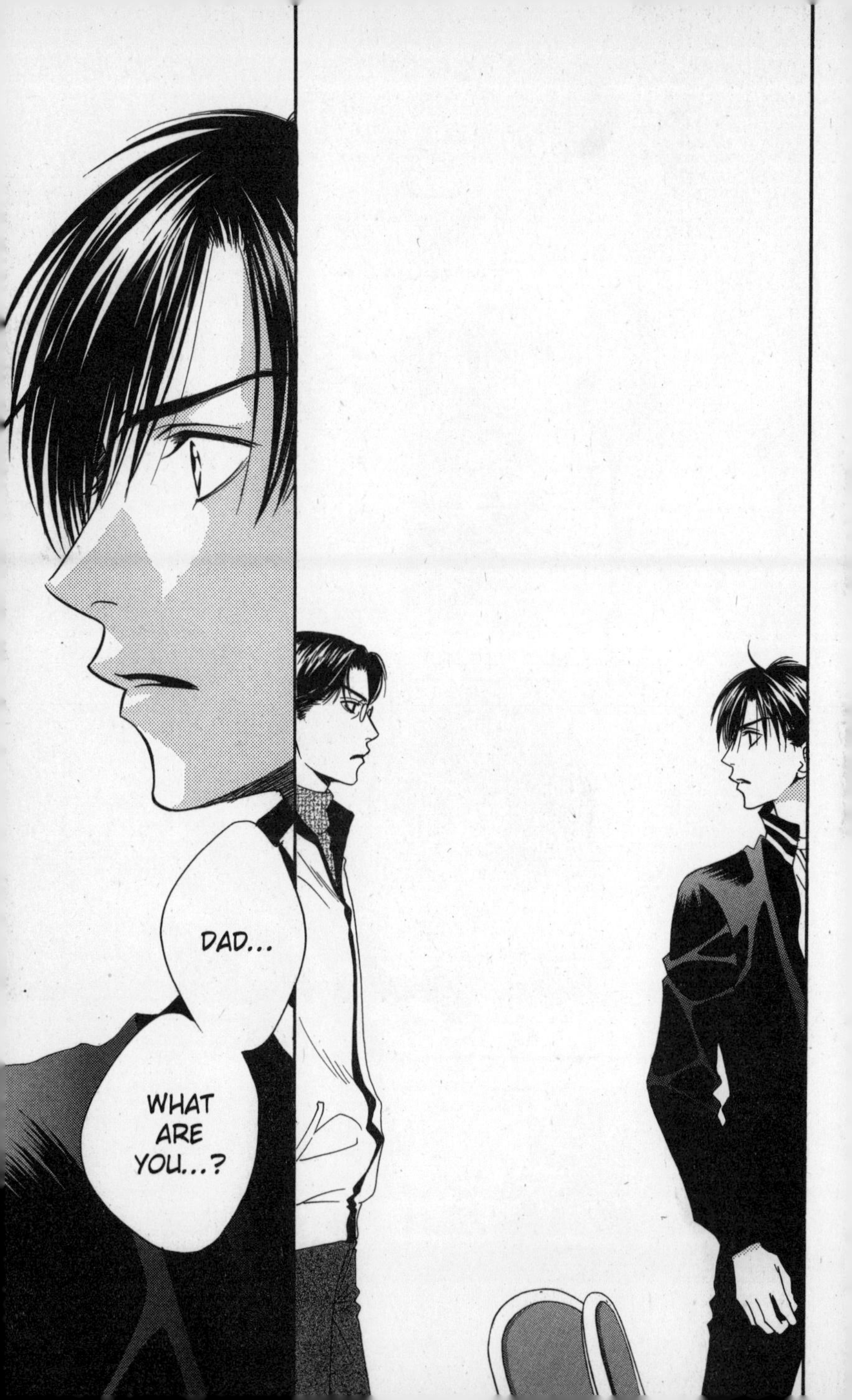
DAD...
WHAT ARE YOU...?

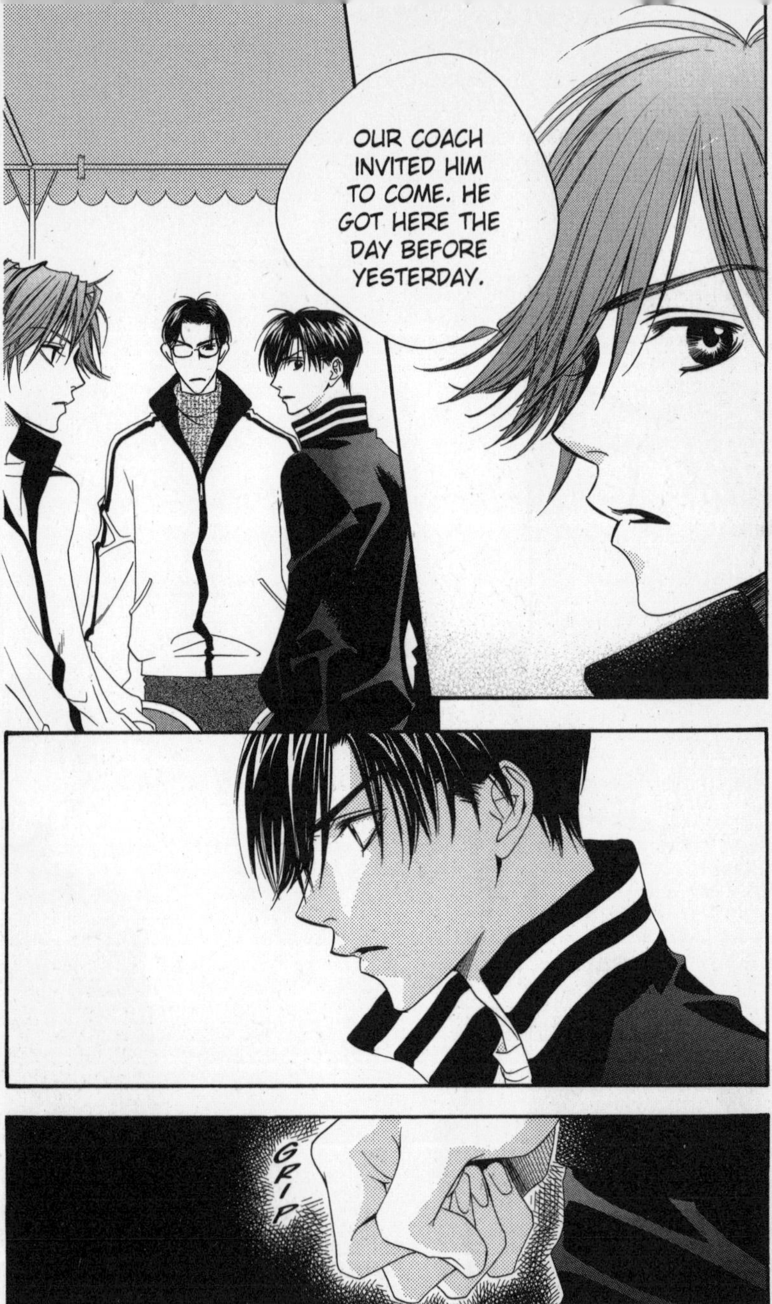
OUR COACH INVITED HIM TO COME. HE GOT HERE THE DAY BEFORE YESTERDAY.
GRIP

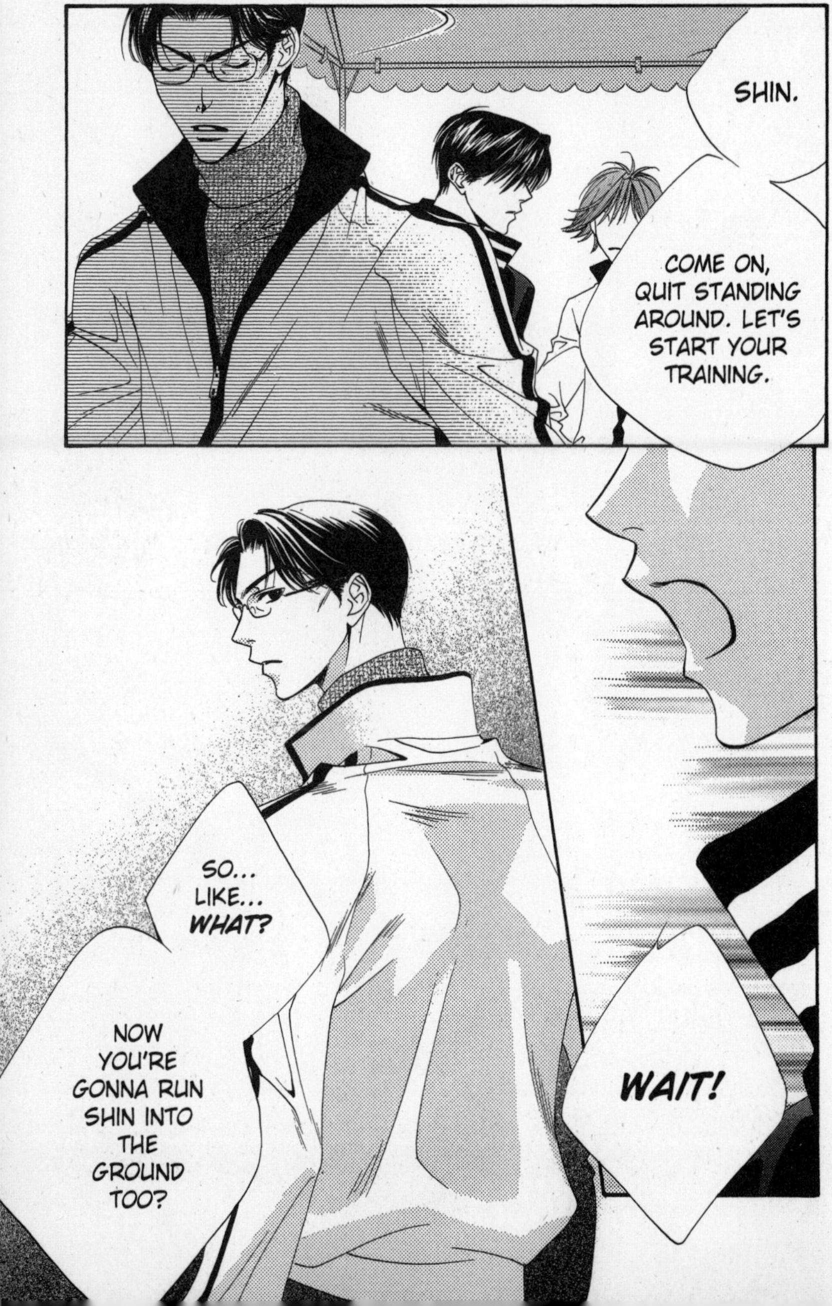
SHIN.
COME ON, QUIT STANDING AROUND. LET'S START YOUR TRAINING.
WAIT!
SO... LIKE... WHAT?
NOW YOU'RE GONNA RUN SHIN INTO THE GROUND TOO?

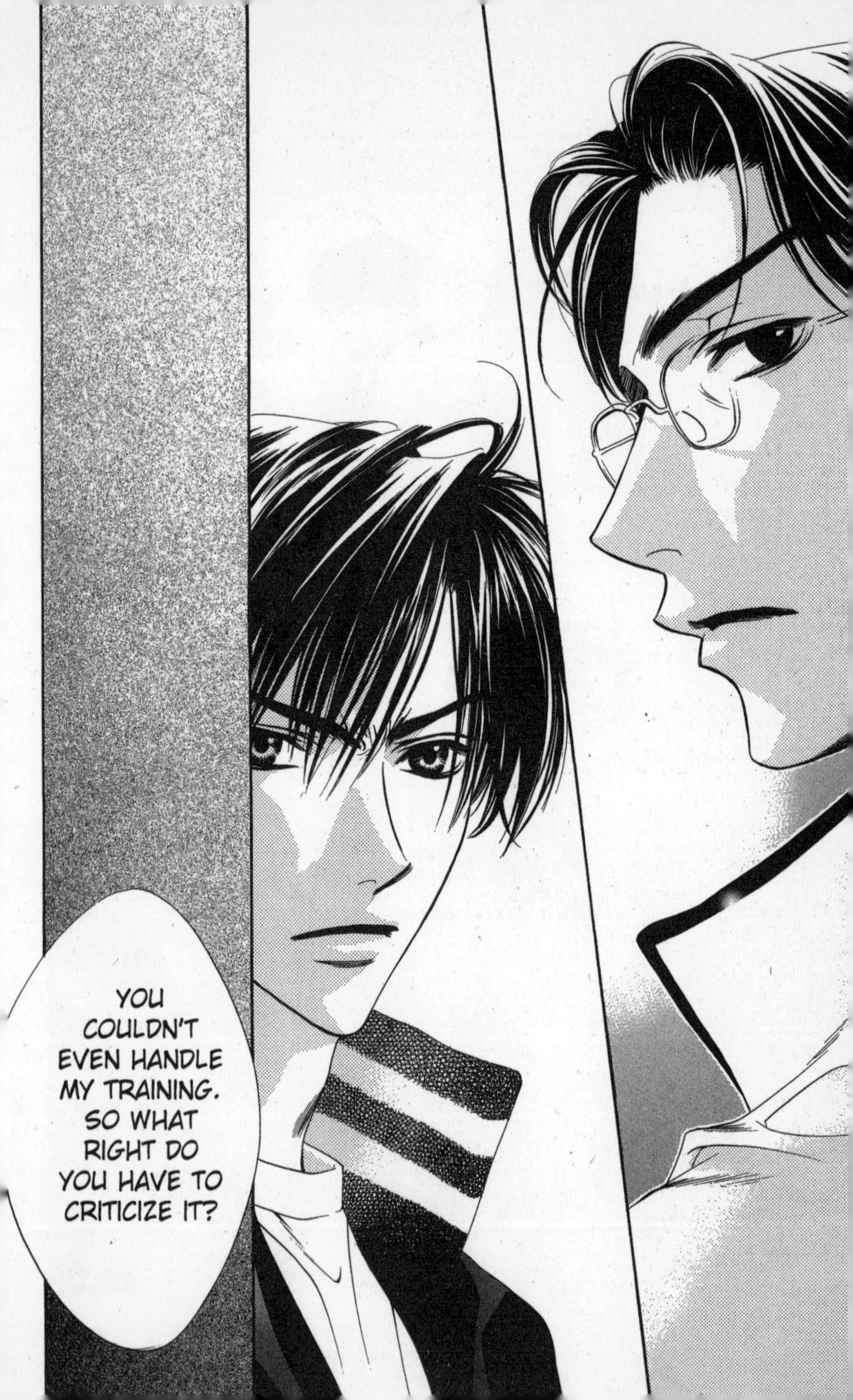
YOU COULDN'T EVEN HANDLE MY TRAINING. SO WHAT RIGHT DO YOU HAVE TO CRITICIZE IT?

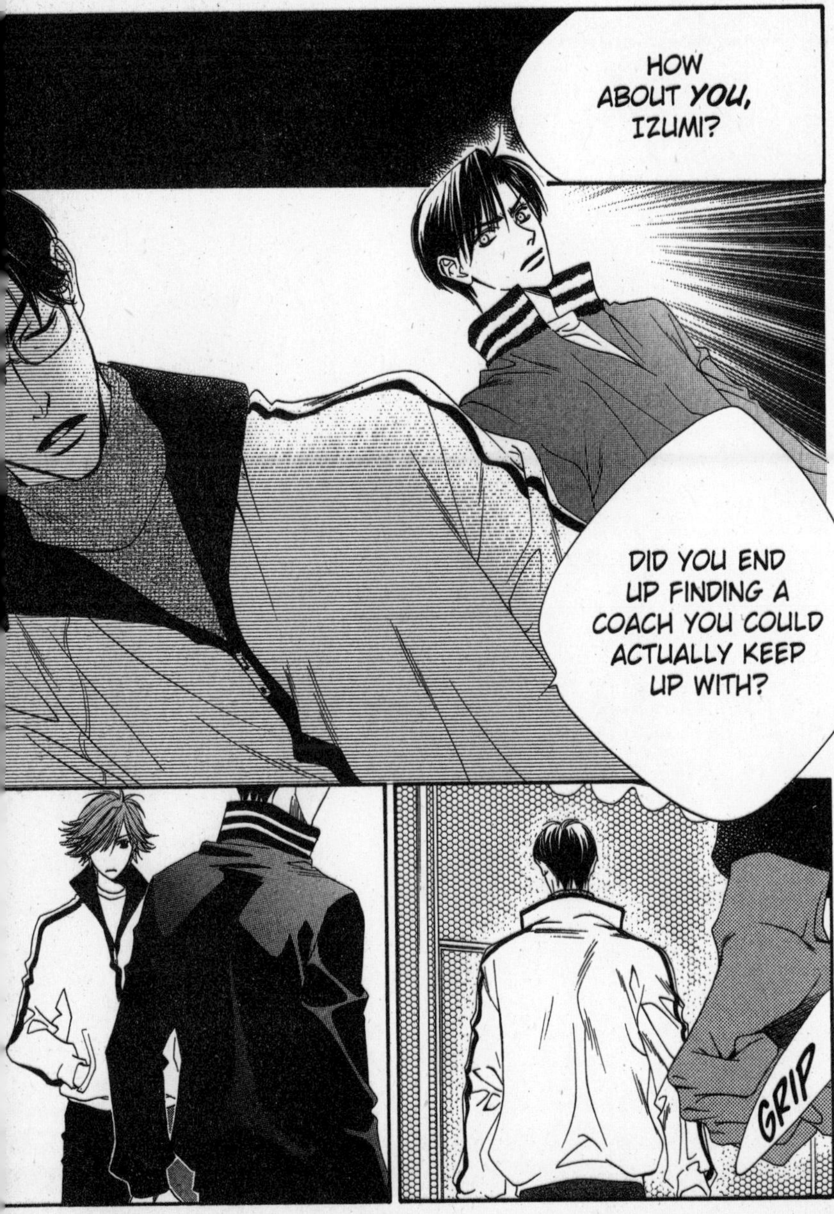
HOW ABOUT YOU, IZUMI?
DID YOU END UP FINDING A COACH YOU COULD ACTUALLY KEEP UP WITH?
GRIP

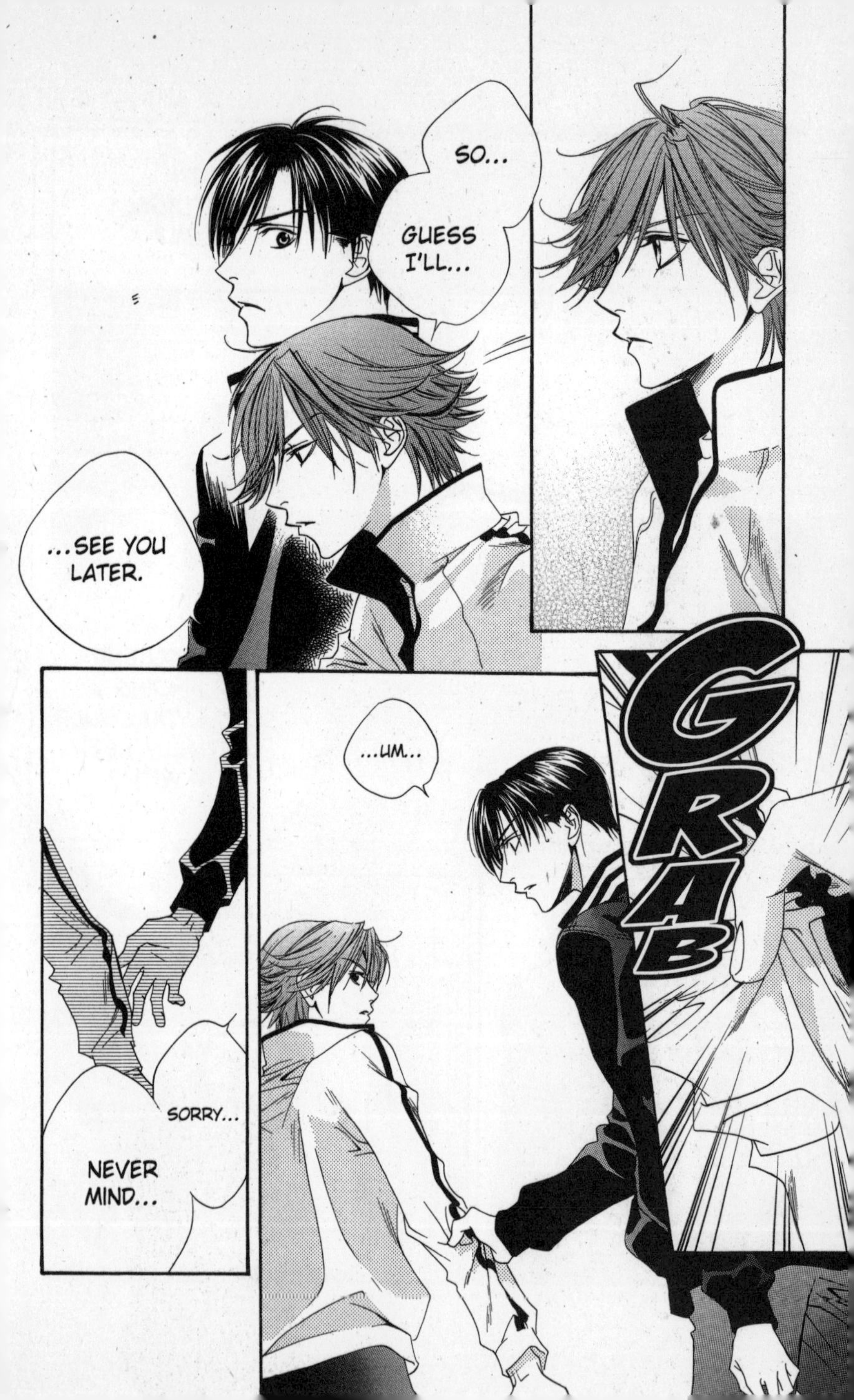
SO...
GUESS I'LL...
...SEE YOU LATER.
GRAB
...UM...
SORRY...
NEVER MIND...

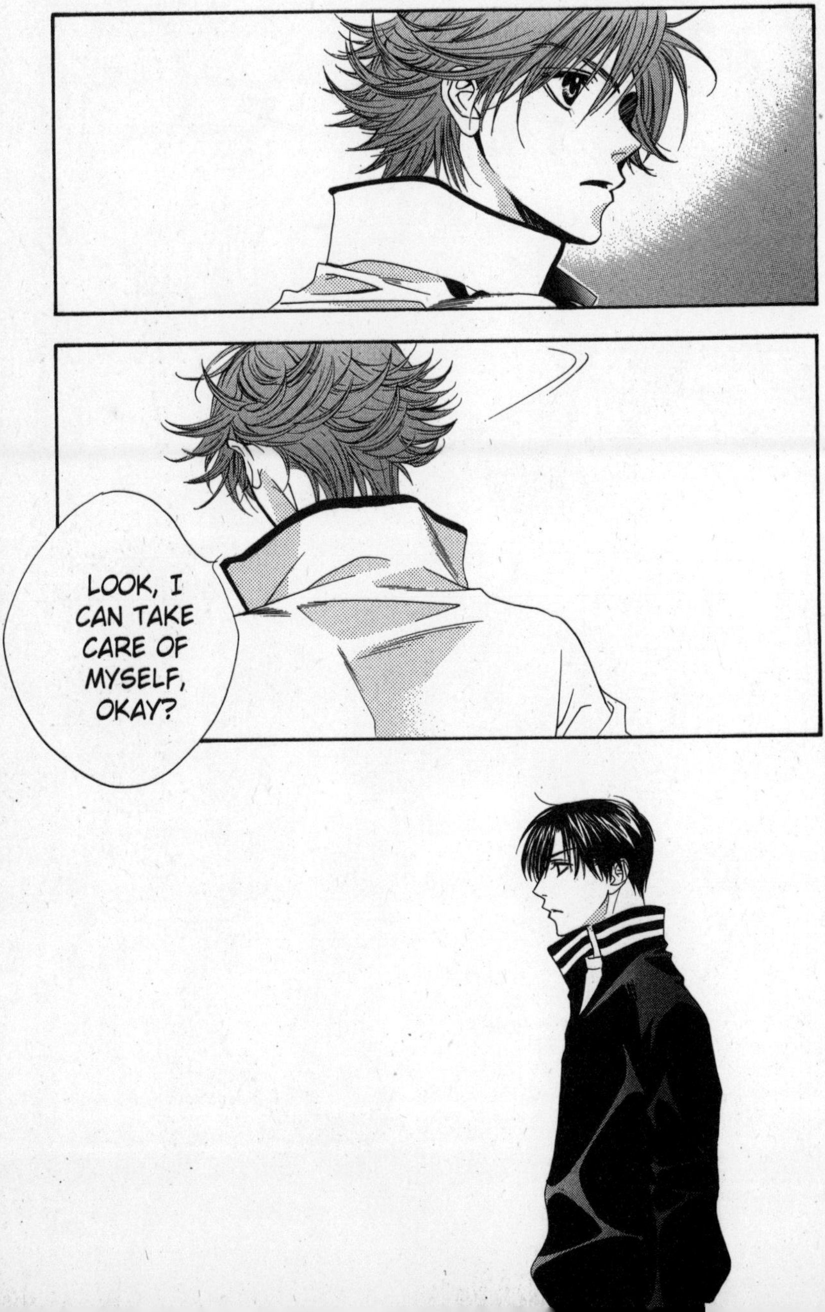
LOOK, I CAN TAKE CARE OF MYSELF, OKAY?

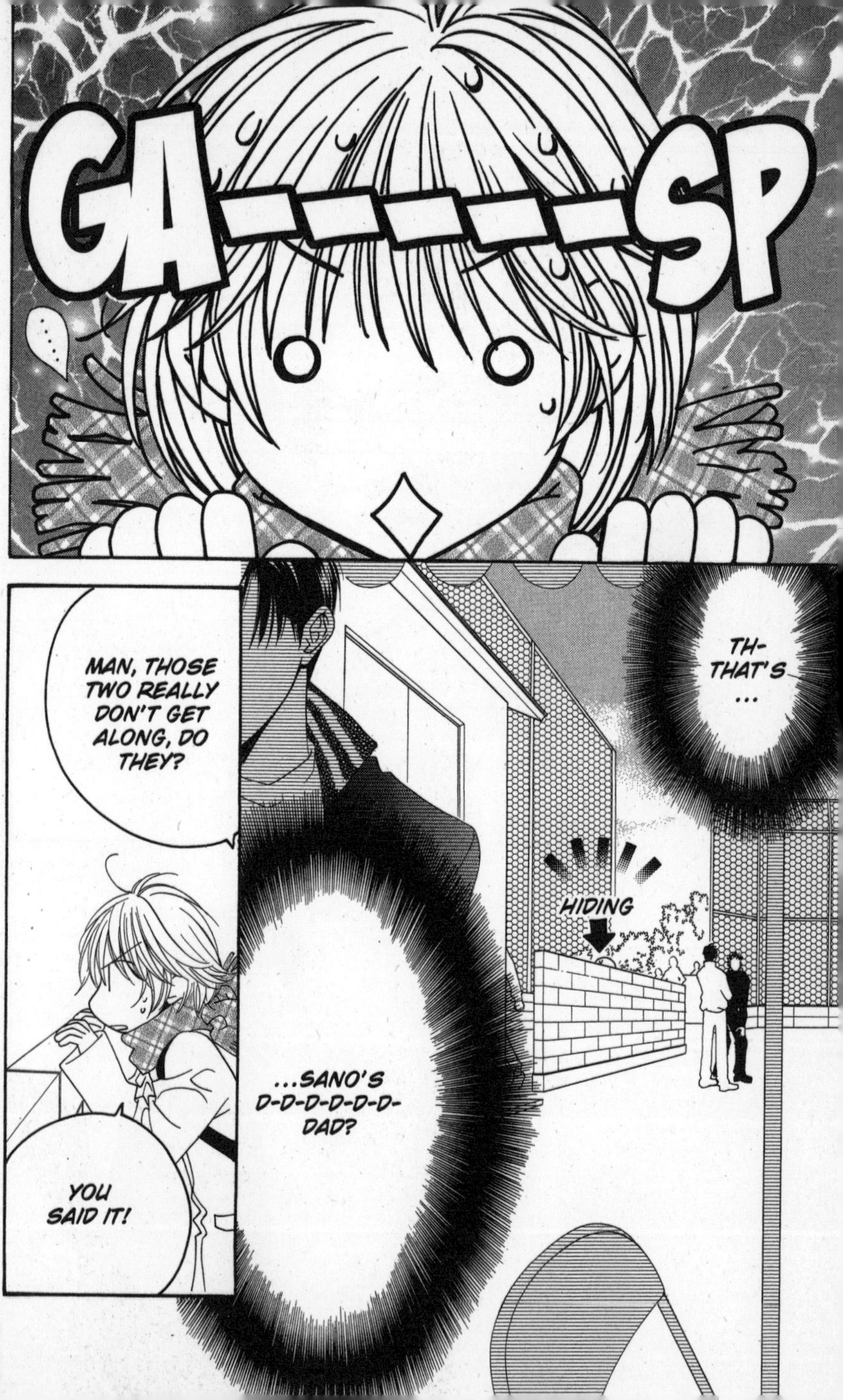
GA-----SP
...
TH-THAT'S...
HIDING
...SANO'S D-D-D-D-D-D-DAD?
MAN, THOSE TWO REALLY DON'T GET ALONG, DO THEY?
YOU SAID IT!

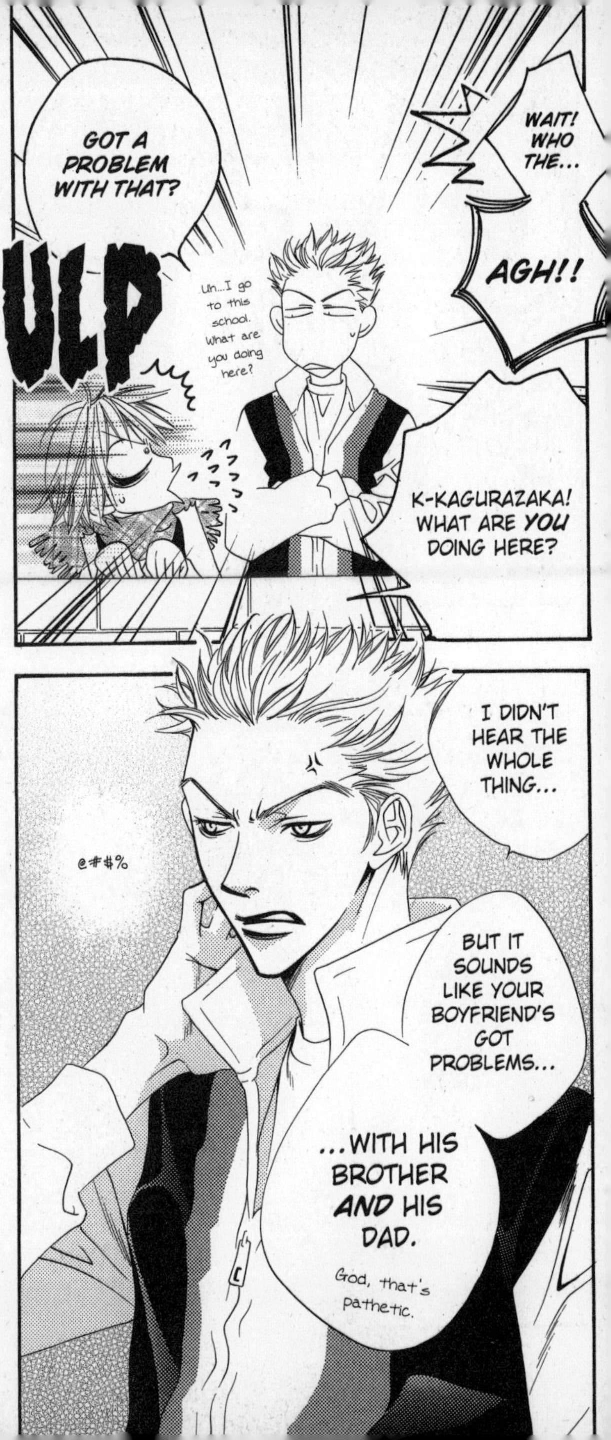
WAIT! WHO THE...
AGH!!
K-KAGURAZAKA! WHAT ARE *YOU* DOING HERE?
Uh...I go to this school. What are you doing here?
GOT A PROBLEM WITH THAT?
ULP
I DIDN'T HEAR THE WHOLE THING...
@#$%
BUT IT SOUNDS LIKE YOUR BOYFRIEND'S GOT PROBLEMS...
...WITH HIS BROTHER *AND* HIS DAD.
God, that's pathetic.

OCHA ZUKE

SANO'S FATHER AND THE TRACK AND FIELD NETWORKING EVENT

Sano's father wasn't originally going to appear in the book so much, but as the story progressed Sano's conflict with his father became more and more important. So, in the end, I had no choice. But Sano's father is supposed to live way up in the north, far away from Osaka High School. So that's why I came up with the networking event story! Ta-da! The only problem is, the story takes place in **winter!** It would have made more sense if it was an indoor sporting event, but...(actually, I'm not really sure if they have indoor sporting events during winter, either). Usually track competitions take place during spring and summer. Heh heh. Oh well... WHO CARES?!

What was I talking about...?

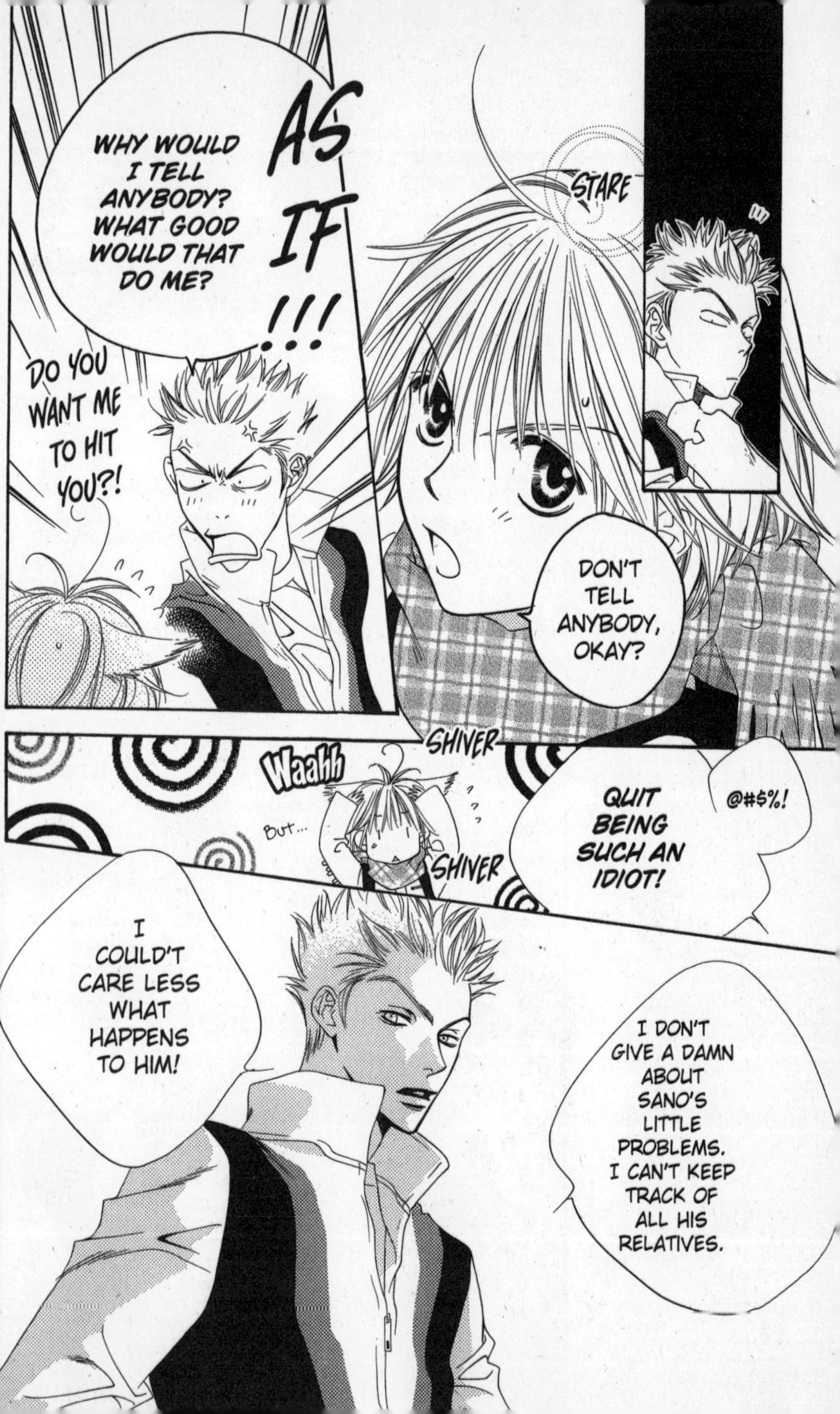
STARE
DON'T TELL ANYBODY, OKAY?
WHY WOULD I TELL ANYBODY? WHAT GOOD WOULD THAT DO ME?
AS IF!!!
DO YOU WANT ME TO HIT YOU?!
@#$%!
QUIT BEING SUCH AN IDIOT!
SHIVER
SHIVER
Waahh
But...
I DON'T GIVE A DAMN ABOUT SANO'S LITTLE PROBLEMS. I CAN'T KEEP TRACK OF ALL HIS RELATIVES.
I COULDN'T CARE LESS WHAT HAPPENS TO HIM!

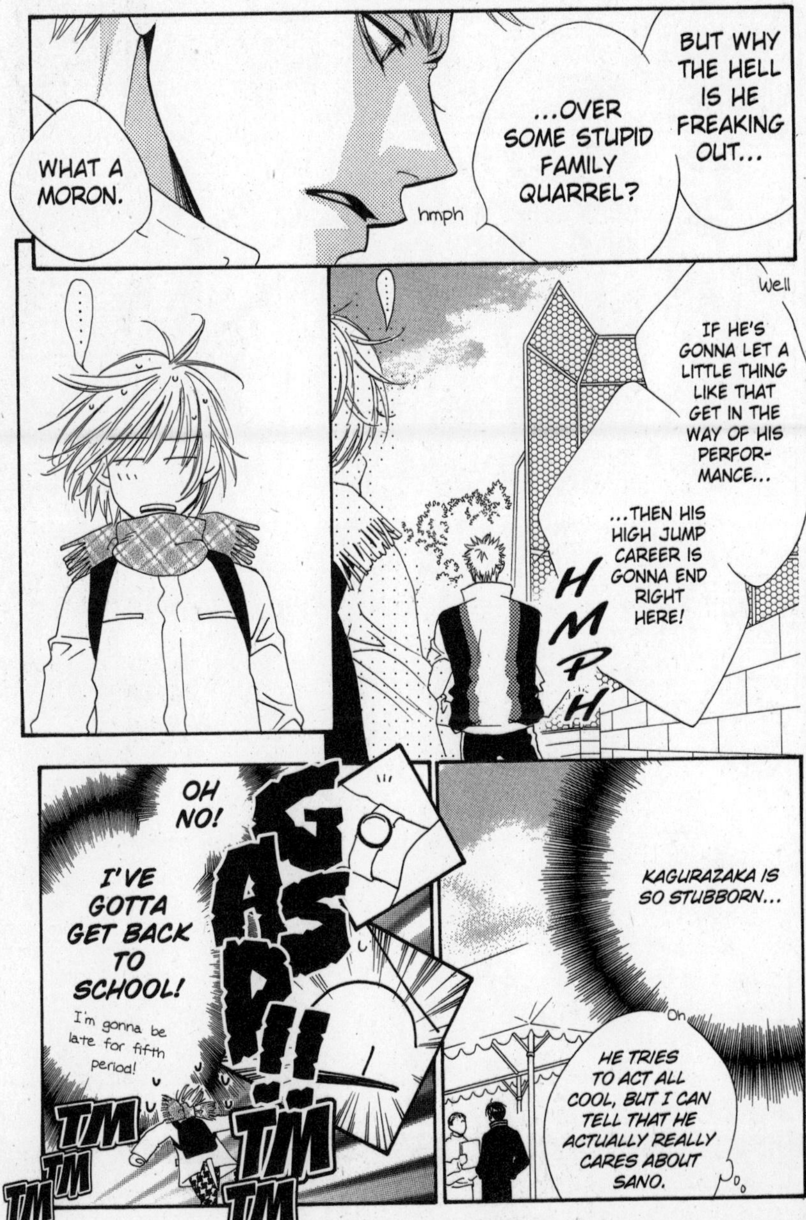
BUT WHY THE HELL IS HE FREAKING OUT...
...OVER SOME STUPID FAMILY QUARREL?
hmph
WHAT A MORON.
Well
IF HE'S GONNA LET A LITTLE THING LIKE THAT GET IN THE WAY OF HIS PERFORMANCE...
...THEN HIS HIGH JUMP CAREER IS GONNA END RIGHT HERE!
HMMPH
!
......
KAGURAZAKA IS SO STUBBORN...
Oh
HE TRIES TO ACT ALL COOL, BUT I CAN TELL THAT HE ACTUALLY REALLY CARES ABOUT SANO.
GASP!!
OH NO!
I'VE GOTTA GET BACK TO SCHOOL!
I'm gonna be late for fifth period!
TM TM TM
TM TM

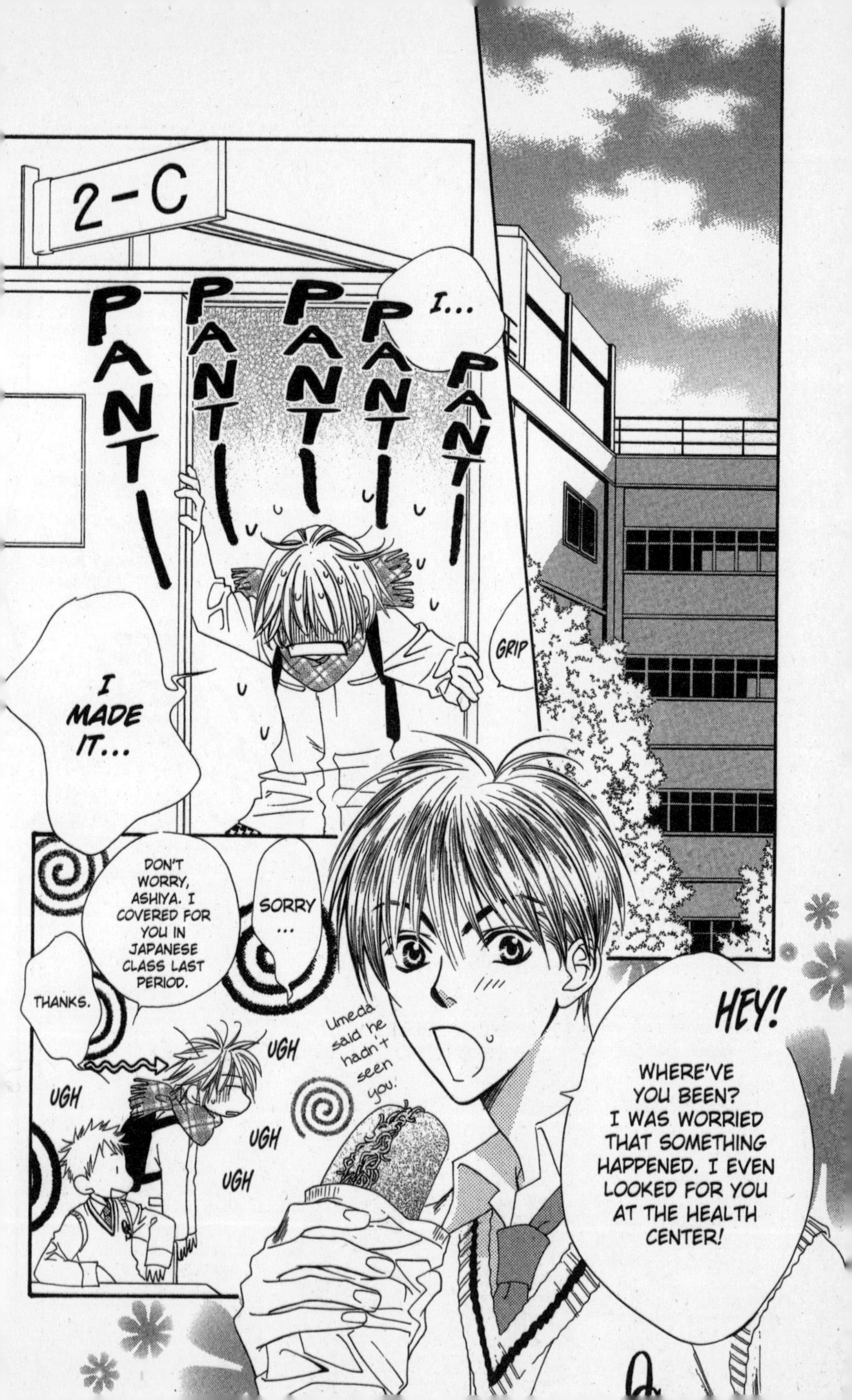
2-C
I...
PANT
PANT
PANT
PANT
PANT
GRIP
I MADE IT...
HEY!
WHERE'VE YOU BEEN? I WAS WORRIED THAT SOMETHING HAPPENED. I EVEN LOOKED FOR YOU AT THE HEALTH CENTER!
Umeda said he hadn't seen you.
SORRY...
DON'T WORRY, ASHIYA. I COVERED FOR YOU IN JAPANESE CLASS LAST PERIOD.
THANKS.
UGH
UGH
UGH
UGH

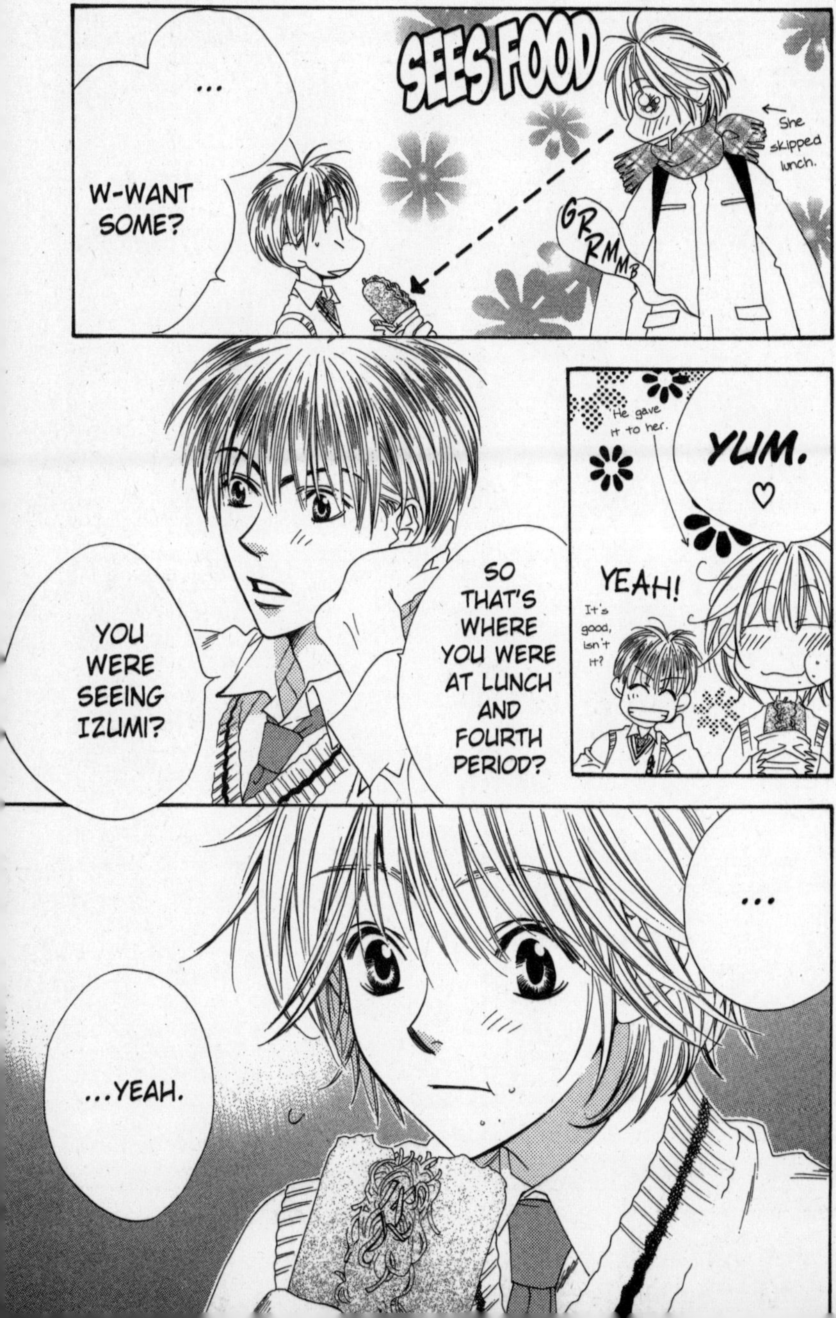
SEES FOOD
She skipped lunch.
GRRMMB
...
W-WANT SOME?
YUM. ♡
He gave it to her.
YEAH!
It's good, isn't it?
SO THAT'S WHERE YOU WERE AT LUNCH AND FOURTH PERIOD?
YOU WERE SEEING IZUMI?
...
...YEAH.

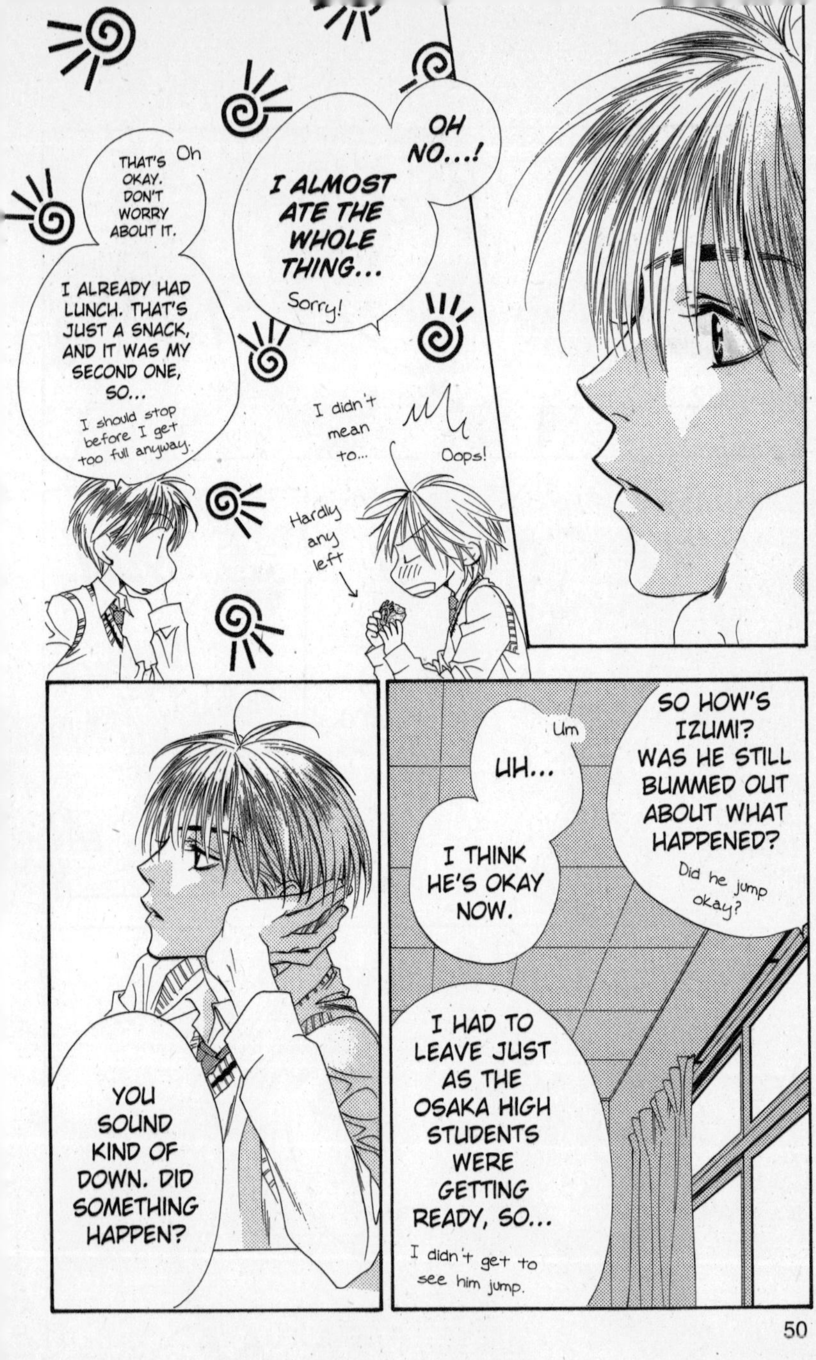
OH NO...!
I ALMOST ATE THE WHOLE THING...
Sorry!
Oh
THAT'S OKAY. DON'T WORRY ABOUT IT.
I ALREADY HAD LUNCH. THAT'S JUST A SNACK, AND IT WAS MY SECOND ONE, SO...
I should stop before I get too full anyway.
Oops!
I didn't mean to...
Hardly any left
SO HOW'S IZUMI? WAS HE STILL BUMMED OUT ABOUT WHAT HAPPENED?
Did he jump okay?
Um
UH...
I THINK HE'S OKAY NOW.
I HAD TO LEAVE JUST AS THE OSAKA HIGH STUDENTS WERE GETTING READY, SO...
I didn't get to see him jump.
YOU SOUND KIND OF DOWN. DID SOMETHING HAPPEN?

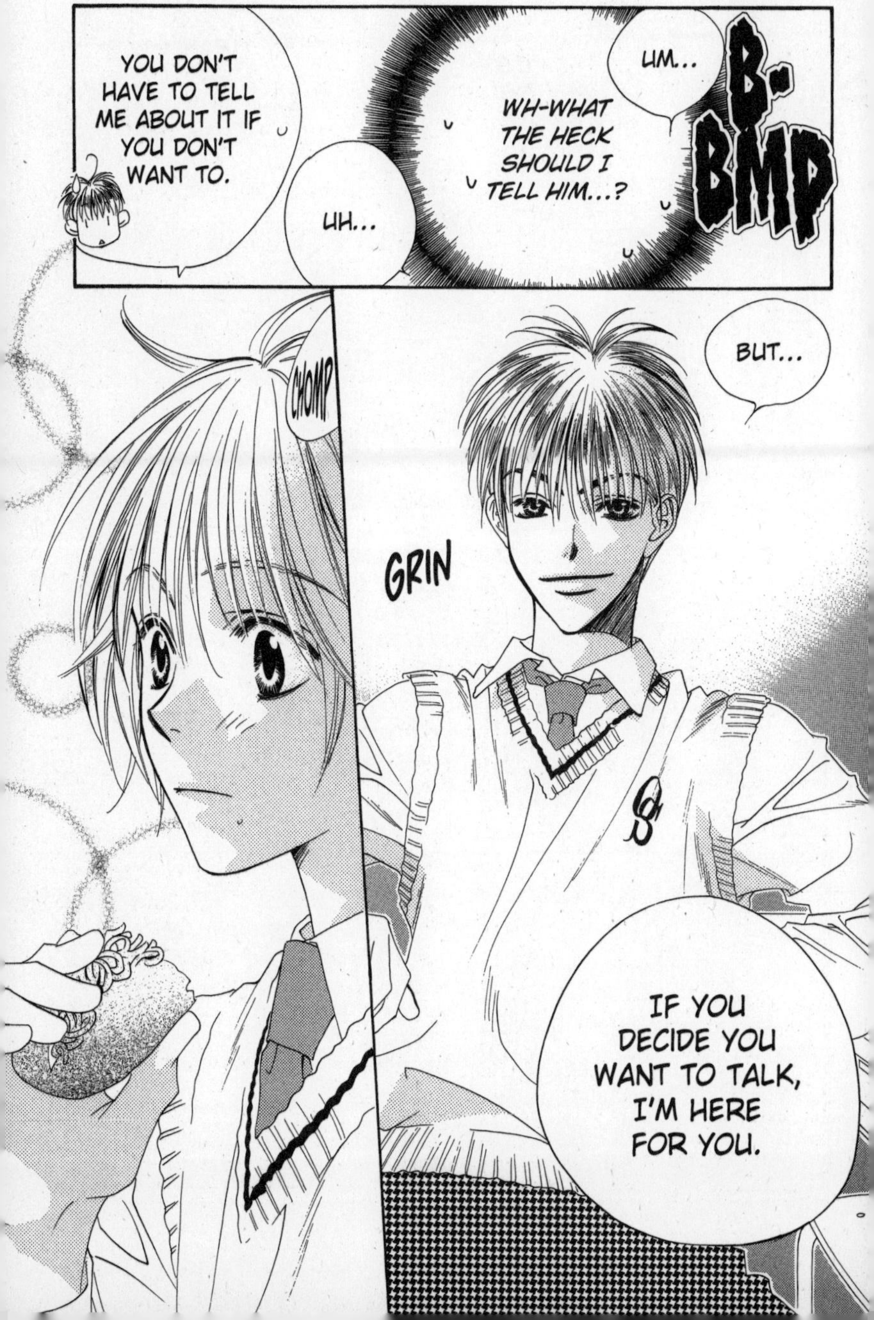
B-BMP
UM...
WH-WHAT THE HECK SHOULD I TELL HIM...?
UH...
YOU DON'T HAVE TO TELL ME ABOUT IT IF YOU DON'T WANT TO.
BUT...
GRIN
IF YOU DECIDE YOU WANT TO TALK, I'M HERE FOR YOU.
CHOMP

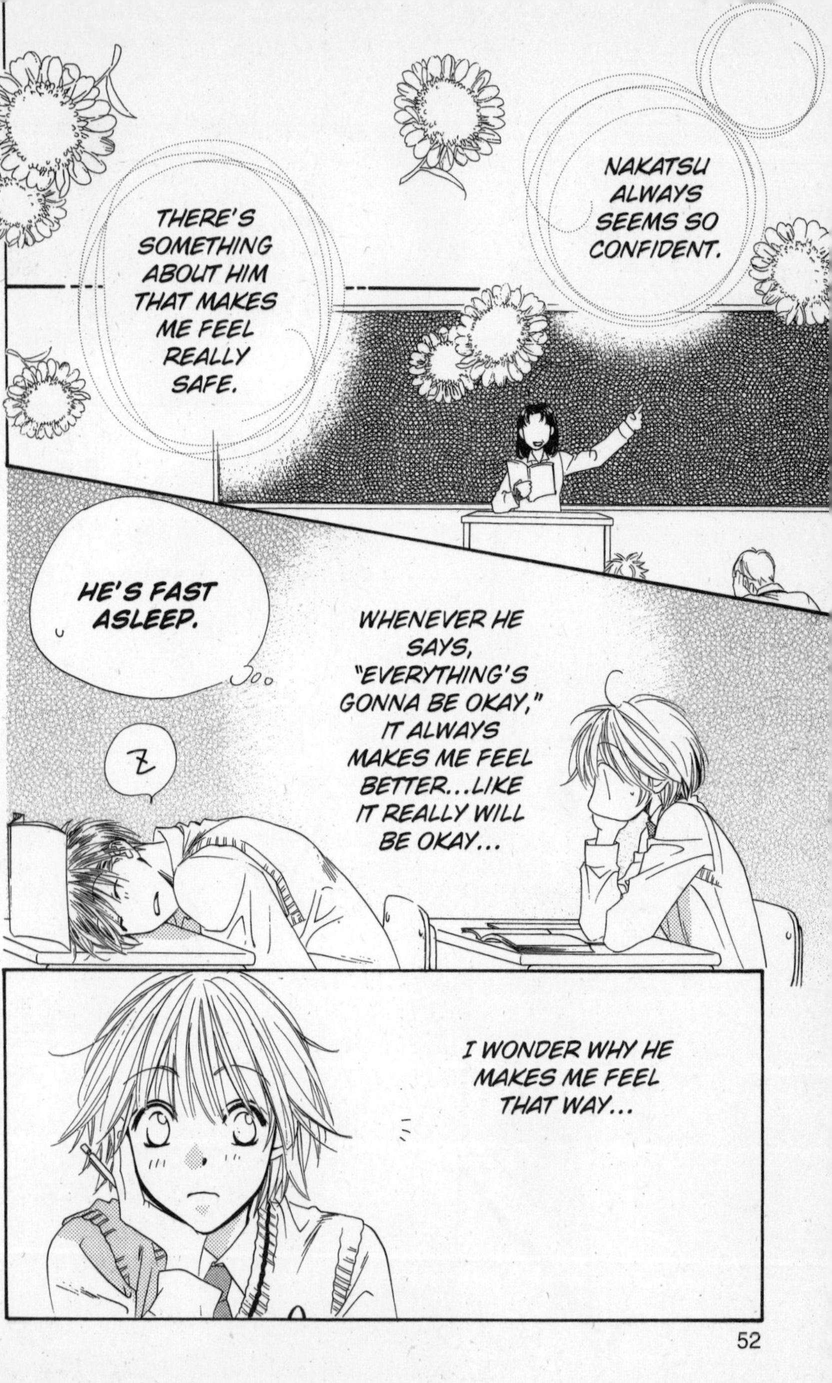
NAKATSU ALWAYS SEEMS SO CONFIDENT.
THERE'S SOMETHING ABOUT HIM THAT MAKES ME FEEL REALLY SAFE.
WHENEVER HE SAYS, "EVERYTHING'S GONNA BE OKAY," IT ALWAYS MAKES ME FEEL BETTER...LIKE IT REALLY WILL BE OKAY...
HE'S FAST ASLEEP.
Z
I WONDER WHY HE MAKES ME FEEL THAT WAY...

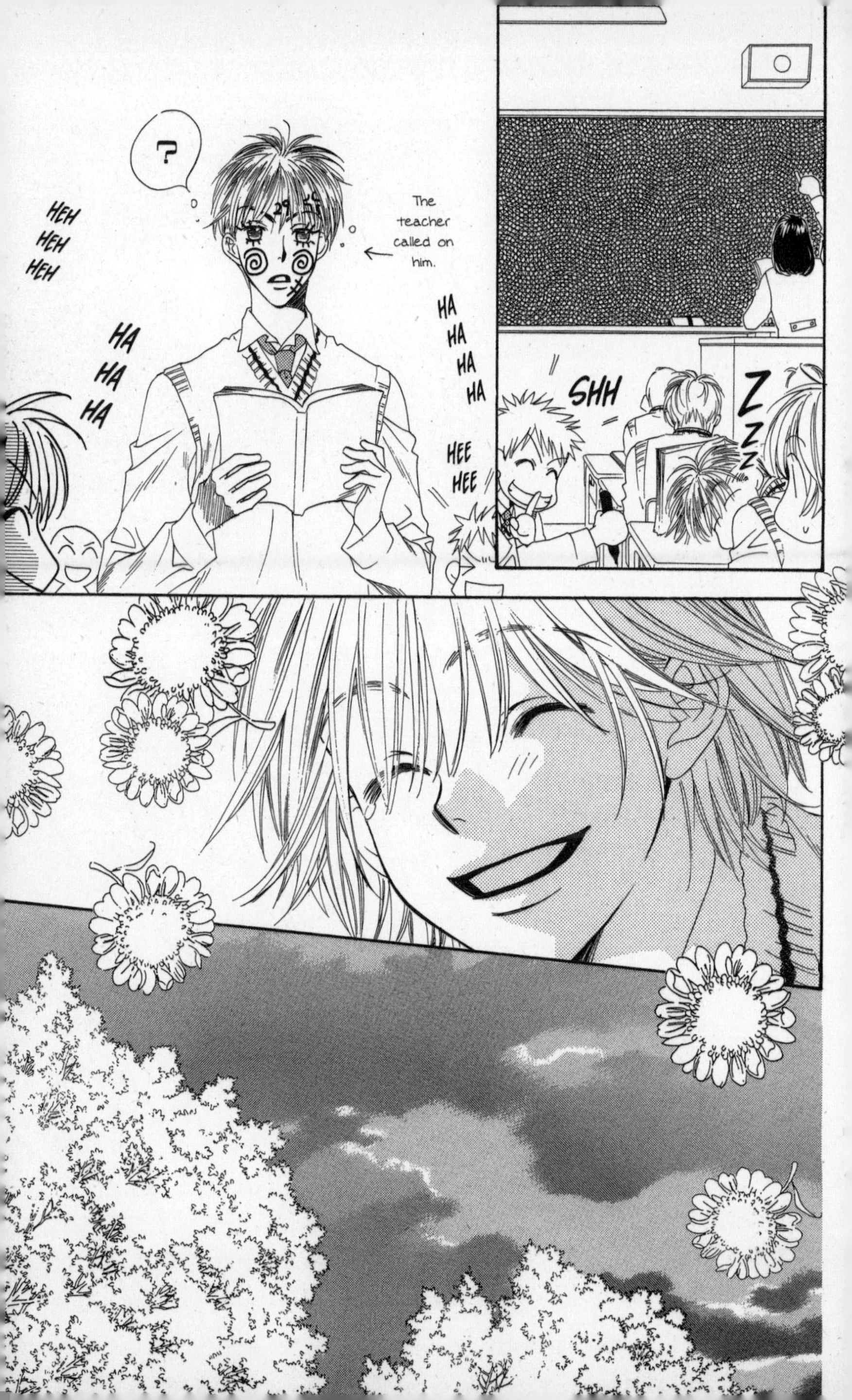
SHH
ZZZ
The teacher called on him.
HA HA HA HA
HEE HEE
?
HEH HEH HEH
HA HA HA

*SIGN = OSAKA HIGH SCHOOL DORMS

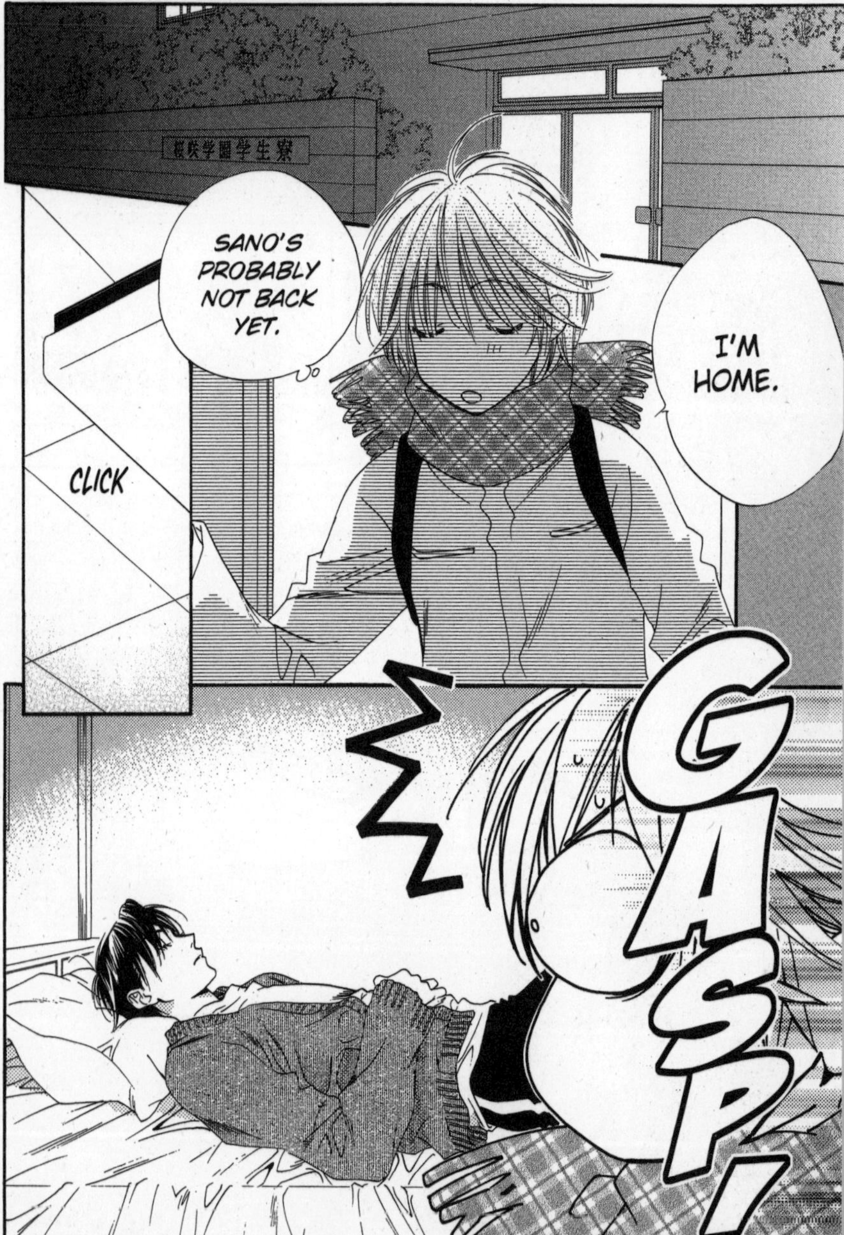
I'M HOME.
SANO'S PROBABLY NOT BACK YET.
CLICK
GASP!

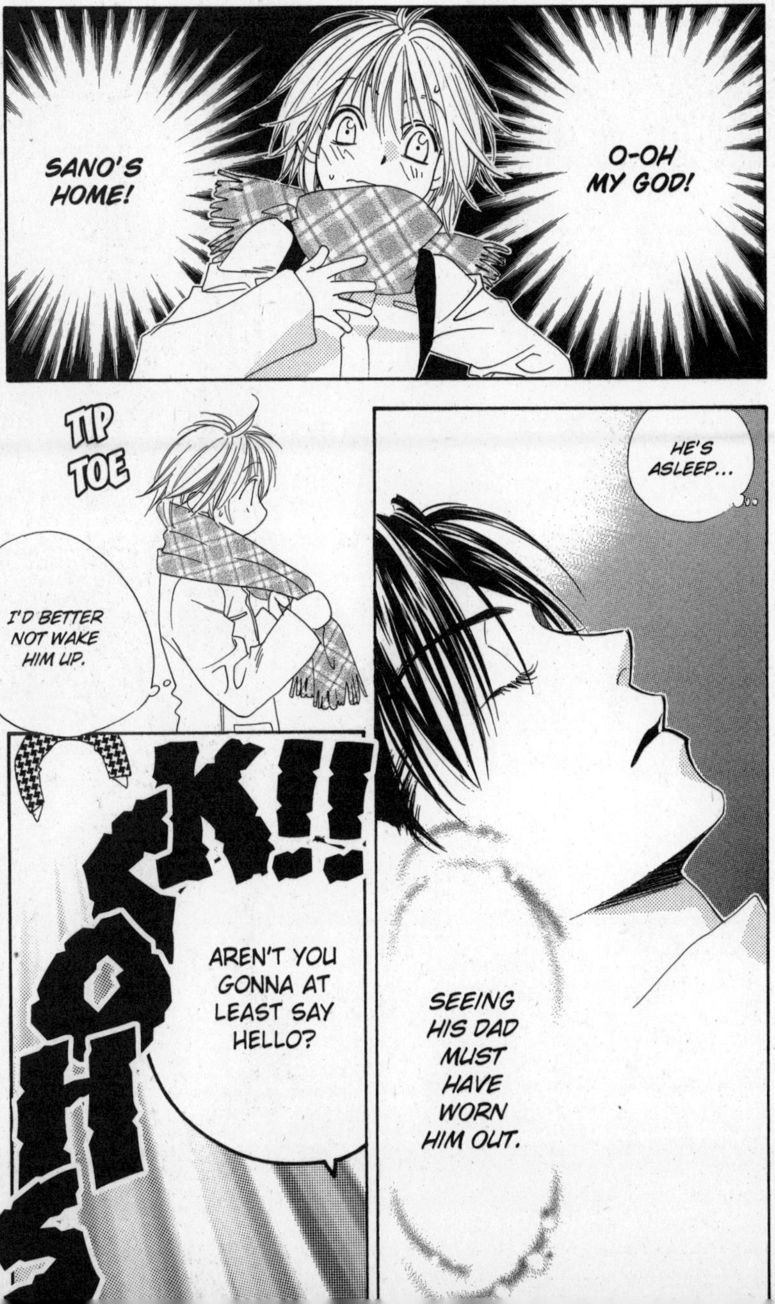
O-OH MY GOD!
SANO'S HOME!
HE'S ASLEEP...
SEEING HIS DAD MUST HAVE WORN HIM OUT.
TIP TOE
I'D BETTER NOT WAKE HIM UP.
SHOCK!!
AREN'T YOU GONNA AT LEAST SAY HELLO?

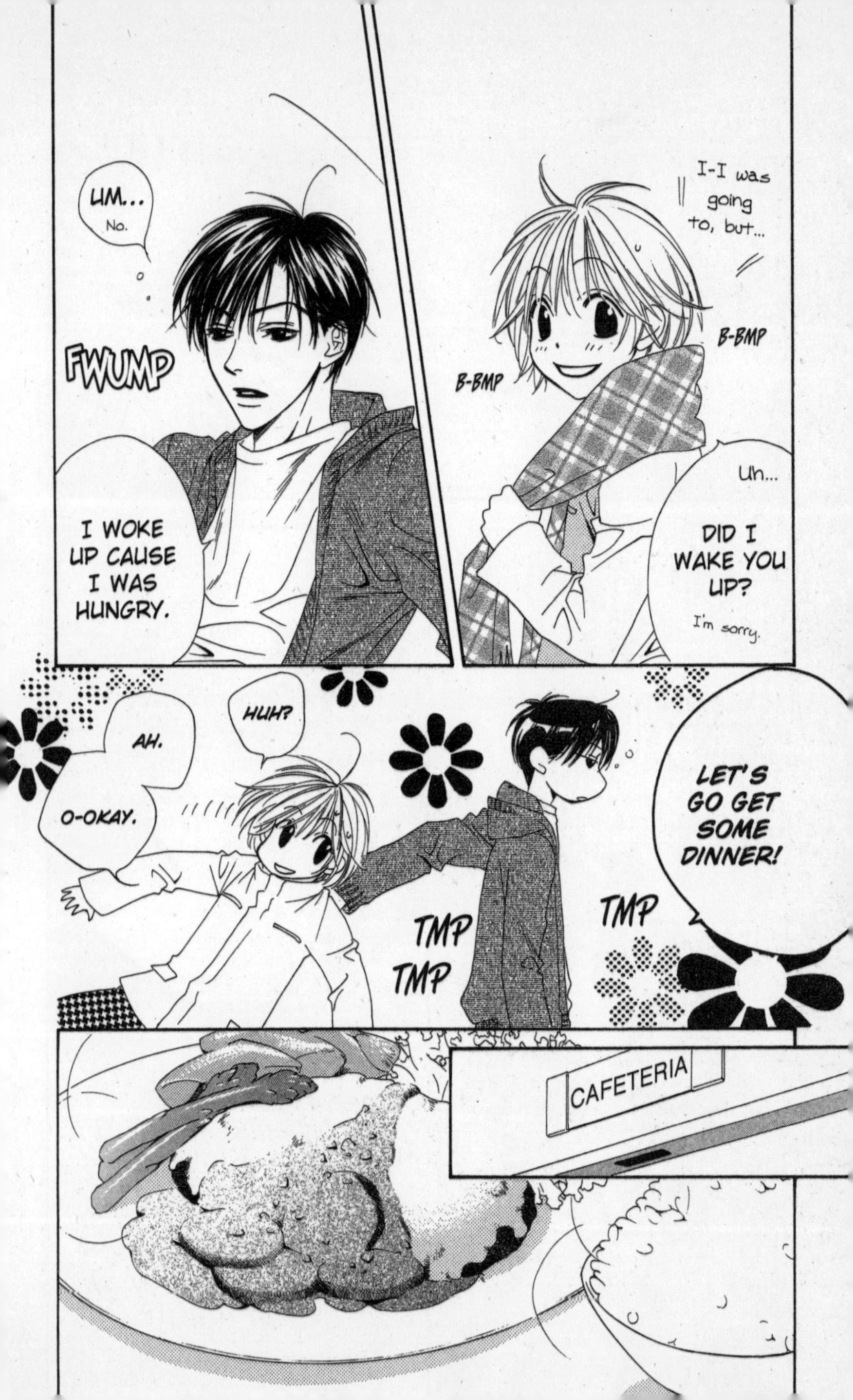
I-I was going to, but...
B-BMP
B-BMP
Uh...
DID I WAKE YOU UP?
I'm sorry.
UM...
No.
FWUMP
I WOKE UP CAUSE I WAS HUNGRY.
LET'S GO GET SOME DINNER!
TMP
TMP
TMP
HUH?
AH.
O-OKAY.
CAFETERIA

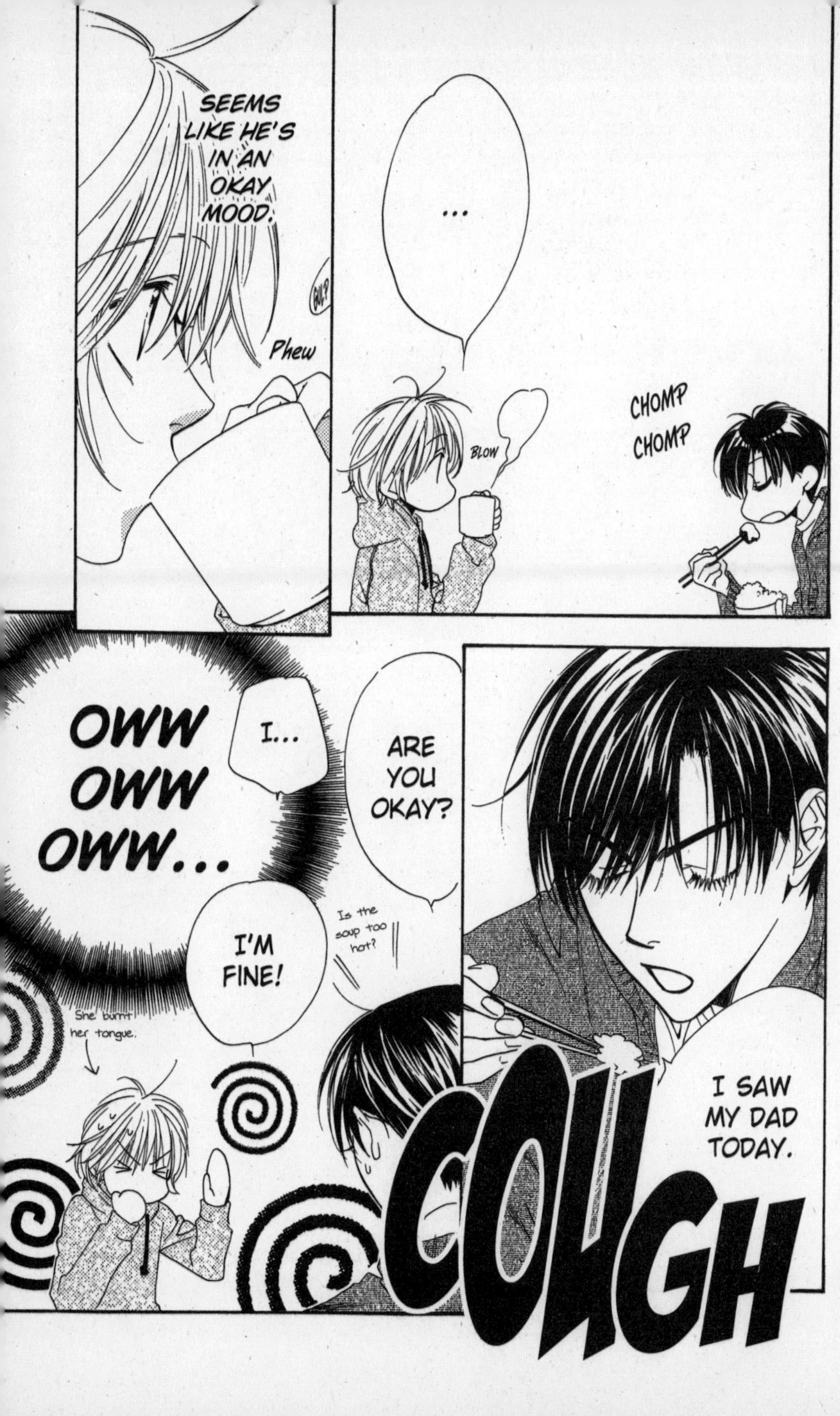
CHOMP CHOMP
...
BLOW
SEEMS LIKE HE'S IN AN OKAY MOOD.
GULP
Phew
I SAW MY DAD TODAY.
COUGH
ARE YOU OKAY?
I...
OWW OWW OWW...
Is the soup too hot?
I'M FINE!
She burnt her tongue.

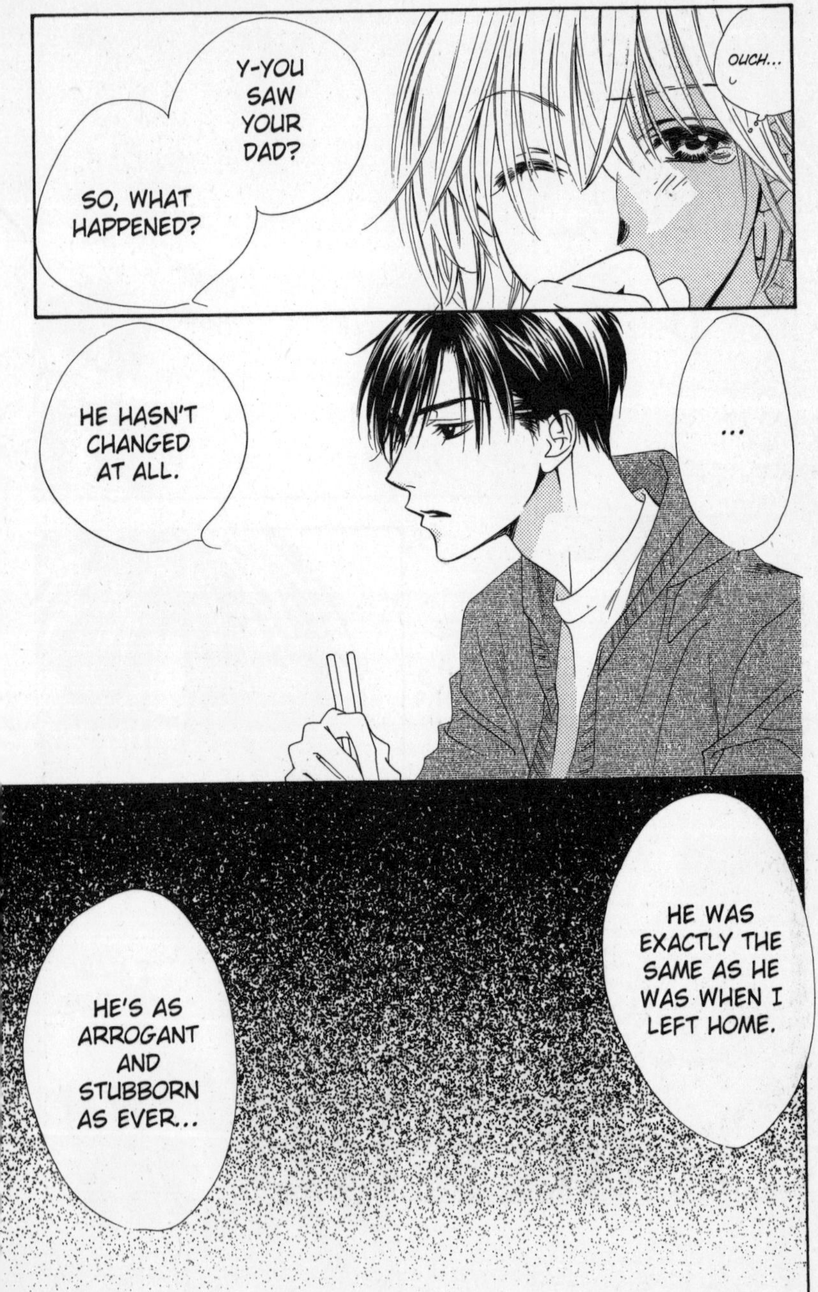
OUCH...
Y-YOU SAW YOUR DAD?
SO, WHAT HAPPENED?
...
HE HASN'T CHANGED AT ALL.
HE WAS EXACTLY THE SAME AS HE WAS WHEN I LEFT HOME.
HE'S AS ARROGANT AND STUBBORN AS EVER...

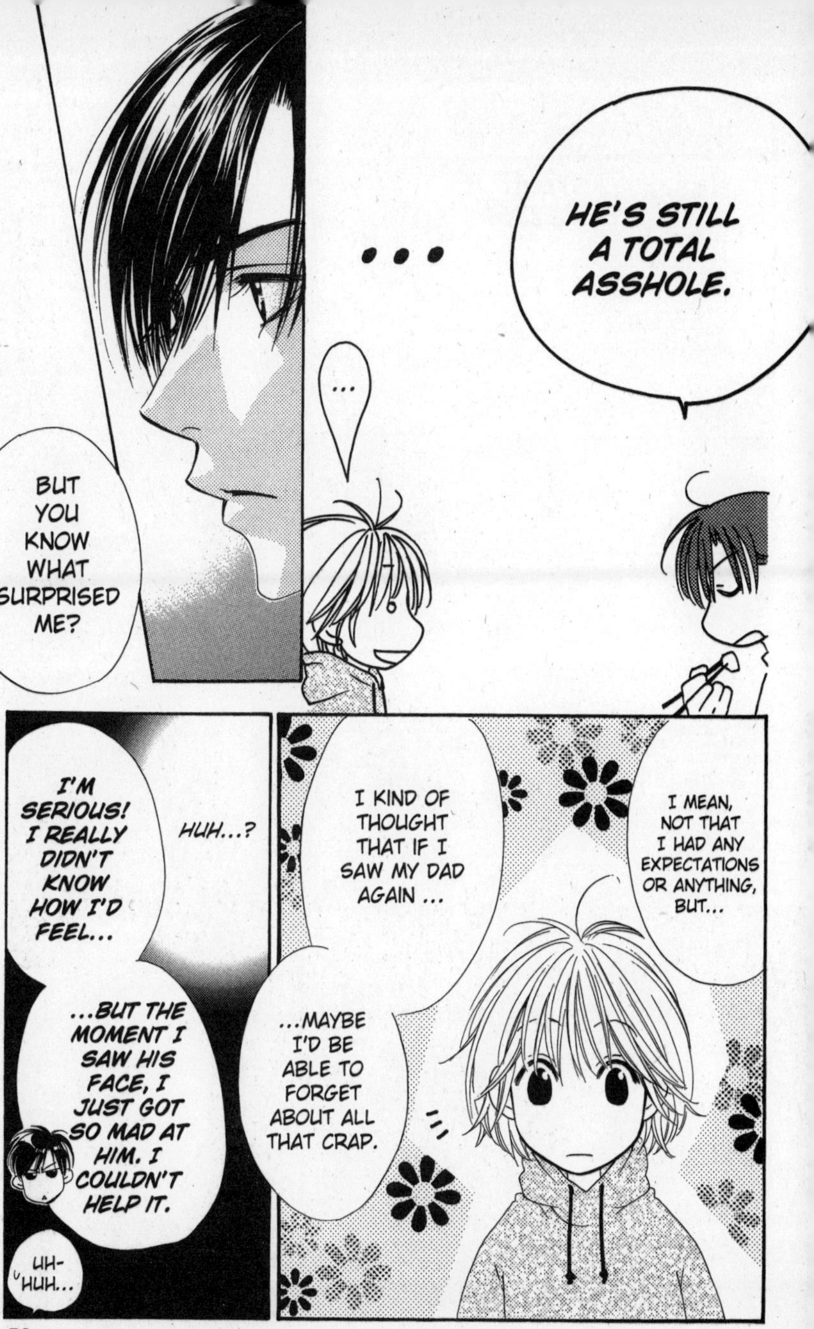
HE'S STILL A TOTAL ASSHOLE.
• • •
...
BUT YOU KNOW WHAT SURPRISED ME?
I MEAN, NOT THAT I HAD ANY EXPECTATIONS OR ANYTHING, BUT...
I KIND OF THOUGHT THAT IF I SAW MY DAD AGAIN ...
...MAYBE I'D BE ABLE TO FORGET ABOUT ALL THAT CRAP.
HUH...?
I'M SERIOUS! I REALLY DIDN'T KNOW HOW I'D FEEL...
...BUT THE MOMENT I SAW HIS FACE, I JUST GOT SO MAD AT HIM. I COULDN'T HELP IT.
UH-HUH...

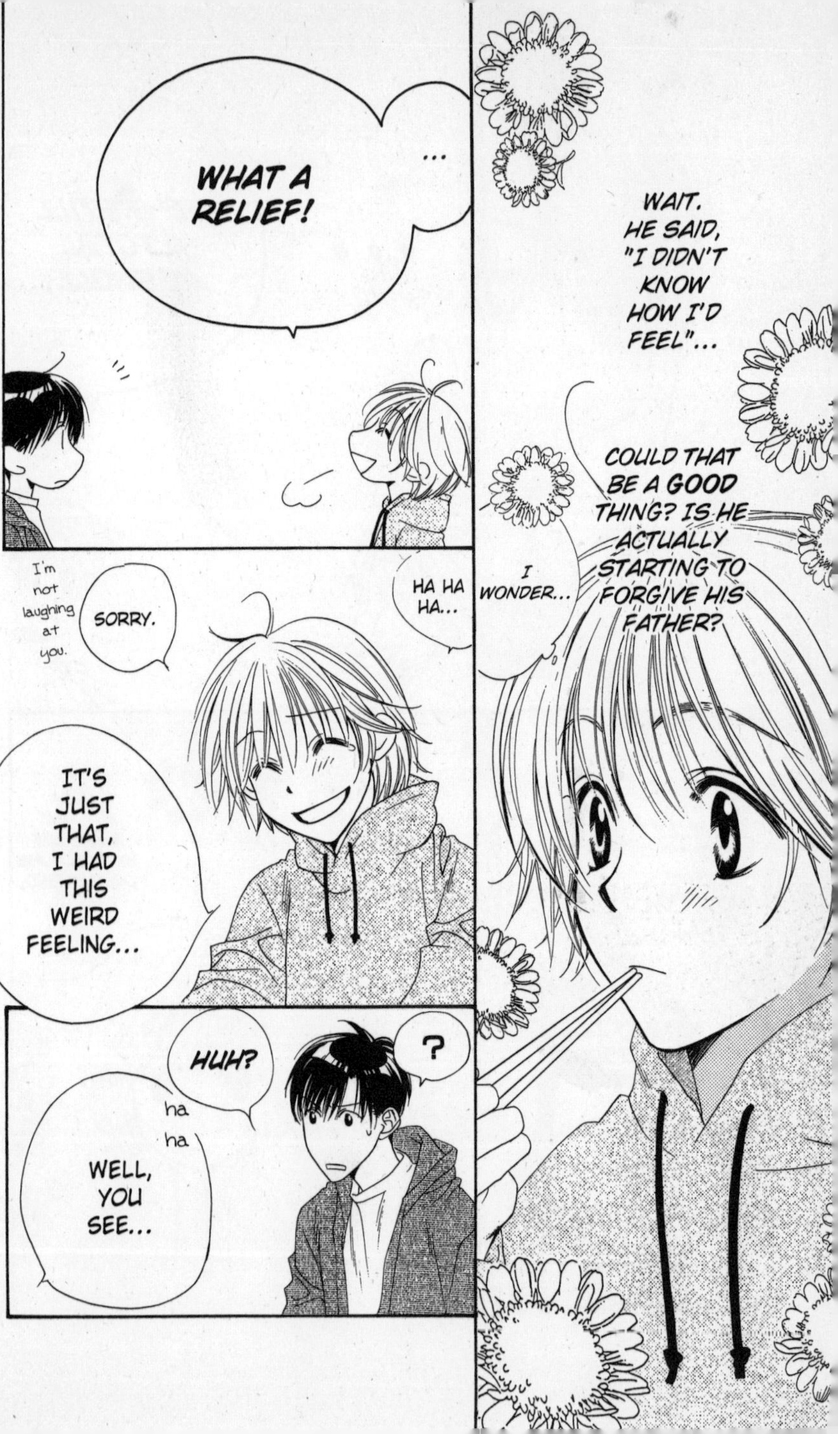
WAIT. HE SAID, "I DIDN'T KNOW HOW I'D FEEL"...
COULD THAT BE A GOOD THING? IS HE ACTUALLY STARTING TO FORGIVE HIS FATHER?
I WONDER...
...
WHAT A RELIEF!
HA HA HA...
SORRY.
I'm not laughing at you.
IT'S JUST THAT, I HAD THIS WEIRD FEELING...
?
HUH?
ha ha
WELL, YOU SEE...

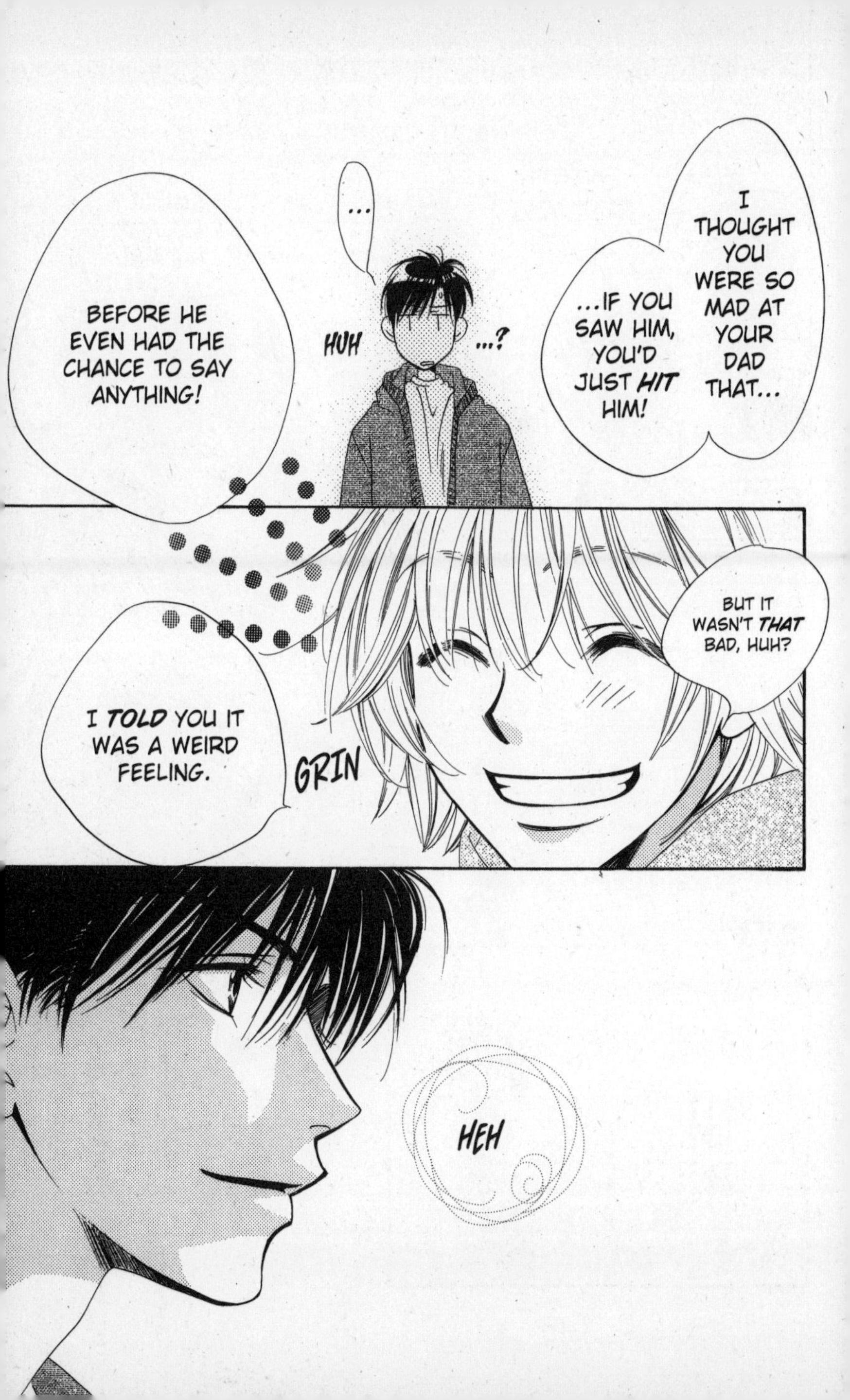
I THOUGHT YOU WERE SO MAD AT YOUR DAD THAT...
...IF YOU SAW HIM, YOU'D JUST HIT HIM!
BEFORE HE EVEN HAD THE CHANCE TO SAY ANYTHING!
...
HUH ...?
BUT IT WASN'T THAT BAD, HUH?
GRIN
I TOLD YOU IT WAS A WEIRD FEELING.
HEH

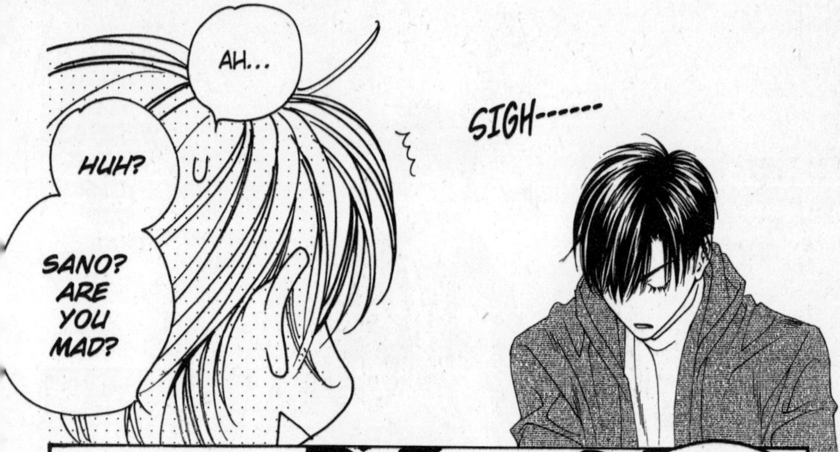
SIGH------
AH...
HUH?
SANO? ARE YOU MAD?

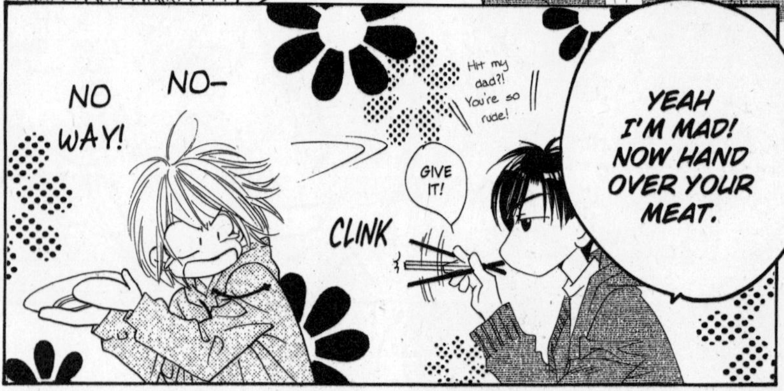
YEAH I'M MAD! NOW HAND OVER YOUR MEAT.
Hit my dad?! You're so rude!
GIVE IT!
CLINK
NO-
NO WAY!

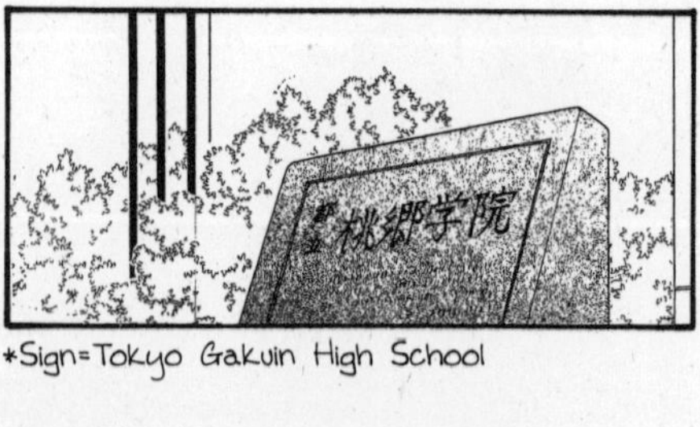
都立 桃郷学院

*Sign=Tokyo Gakuin High School

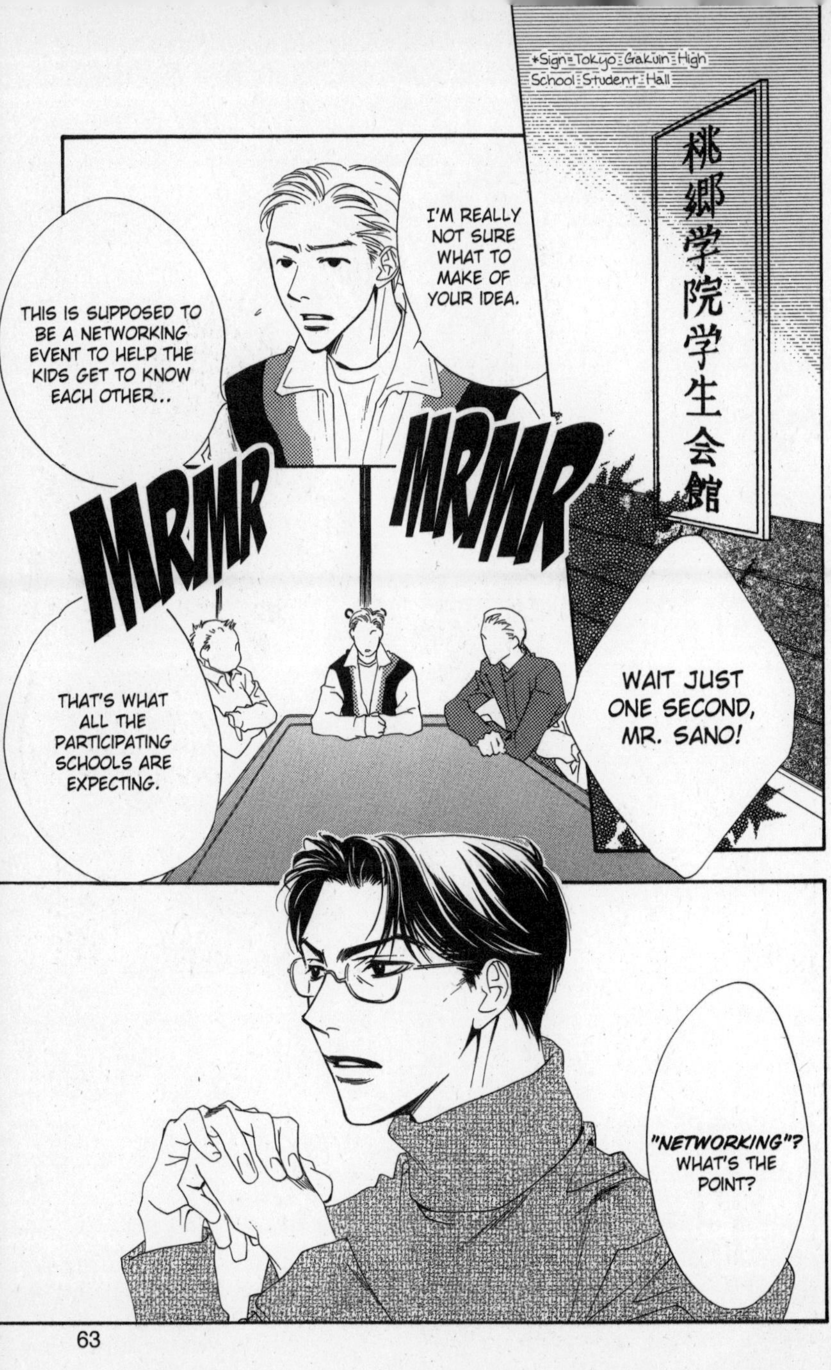
*Sign: Tokyo Gakuin High School Student Hall
桃郷学院学生会館
I'M REALLY NOT SURE WHAT TO MAKE OF YOUR IDEA.
THIS IS SUPPOSED TO BE A NETWORKING EVENT TO HELP THE KIDS GET TO KNOW EACH OTHER...
MRMR
MRMR
THAT'S WHAT ALL THE PARTICIPATING SCHOOLS ARE EXPECTING.
WAIT JUST ONE SECOND, MR. SANO!
"NETWORKING"? WHAT'S THE POINT?

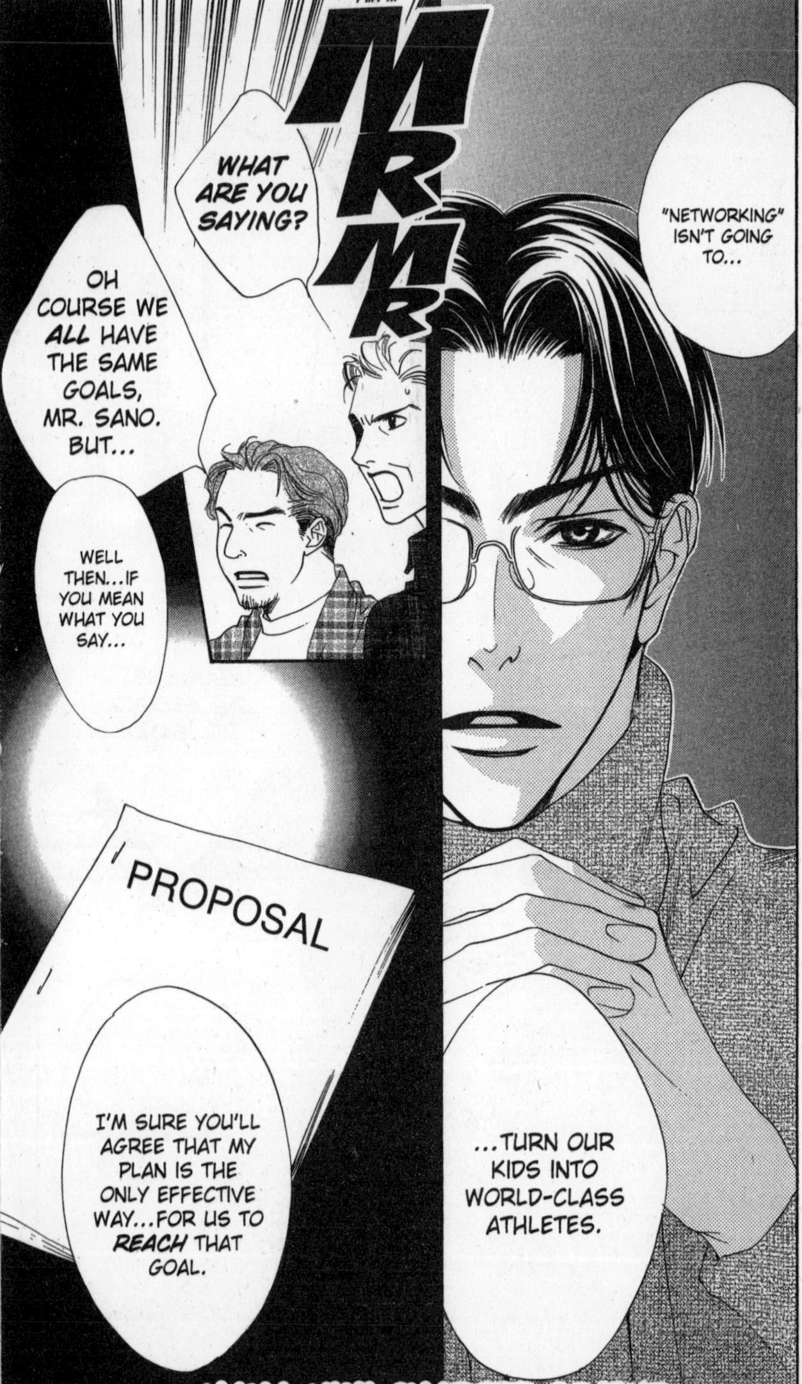

"NETWORKING" ISN'T GOING TO...
...TURN OUR KIDS INTO WORLD-CLASS ATHLETES.
MRMR
WHAT ARE YOU SAYING?
OH COURSE WE ALL HAVE THE SAME GOALS, MR. SANO. BUT...
WELL THEN...IF YOU MEAN WHAT YOU SAY...
PROPOSAL
I'M SURE YOU'LL AGREE THAT MY PLAN IS THE ONLY EFFECTIVE WAY...FOR US TO REACH THAT GOAL.

HANA-KIMI CHAPTER 93/END

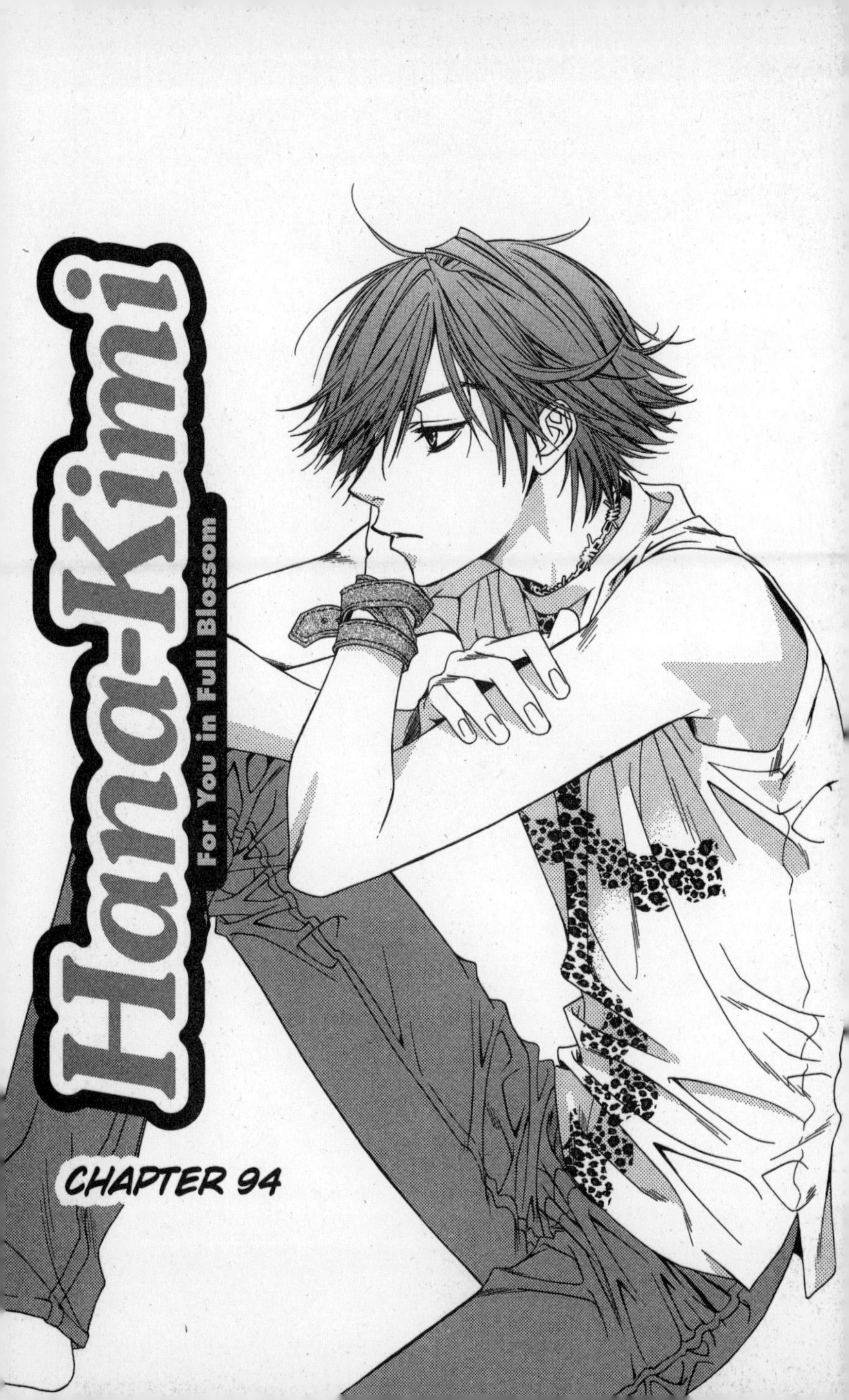
Hana-Kimi
For You in Full Blossom
CHAPTER 94

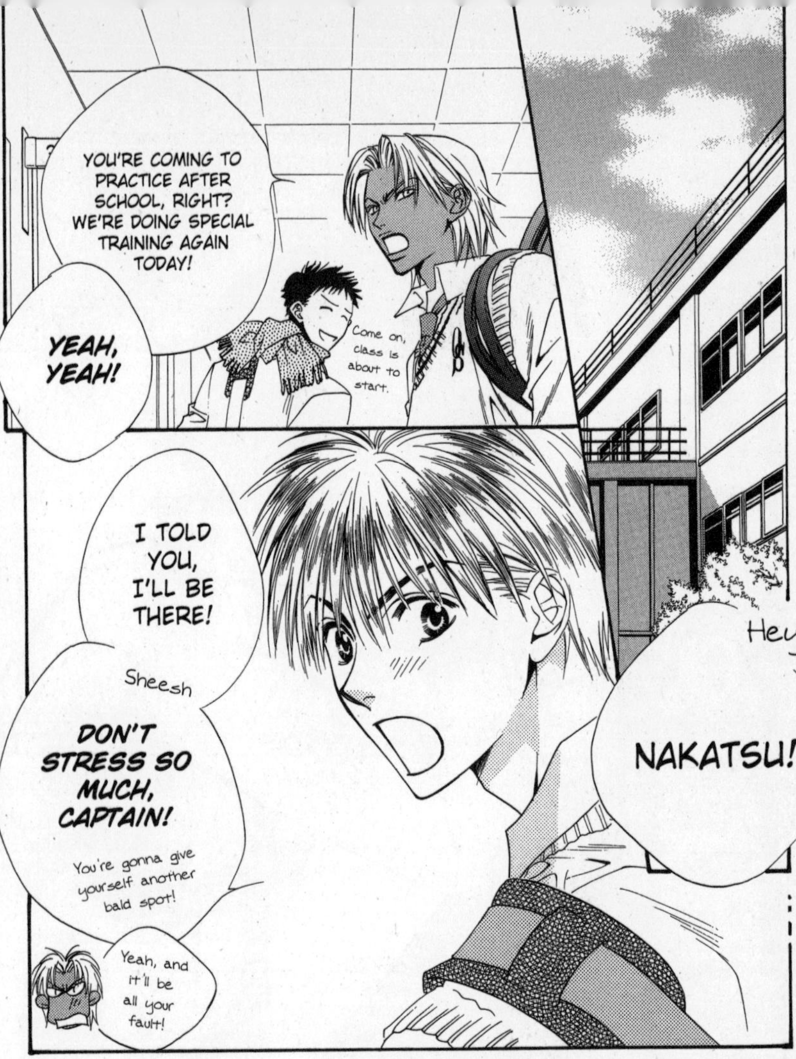
Hey
NAKATSU!
YOU'RE COMING TO PRACTICE AFTER SCHOOL, RIGHT? WE'RE DOING SPECIAL TRAINING AGAIN TODAY!
Come on, class is about to start.
YEAH, YEAH!
I TOLD YOU, I'LL BE THERE!
Sheesh
DON'T STRESS SO MUCH, CAPTAIN!
You're gonna give yourself another bald spot!
Yeah, and it'll be all your fault!

ONMYO-ZA

I recently discovered this band. I happened to see (hear?) their music video on TV one day, but I had no idea who they were. A few days later, I discovered their CD at a record store...it must be fate! They're a metal band with two vocalists (a guy and a girl). They play melodic rock songs with very traditional Japanese lyrics. Their costumes are really traditional too, and they match perfectly with their music.

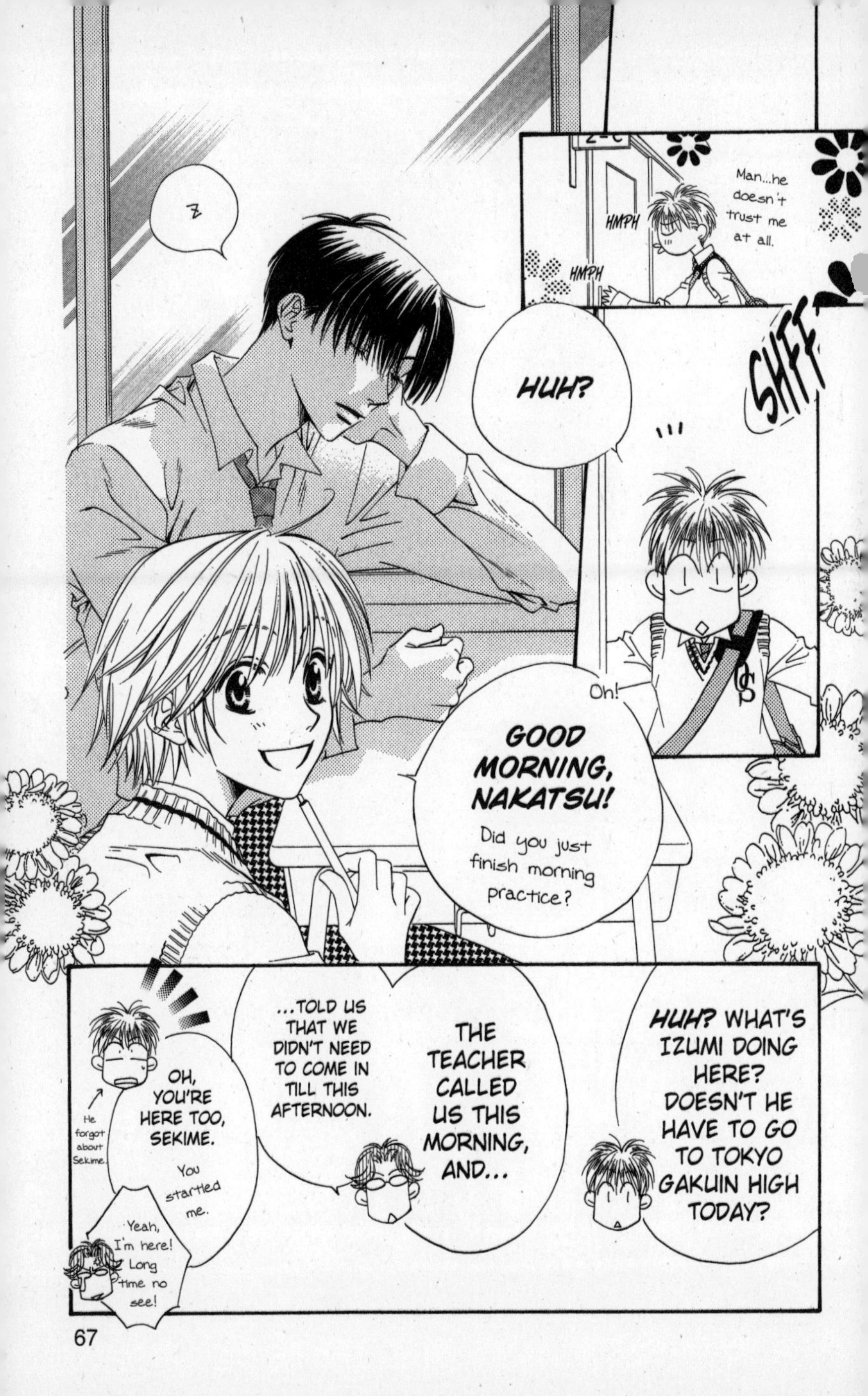
HMPH
HMPH
Man...he doesn't trust me at all.
SHFF
Z
HUH?
Oh!
GOOD MORNING, NAKATSU!
Did you just finish morning practice?
HUH? WHAT'S IZUMI DOING HERE? DOESN'T HE HAVE TO GO TO TOKYO GAKUIN HIGH TODAY?
THE TEACHER CALLED US THIS MORNING, AND...
...TOLD US THAT WE DIDN'T NEED TO COME IN TILL THIS AFTERNOON.
OH, YOU'RE HERE TOO, SEKIME.
You startled me.
He forgot about Sekime.
Yeah, I'm here! Long time no see!

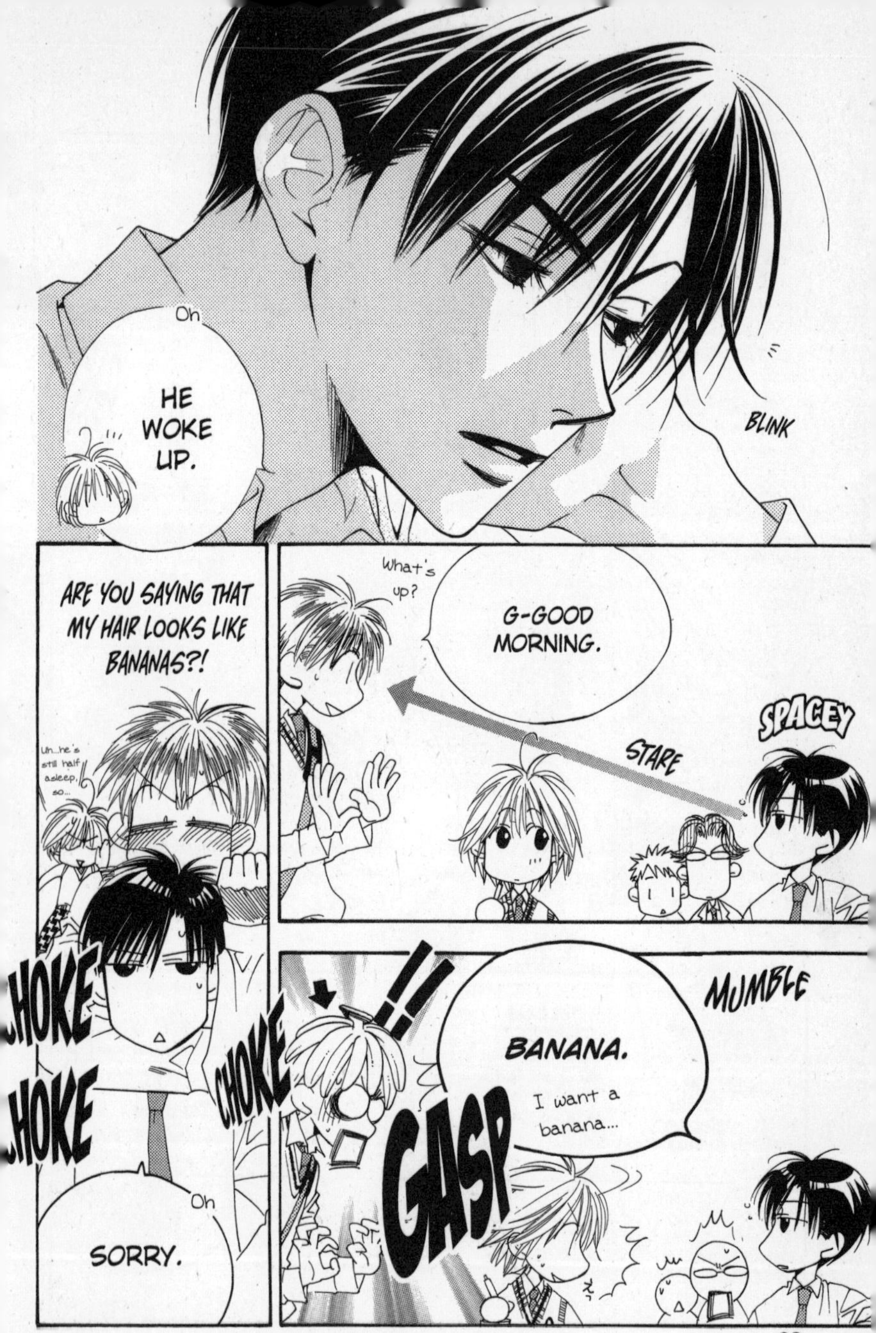
BLINK
Oh
HE WOKE UP.
SPACEY
STARE
G-GOOD MORNING.
What's up?
MUMBLE
BANANA.
I want a banana...
GASP
CHOKE
ARE YOU SAYING THAT MY HAIR LOOKS LIKE BANANAS?!
Uh...he's still half asleep, so...
CHOKE
CHOKE
Oh
SORRY.

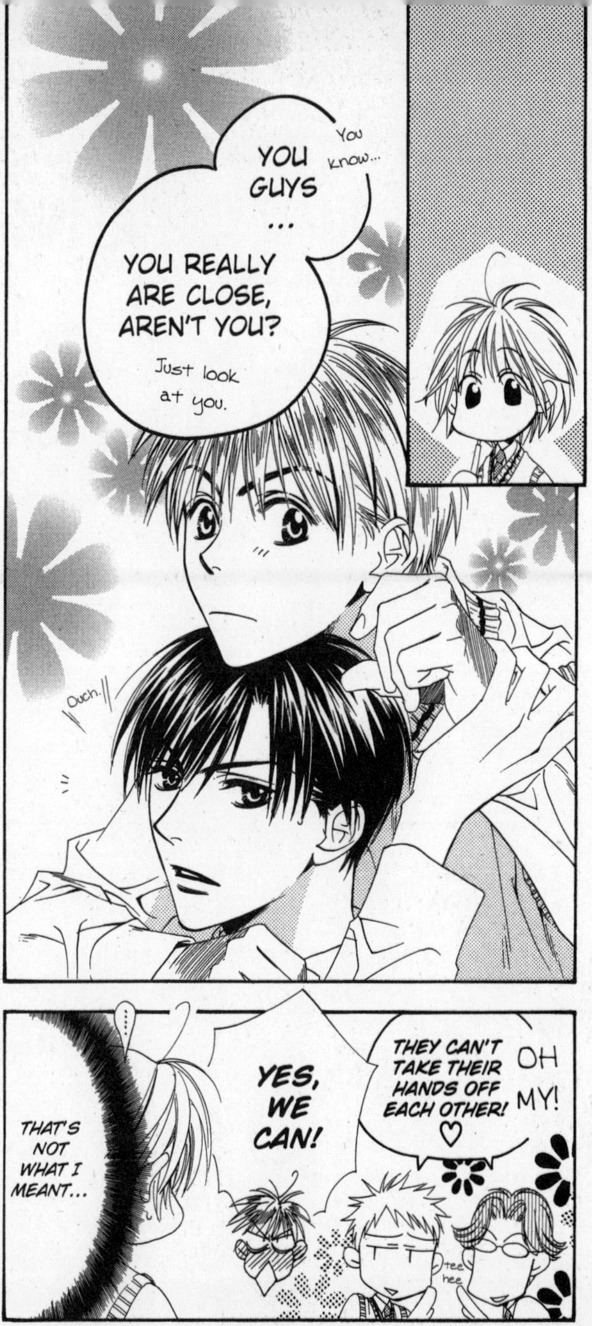
YOU GUYS ... YOU REALLY ARE CLOSE, AREN'T YOU?
You know...
Just look at you.
Ouch.
OH MY!
THEY CAN'T TAKE THEIR HANDS OFF EACH OTHER! ♡
tee hee
YES, WE CAN!
THAT'S NOT WHAT I MEANT...

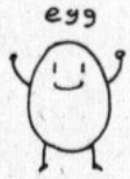
egg

SANO'S FATHER AND THE TRACK AND FIELD NETWORKING EVENT: PART 2

...So basically, I came up with a way to make Sano's father leave his hometown, and that's how this story was created! But then I realized there was a big problem. That's right, I'm talking about having to decide, what does Sano's father look like? After many tries, I finally came up with the right look for him. (I know you're probably thinking, "Many tries? He doesn't look that special.") There's one other thing that I'm sure some of you have noticed already, but since nobody has said anything, I'm gonna bring it to everyone's attention. Every story since volume three has taken place during fall or winter. That's right...heh... it's been fall or winter all this time.

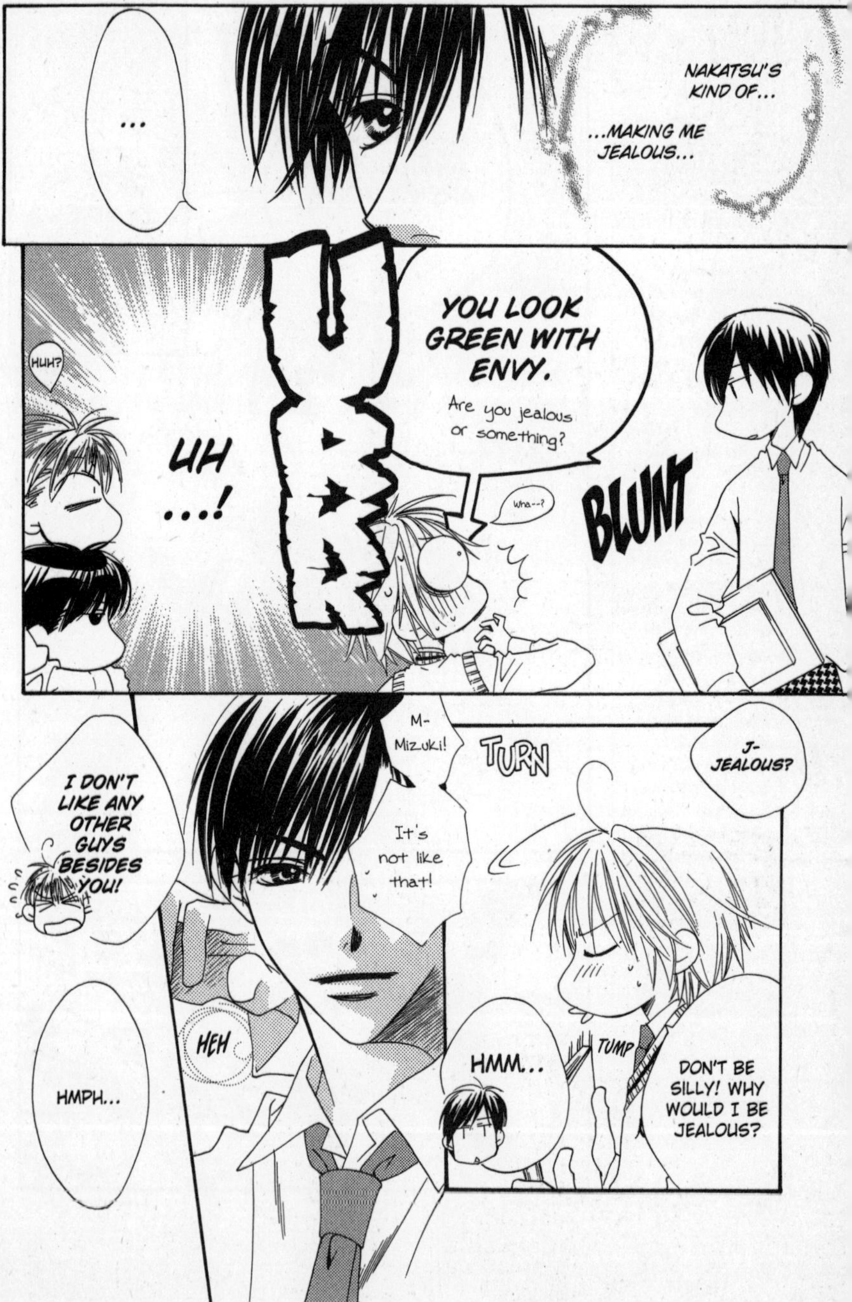
NAKATSU'S KIND OF...
...MAKING ME JEALOUS...
...
YOU LOOK GREEN WITH ENVY.
Are you jealous or something?
BLUNT
Wha--?
UH ...!
HUH?
J- JEALOUS?
TURN
M- Mizuki!
It's not like that!
DON'T BE SILLY! WHY WOULD I BE JEALOUS?
TUMP
HMM...
I DON'T LIKE ANY OTHER GUYS BESIDES YOU!
HEH
HMPH...

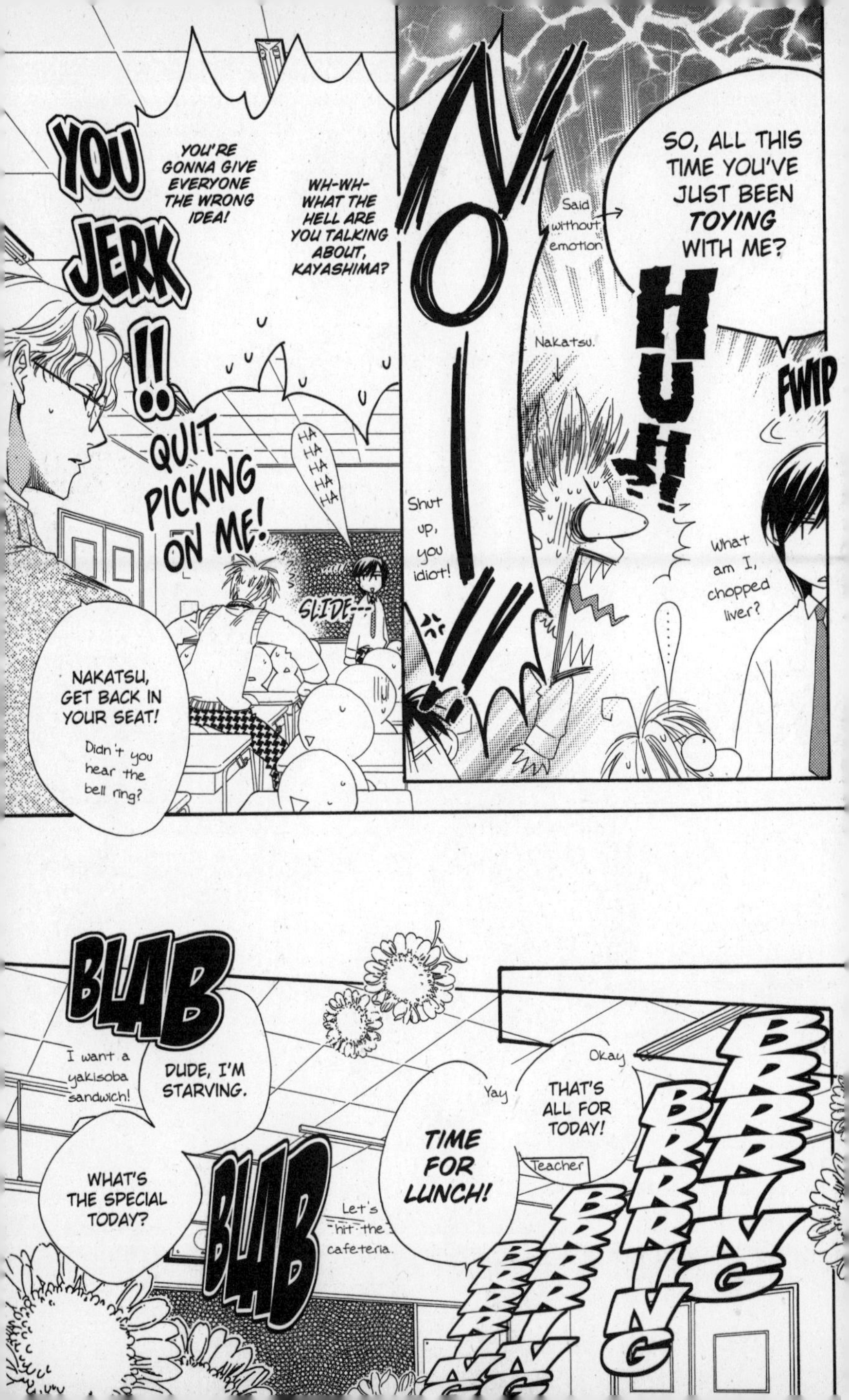
SO, ALL THIS TIME YOU'VE JUST BEEN TOYING WITH ME?
Said without emotion
HUH!
FWIP
Nakatsu.
NO!!
What am I, chopped liver?
Shut up, you idiot!
...
WH-WH-WHAT THE HELL ARE YOU TALKING ABOUT, KAYASHIMA?
YOU'RE GONNA GIVE EVERYONE THE WRONG IDEA!
YOU JERK!!
QUIT PICKING ON ME!
HA HA HA HA HA
SLIDE
NAKATSU, GET BACK IN YOUR SEAT!
Didn't you hear the bell ring?
BRRRING
BRRRING
BRRRING
Okay
THAT'S ALL FOR TODAY!
Teacher
Yay
TIME FOR LUNCH!
Let's hit the cafeteria.
BLAB
DUDE, I'M STARVING.
I want a yakisoba sandwich!
WHAT'S THE SPECIAL TODAY?
BLAB

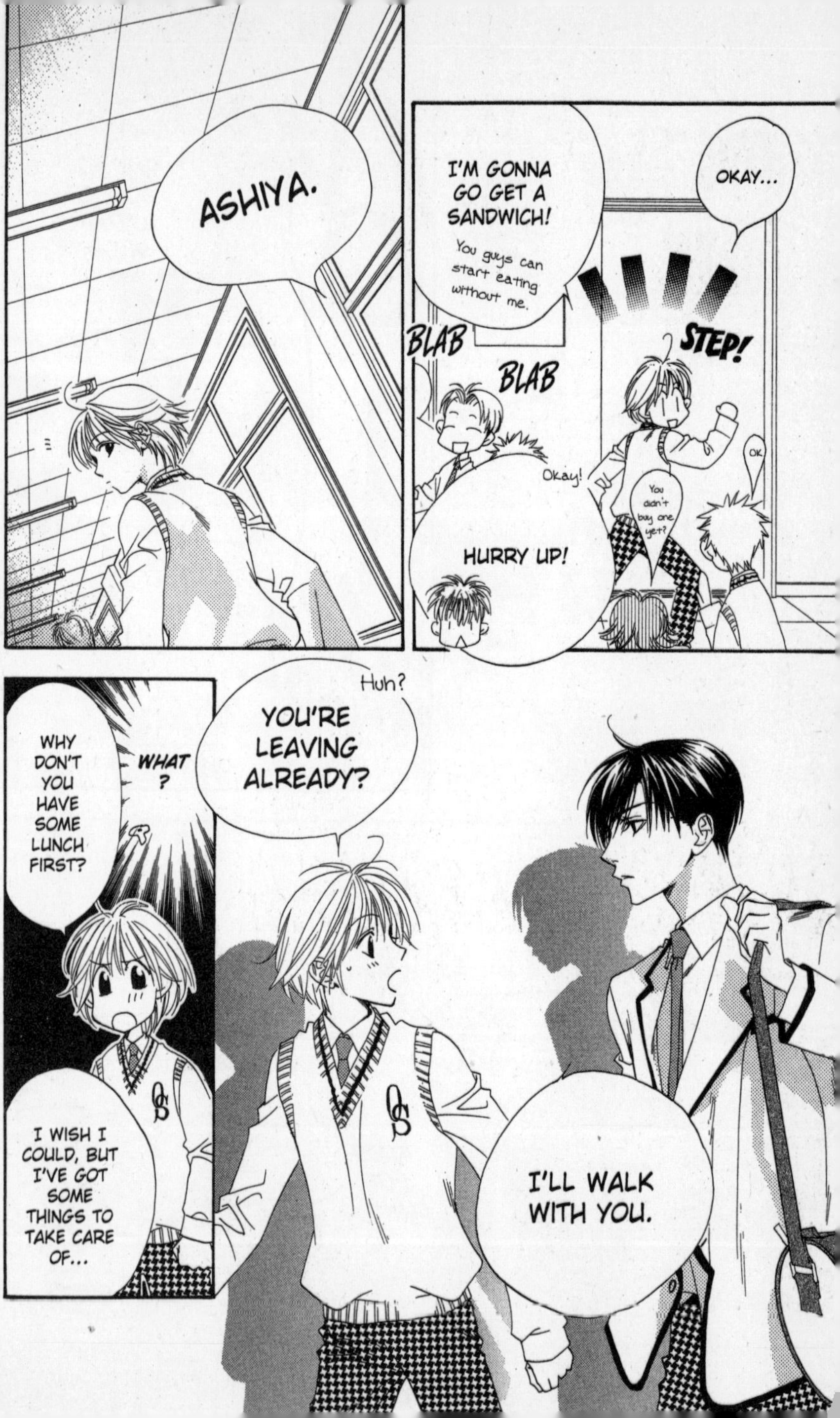
OKAY...
I'M GONNA GO GET A SANDWICH!
You guys can start eating without me.
STEP!
BLAB
BLAB
OK
You didn't buy one yet?
Okay!
HURRY UP!
ASHIYA.
Huh?
YOU'RE LEAVING ALREADY?
WHY DON'T YOU HAVE SOME LUNCH FIRST?
WHAT?
I WISH I COULD, BUT I'VE GOT SOME THINGS TO TAKE CARE OF...
I'LL WALK WITH YOU.

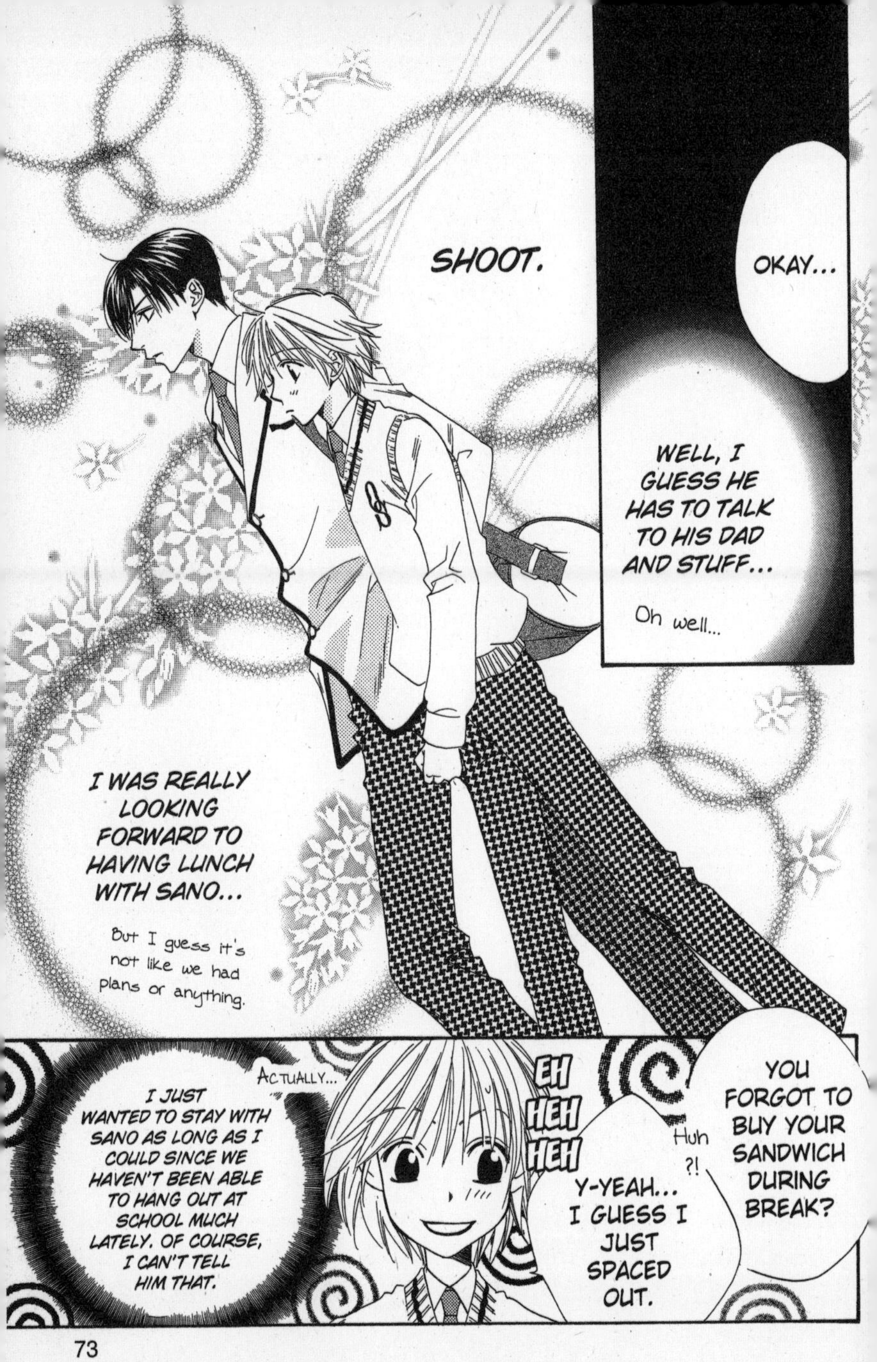
OKAY...
WELL, I GUESS HE HAS TO TALK TO HIS DAD AND STUFF...
Oh well...
SHOOT.
I WAS REALLY LOOKING FORWARD TO HAVING LUNCH WITH SANO...
But I guess it's not like we had plans or anything.
YOU FORGOT TO BUY YOUR SANDWICH DURING BREAK?
Huh ?!
Y-YEAH... I GUESS I JUST SPACED OUT.
EH HEH HEH
ACTUALLY...
I JUST WANTED TO STAY WITH SANO AS LONG AS I COULD SINCE WE HAVEN'T BEEN ABLE TO HANG OUT AT SCHOOL MUCH LATELY. OF COURSE, I CAN'T TELL HIM THAT.

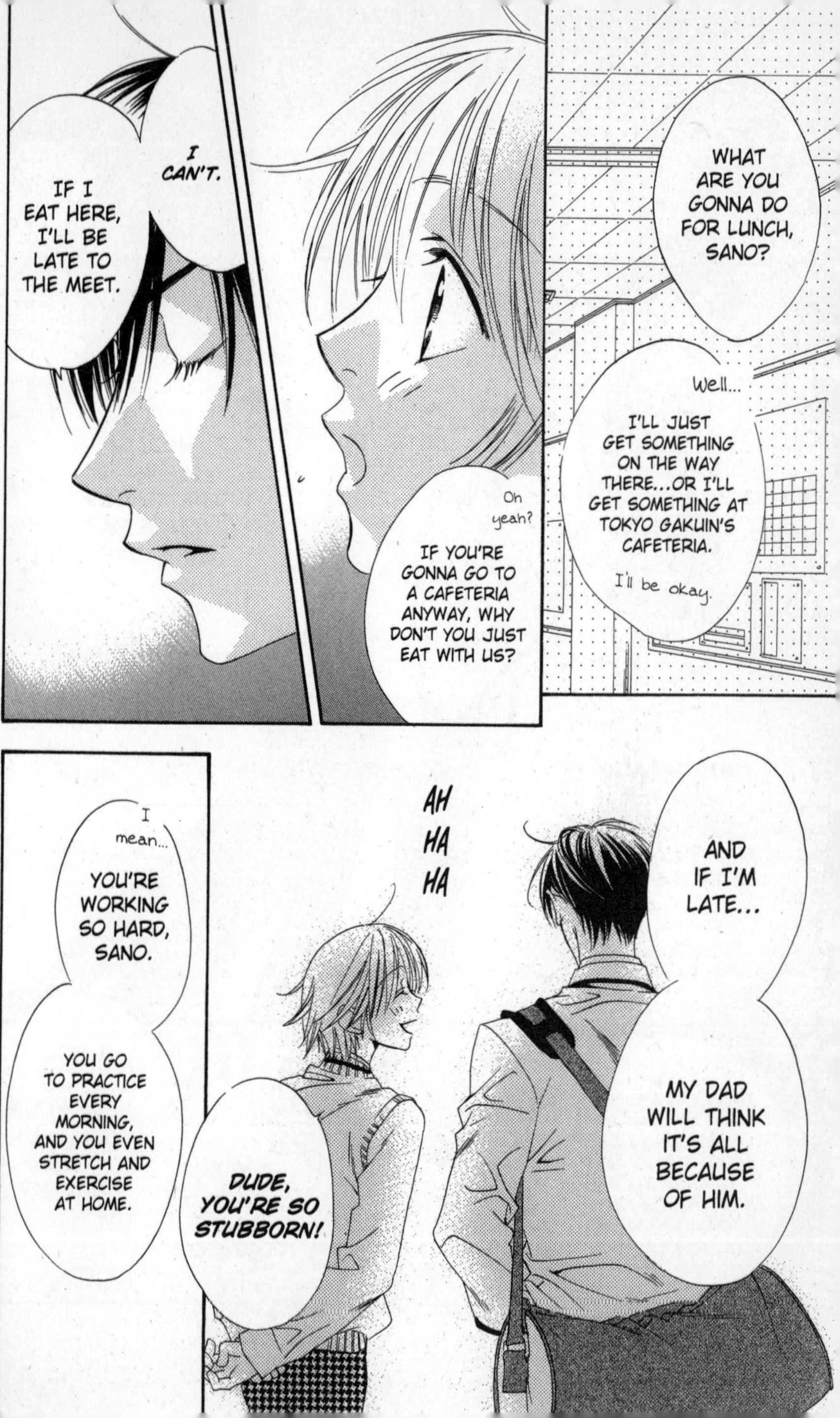
WHAT ARE YOU GONNA DO FOR LUNCH, SANO?
Well...
I'LL JUST GET SOMETHING ON THE WAY THERE...OR I'LL GET SOMETHING AT TOKYO GAKUIN'S CAFETERIA.
I'll be okay.
Oh yeah?
IF YOU'RE GONNA GO TO A CAFETERIA ANYWAY, WHY DON'T YOU JUST EAT WITH US?
I CAN'T.
IF I EAT HERE, I'LL BE LATE TO THE MEET.
AND IF I'M LATE...
MY DAD WILL THINK IT'S ALL BECAUSE OF HIM.
AH HA HA
DUDE, YOU'RE SO STUBBORN!
I mean...
YOU'RE WORKING SO HARD, SANO.
YOU GO TO PRACTICE EVERY MORNING, AND YOU EVEN STRETCH AND EXERCISE AT HOME.

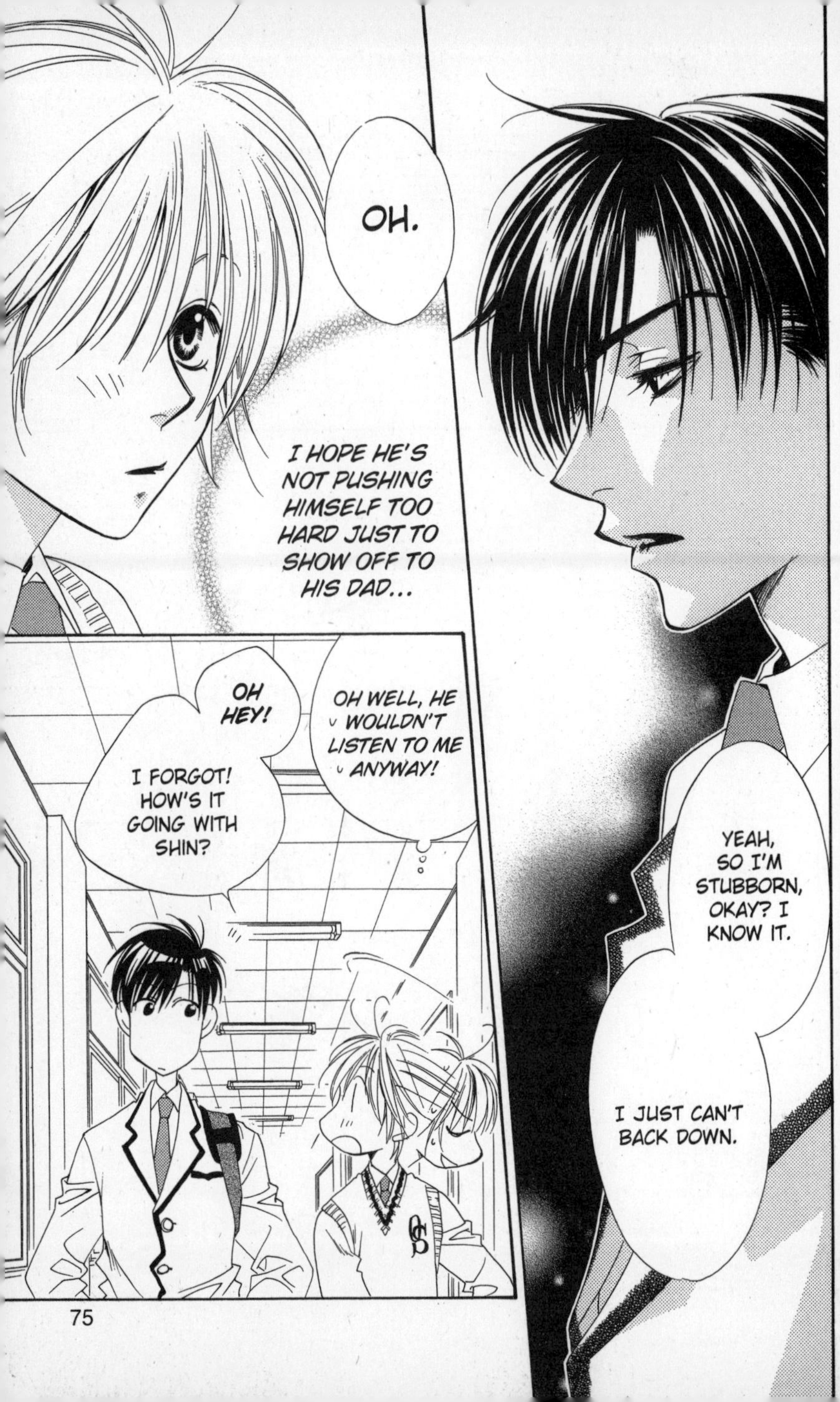
YEAH, SO I'M STUBBORN, OKAY? I KNOW IT.
I JUST CAN'T BACK DOWN.
OH.
I HOPE HE'S NOT PUSHING HIMSELF TOO HARD JUST TO SHOW OFF TO HIS DAD...
OH WELL, HE WOULDN'T LISTEN TO ME ANYWAY!
OH HEY!
I FORGOT! HOW'S IT GOING WITH SHIN?

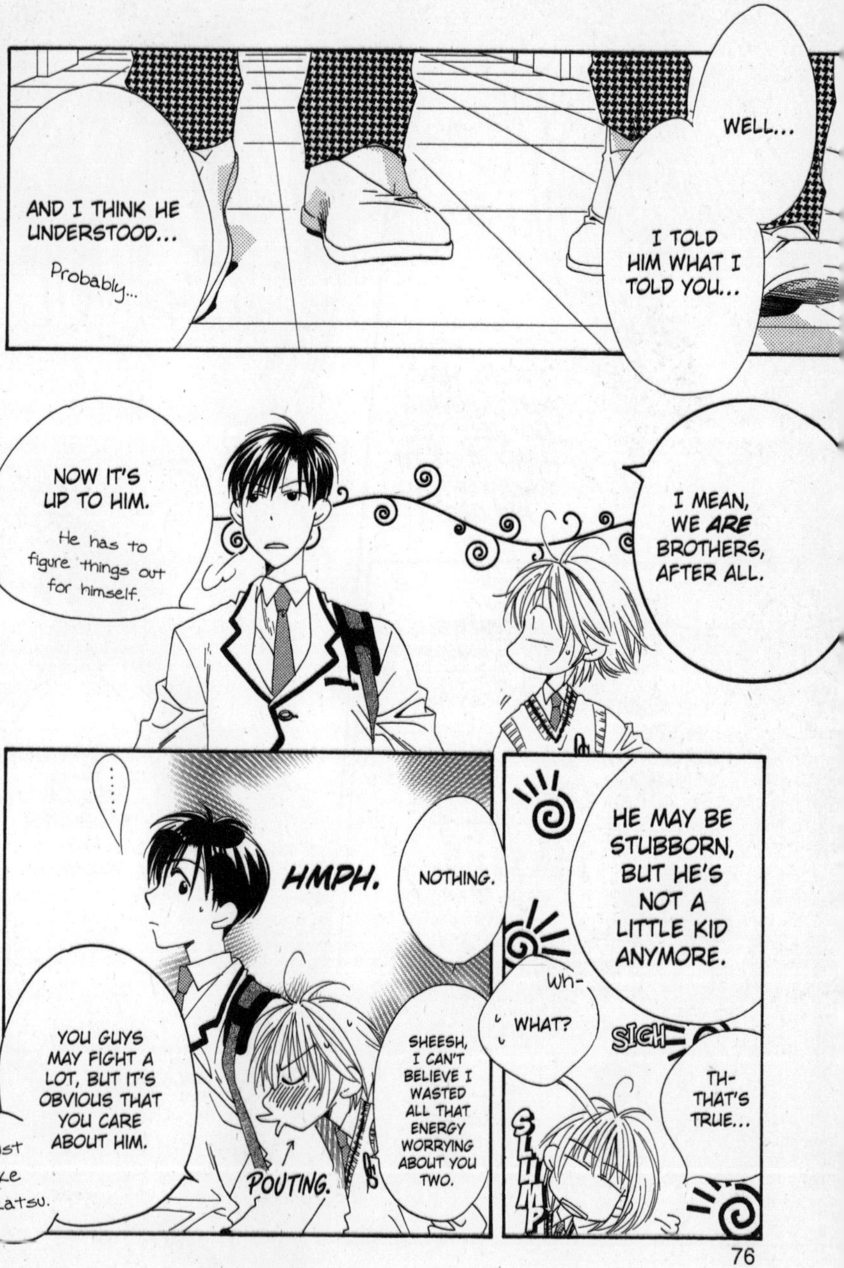
WELL...
I TOLD HIM WHAT I TOLD YOU...
AND I THINK HE UNDERSTOOD...
Probably...
I MEAN, WE ARE BROTHERS, AFTER ALL.
NOW IT'S UP TO HIM.
He has to figure things out for himself.
HE MAY BE STUBBORN, BUT HE'S NOT A LITTLE KID ANYMORE.
SIGH
TH- THAT'S TRUE...
Wh-
WHAT?
SLUMP
NOTHING.
HMPH.
......
SHEESH, I CAN'T BELIEVE I WASTED ALL THAT ENERGY WORRYING ABOUT YOU TWO.
POUTING.
YOU GUYS MAY FIGHT A LOT, BUT IT'S OBVIOUS THAT YOU CARE ABOUT HIM.
Just like Nakatsu.

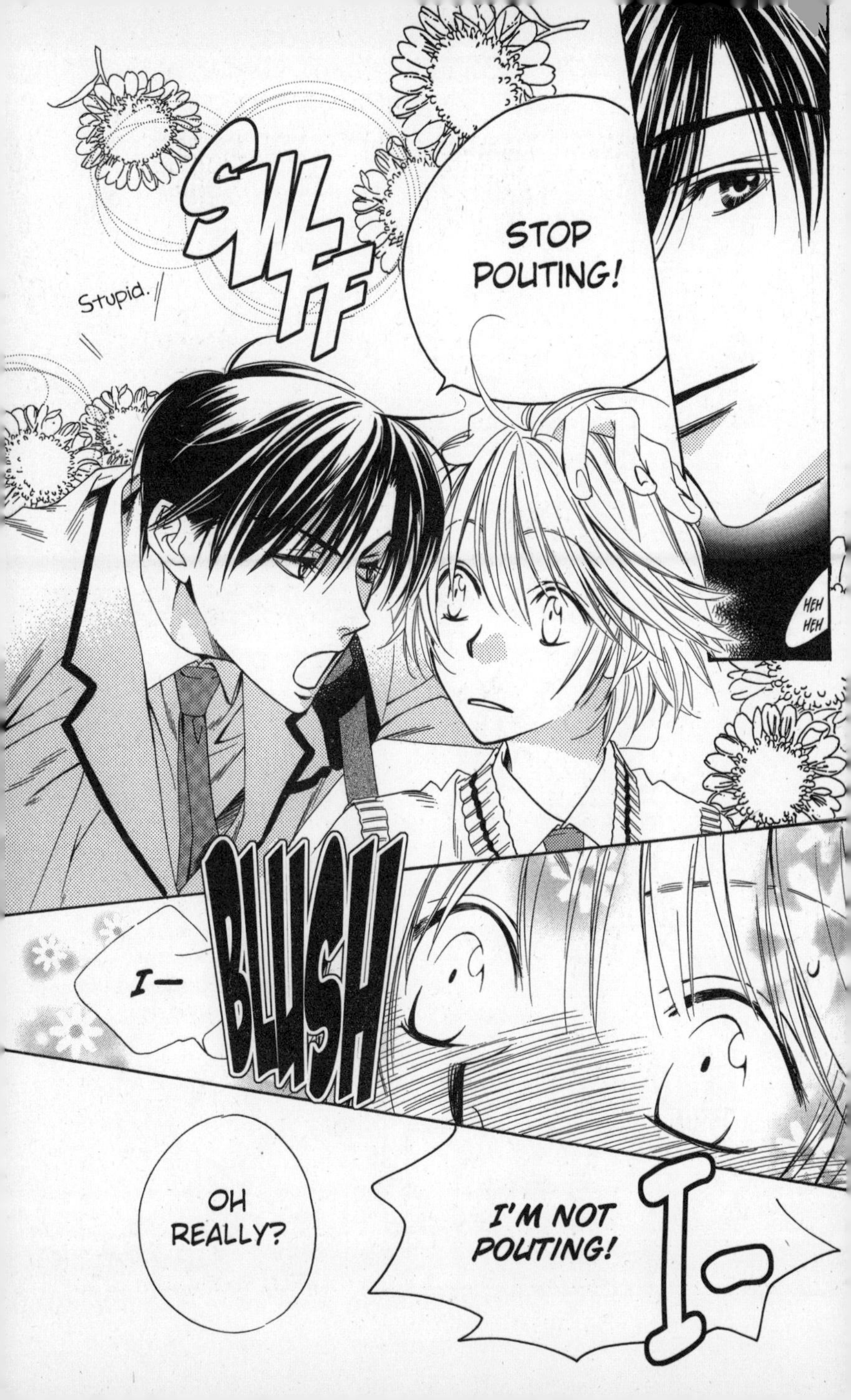
HEH HEH
STOP POUTING!
SNIFF
Stupid.
BLUSH
I—
I-
I'M NOT POUTING!
OH REALLY?

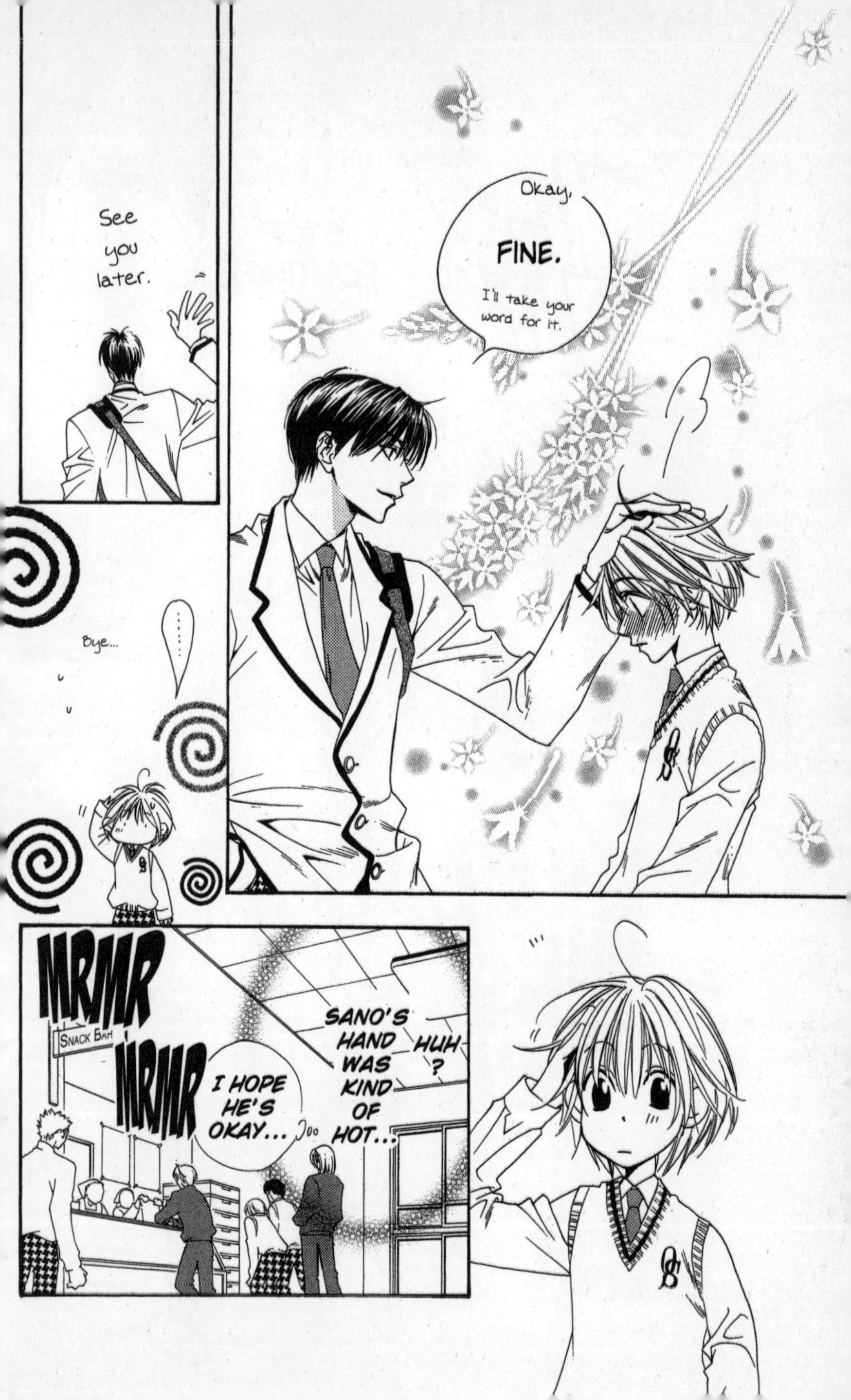
Okay, FINE. I'll take your word for it.
See you later.
Bye...
......
HUH?
SANO'S HAND WAS KIND OF HOT...
MRMR MRMR
SNACK BAR
I HOPE HE'S OKAY...

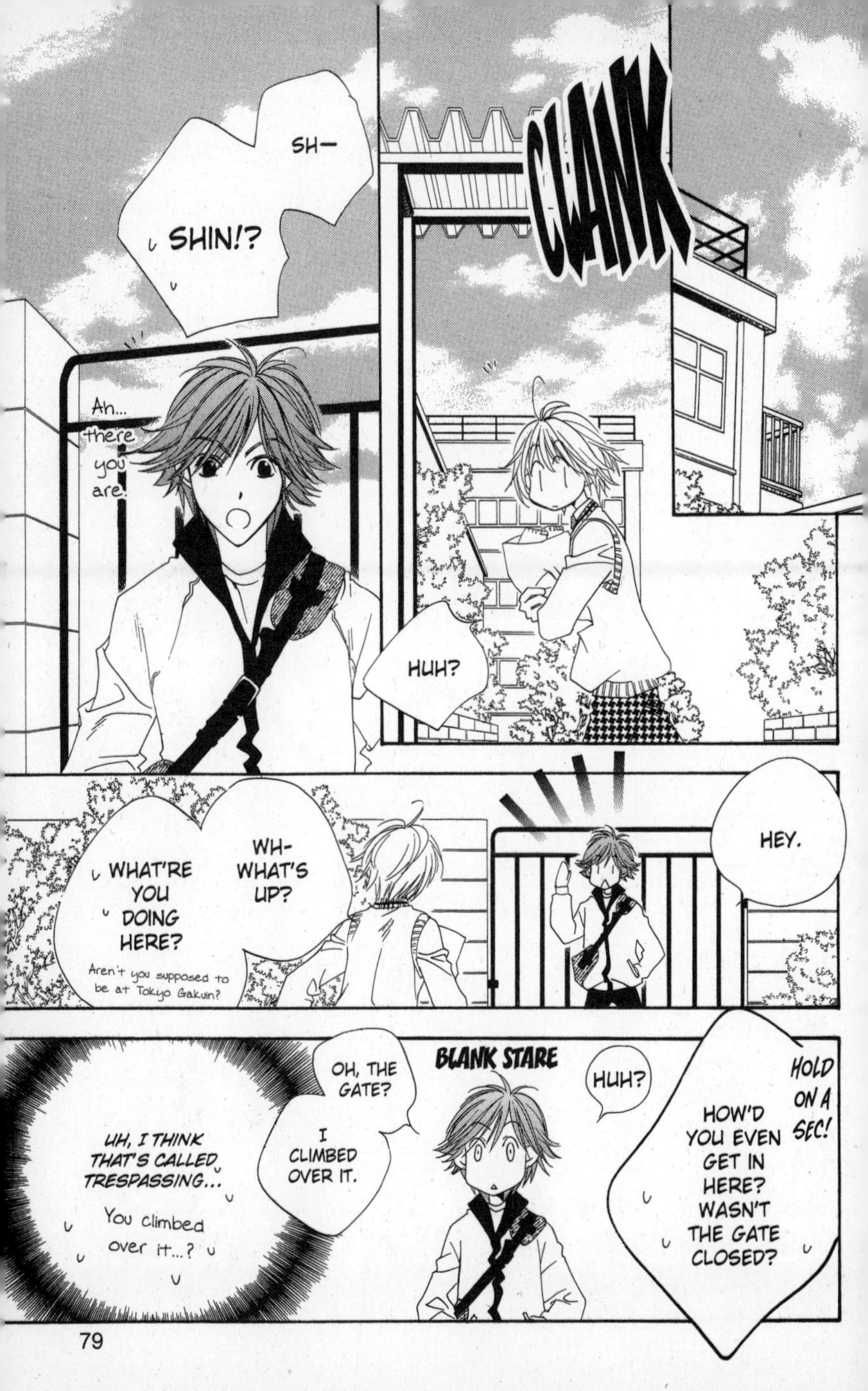
CLANK
HUH?
SH—
SHIN!?
An... there you are.
HEY.
WH- WHAT'S UP?
WHAT'RE YOU DOING HERE?
Aren't you supposed to be at Tokyo Gakuin?
HOLD ON A SEC!
HOW'D YOU EVEN GET IN HERE? WASN'T THE GATE CLOSED?
HUH?
BLANK STARE
OH, THE GATE?
I CLIMBED OVER IT.
UH, I THINK THAT'S CALLED TRESPASSING...
You climbed over it...?

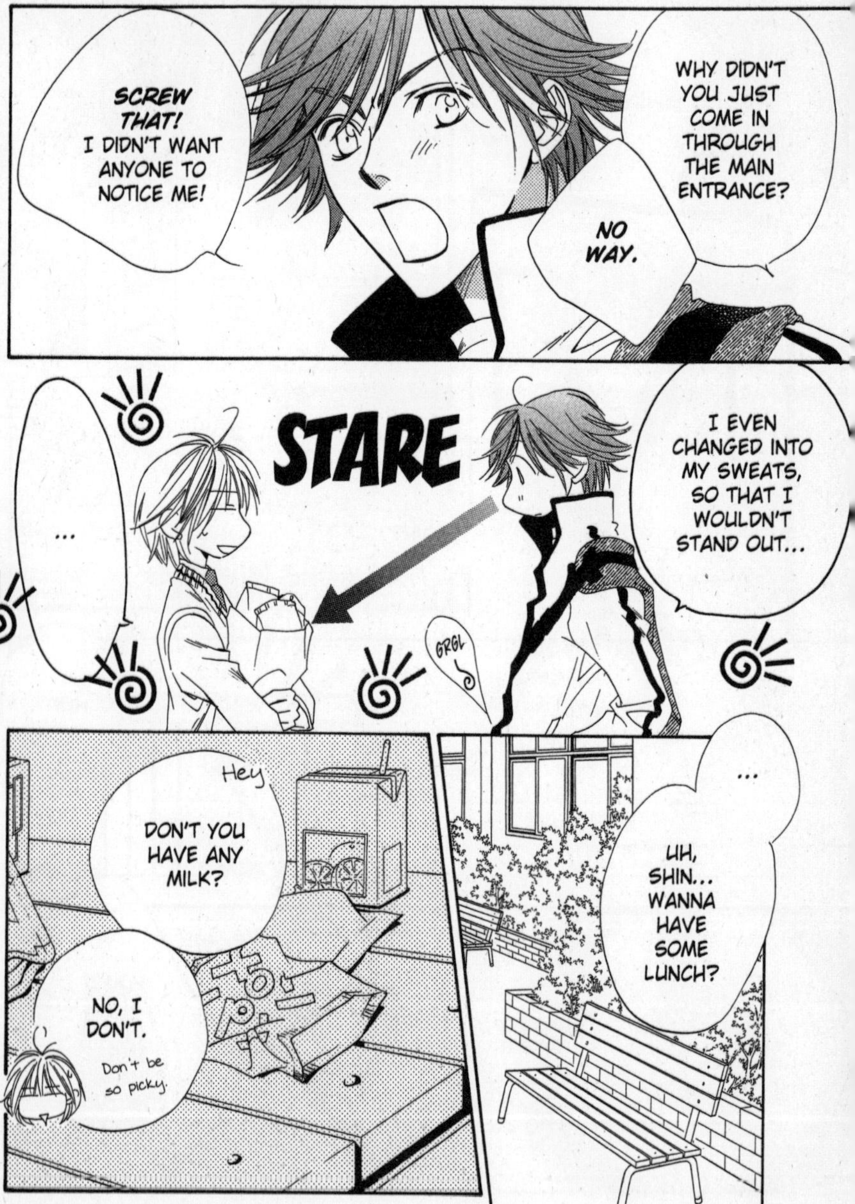
WHY DIDN'T YOU JUST COME IN THROUGH THE MAIN ENTRANCE?
NO WAY.
SCREW THAT! I DIDN'T WANT ANYONE TO NOTICE ME!
I EVEN CHANGED INTO MY SWEATS, SO THAT I WOULDN'T STAND OUT...
STARE
GRGL
...
...
UH, SHIN... WANNA HAVE SOME LUNCH?
Hey
DON'T YOU HAVE ANY MILK?
NO, I DON'T.
Don't be so picky.

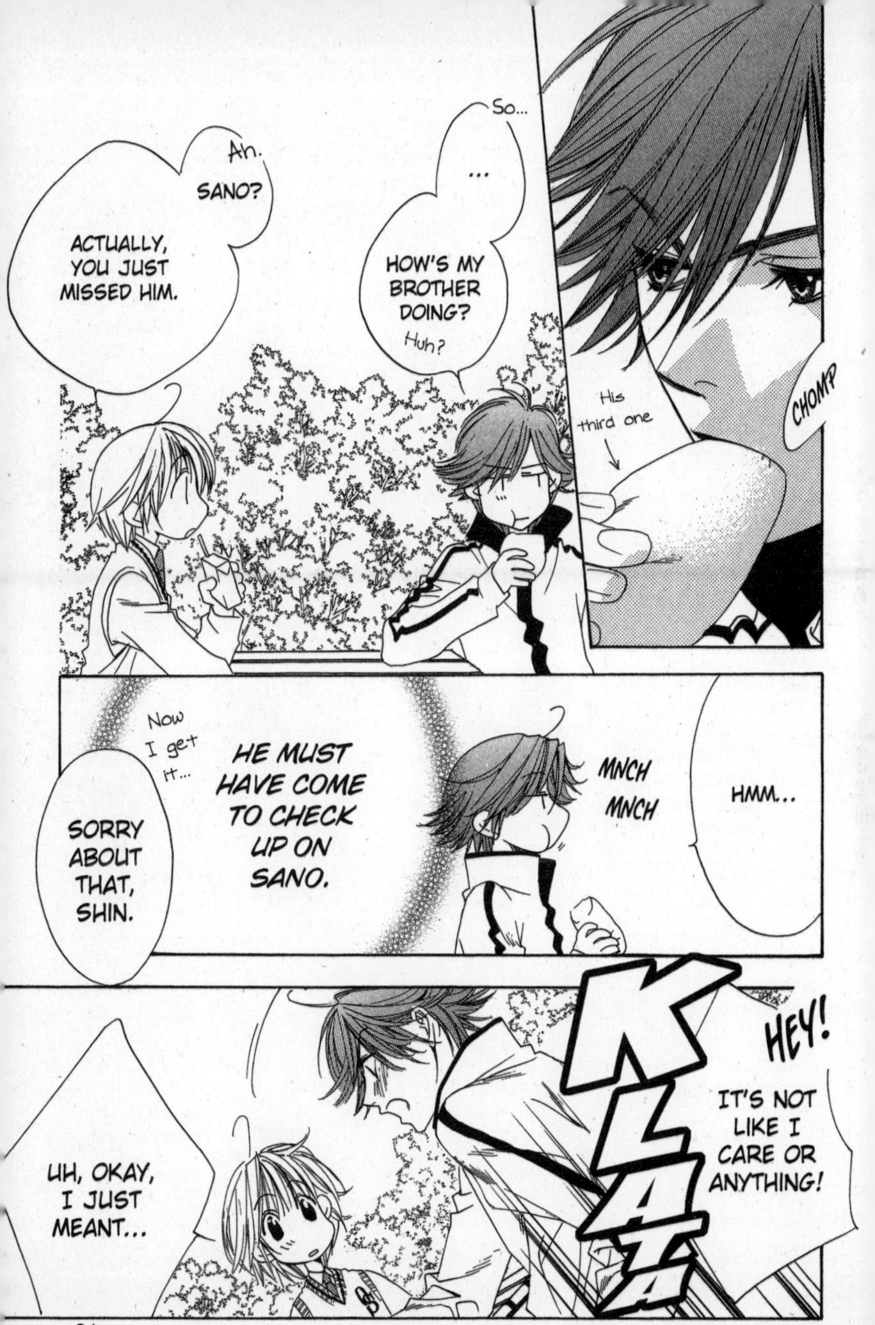
CHOMP
His third one
So...
...
HOW'S MY BROTHER DOING?
Huh?
Ah.
SANO?
ACTUALLY, YOU JUST MISSED HIM.
HMM...
MNCH MNCH
HE MUST HAVE COME TO CHECK UP ON SANO.
Now I get it...
SORRY ABOUT THAT, SHIN.
HEY!
IT'S NOT LIKE I CARE OR ANYTHING!
KLAAA
UH, OKAY, I JUST MEANT...

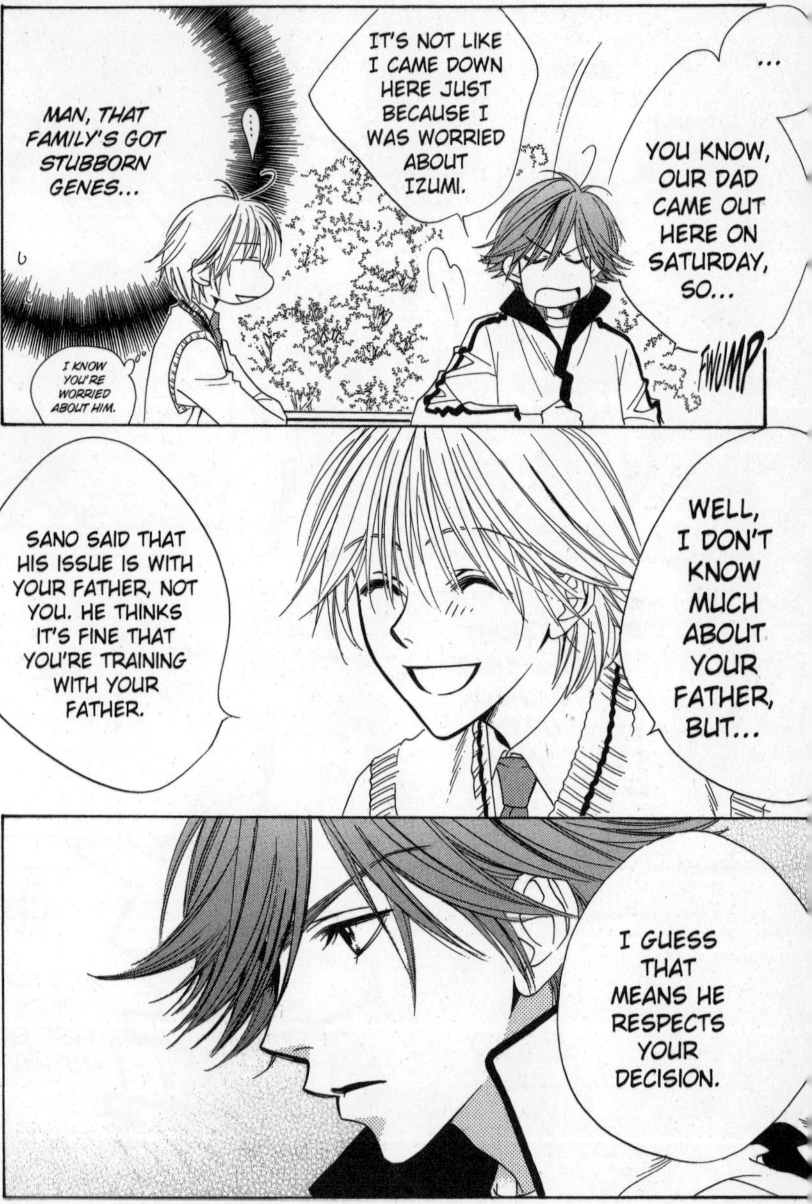
...
YOU KNOW, OUR DAD CAME OUT HERE ON SATURDAY, SO...
FWUMP
IT'S NOT LIKE I CAME DOWN HERE JUST BECAUSE I WAS WORRIED ABOUT IZUMI.
MAN, THAT FAMILY'S GOT STUBBORN GENES...
I KNOW YOU'RE WORRIED ABOUT HIM.
WELL, I DON'T KNOW MUCH ABOUT YOUR FATHER, BUT...
SANO SAID THAT HIS ISSUE IS WITH YOUR FATHER, NOT YOU. HE THINKS IT'S FINE THAT YOU'RE TRAINING WITH YOUR FATHER.
I GUESS THAT MEANS HE RESPECTS YOUR DECISION.

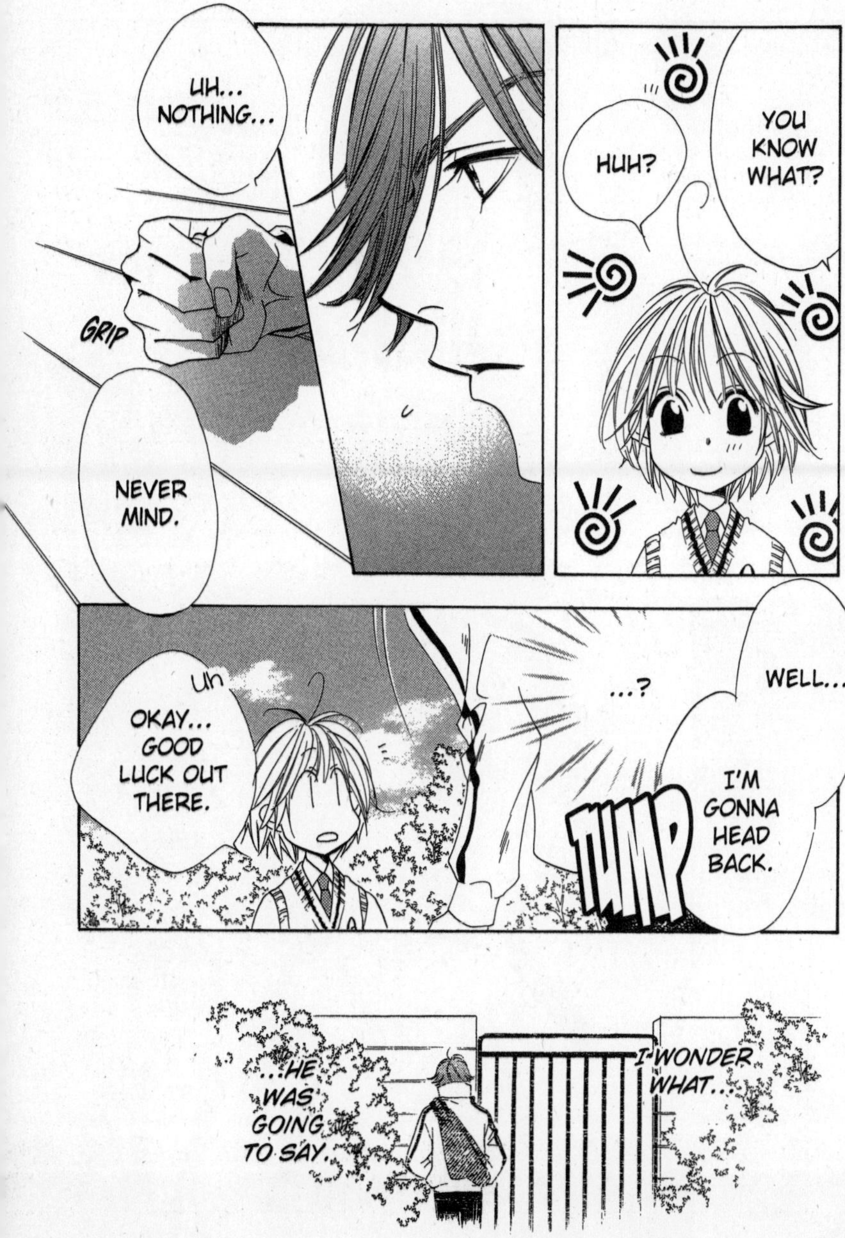
YOU KNOW WHAT?
HUH?
UH... NOTHING...
GRIP
NEVER MIND.
WELL...
I'M GONNA HEAD BACK.
TUMP
...?
Uh
OKAY... GOOD LUCK OUT THERE.
I WONDER WHAT...
...HE WAS GOING TO SAY.

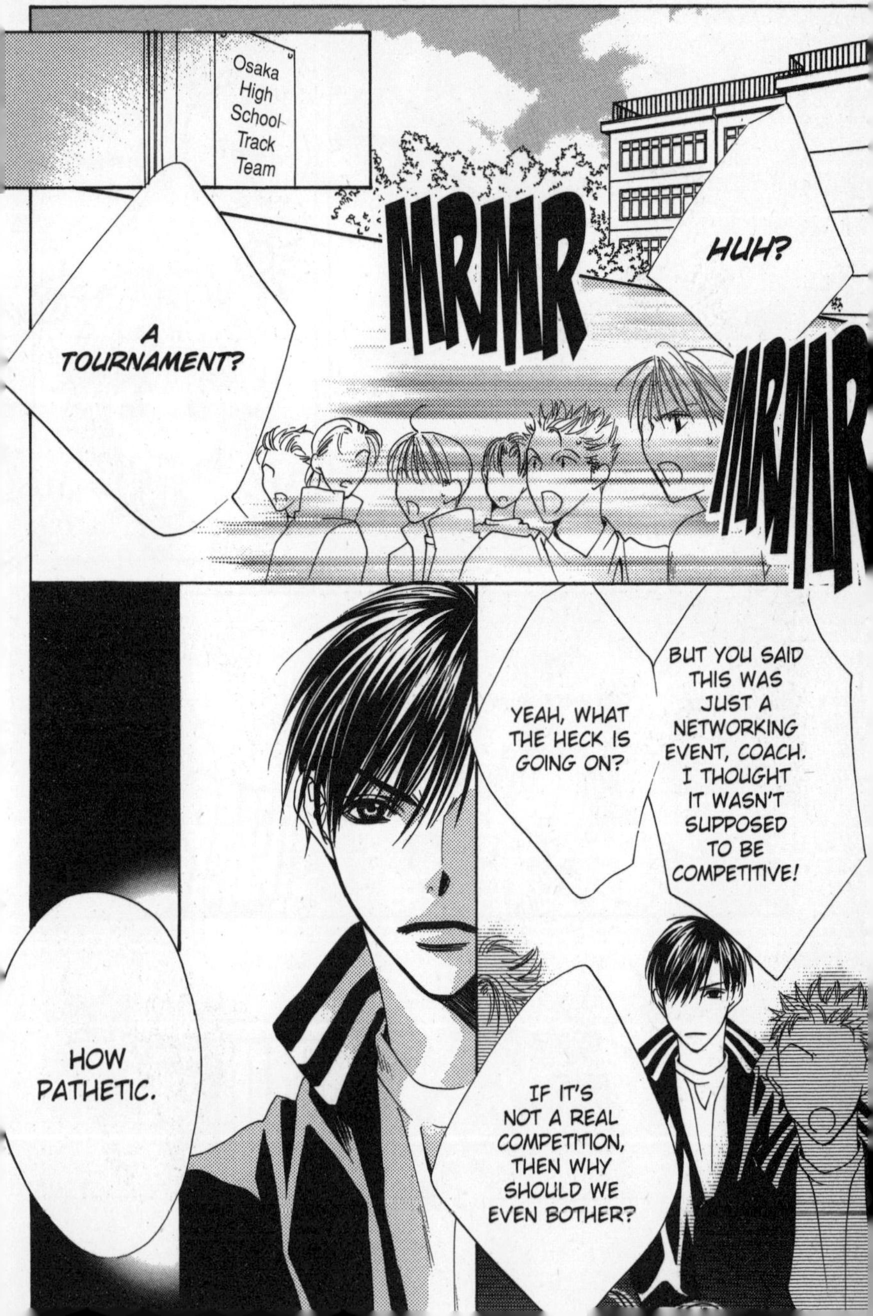
Osaka High School Track Team
HUH?
MRMR
MRMR
A TOURNAMENT?
BUT YOU SAID THIS WAS JUST A NETWORKING EVENT, COACH. I THOUGHT IT WASN'T SUPPOSED TO BE COMPETITIVE!
YEAH, WHAT THE HECK IS GOING ON?
IF IT'S NOT A REAL COMPETITION, THEN WHY SHOULD WE EVEN BOTHER?
HOW PATHETIC.

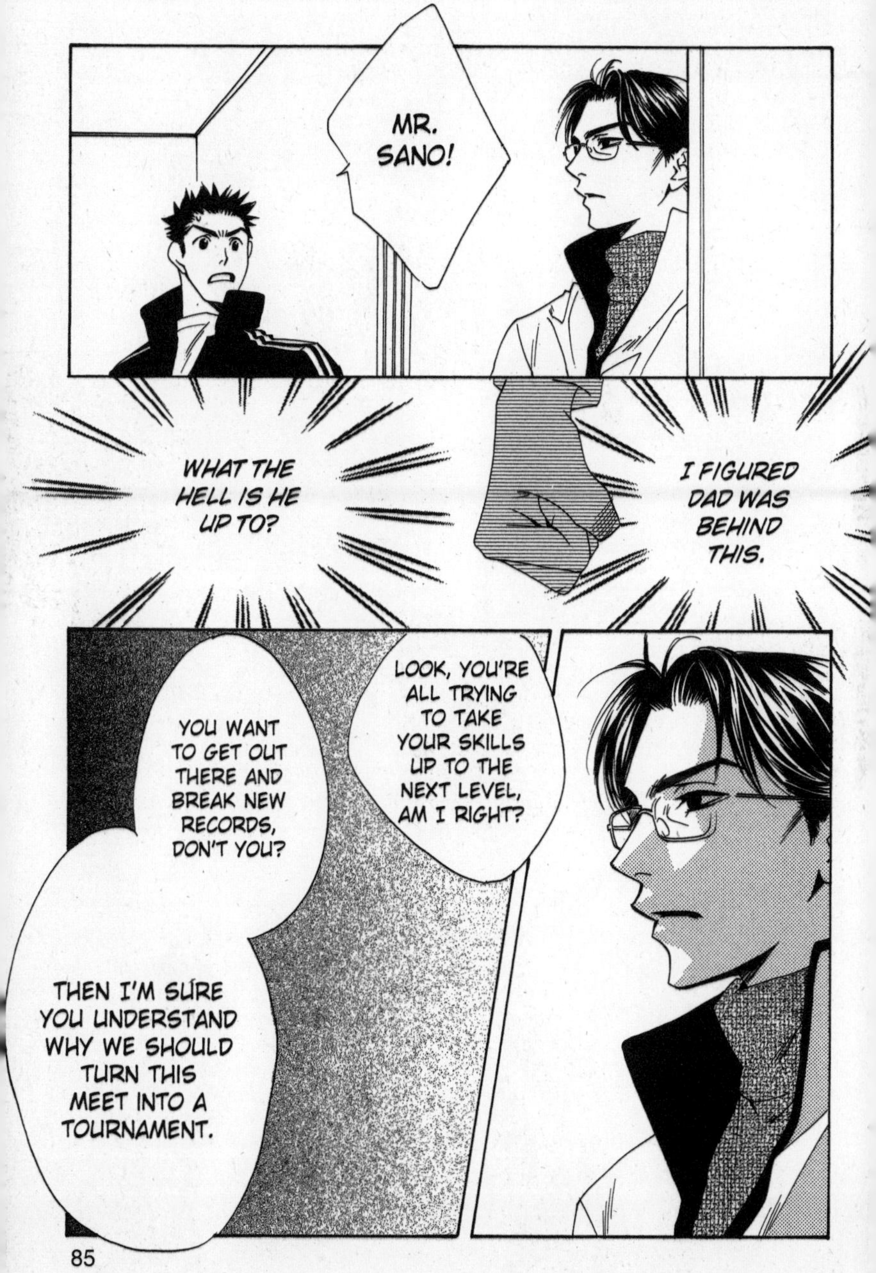
MR. SANO!
I FIGURED DAD WAS BEHIND THIS.
WHAT THE HELL IS HE UP TO?
LOOK, YOU'RE ALL TRYING TO TAKE YOUR SKILLS UP TO THE NEXT LEVEL, AM I RIGHT?
YOU WANT TO GET OUT THERE AND BREAK NEW RECORDS, DON'T YOU?
THEN I'M SURE YOU UNDERSTAND WHY WE SHOULD TURN THIS MEET INTO A TOURNAMENT.

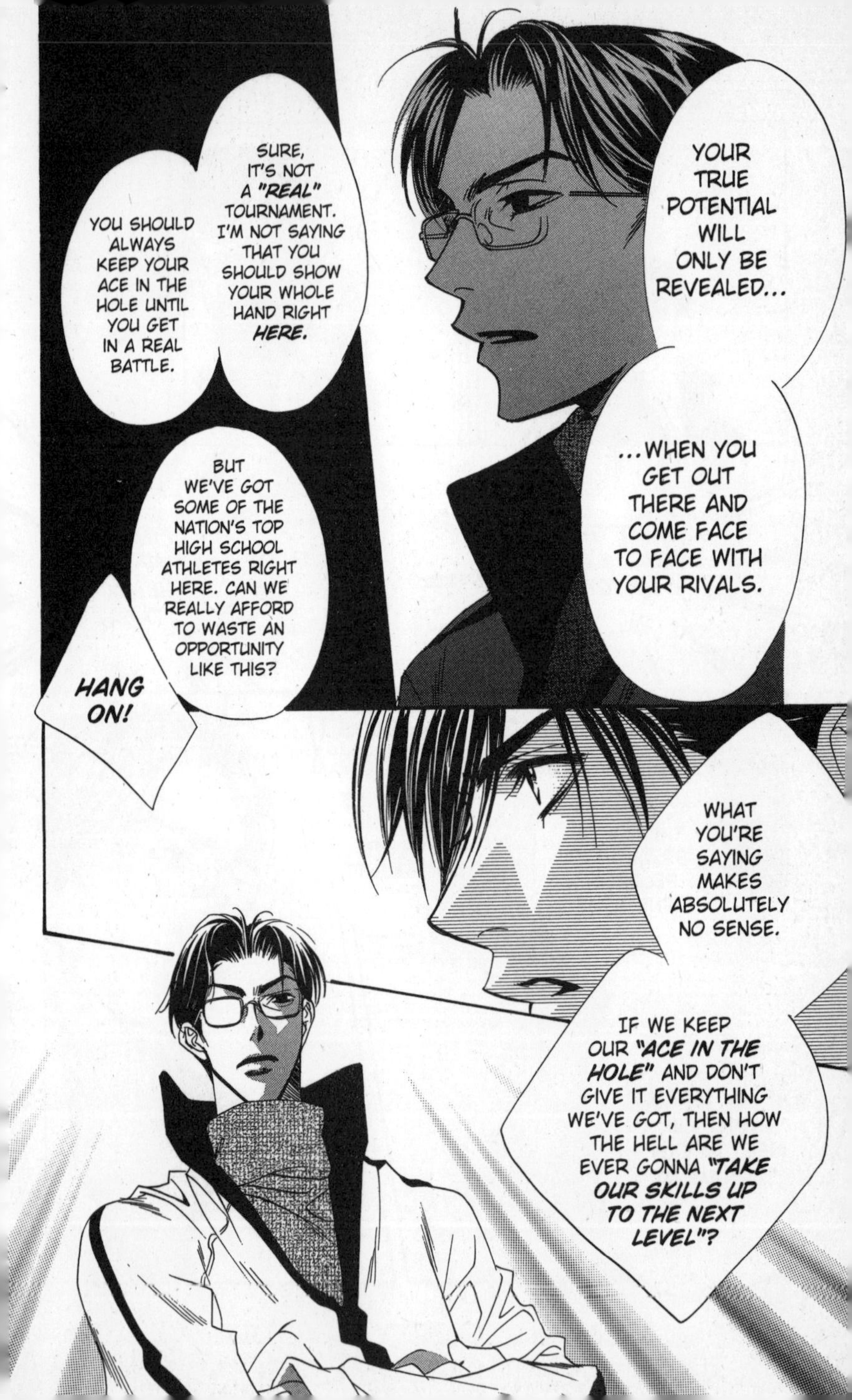
YOUR TRUE POTENTIAL WILL ONLY BE REVEALED...
...WHEN YOU GET OUT THERE AND COME FACE TO FACE WITH YOUR RIVALS.
SURE, IT'S NOT A "REAL" TOURNAMENT. I'M NOT SAYING THAT YOU SHOULD SHOW YOUR WHOLE HAND RIGHT HERE.
YOU SHOULD ALWAYS KEEP YOUR ACE IN THE HOLE UNTIL YOU GET IN A REAL BATTLE.
BUT WE'VE GOT SOME OF THE NATION'S TOP HIGH SCHOOL ATHLETES RIGHT HERE. CAN WE REALLY AFFORD TO WASTE AN OPPORTUNITY LIKE THIS?
HANG ON!
WHAT YOU'RE SAYING MAKES ABSOLUTELY NO SENSE.
IF WE KEEP OUR "ACE IN THE HOLE" AND DON'T GIVE IT EVERYTHING WE'VE GOT, THEN HOW THE HELL ARE WE EVER GONNA "TAKE OUR SKILLS UP TO THE NEXT LEVEL"?

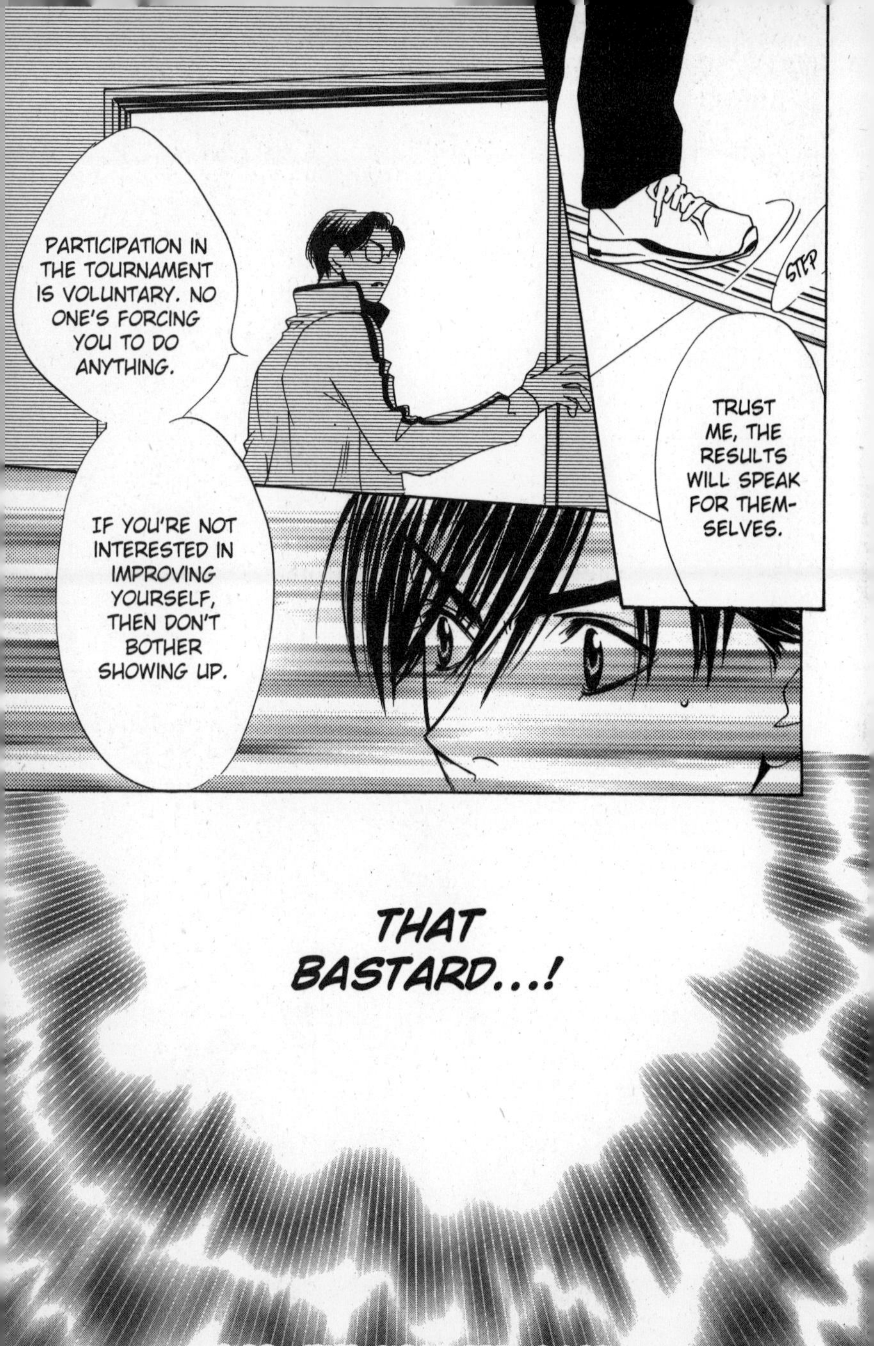
STEP
TRUST ME, THE RESULTS WILL SPEAK FOR THEM-SELVES.
PARTICIPATION IN THE TOURNAMENT IS VOLUNTARY. NO ONE'S FORCING YOU TO DO ANYTHING.
IF YOU'RE NOT INTERESTED IN IMPROVING YOURSELF, THEN DON'T BOTHER SHOWING UP.
THAT BASTARD...!

HANA-KIMI CHAPTER 94/END

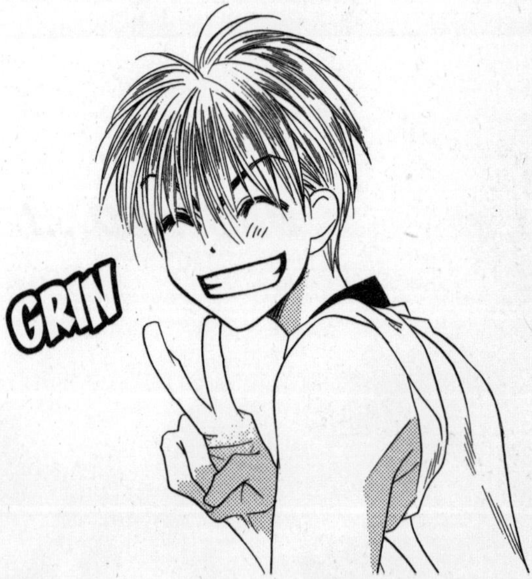
GRIN

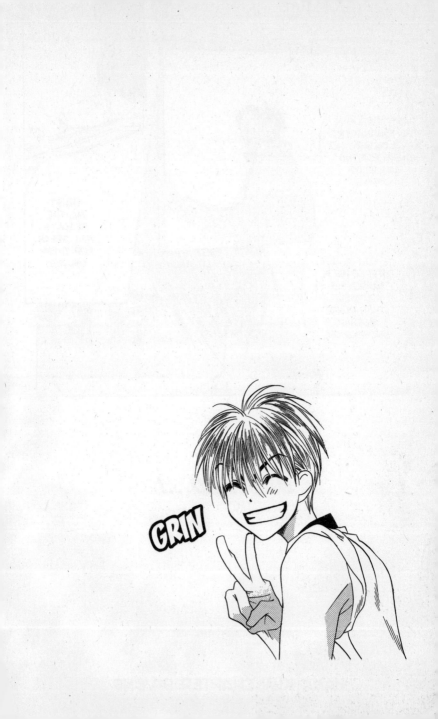

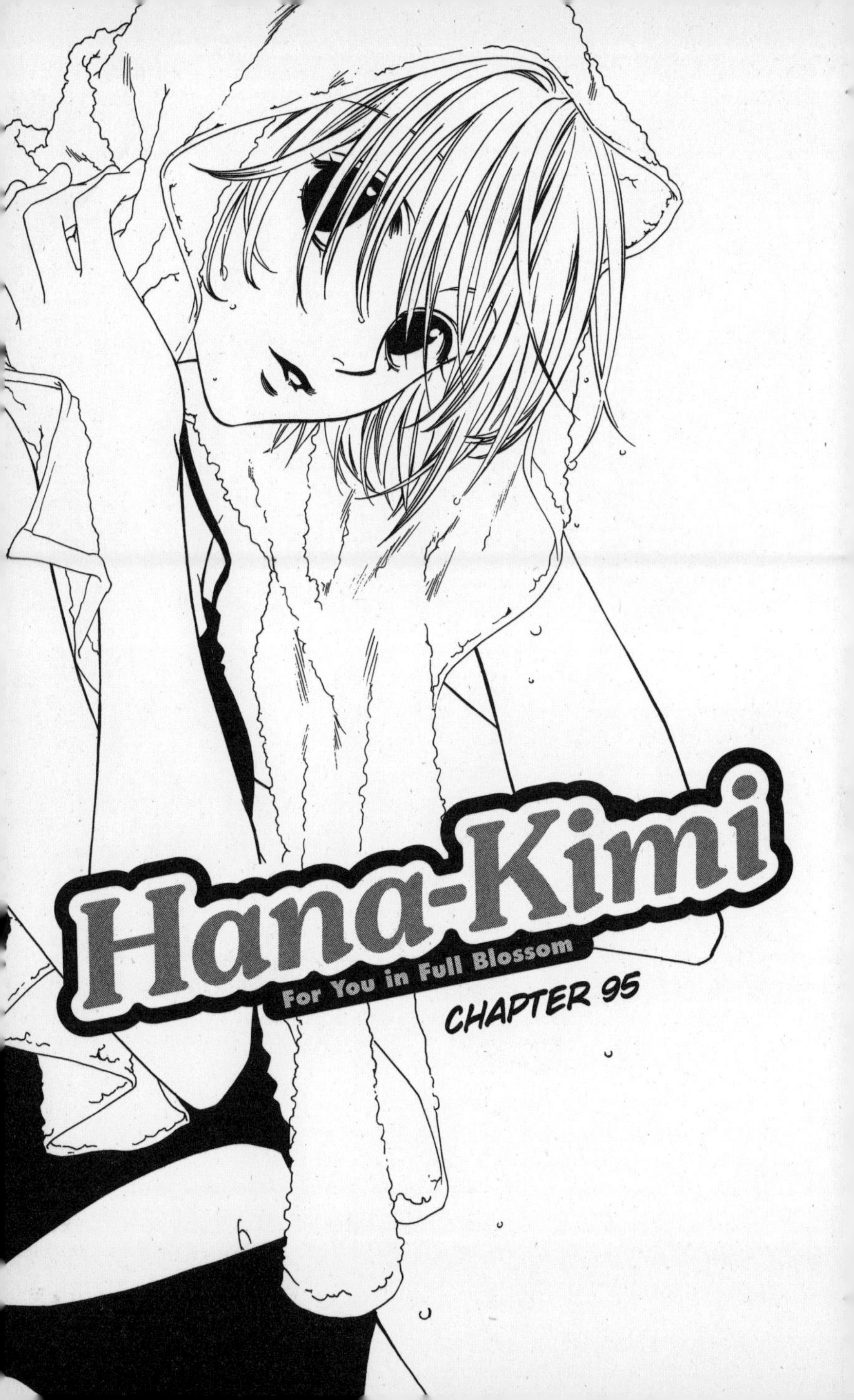
Hana-Kimi
For You in Full Blossom
CHAPTER 95

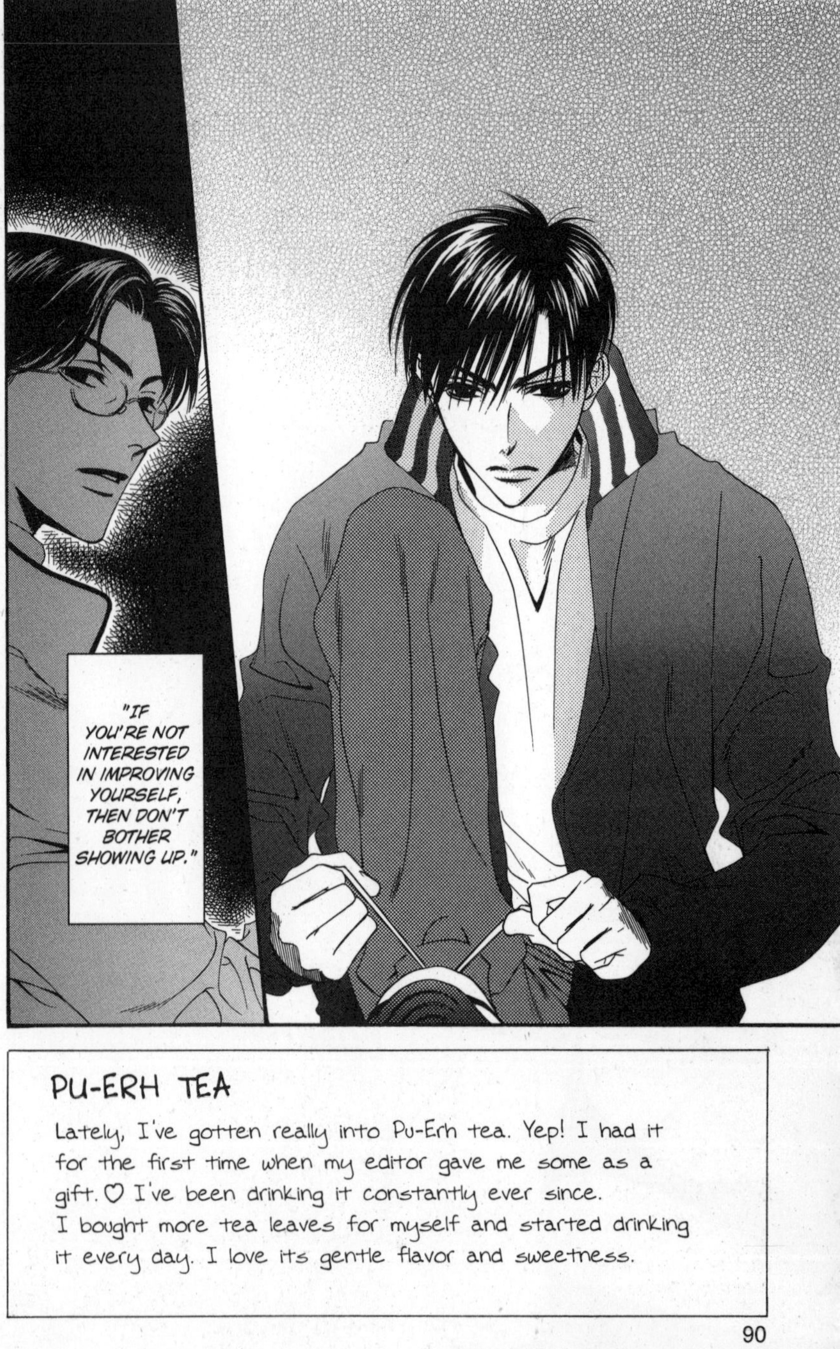
"IF YOU'RE NOT INTERESTED IN IMPROVING YOURSELF, THEN DON'T BOTHER SHOWING UP."

PU-ERH TEA

Lately, I've gotten really into Pu-Erh tea. Yep! I had it for the first time when my editor gave me some as a gift. ♡ I've been drinking it constantly ever since.
I bought more tea leaves for myself and started drinking it every day. I love its gentle flavor and sweetness.

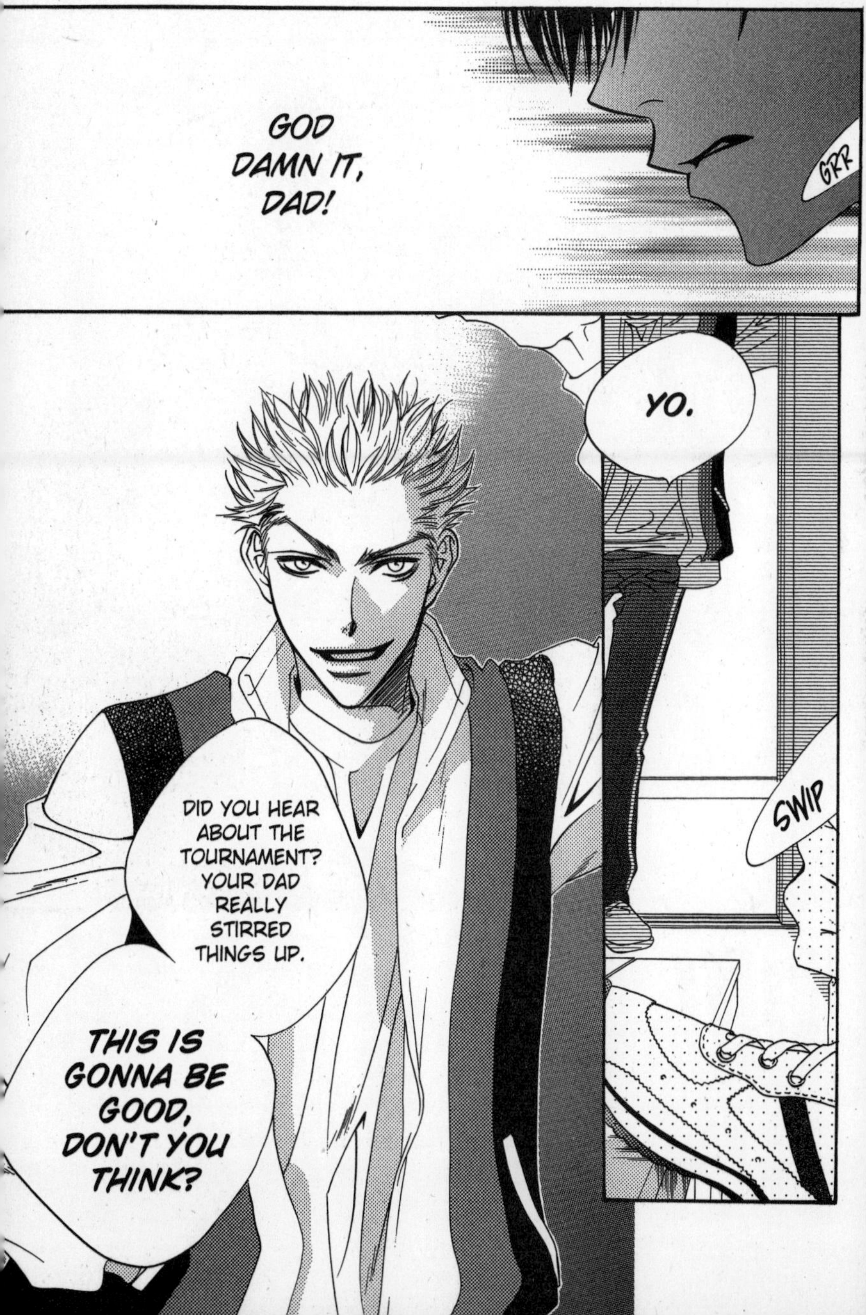
GRR
GOD DAMN IT, DAD!
YO.
SWIP
DID YOU HEAR ABOUT THE TOURNAMENT? YOUR DAD REALLY STIRRED THINGS UP.
THIS IS GONNA BE GOOD, DON'T YOU THINK?

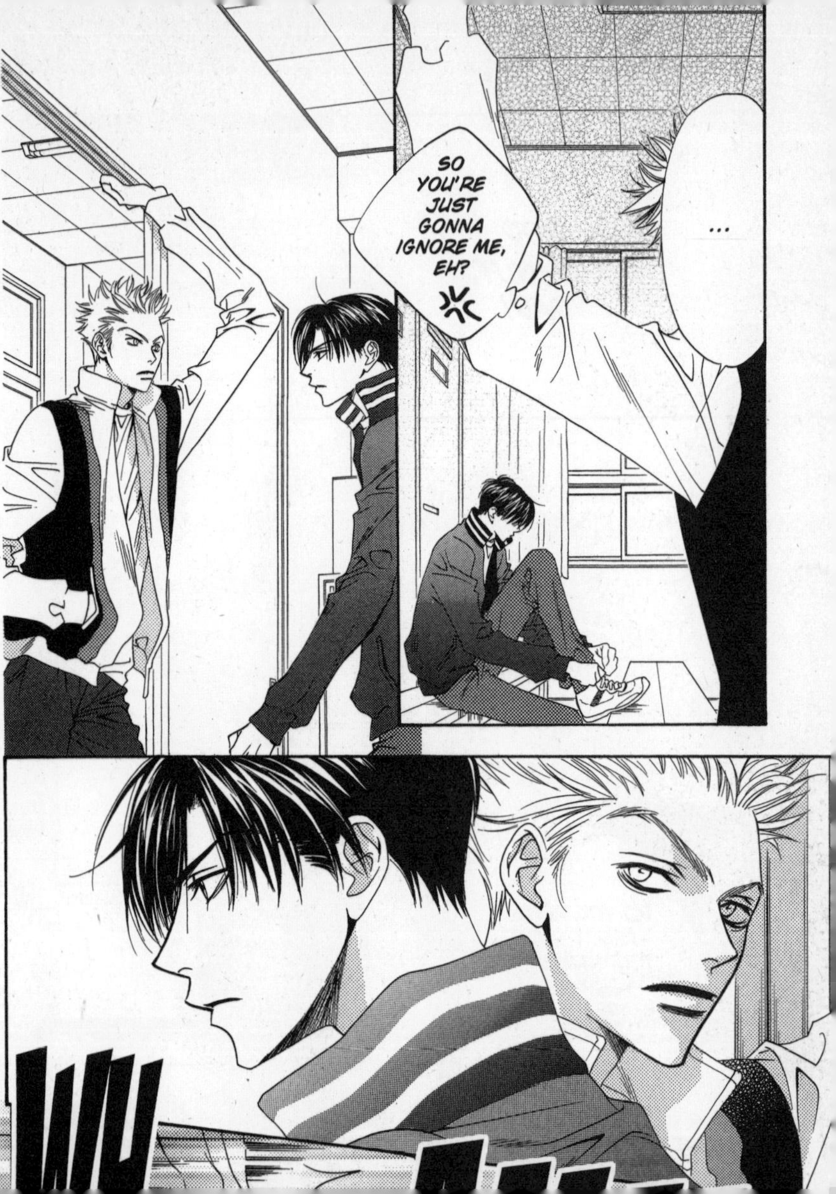
SO YOU'RE JUST GONNA IGNORE ME, EH?
...

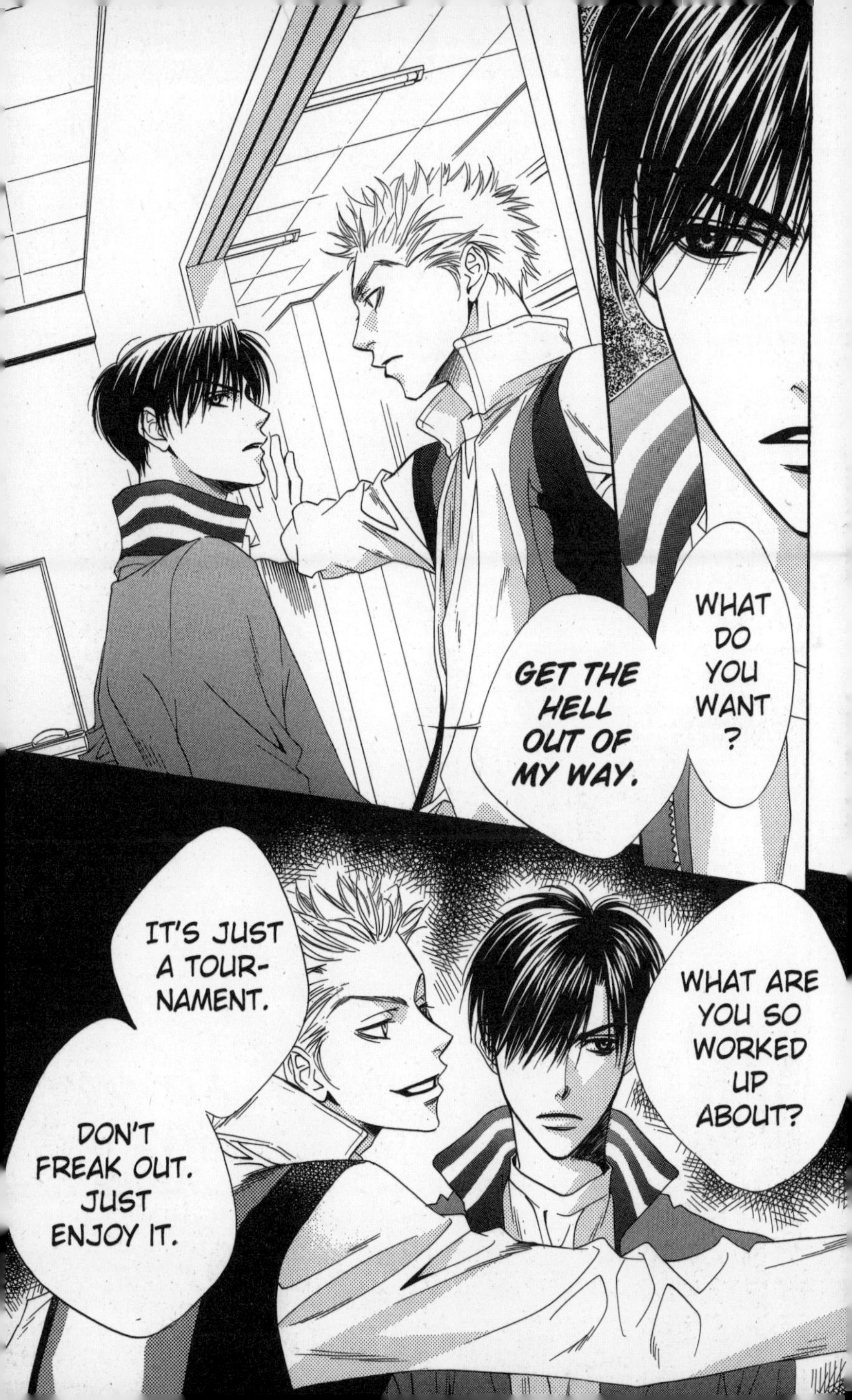
WHAT DO YOU WANT?
GET THE HELL OUT OF MY WAY.
WHAT ARE YOU SO WORKED UP ABOUT?
IT'S JUST A TOURNAMENT.
DON'T FREAK OUT. JUST ENJOY IT.

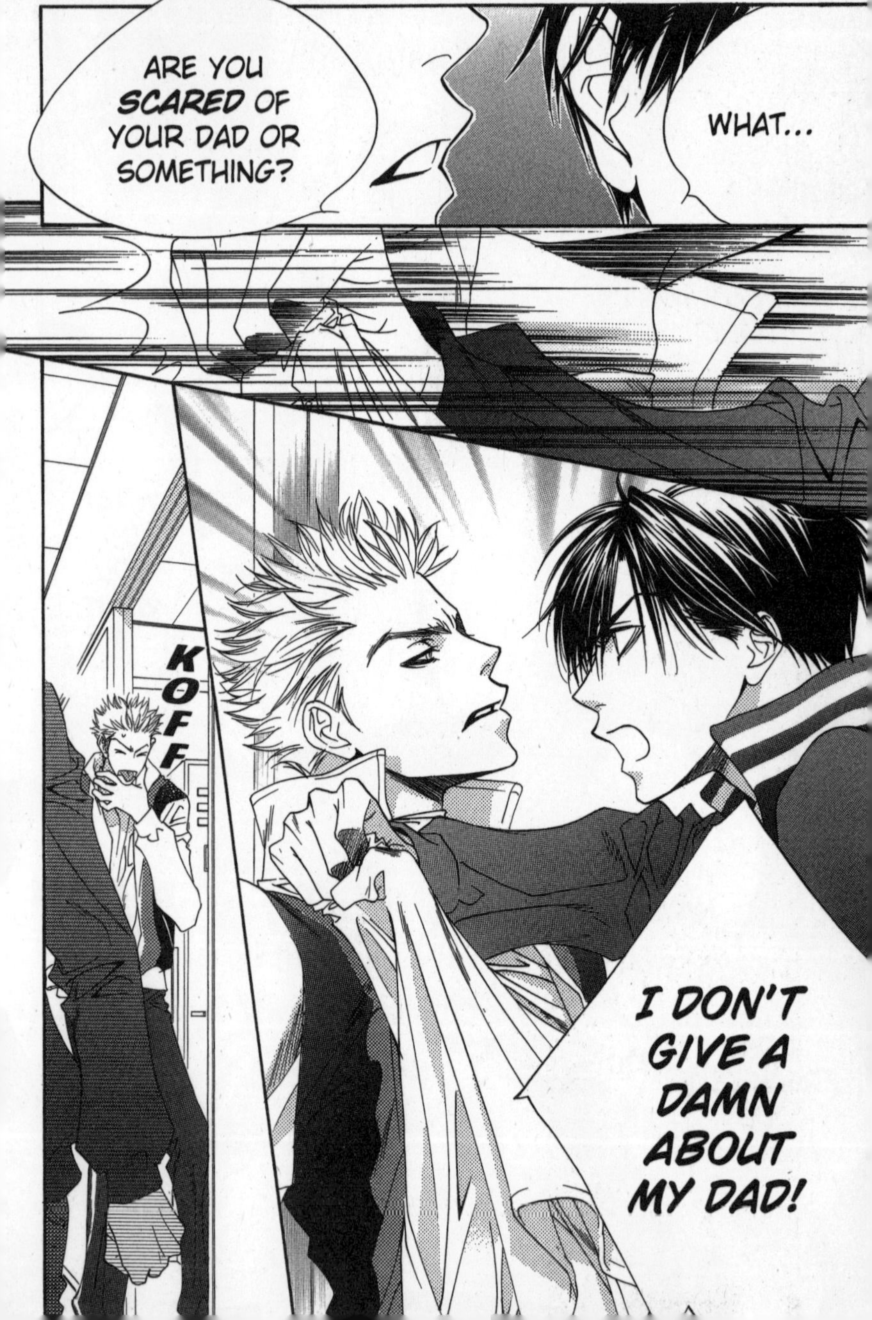
WHAT...
ARE YOU SCARED OF YOUR DAD OR SOMETHING?
I DON'T GIVE A DAMN ABOUT MY DAD!
KOFF

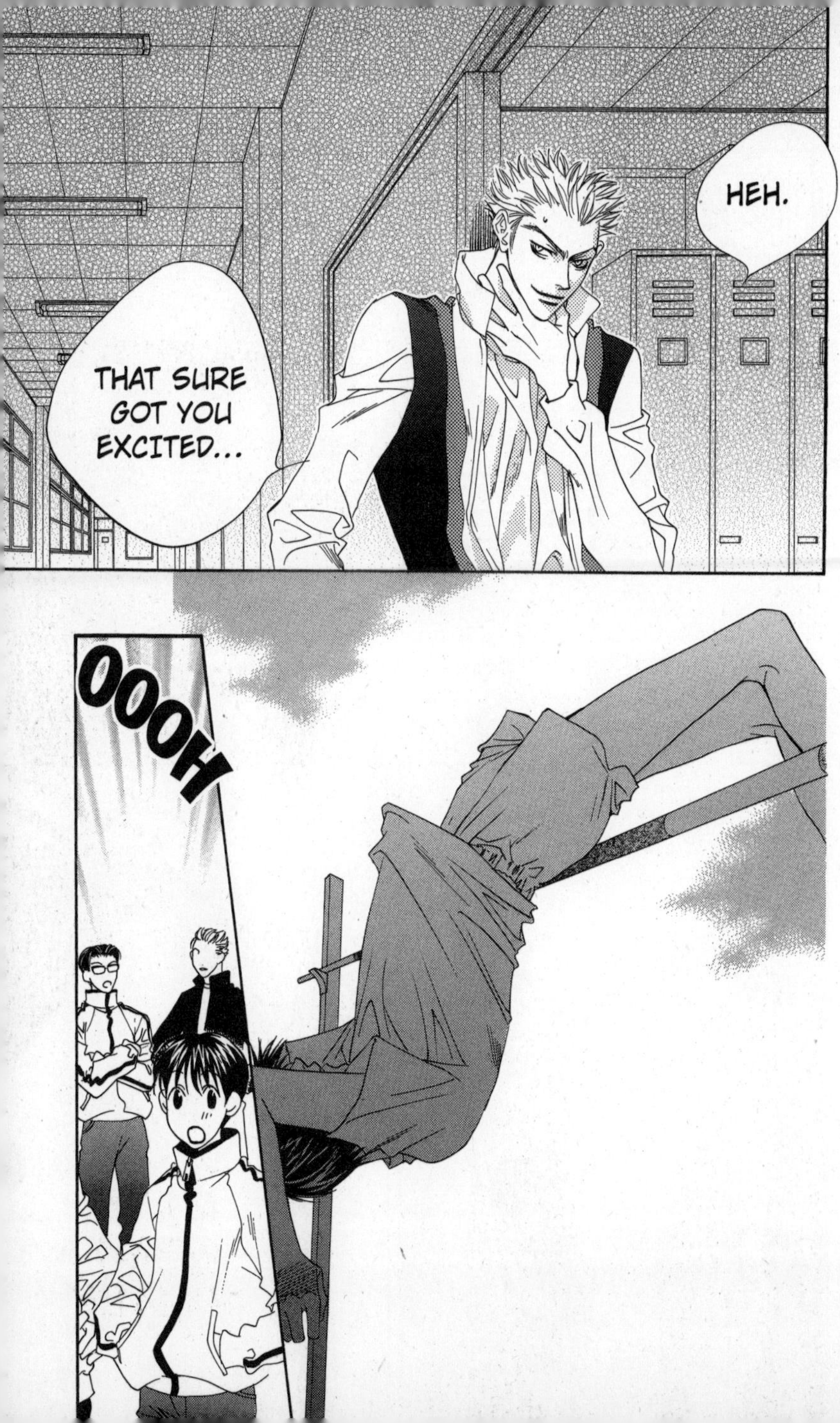
HEH.
THAT SURE GOT YOU EXCITED...
OOOH

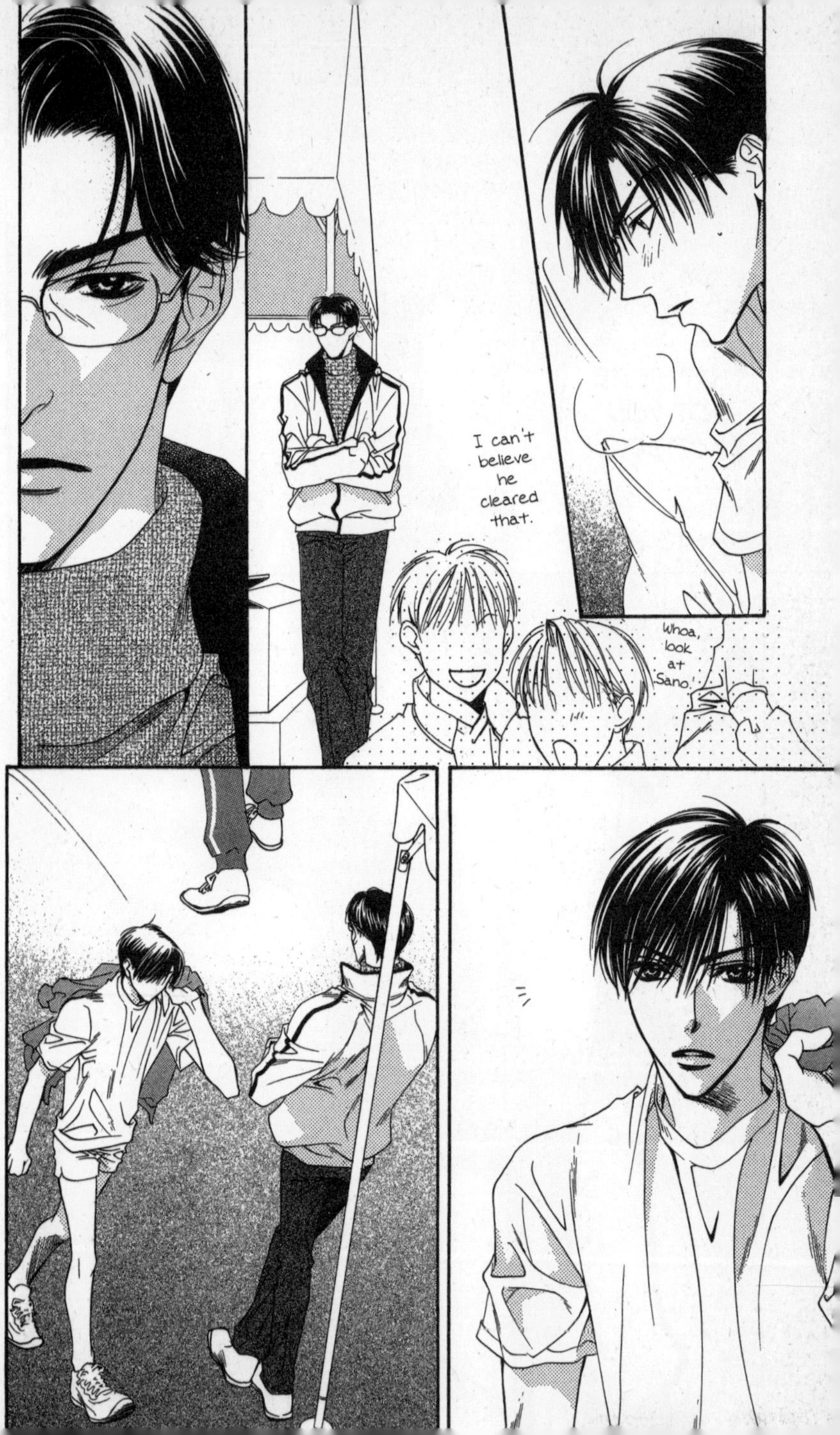
I can't believe he cleared that.
Whoa, look at Sano.

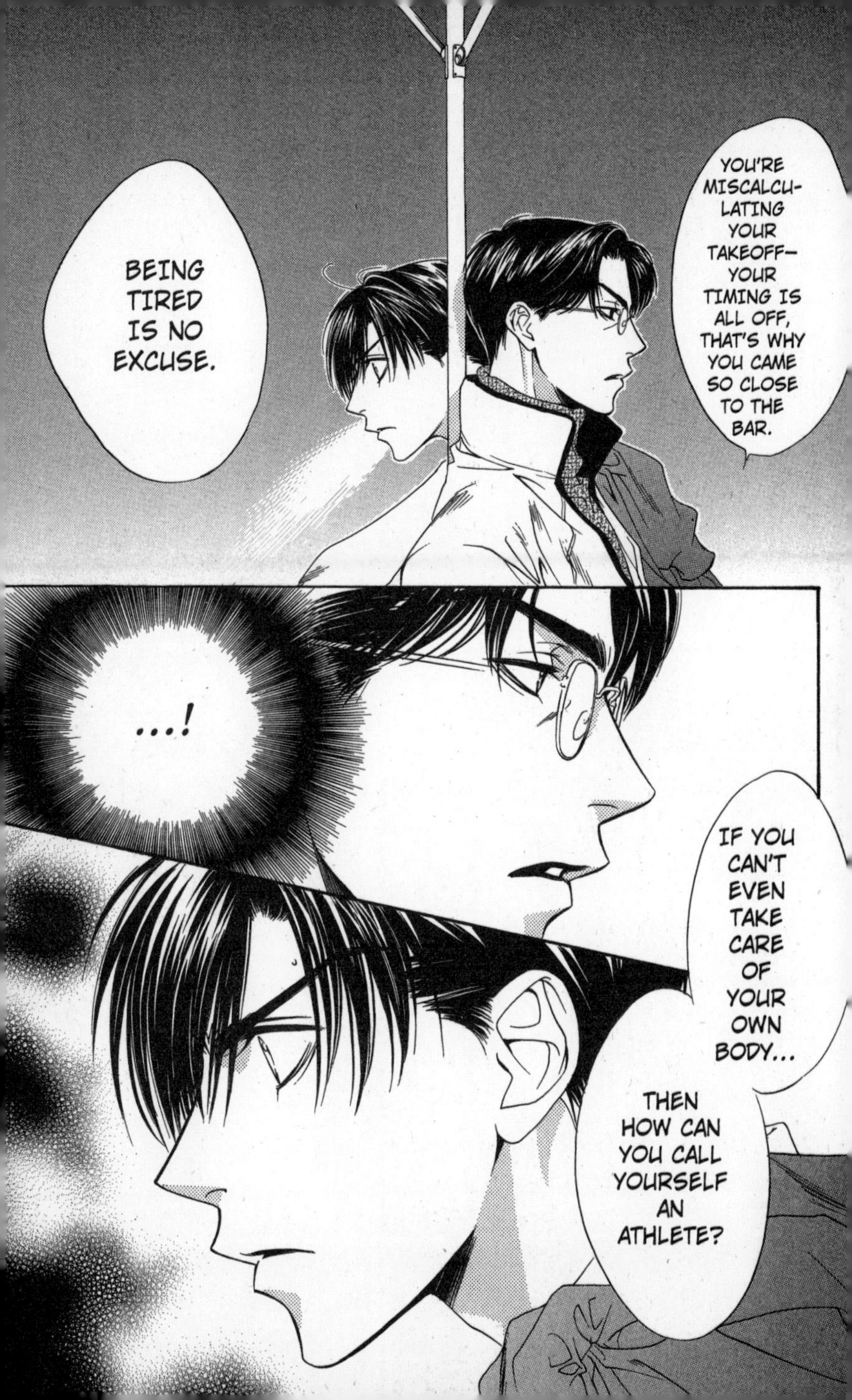
YOU'RE MISCALCU-LATING YOUR TAKEOFF—YOUR TIMING IS ALL OFF, THAT'S WHY YOU CAME SO CLOSE TO THE BAR.
BEING TIRED IS NO EXCUSE.
...!
IF YOU CAN'T EVEN TAKE CARE OF YOUR OWN BODY...
THEN HOW CAN YOU CALL YOURSELF AN ATHLETE?

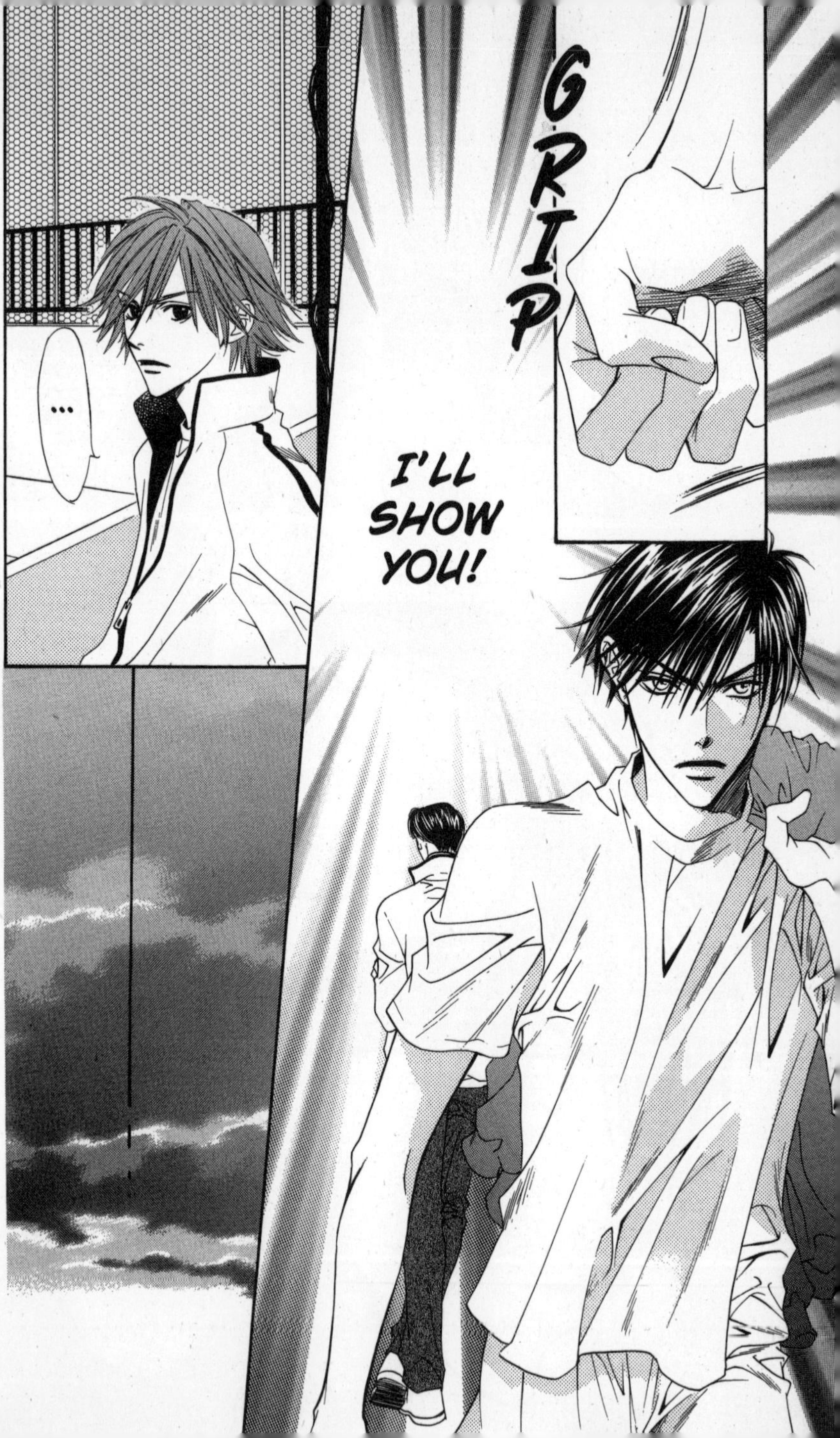
GRIP
I'LL SHOW YOU!
...

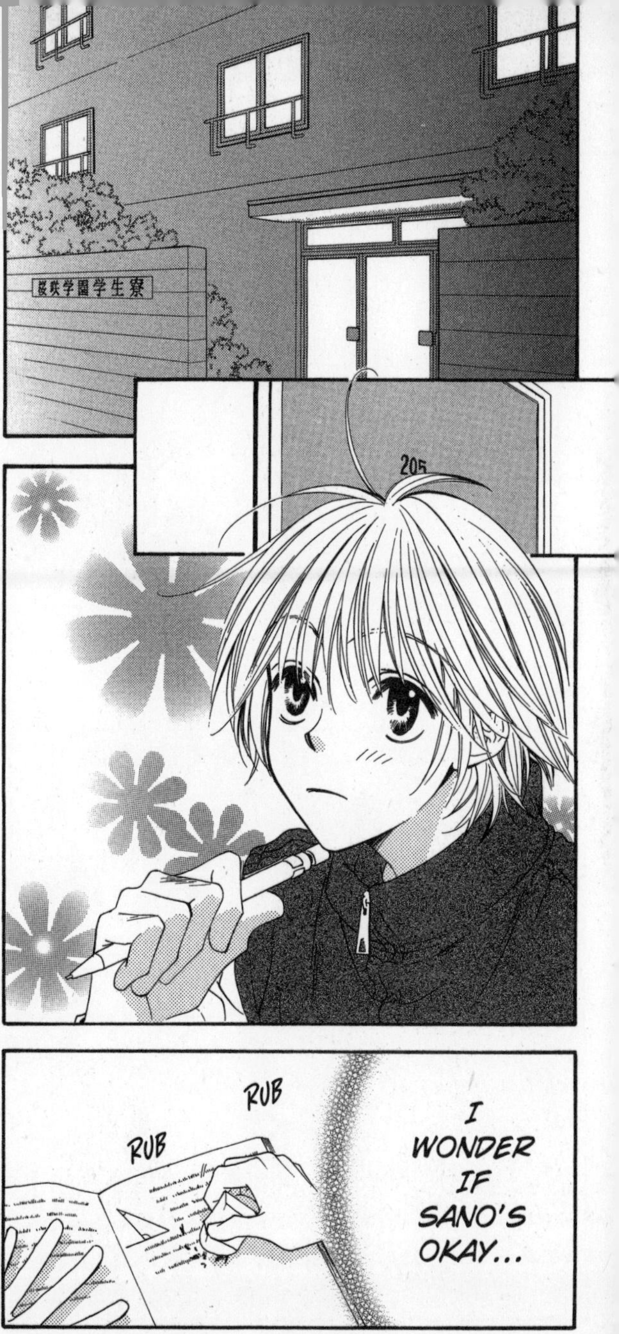
桜咲学園学生寮
205
I WONDER IF SANO'S OKAY...
RUB
RUB

SHINJI NOE

Birthday: July 11th
Grade: Second Year Japanese H.S. (equivalent of 11th grade in America)
Blood Type: A
Sign: Cancer
Height: 167 cm (5'6")
Favorite Foods: Curry, Katsudon, Bananas
Favorite Celebrities: Noriko Kuwashima, Yui Horie, Maya Sakamoto (all are voice actresses)
Favorite Colors: Orange, Khaki
Favorite Subject: English
Least Favorite Animals: Hairy animals other than insects
Least Favorite Foods: Carrots, Celery, Herbs
Dislikes: The Occult
Clubs and Affiliations: The Manga Club
Flower: The Pansy

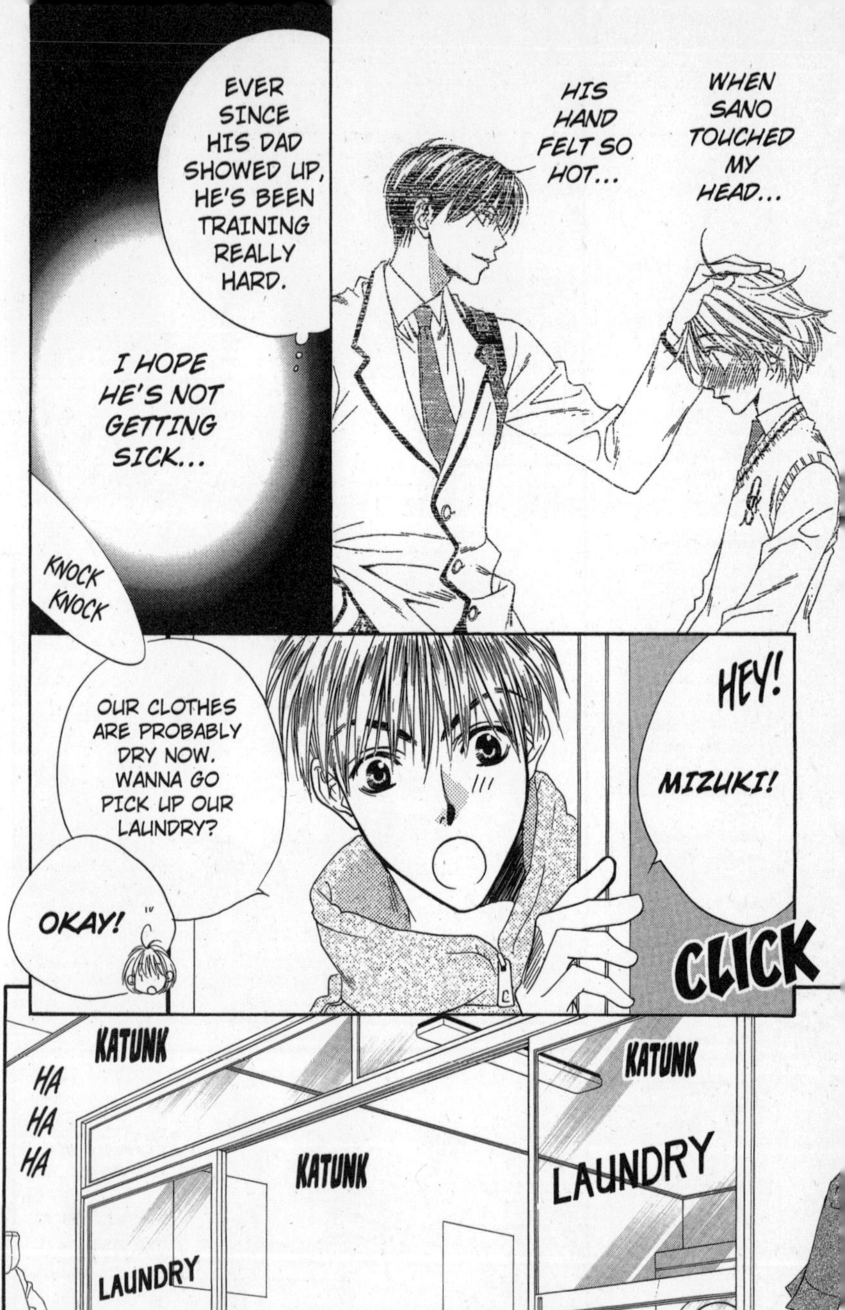
WHEN SANO TOUCHED MY HEAD...
HIS HAND FELT SO HOT...
EVER SINCE HIS DAD SHOWED UP, HE'S BEEN TRAINING REALLY HARD.
I HOPE HE'S NOT GETTING SICK...
KNOCK KNOCK
HEY!
MIZUKI!
CLICK
OUR CLOTHES ARE PROBABLY DRY NOW. WANNA GO PICK UP OUR LAUNDRY?
OKAY!
KATUNK
LAUNDRY
KATUNK
KATUNK
HA HA HA
LAUNDRY

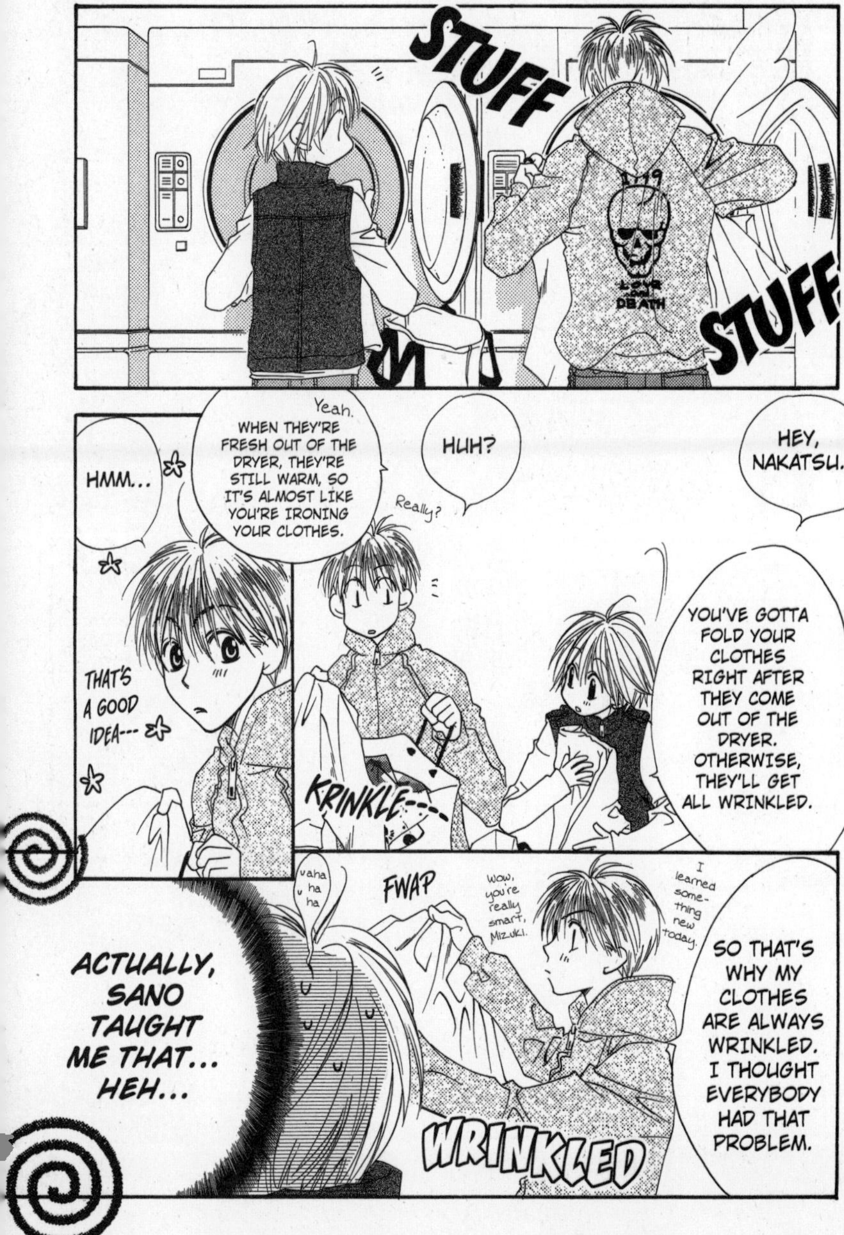
STUFF
STUFF
HEY, NAKATSU.
HUH?
YOU'VE GOTTA FOLD YOUR CLOTHES RIGHT AFTER THEY COME OUT OF THE DRYER. OTHERWISE, THEY'LL GET ALL WRINKLED.
KRINKLE---
Really?
Yeah.
WHEN THEY'RE FRESH OUT OF THE DRYER, THEY'RE STILL WARM, SO IT'S ALMOST LIKE YOU'RE IRONING YOUR CLOTHES.
HMM...
THAT'S A GOOD IDEA---
SO THAT'S WHY MY CLOTHES ARE ALWAYS WRINKLED. I THOUGHT EVERYBODY HAD THAT PROBLEM.
I learned something new today.
Wow, you're really smart, Mizuki.
FWAP
WRINKLED
vaha ha ha
ACTUALLY, SANO TAUGHT ME THAT... HEH...

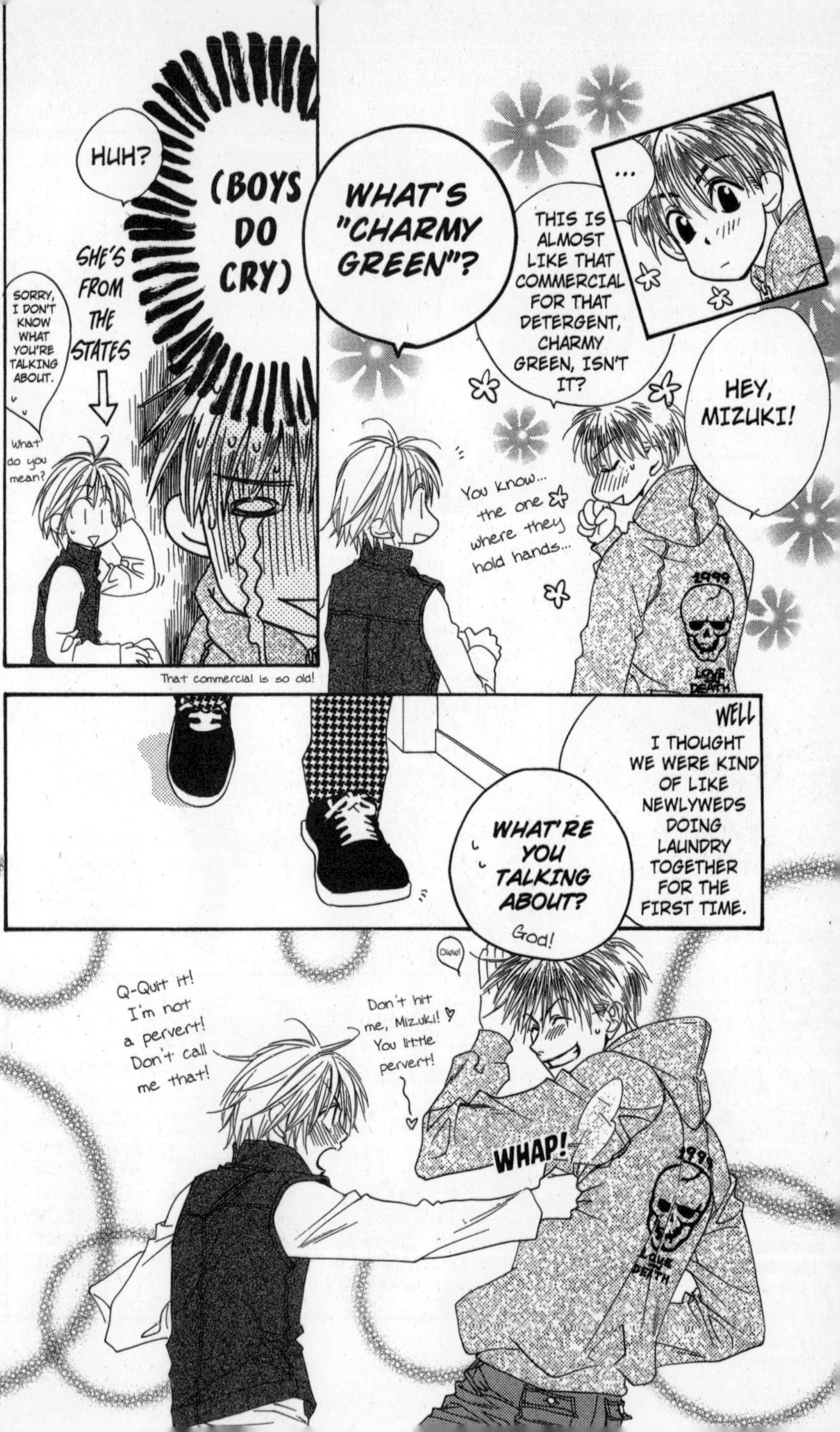
...
HEY, MIZUKI!
THIS IS ALMOST LIKE THAT COMMERCIAL FOR THAT DETERGENT, CHARMY GREEN, ISN'T IT?
You know... the one where they hold hands...
WHAT'S "CHARMY GREEN"?
(BOYS DO CRY)
HUH?
SHE'S FROM THE STATES
SORRY, I DON'T KNOW WHAT YOU'RE TALKING ABOUT.
What do you mean?
That commercial is so old!
WELL I THOUGHT WE WERE KIND OF LIKE NEWLYWEDS DOING LAUNDRY TOGETHER FOR THE FIRST TIME.
WHAT'RE YOU TALKING ABOUT?
God!
Oww!
WHAP!
Don't hit me, Mizuki! You little pervert!
Q-Quit it! I'm not a pervert! Don't call me that!

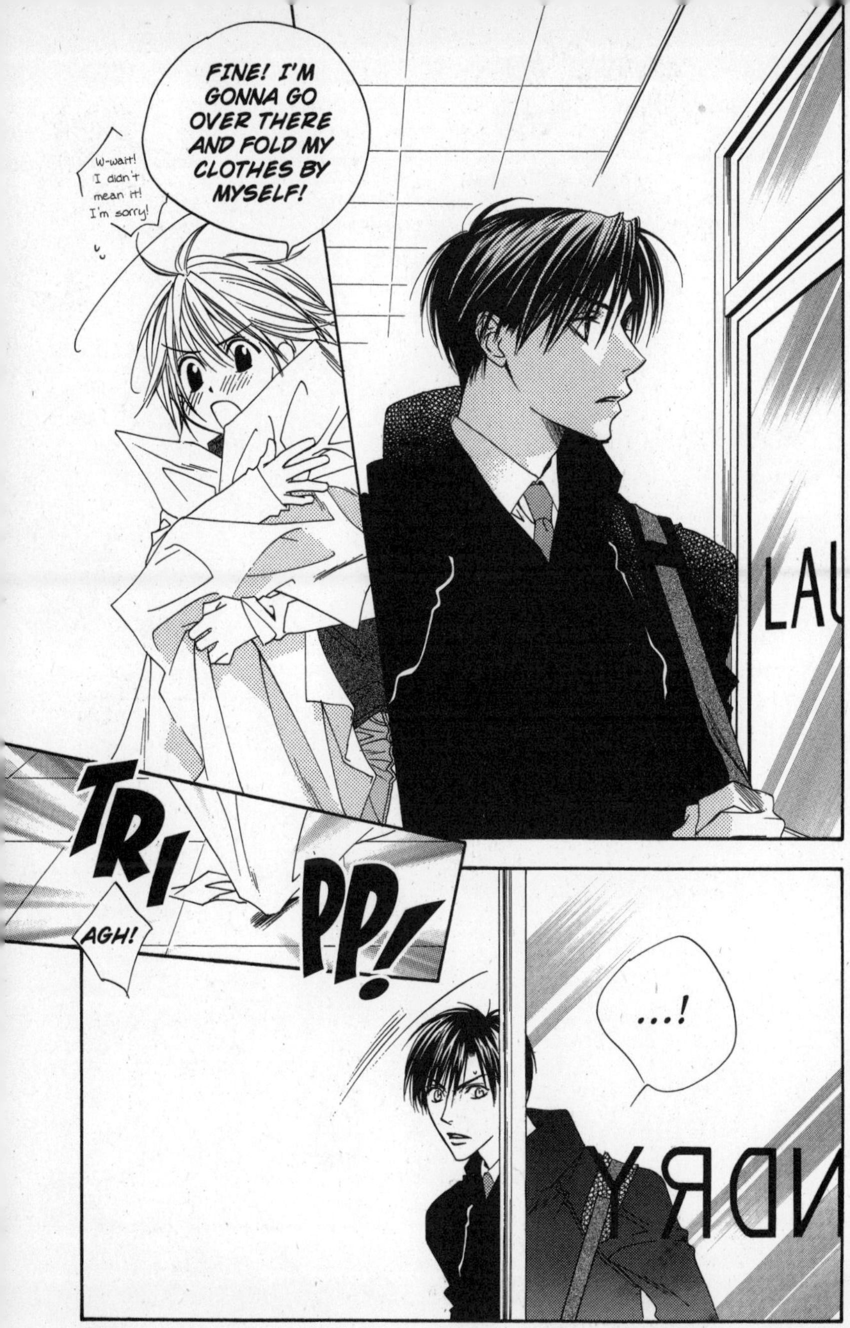
FINE! I'M GONNA GO OVER THERE AND FOLD MY CLOTHES BY MYSELF!
W-wait! I didn't mean it! I'm sorry!
LAU
TRIPP!
AGH!
...!

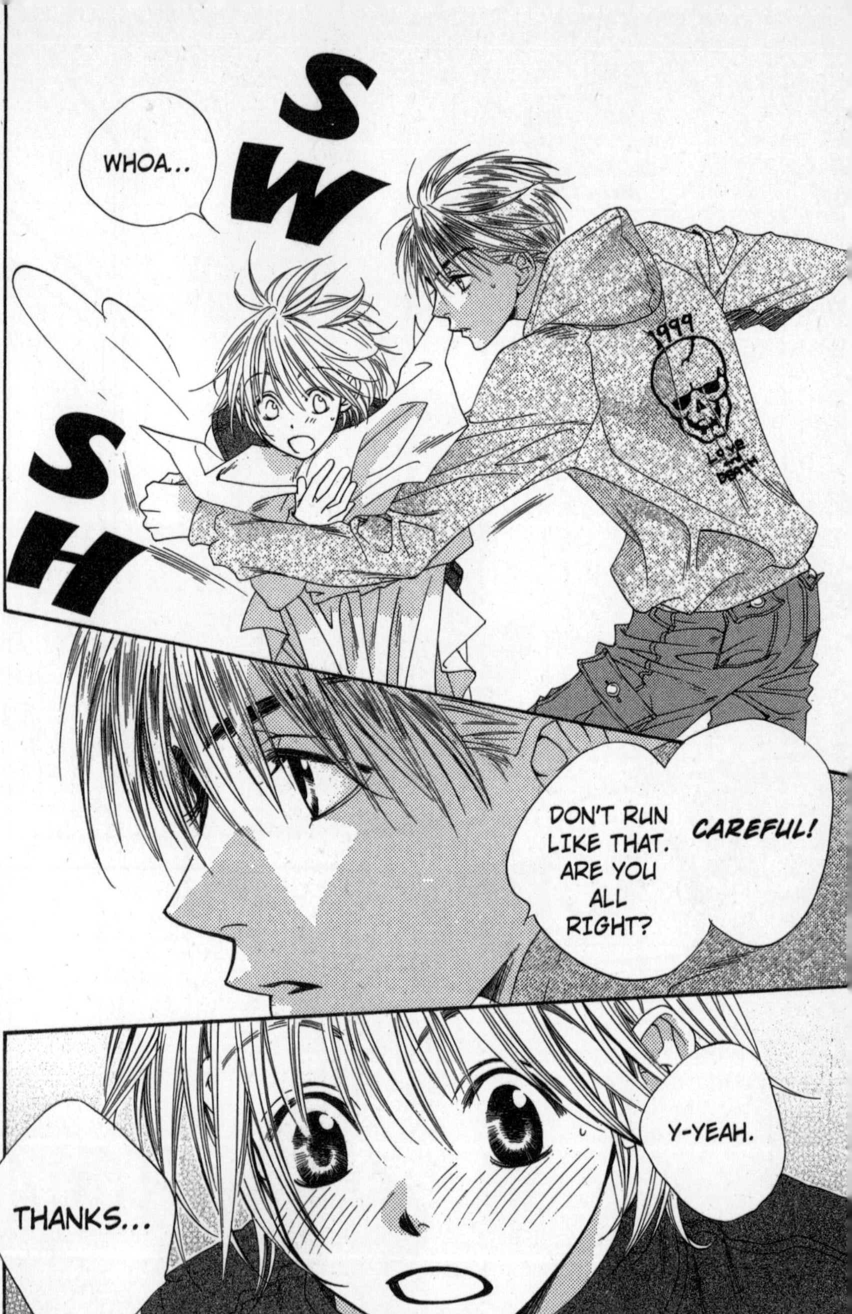
SW
WHOA...
SH
CAREFUL!
DON'T RUN LIKE THAT. ARE YOU ALL RIGHT?
Y-YEAH.
THANKS...

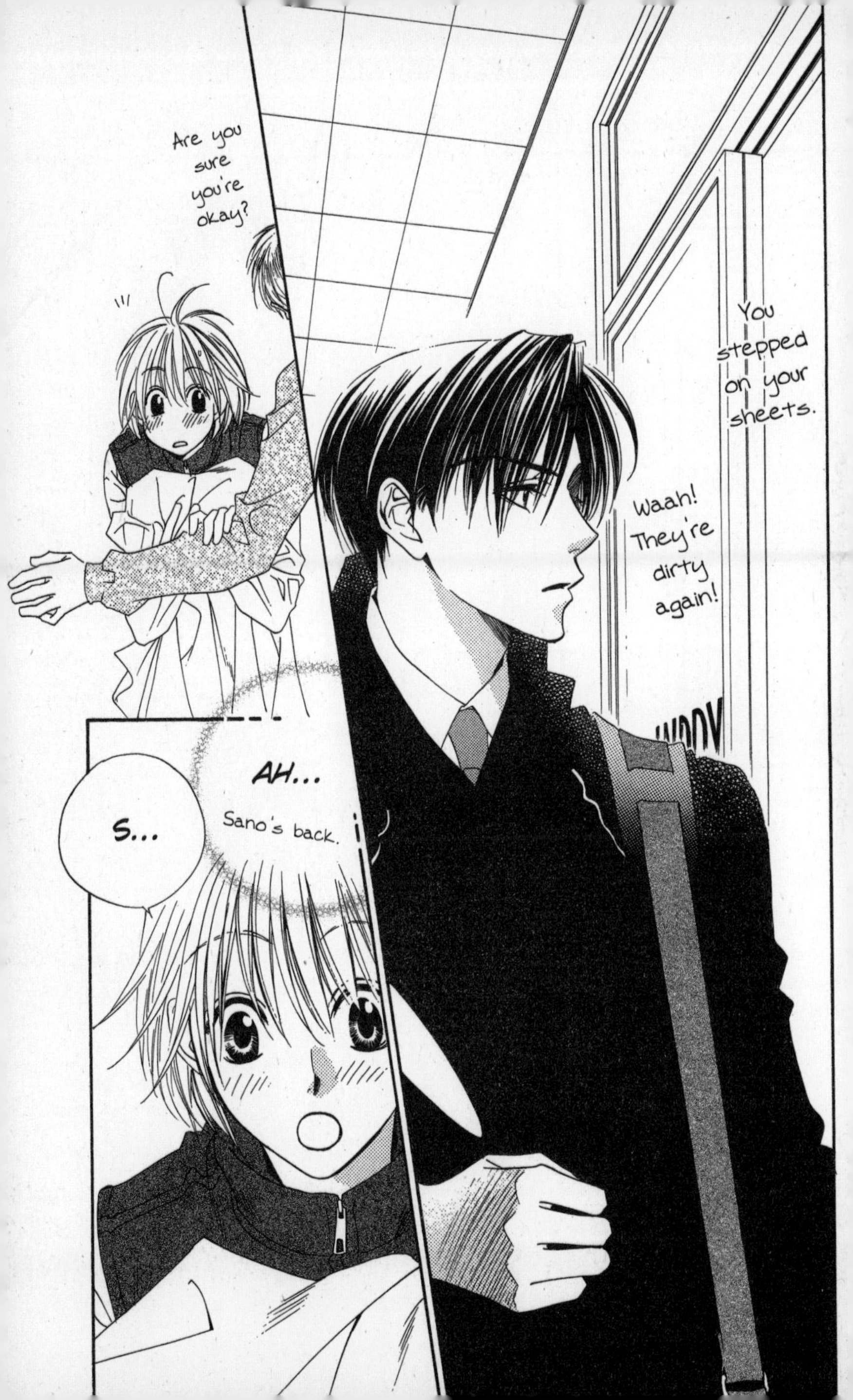
You stepped on your sheets.
Waah! They're dirty again!
Are you sure you're okay?
S...
AH...
Sano's back.

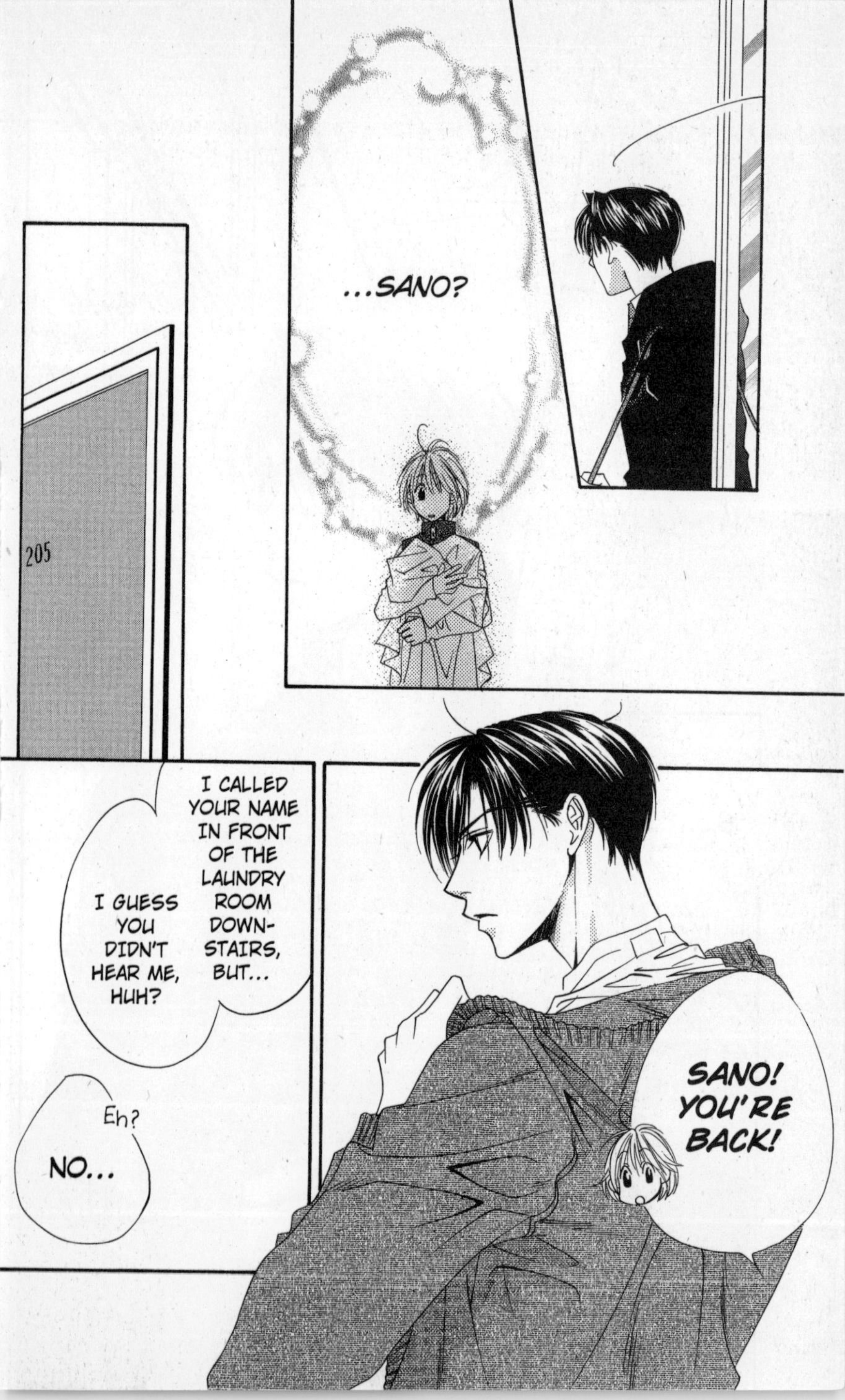
...SANO?
205
SANO! YOU'RE BACK!
I CALLED YOUR NAME IN FRONT OF THE LAUNDRY ROOM DOWN-STAIRS, BUT...
I GUESS YOU DIDN'T HEAR ME, HUH?
Eh?
NO...

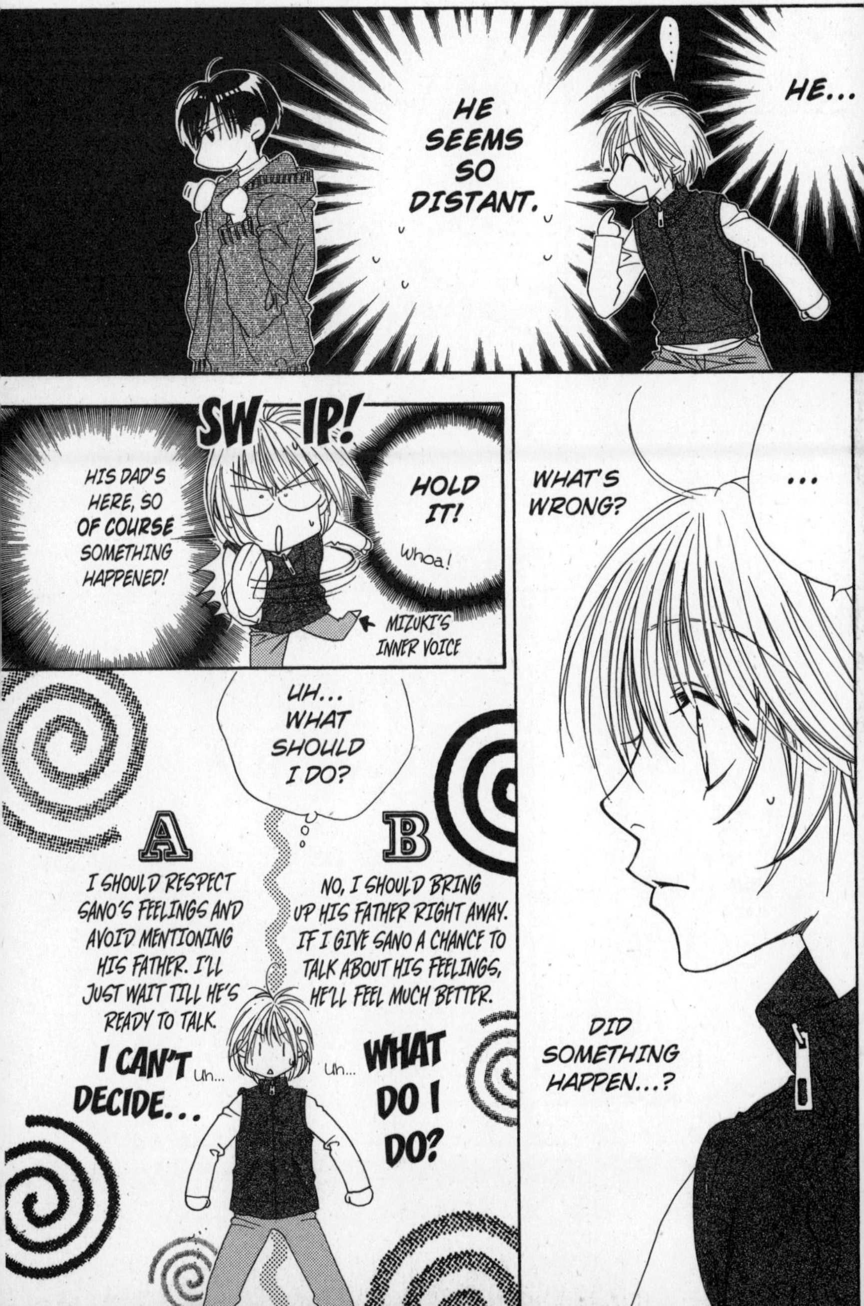
HE...
!
HE SEEMS SO DISTANT.
...
WHAT'S WRONG?
DID SOMETHING HAPPEN...?
SW IP!
HOLD IT!
Whoa!
HIS DAD'S HERE, SO OF COURSE SOMETHING HAPPENED!
MIZUKI'S INNER VOICE
UH... WHAT SHOULD I DO?
B
NO, I SHOULD BRING UP HIS FATHER RIGHT AWAY. IF I GIVE SANO A CHANCE TO TALK ABOUT HIS FEELINGS, HE'LL FEEL MUCH BETTER.
A
I SHOULD RESPECT SANO'S FEELINGS AND AVOID MENTIONING HIS FATHER. I'LL JUST WAIT TILL HE'S READY TO TALK.
WHAT DO I DO?
Uh...
Uh...
I CAN'T DECIDE...

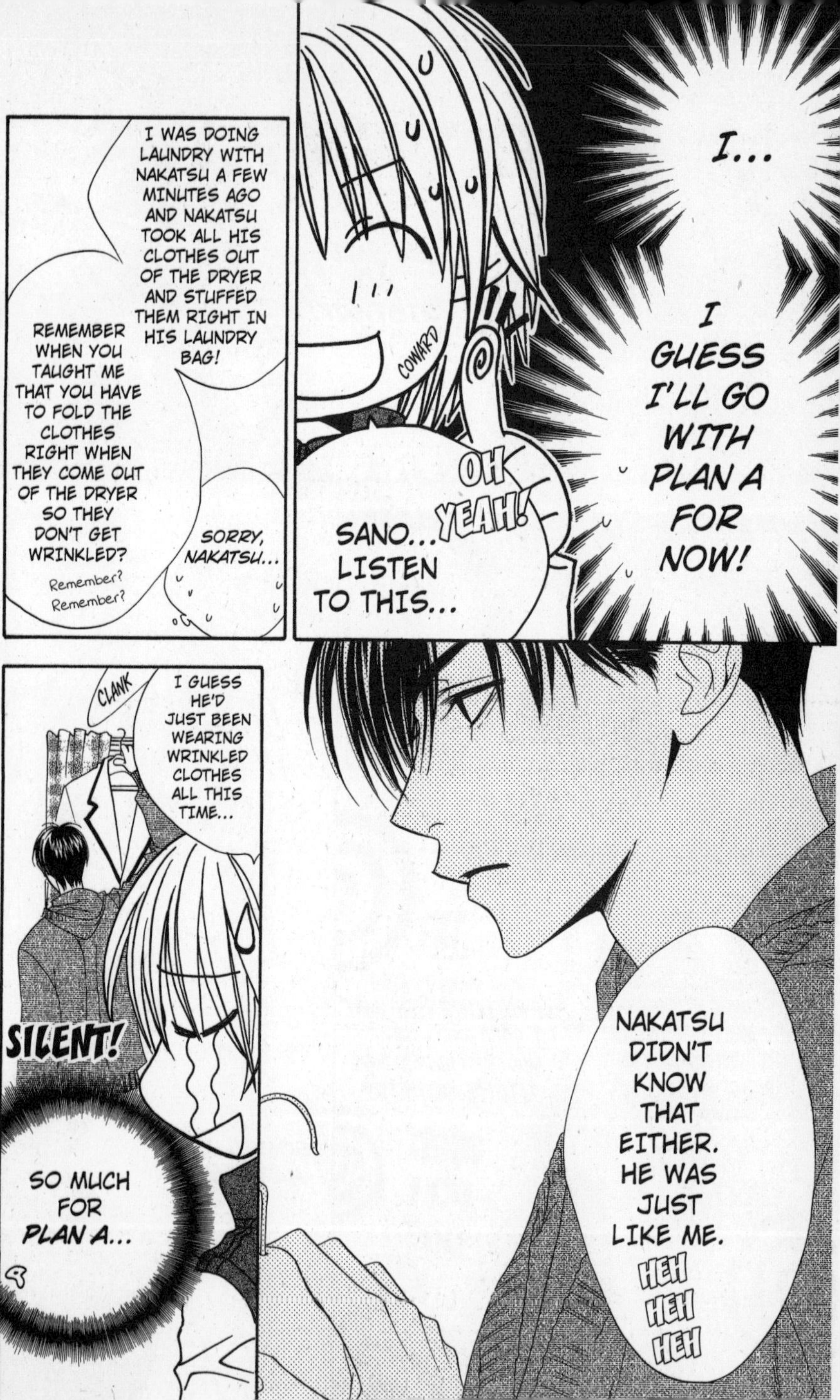
I...
I GUESS I'LL GO WITH PLAN A FOR NOW!
COWARD
OH YEAH!
SANO... LISTEN TO THIS...
I WAS DOING LAUNDRY WITH NAKATSU A FEW MINUTES AGO AND NAKATSU TOOK ALL HIS CLOTHES OUT OF THE DRYER AND STUFFED THEM RIGHT IN HIS LAUNDRY BAG!
REMEMBER WHEN YOU TAUGHT ME THAT YOU HAVE TO FOLD THE CLOTHES RIGHT WHEN THEY COME OUT OF THE DRYER SO THEY DON'T GET WRINKLED?
Remember? Remember?
SORRY, NAKATSU...
NAKATSU DIDN'T KNOW THAT EITHER. HE WAS JUST LIKE ME.
HEH HEH HEH
CLANK
I GUESS HE'D JUST BEEN WEARING WRINKLED CLOTHES ALL THIS TIME...
SILENT!
SO MUCH FOR PLAN A...

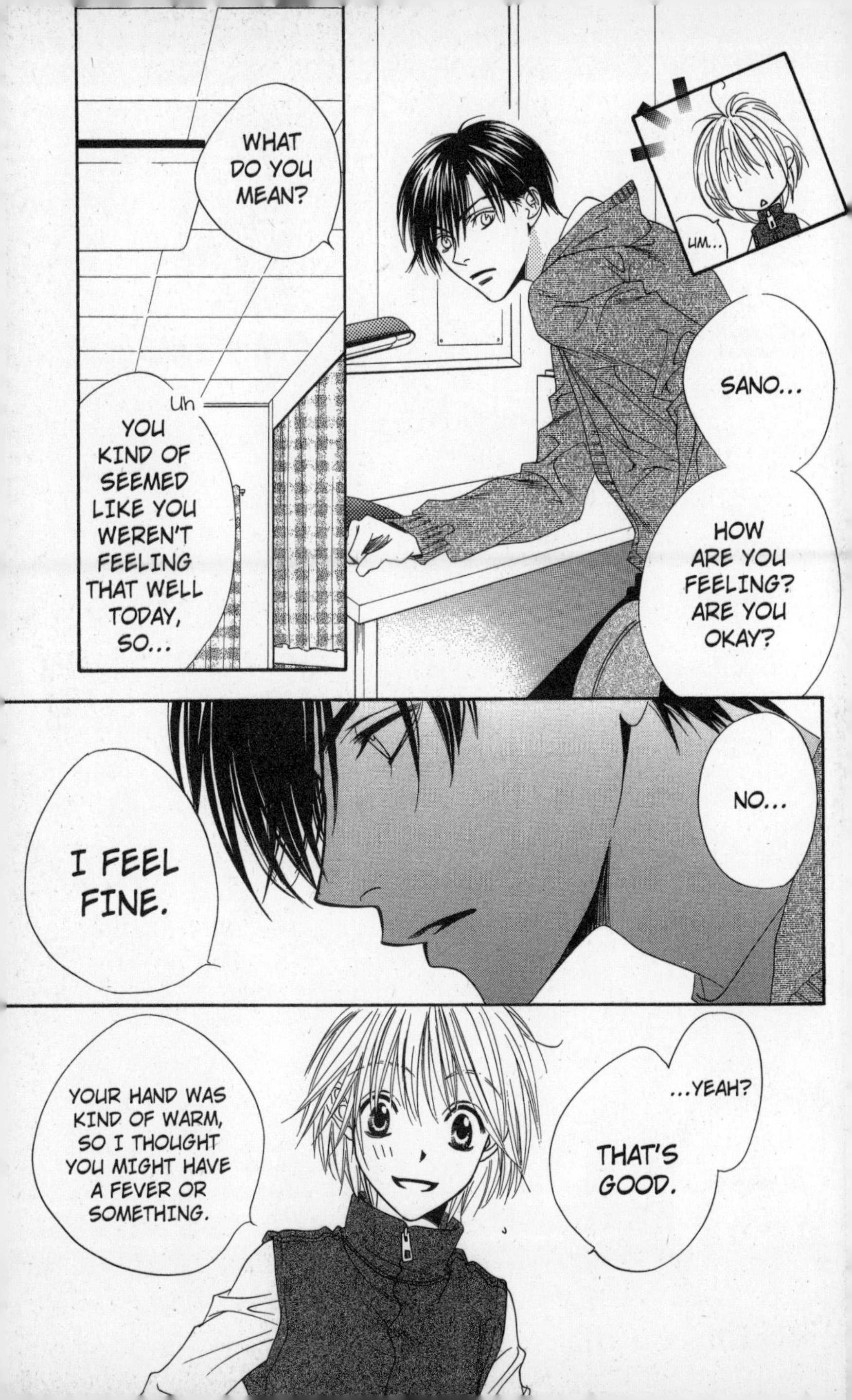
UM...
SANO...
HOW ARE YOU FEELING? ARE YOU OKAY?
WHAT DO YOU MEAN?
Uh
YOU KIND OF SEEMED LIKE YOU WEREN'T FEELING THAT WELL TODAY, SO...
NO...
I FEEL FINE.
...YEAH?
THAT'S GOOD.
YOUR HAND WAS KIND OF WARM, SO I THOUGHT YOU MIGHT HAVE A FEVER OR SOMETHING.

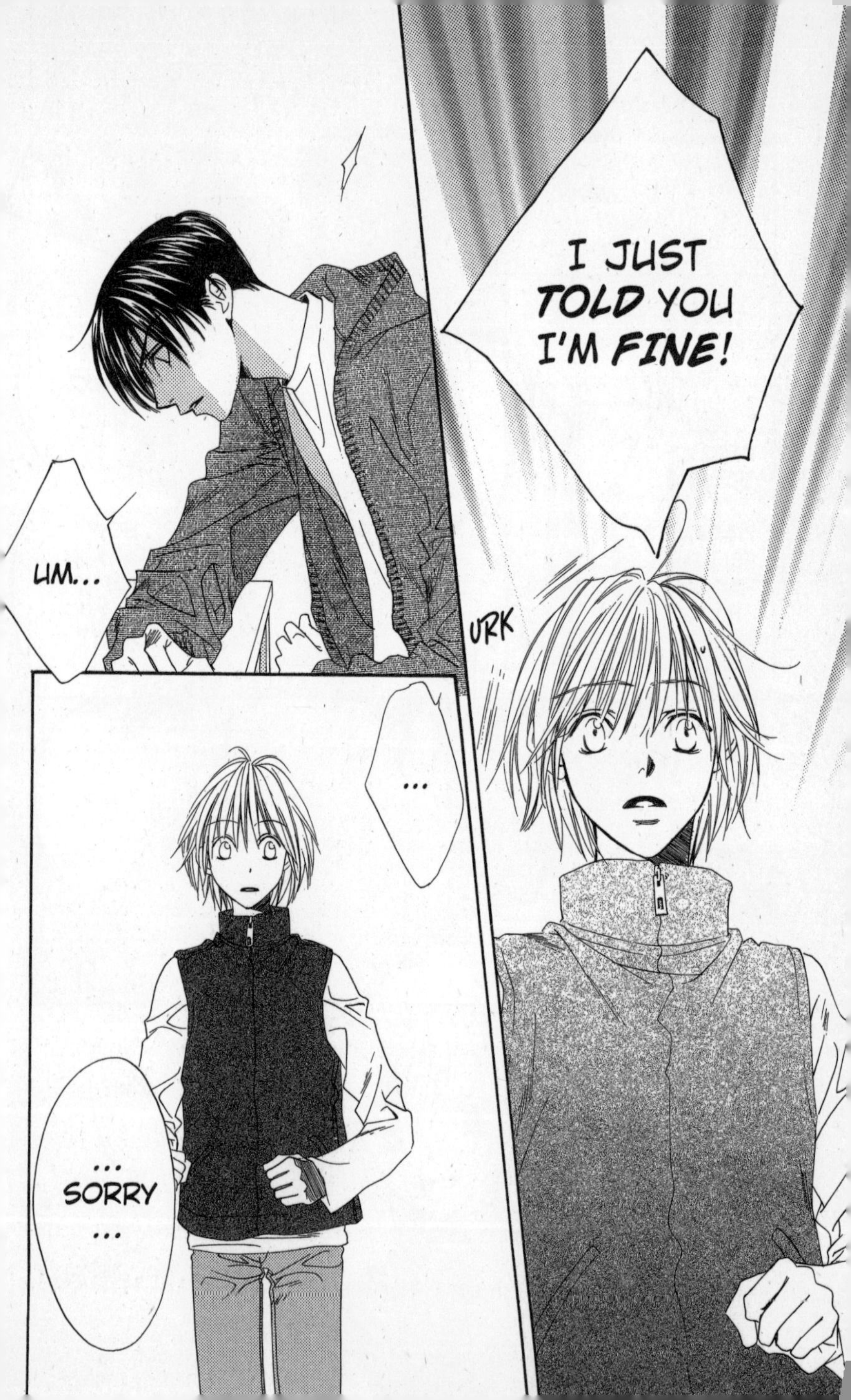
I JUST TOLD YOU I'M FINE!
URK
UM...
...
... SORRY ...

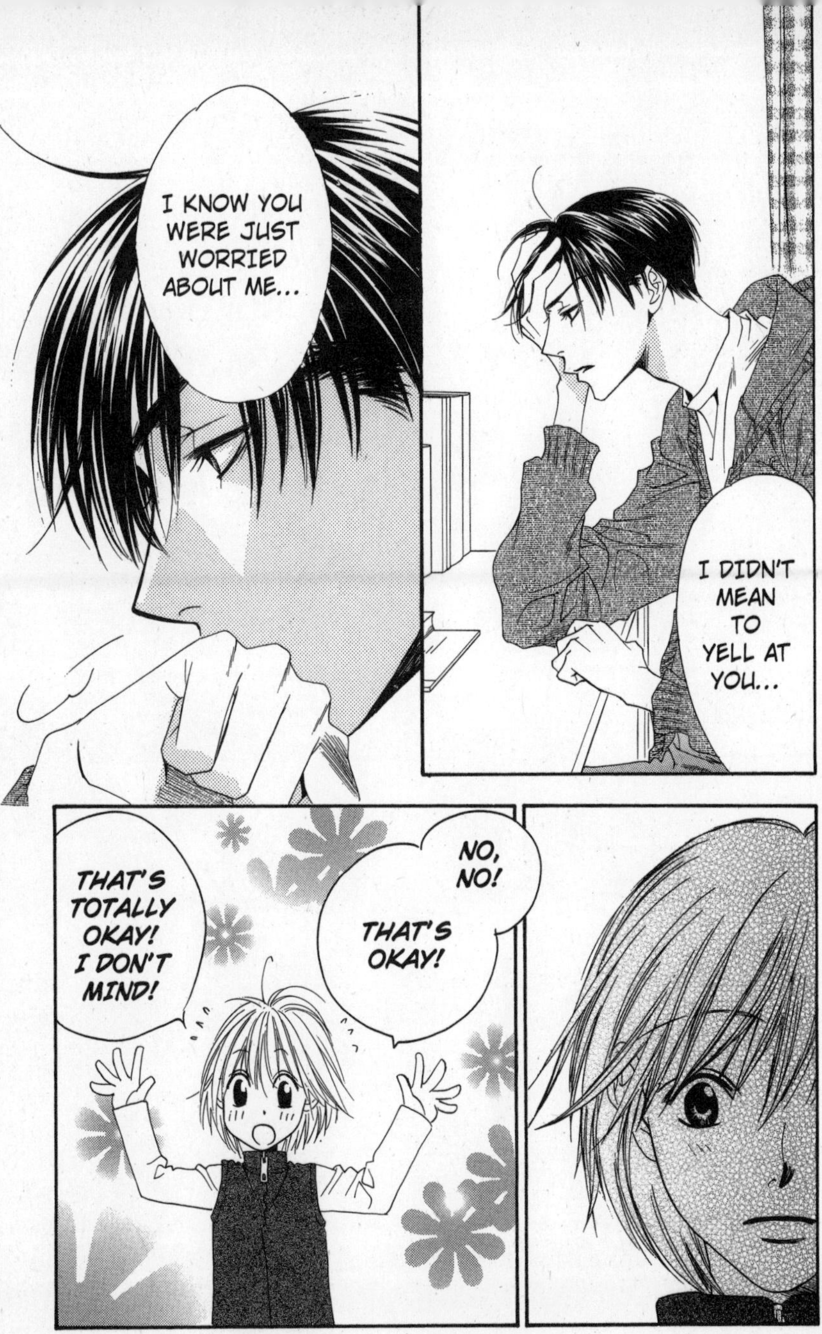
I DIDN'T MEAN TO YELL AT YOU...
I KNOW YOU WERE JUST WORRIED ABOUT ME...
NO, NO!
THAT'S OKAY!
THAT'S TOTALLY OKAY! I DON'T MIND!

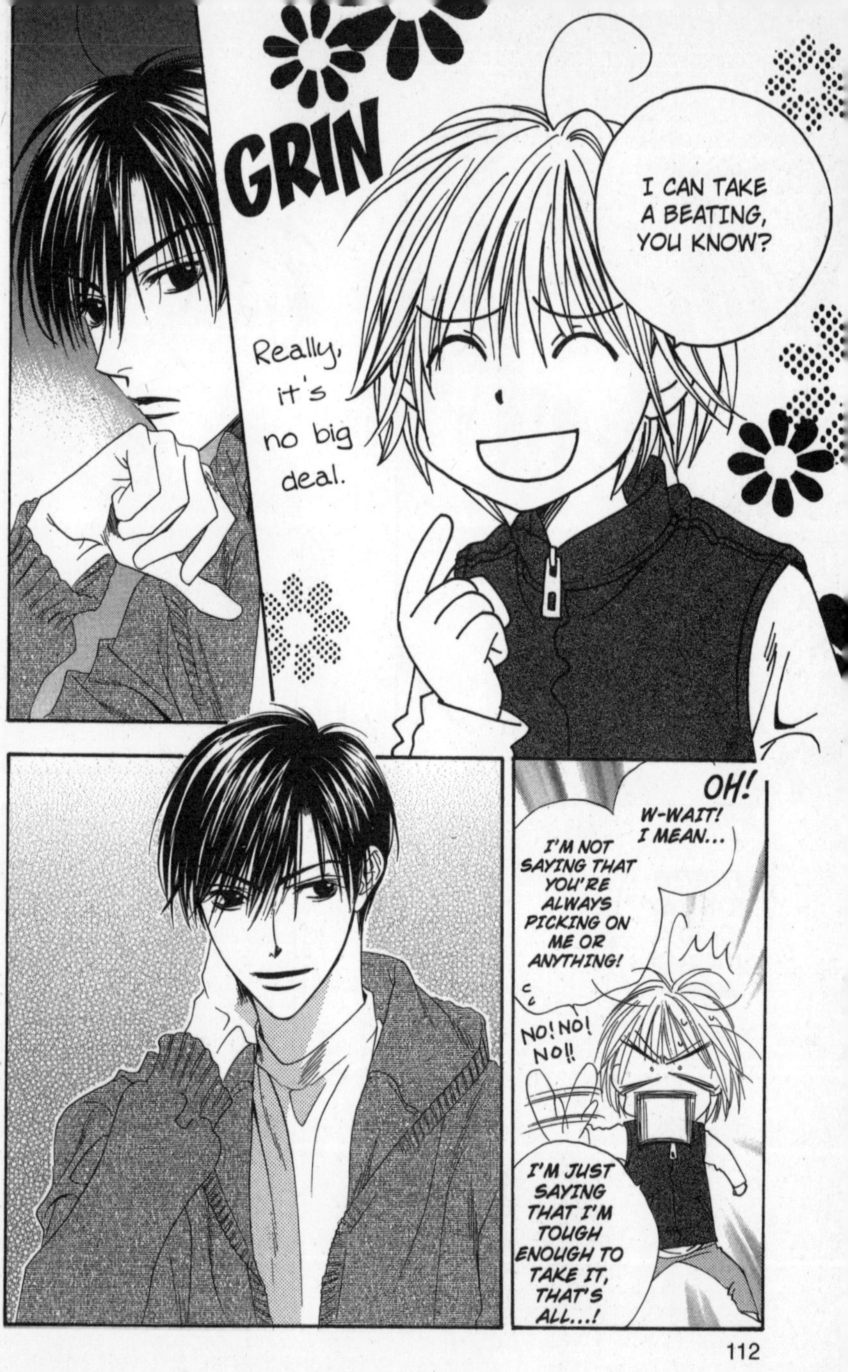
I CAN TAKE A BEATING, YOU KNOW?
GRIN
Really, it's no big deal.
OH!
W-WAIT! I MEAN...
I'M NOT SAYING THAT YOU'RE ALWAYS PICKING ON ME OR ANYTHING!
NO! NO! NO!!
I'M JUST SAYING THAT I'M TOUGH ENOUGH TO TAKE IT, THAT'S ALL...!

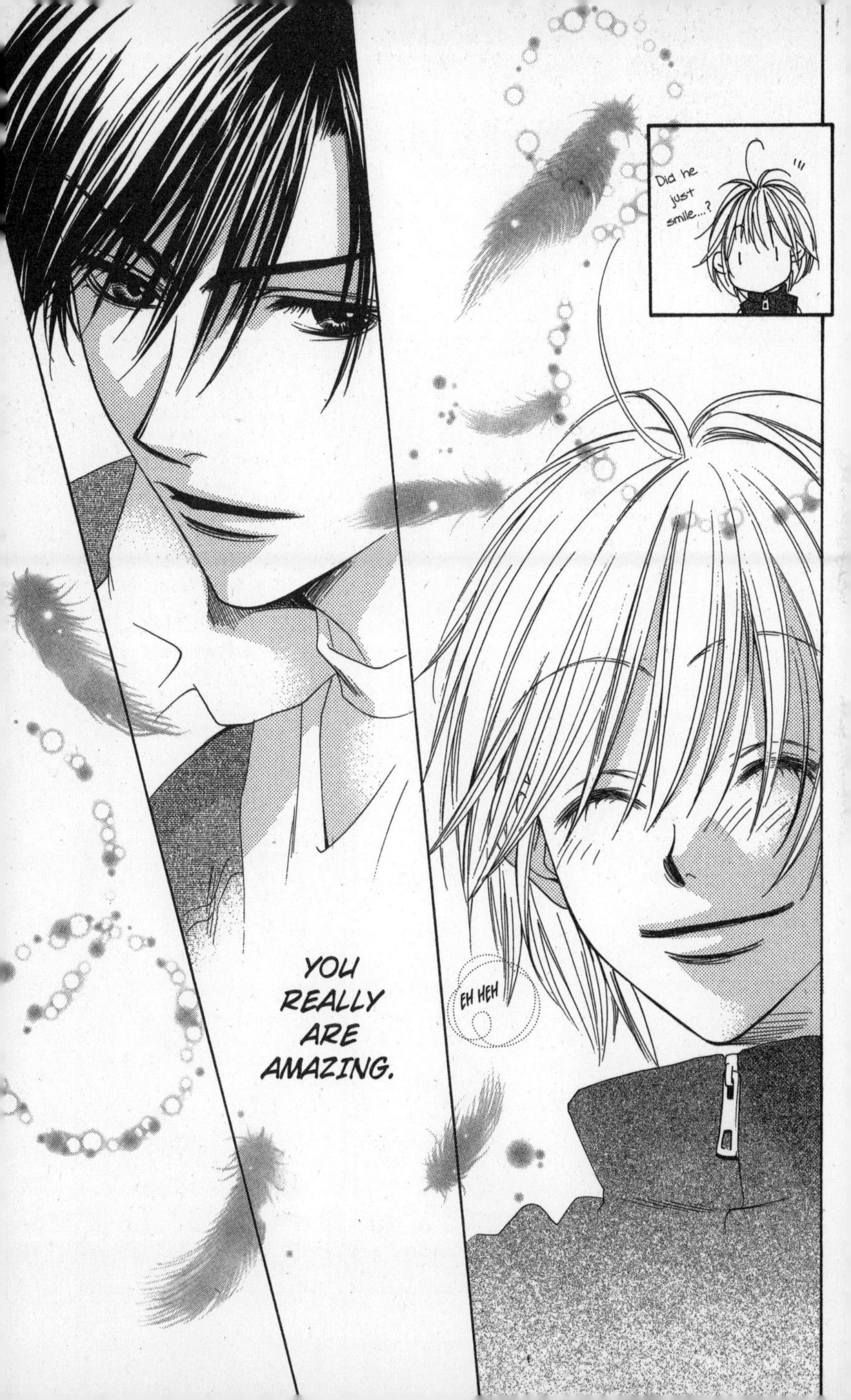
Did he just smile...?
EH HEH
YOU REALLY ARE AMAZING.

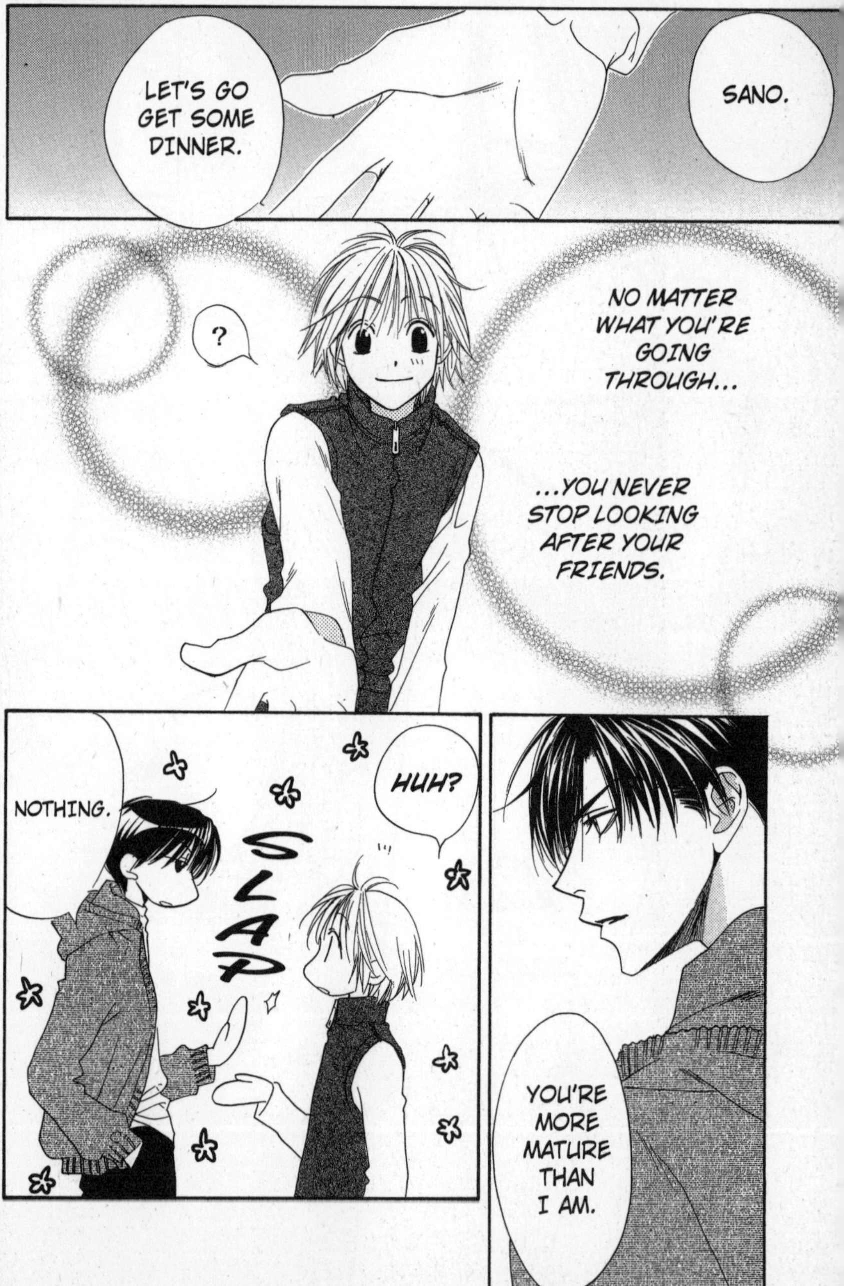
SANO.
LET'S GO GET SOME DINNER.
NO MATTER WHAT YOU'RE GOING THROUGH...
?
...YOU NEVER STOP LOOKING AFTER YOUR FRIENDS.
YOU'RE MORE MATURE THAN I AM.
HUH?
NOTHING.
SLAP

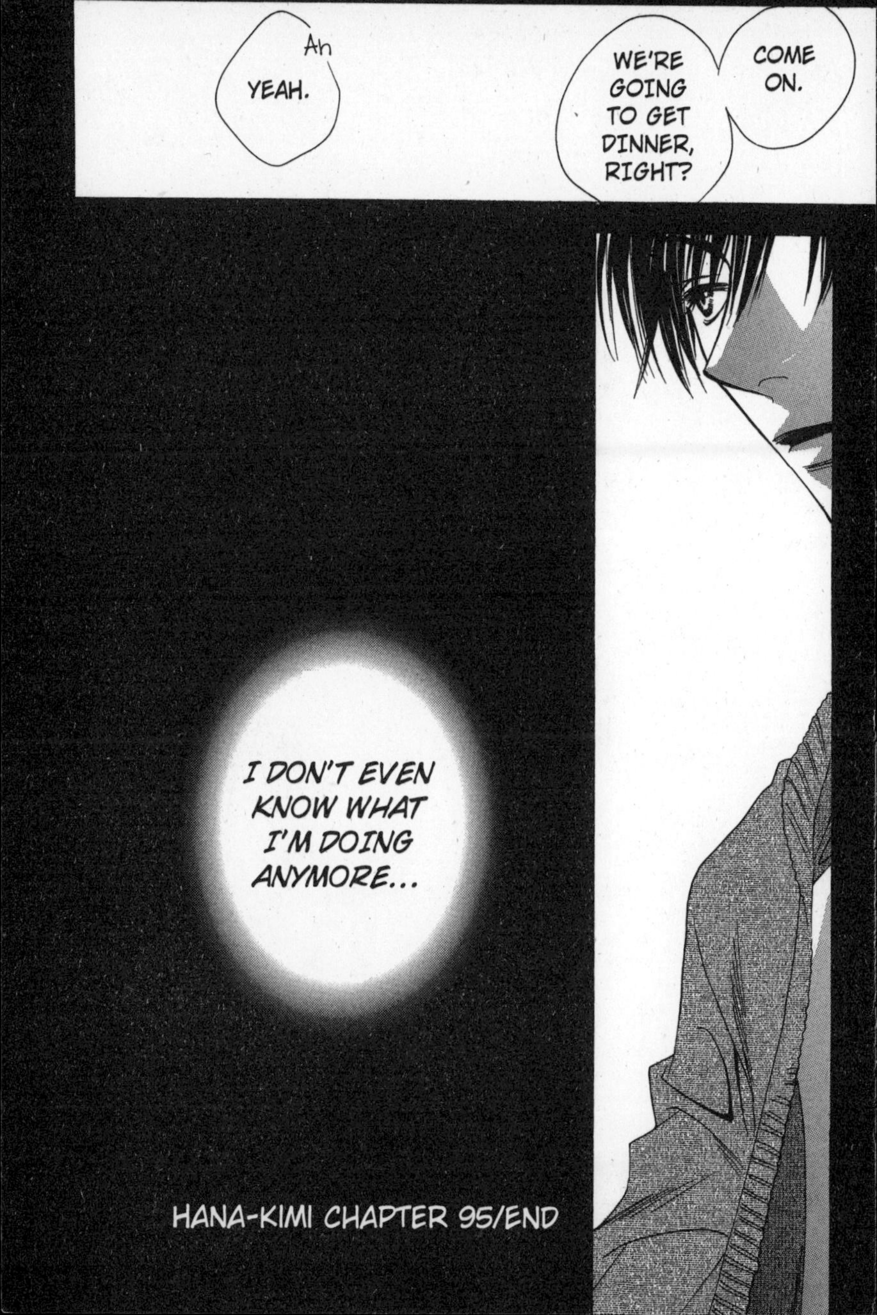
COME ON.
WE'RE GOING TO GET DINNER, RIGHT?
Ah
YEAH.
I DON'T EVEN KNOW WHAT I'M DOING ANYMORE...
HANA-KIMI CHAPTER 95/END

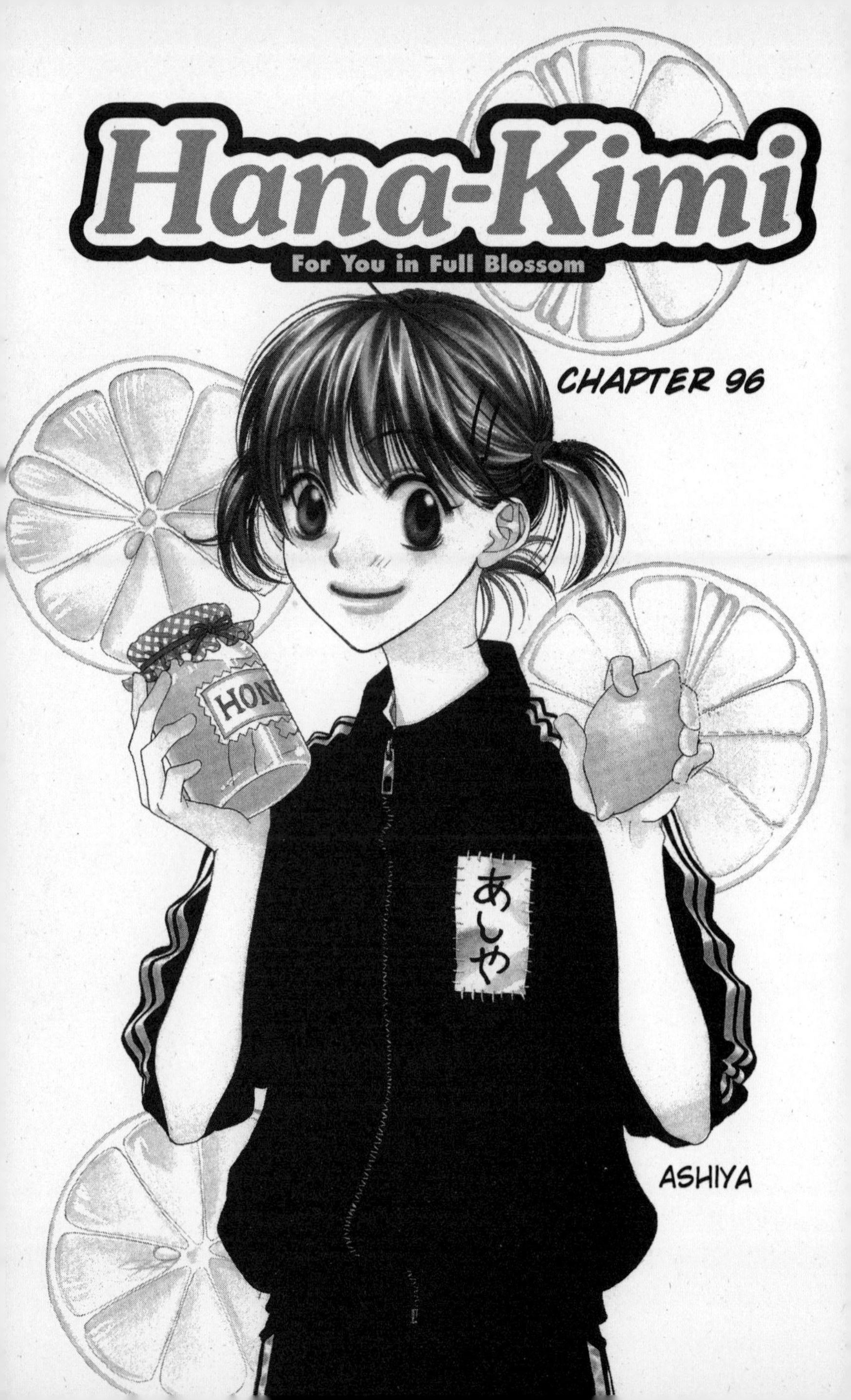
Hana-Kimi
For You in Full Blossom
CHAPTER 96
HON
あしや
ASHIYA

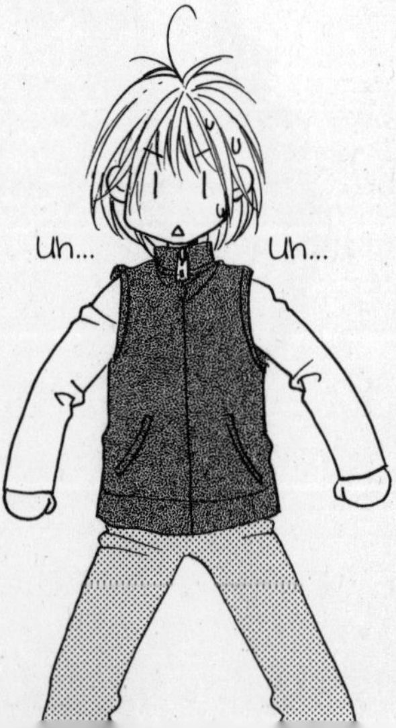
Uh...
Uh...

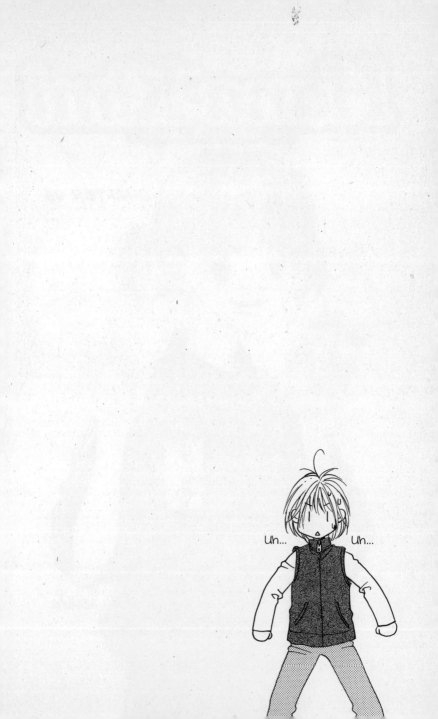

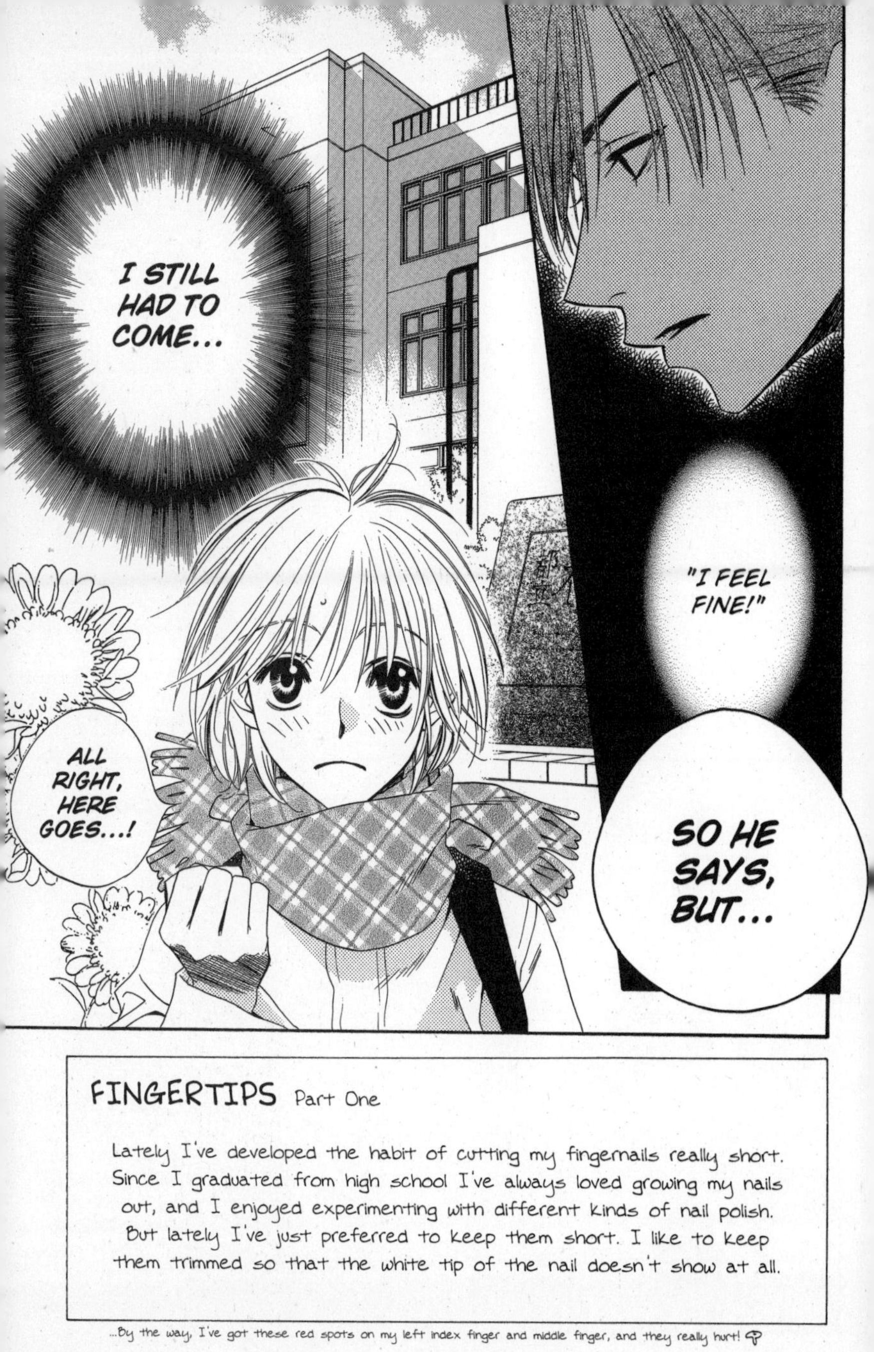
"I FEEL FINE!"
SO HE SAYS, BUT...
I STILL HAD TO COME...
ALL RIGHT, HERE GOES...!

FINGERTIPS Part One

Lately I've developed the habit of cutting my fingernails really short. Since I graduated from high school I've always loved growing my nails out, and I enjoyed experimenting with different kinds of nail polish. But lately I've just preferred to keep them short. I like to keep them trimmed so that the white tip of the nail doesn't show at all.

...By the way, I've got these red spots on my left index finger and middle finger, and they really hurt!

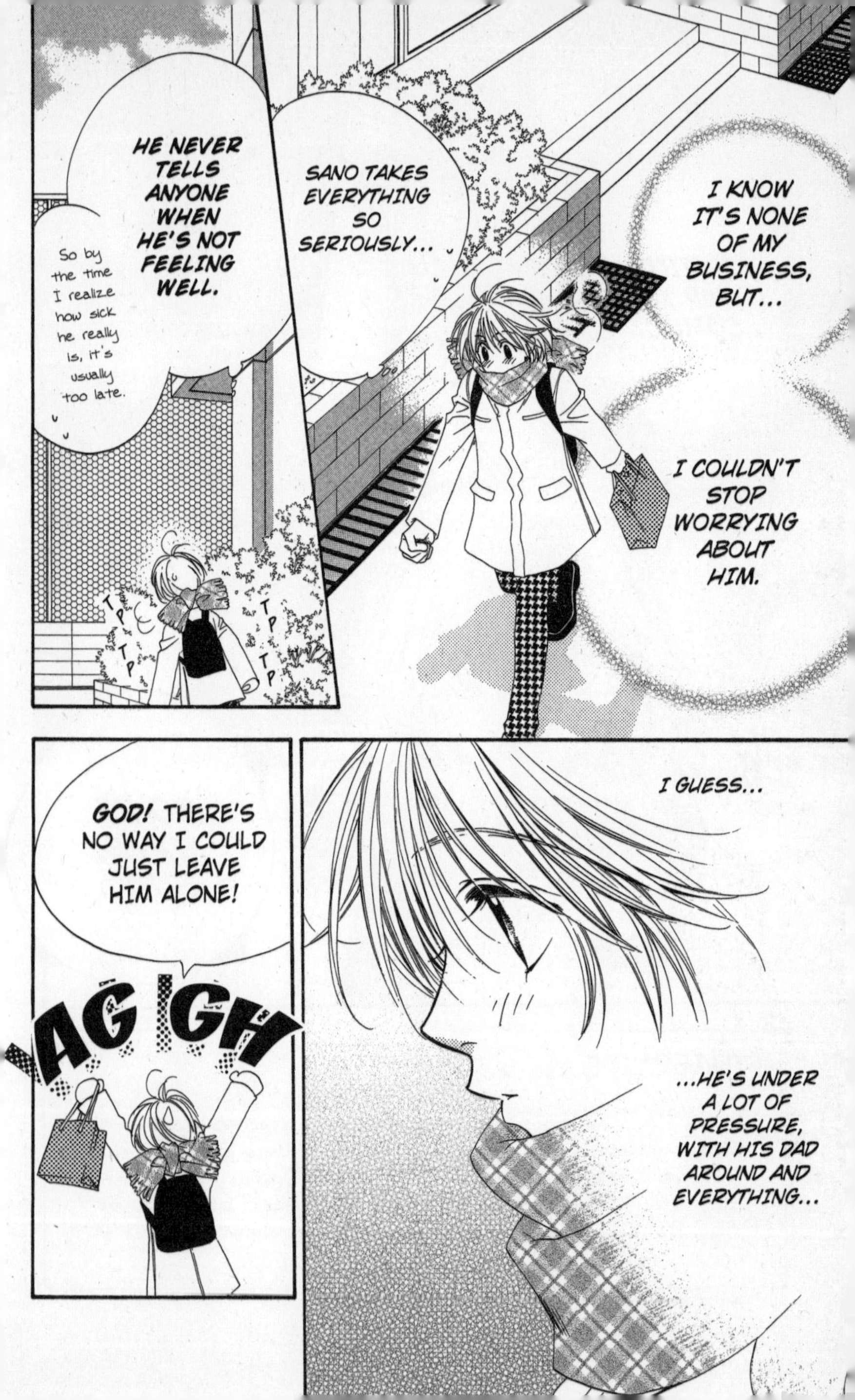
I KNOW IT'S NONE OF MY BUSINESS, BUT...
I COULDN'T STOP WORRYING ABOUT HIM.
SANO TAKES EVERYTHING SO SERIOUSLY...
HE NEVER TELLS ANYONE WHEN HE'S NOT FEELING WELL.
So by the time I realize how sick he really is, it's usually too late.
TP TP TP
TP TP TP
I GUESS...
...HE'S UNDER A LOT OF PRESSURE, WITH HIS DAD AROUND AND EVERYTHING...
GOD! THERE'S NO WAY I COULD JUST LEAVE HIM ALONE!
AGGH

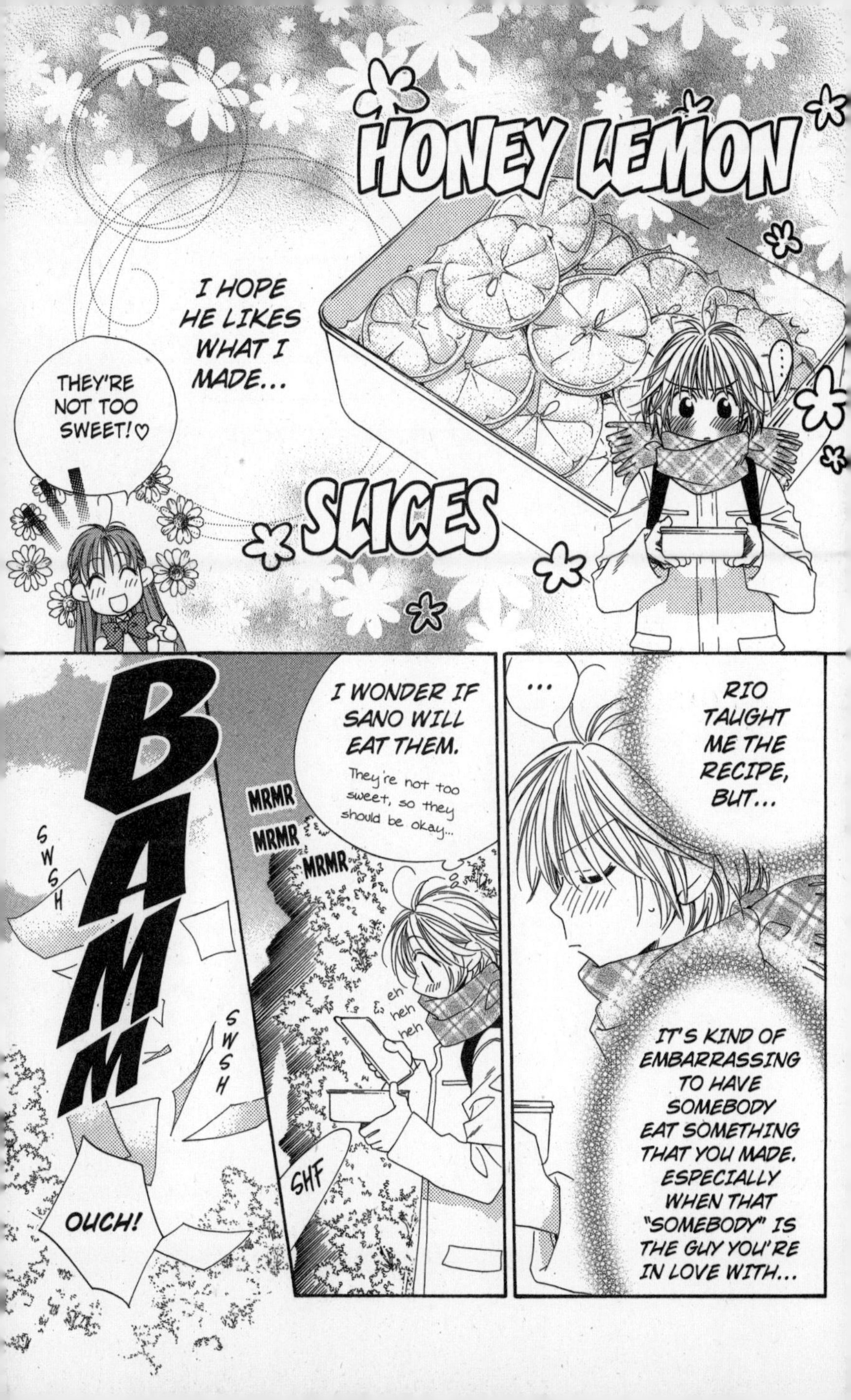
HONEY LEMON SLICES
I HOPE HE LIKES WHAT I MADE...
THEY'RE NOT TOO SWEET! ♡
...
RIO TAUGHT ME THE RECIPE, BUT...
IT'S KIND OF EMBARRASSING TO HAVE SOMEBODY EAT SOMETHING THAT YOU MADE. ESPECIALLY WHEN THAT "SOMEBODY" IS THE GUY YOU'RE IN LOVE WITH...
I WONDER IF SANO WILL EAT THEM.
They're not too sweet, so they should be okay...
MRMR
MRMR
MRMR
eh heh heh
SHF
BAMM
SWSH
SWSH
OUCH!

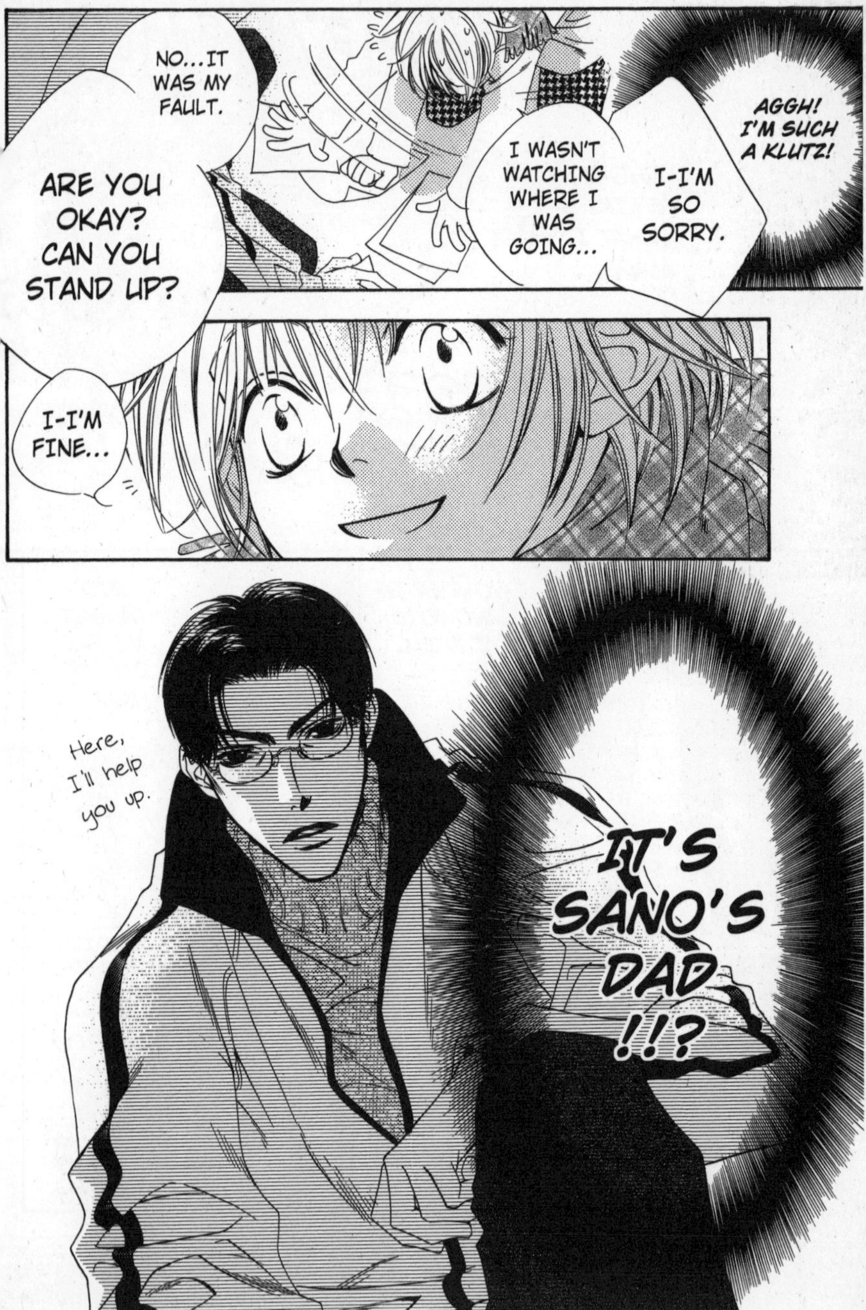
AGGH! I'M SUCH A KLUTZ!
I-I'M SO SORRY.
I WASN'T WATCHING WHERE I WAS GOING...
NO...IT WAS MY FAULT.
ARE YOU OKAY? CAN YOU STAND UP?
I-I'M FINE...
IT'S SANO'S DAD !!?
Here, I'll help you up.

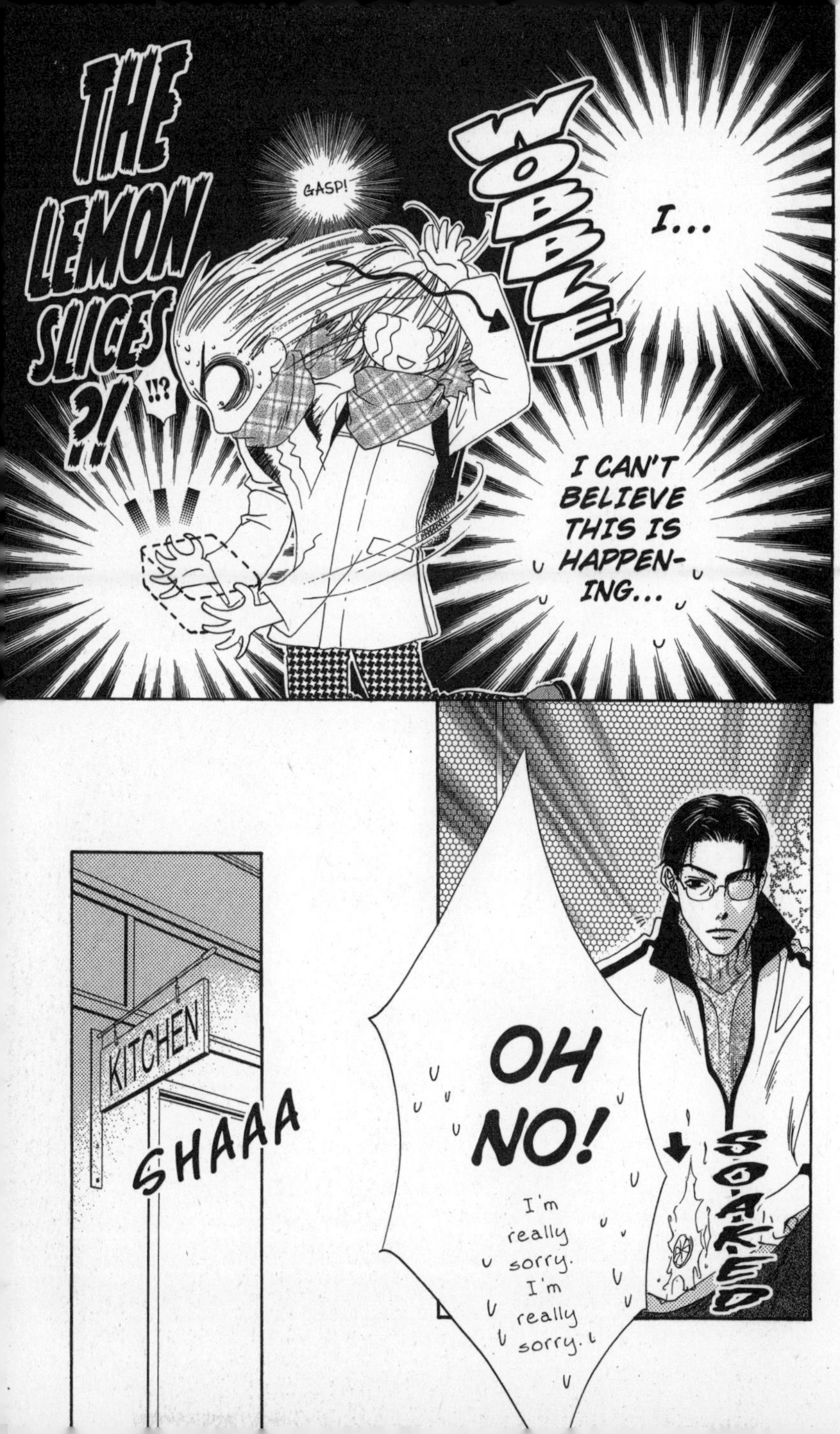
I...
WOBBLE
I CAN'T BELIEVE THIS IS HAPPENING...
GASP!
THE LEMON SLICES?!
!!?
SOAKED
OH NO!
I'm really sorry. I'm really sorry.
KITCHEN
SHAAA

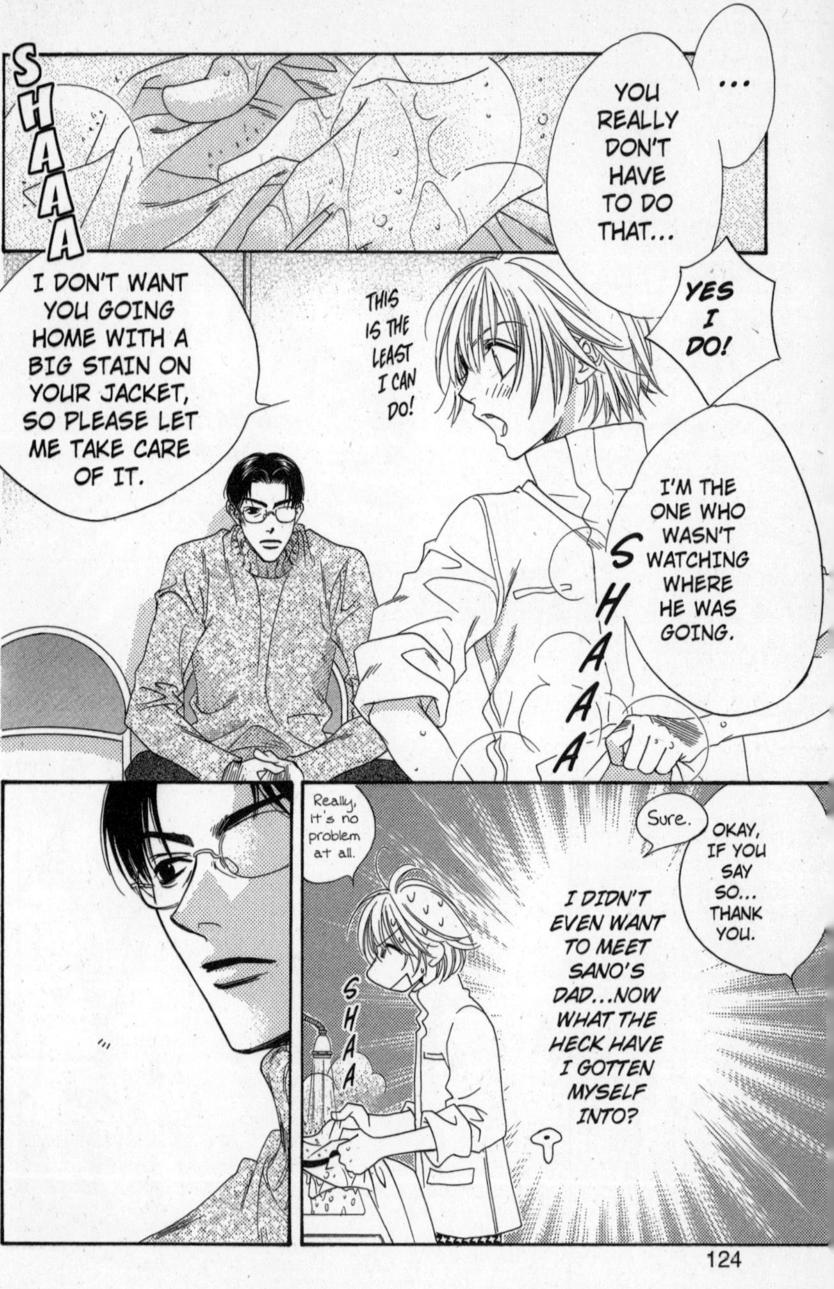
...
YOU REALLY DON'T HAVE TO DO THAT...
SHAAAA
YES I DO!
I'M THE ONE WHO WASN'T WATCHING WHERE HE WAS GOING.
SHAAAA
THIS IS THE LEAST I CAN DO!
I DON'T WANT YOU GOING HOME WITH A BIG STAIN ON YOUR JACKET, SO PLEASE LET ME TAKE CARE OF IT.
OKAY, IF YOU SAY SO... THANK YOU.
Sure.
I DIDN'T EVEN WANT TO MEET SANO'S DAD...NOW WHAT THE HECK HAVE I GOTTEN MYSELF INTO?
Really, it's no problem at all.
SHAA

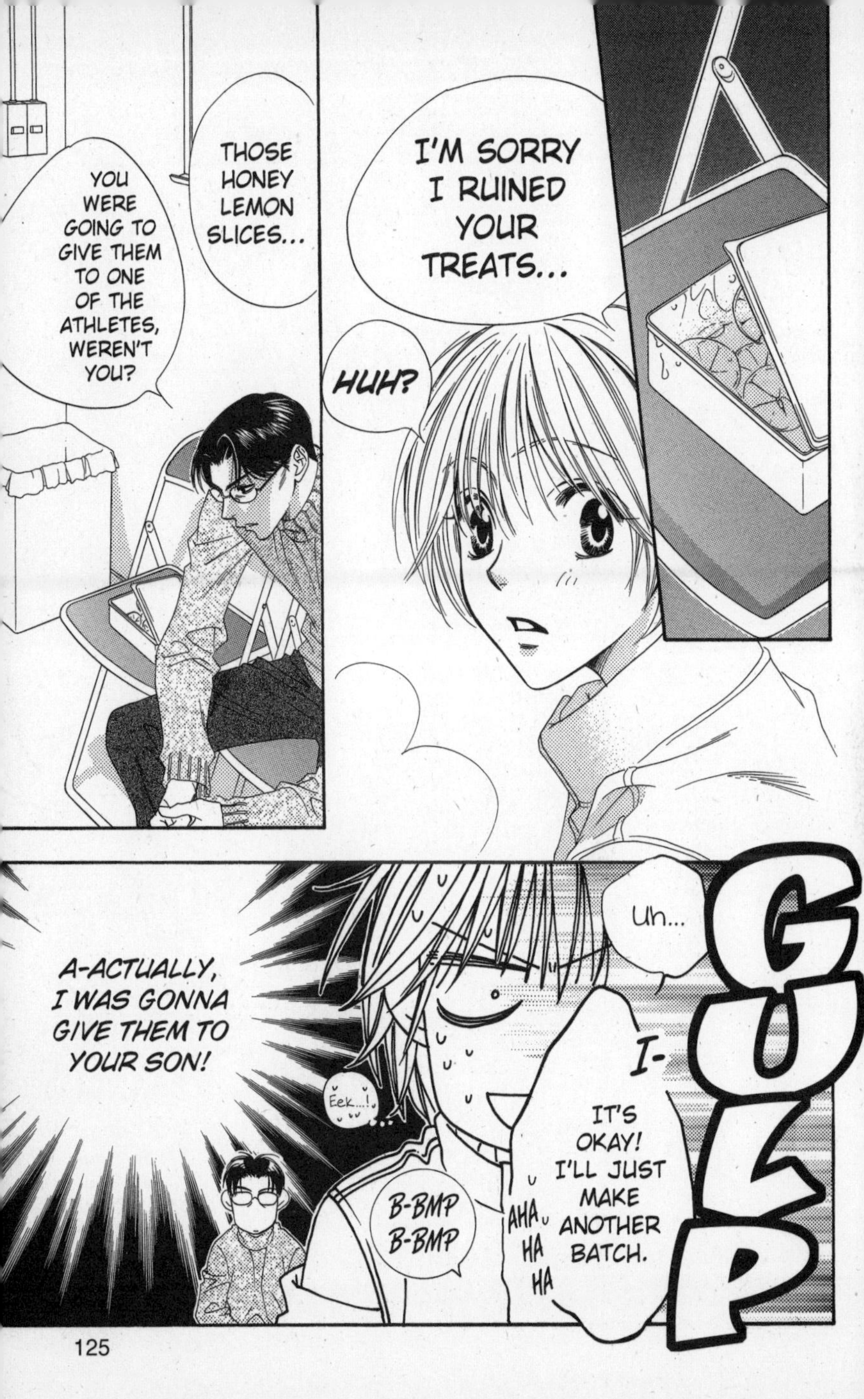

I'M SORRY I RUINED YOUR TREATS...
HUH?
THOSE HONEY LEMON SLICES...
YOU WERE GOING TO GIVE THEM TO ONE OF THE ATHLETES, WEREN'T YOU?
GULP
Uh...
I-
IT'S OKAY! I'LL JUST MAKE ANOTHER BATCH.
AHA HA HA
B-BMP B-BMP
Eek...!
A-ACTUALLY, I WAS GONNA GIVE THEM TO YOUR SON!

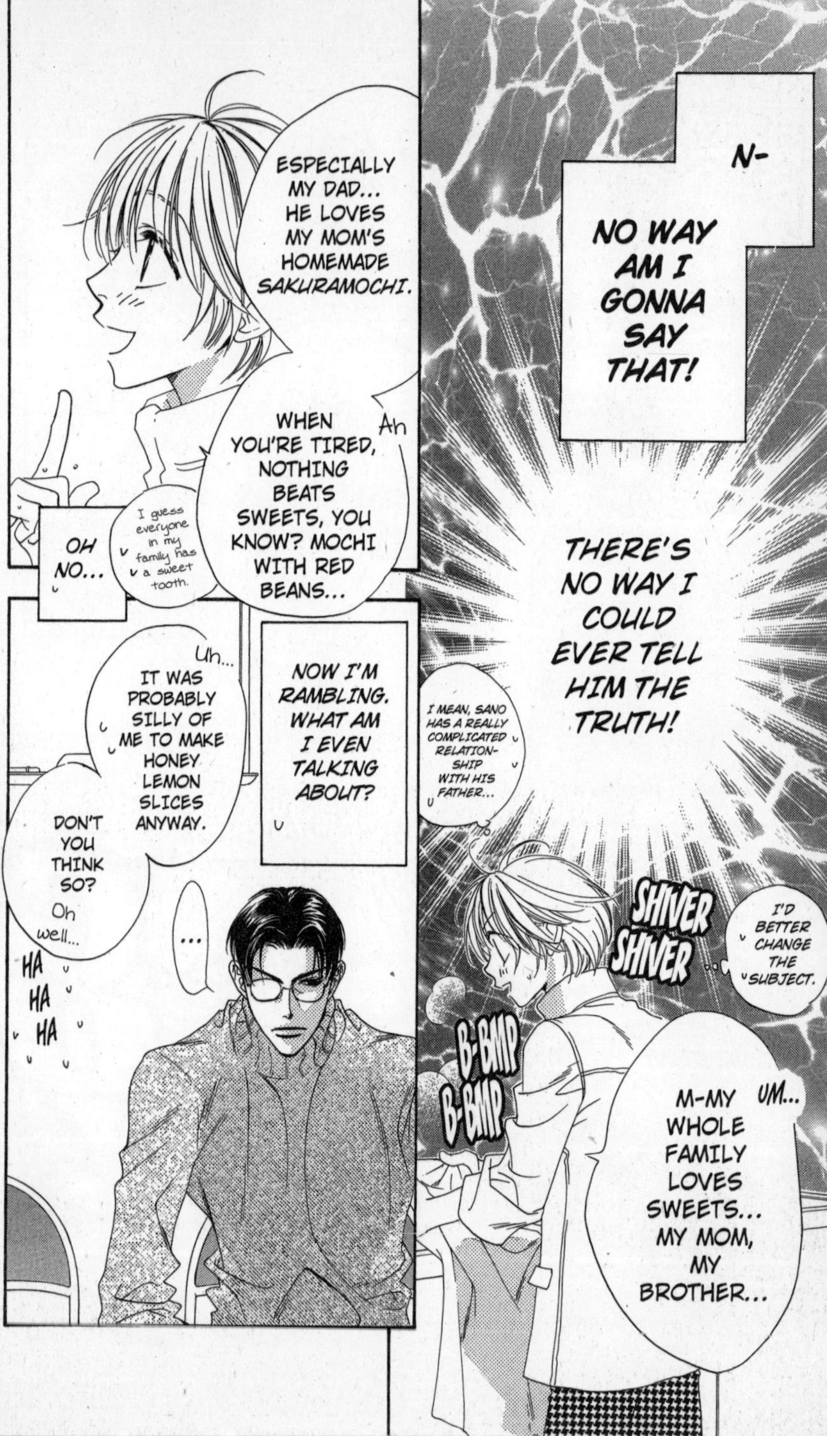
N-
NO WAY AM I GONNA SAY THAT!
THERE'S NO WAY I COULD EVER TELL HIM THE TRUTH!
I MEAN, SANO HAS A REALLY COMPLICATED RELATION-SHIP WITH HIS FATHER...
SHIVER SHIVER
I'D BETTER CHANGE THE SUBJECT.
B-BMP B-BMP
UM...
M-MY WHOLE FAMILY LOVES SWEETS... MY MOM, MY BROTHER...
ESPECIALLY MY DAD... HE LOVES MY MOM'S HOMEMADE SAKURAMOCHI.
Ah
WHEN YOU'RE TIRED, NOTHING BEATS SWEETS, YOU KNOW? MOCHI WITH RED BEANS...
I guess everyone in my family has a sweet tooth.
OH NO...
NOW I'M RAMBLING. WHAT AM I EVEN TALKING ABOUT?
Uh...
IT WAS PROBABLY SILLY OF ME TO MAKE HONEY LEMON SLICES ANYWAY.
DON'T YOU THINK SO?
Oh well...
HA HA HA
...

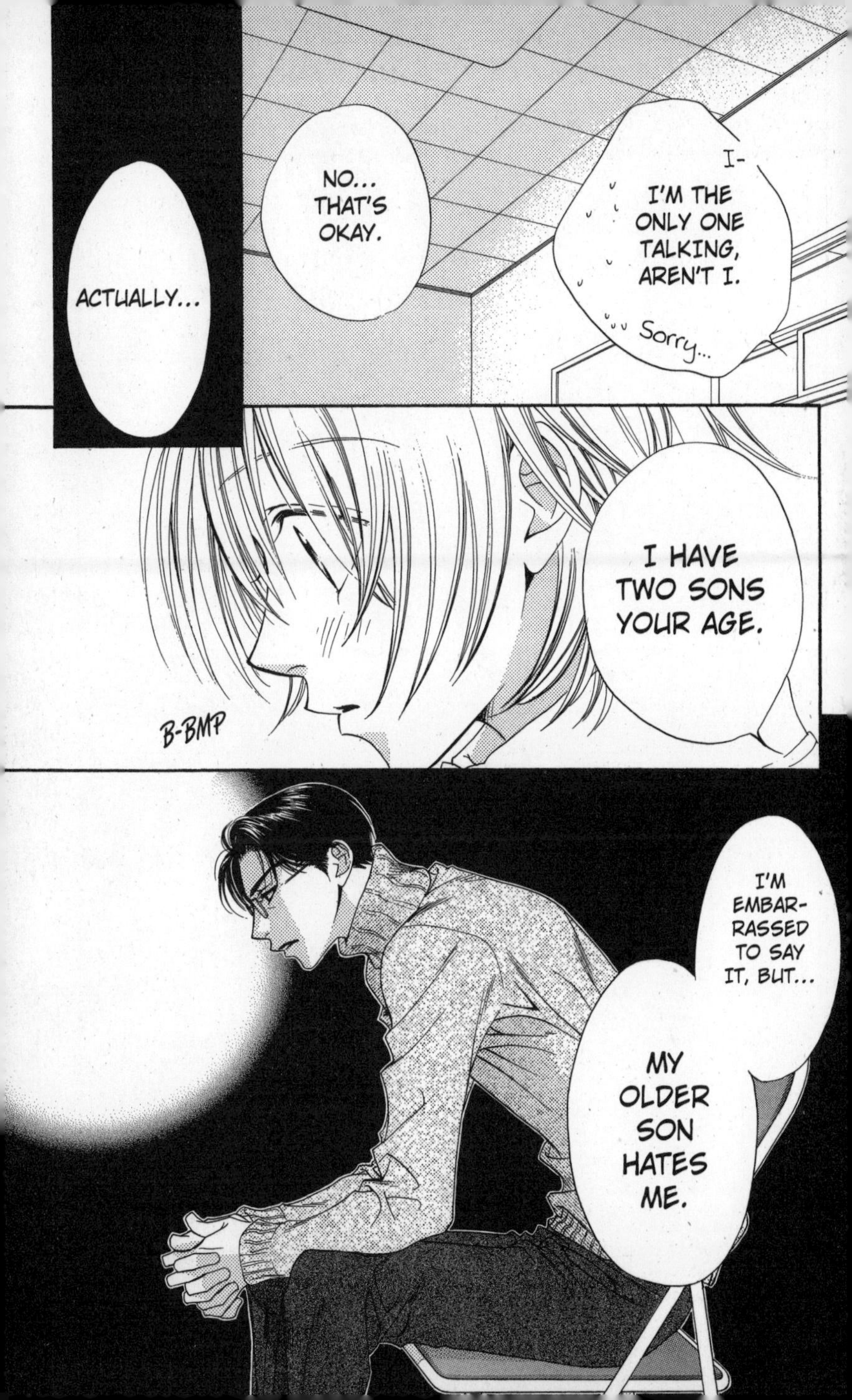
I-
I'M THE ONLY ONE TALKING, AREN'T I.
Sorry...
NO... THAT'S OKAY.
ACTUALLY...
I HAVE TWO SONS YOUR AGE.
B-BMP
I'M EMBAR-RASSED TO SAY IT, BUT...
MY OLDER SON HATES ME.

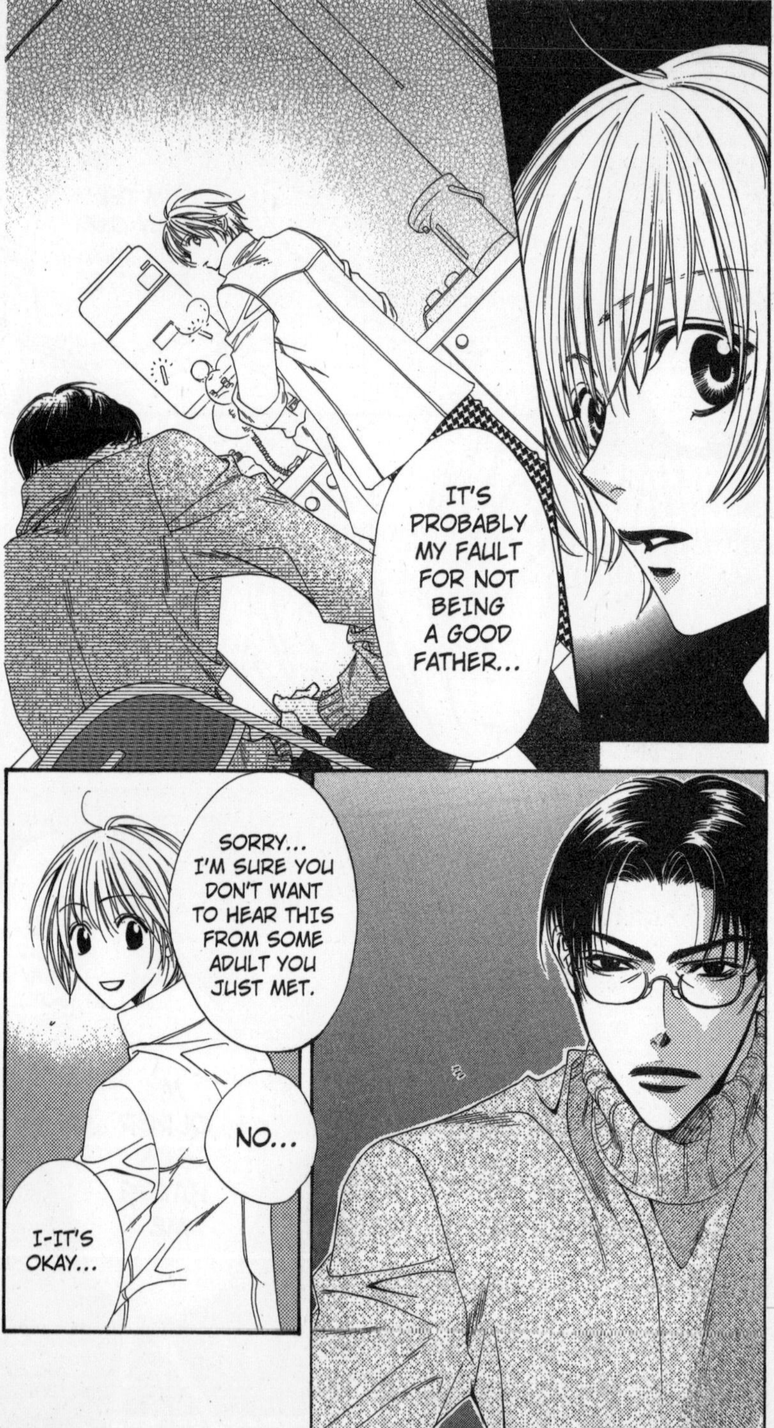
IT'S PROBABLY MY FAULT FOR NOT BEING A GOOD FATHER...
SORRY... I'M SURE YOU DON'T WANT TO HEAR THIS FROM SOME ADULT YOU JUST MET.
NO...
I-IT'S OKAY...

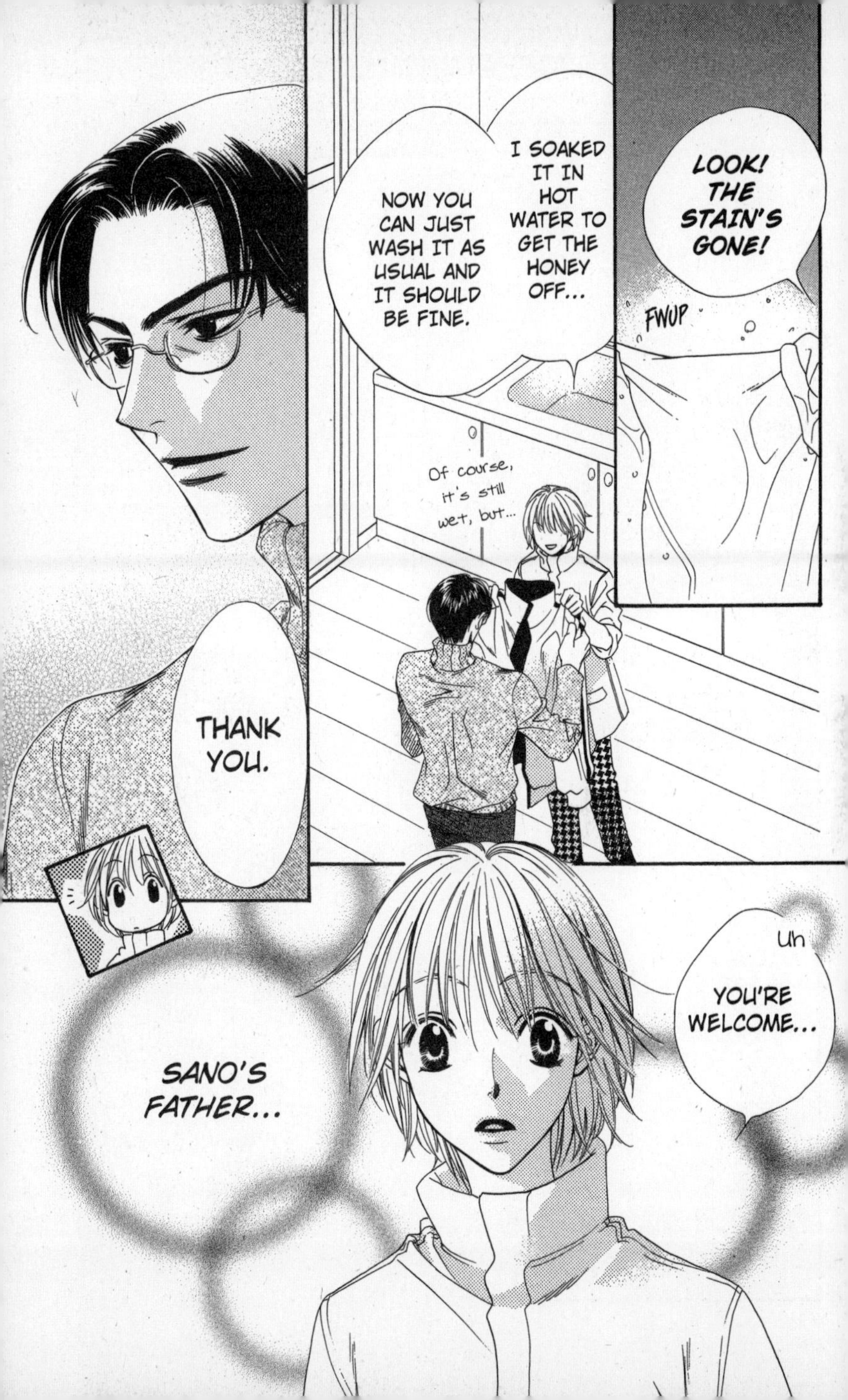
LOOK! THE STAIN'S GONE!
FWUP
I SOAKED IT IN HOT WATER TO GET THE HONEY OFF...
NOW YOU CAN JUST WASH IT AS USUAL AND IT SHOULD BE FINE.
Of course, it's still wet, but...
THANK YOU.
Uh
YOU'RE WELCOME...
SANO'S FATHER...

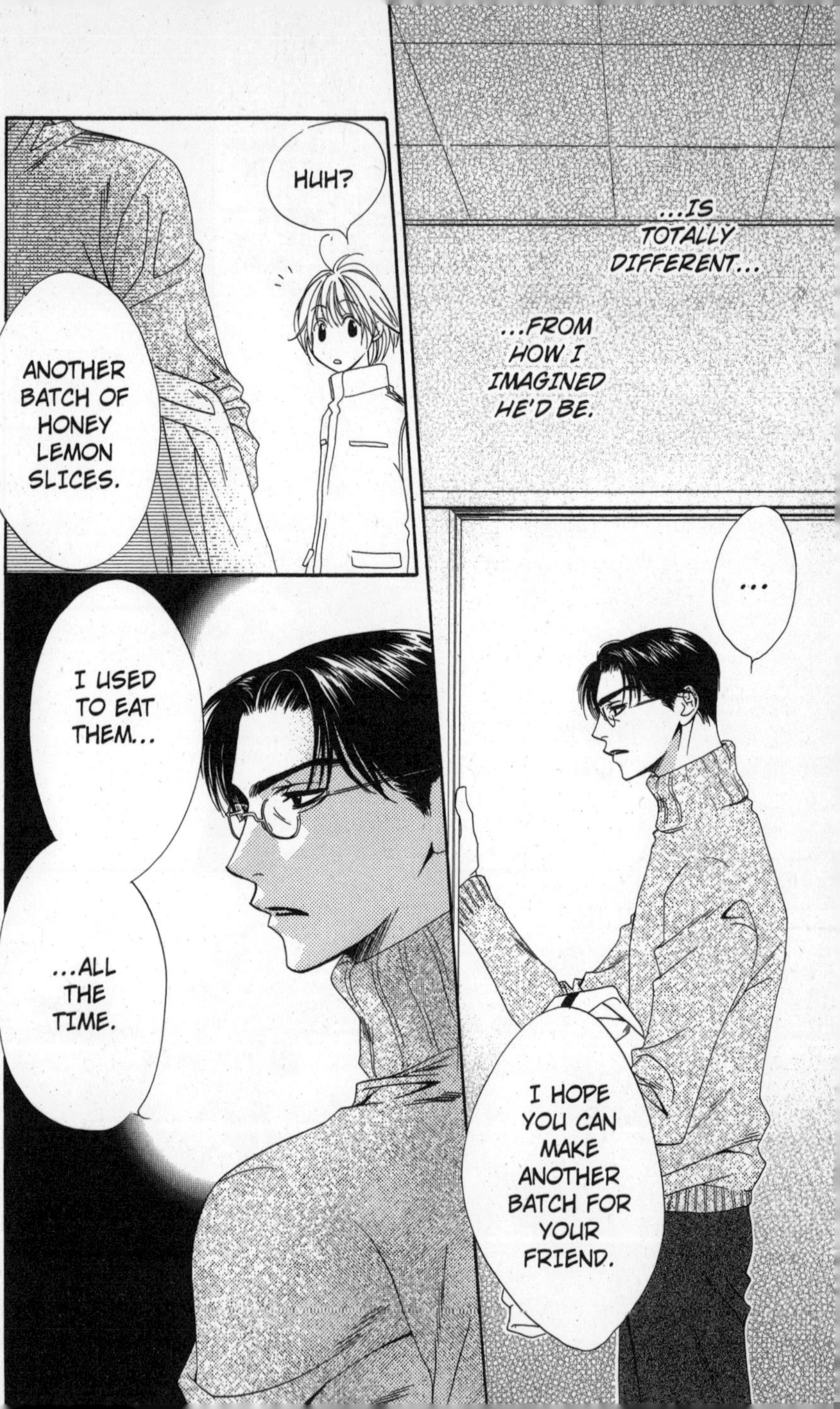
...IS TOTALLY DIFFERENT...
...FROM HOW I IMAGINED HE'D BE.
HUH?
ANOTHER BATCH OF HONEY LEMON SLICES.
...
I HOPE YOU CAN MAKE ANOTHER BATCH FOR YOUR FRIEND.
I USED TO EAT THEM...
...ALL THE TIME.

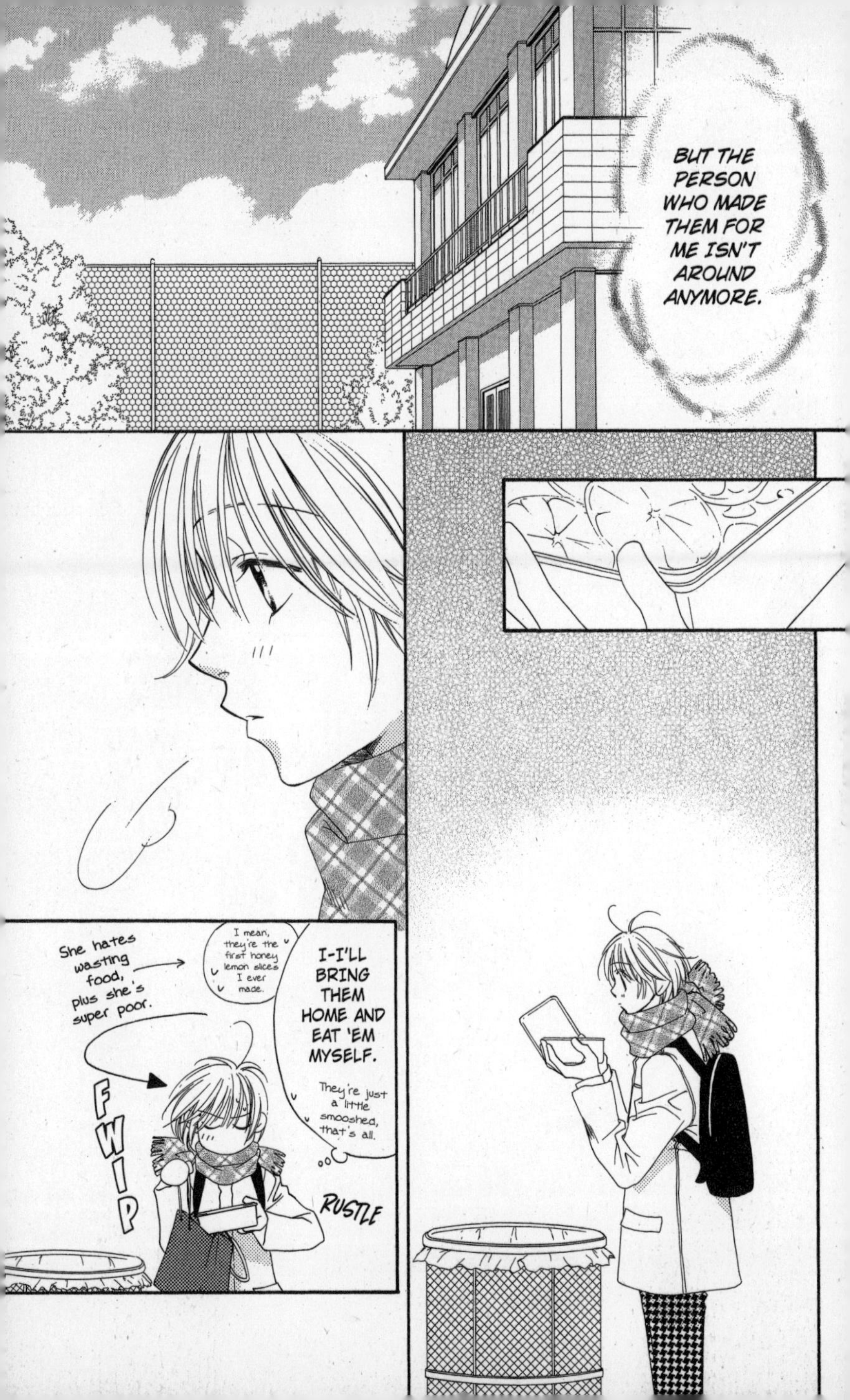

BUT THE PERSON WHO MADE THEM FOR ME ISN'T AROUND ANYMORE.
I-I'LL BRING THEM HOME AND EAT 'EM MYSELF.
They're just a little smooshed, that's all.
I mean, they're the first honey lemon slices I ever made.
She hates wasting food, plus she's super poor.
RUSTLE
FWIP

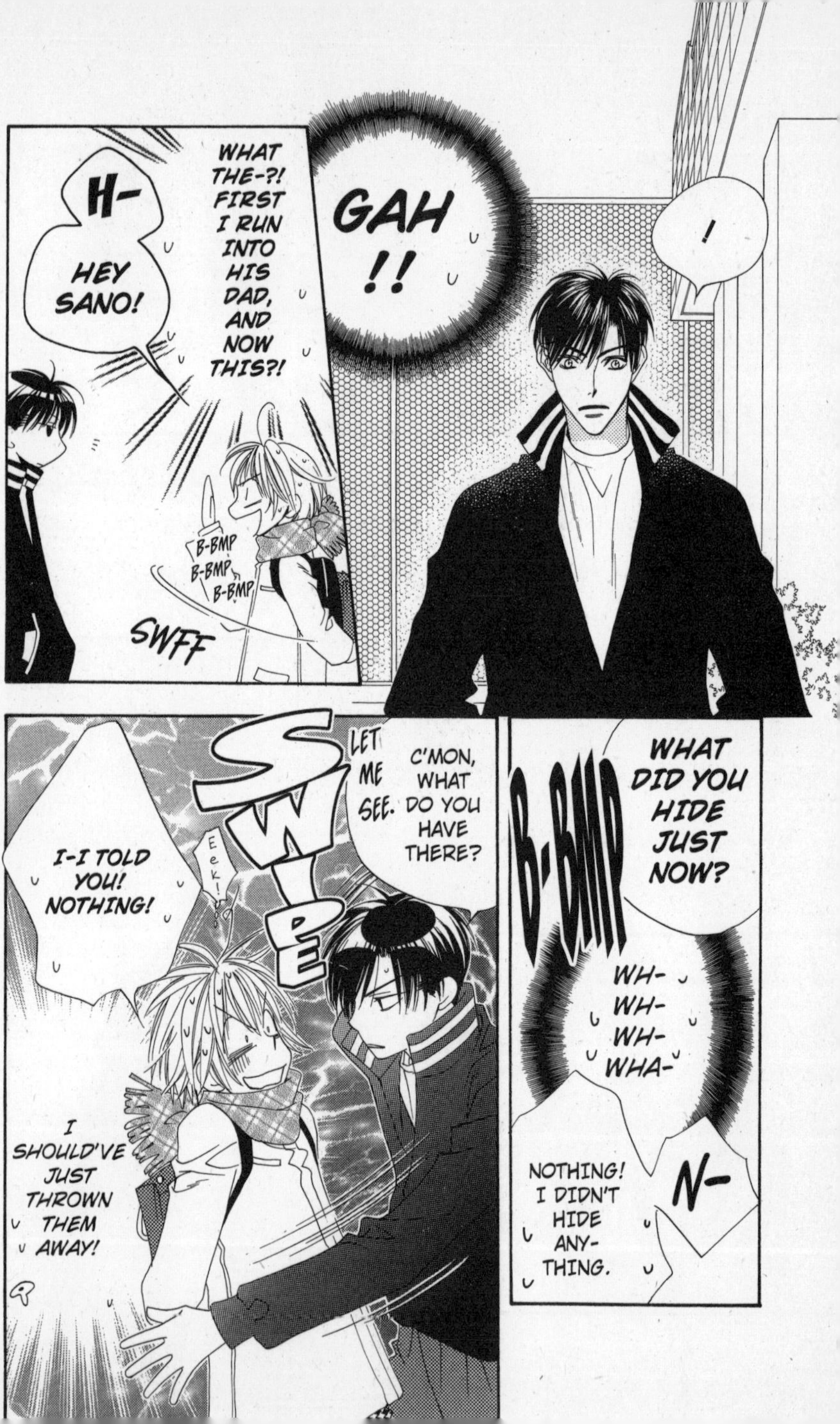
!
GAH!!
WHAT THE-?! FIRST I RUN INTO HIS DAD, AND NOW THIS?!
H- HEY SANO!
B-BMP B-BMP B-BMP
SWFF
WHAT DID YOU HIDE JUST NOW?
B-BMP
WH- WH- WH- WHA-
N-
NOTHING! I DIDN'T HIDE ANY-THING.
C'MON, WHAT DO YOU HAVE THERE?
LET ME SEE.
SWIPE
Eek!
I-I TOLD YOU! NOTHING!
I SHOULD'VE JUST THROWN THEM AWAY!

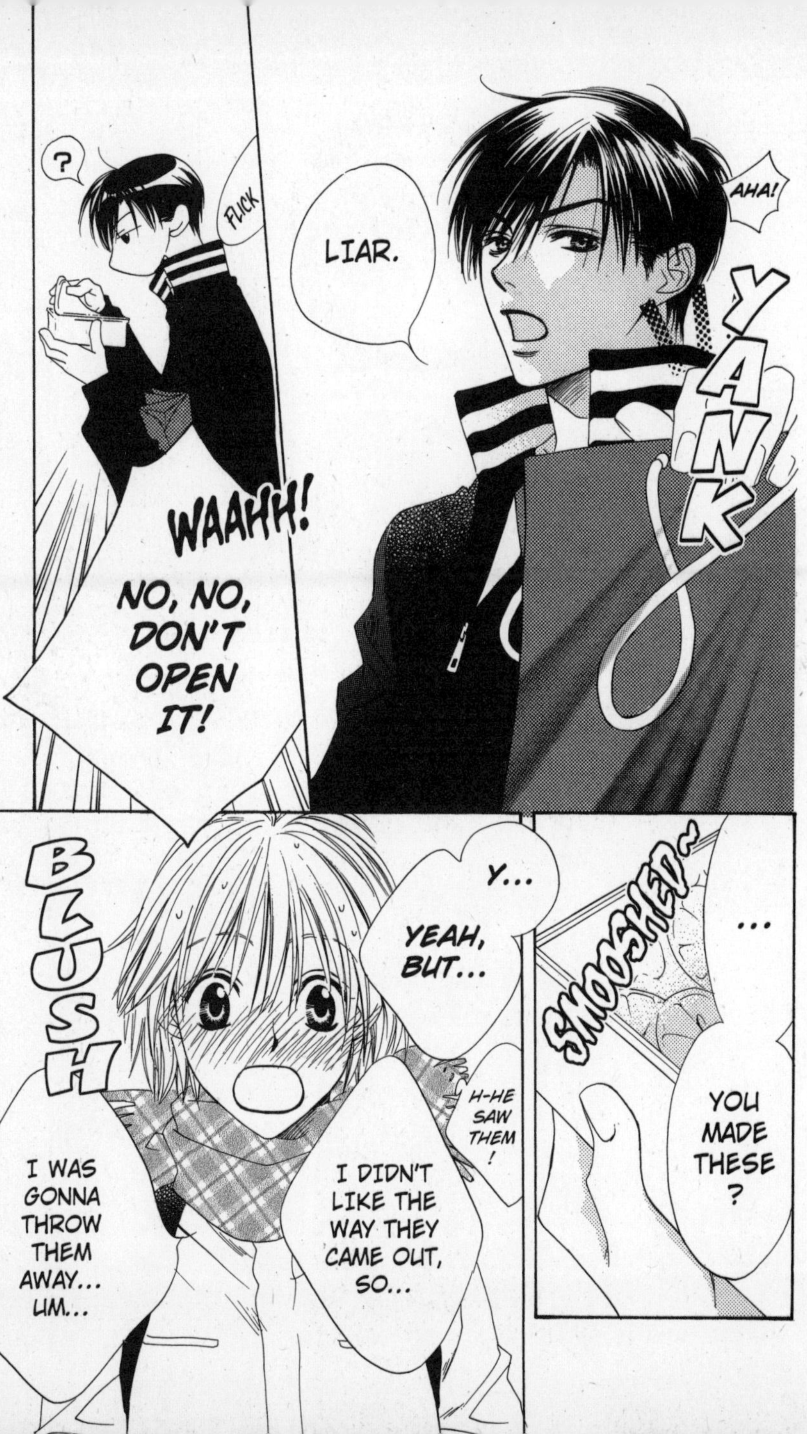
AHA!
YANK
LIAR.
?
FLICK
WAAHH!
NO, NO, DON'T OPEN IT!
SMOOSHED~
...
YOU MADE THESE?
BLUSH
Y...
YEAH, BUT...
H-HE SAW THEM!
I DIDN'T LIKE THE WAY THEY CAME OUT, SO...
I WAS GONNA THROW THEM AWAY... UM...

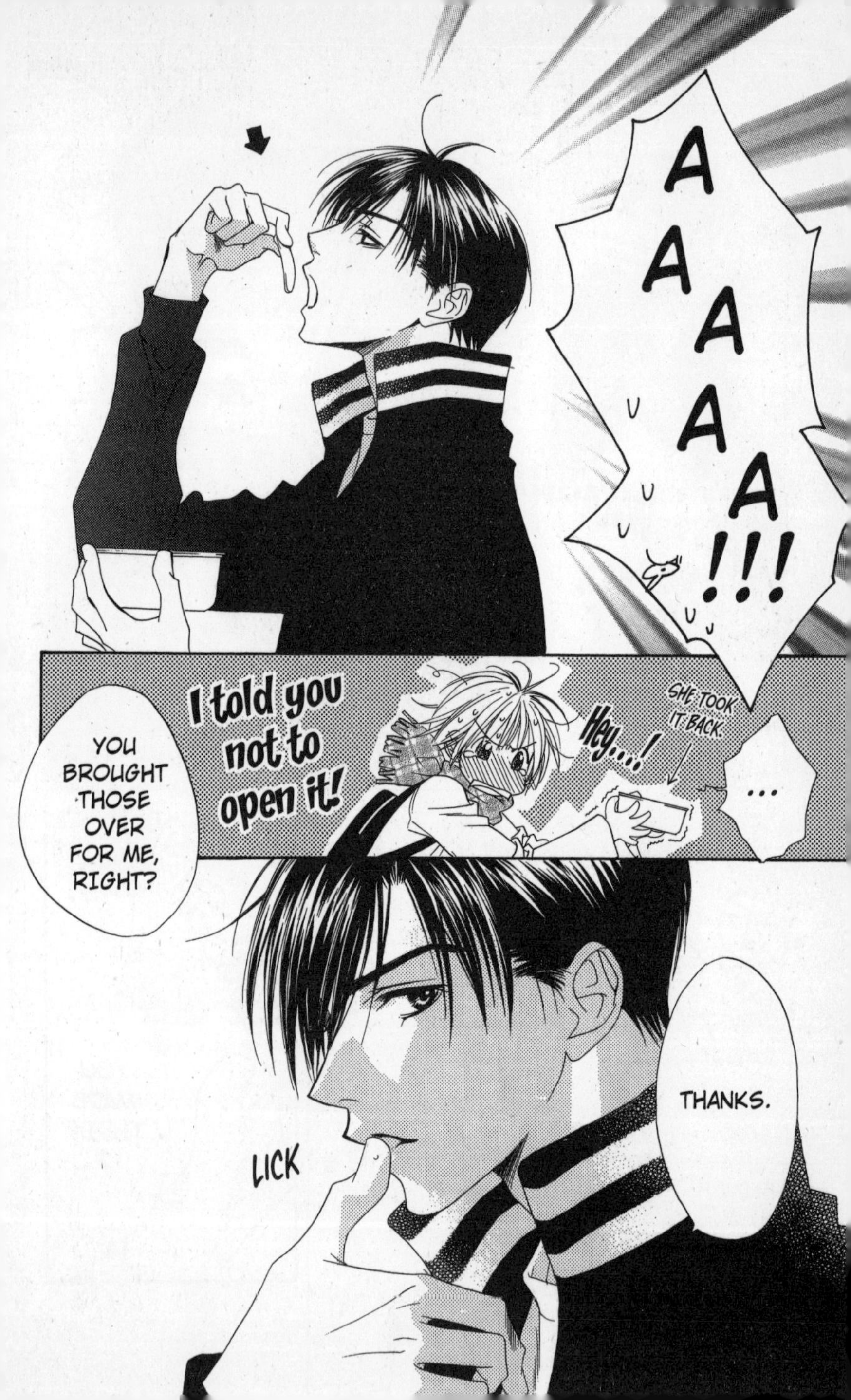
AAAAA!!!
...
SHE TOOK IT BACK.
Hey...!
I told you not to open it!
YOU BROUGHT THOSE OVER FOR ME, RIGHT?
THANKS.
LICK

UM...
I TRIED NOT TO MAKE THEM TOO SWEET...
How are they?
THEY'RE PERFECT.
Just right.
THEY'RE REALLY GOOD.
REALLY?
SIGH
I'M SO HAPPY!
HEH HEH HEH! HE LIKES THEM!
YAY!
Okay then!
I'LL MAKE THEM EVEN BETTER NEXT TIME!
OH...

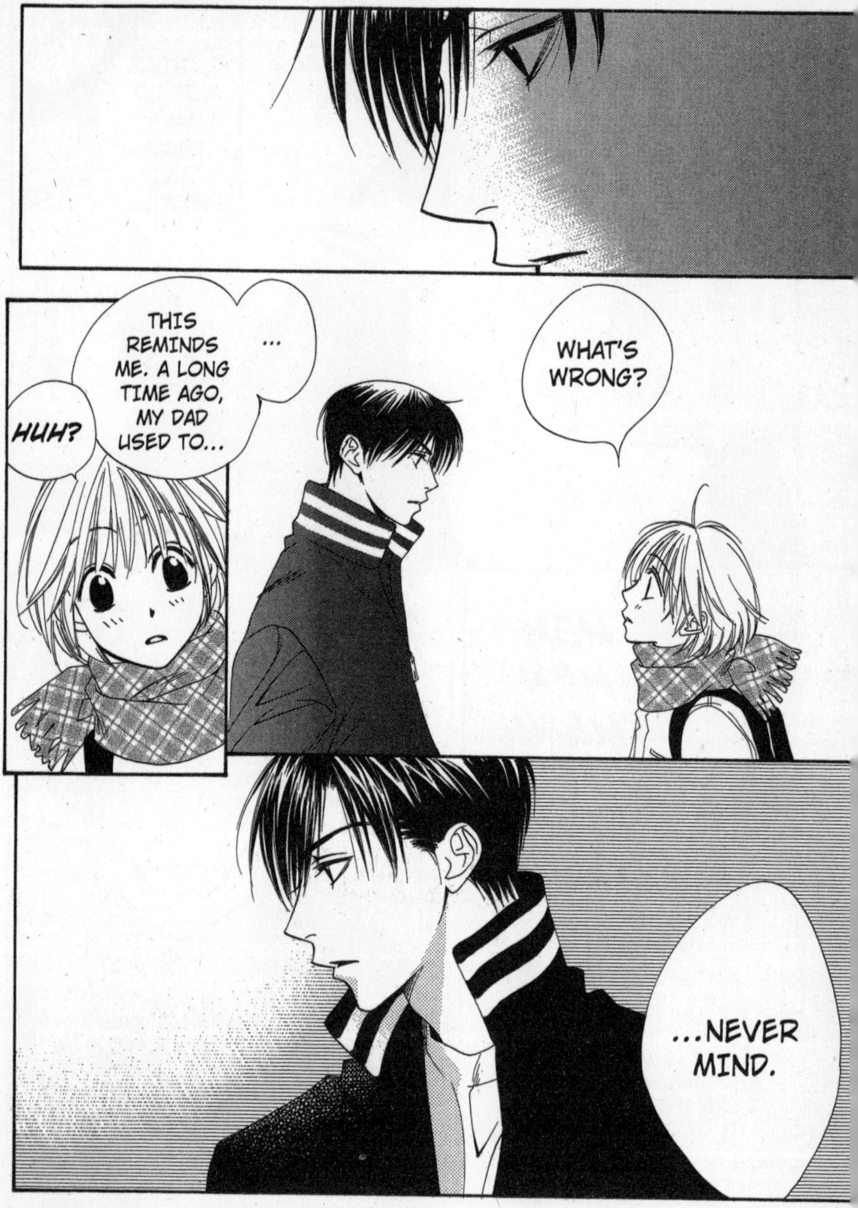

WHAT'S WRONG?
...
THIS REMINDS ME. A LONG TIME AGO, MY DAD USED TO...
HUH?
...NEVER MIND.

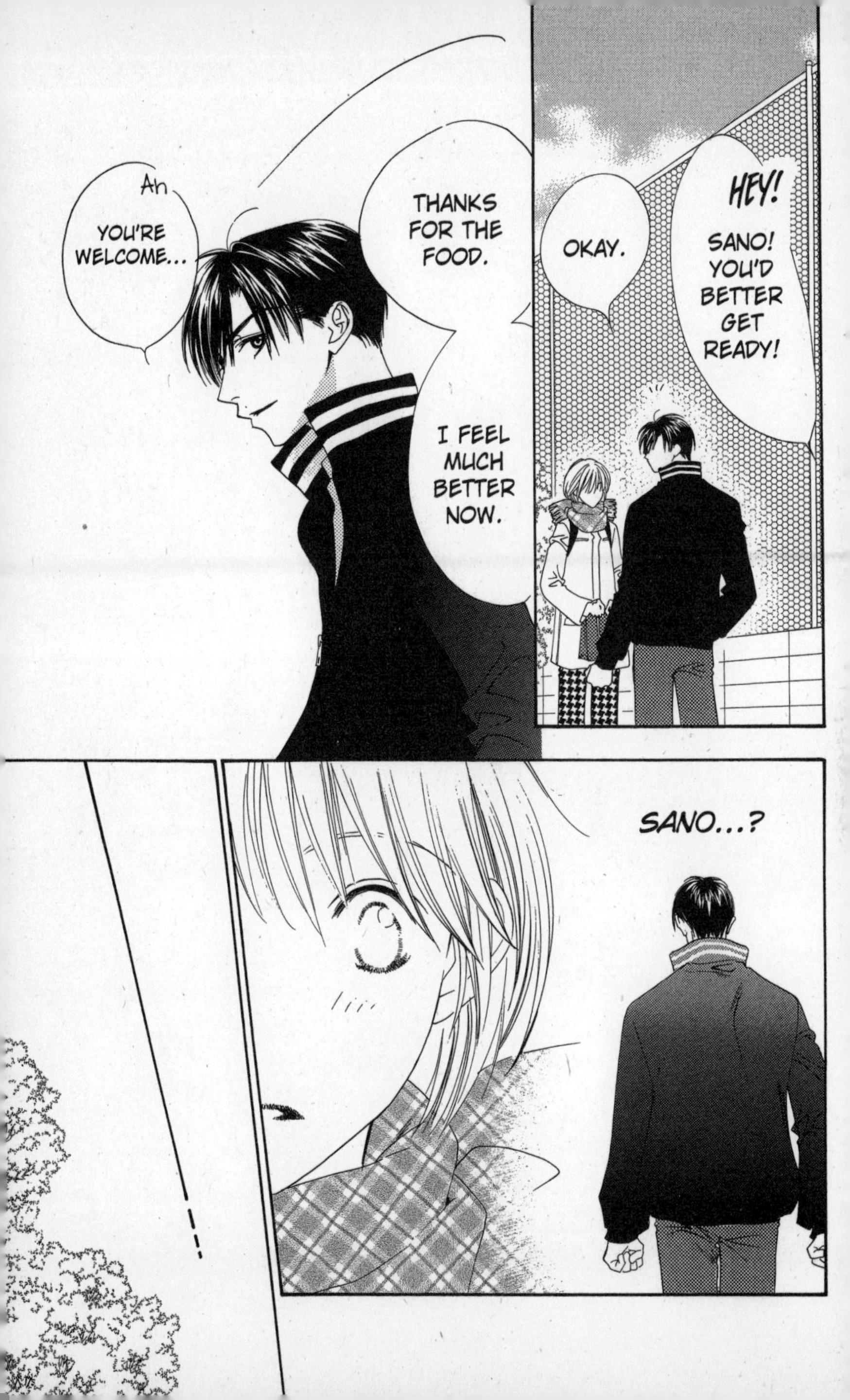
HEY!
SANO! YOU'D BETTER GET READY!
OKAY.
THANKS FOR THE FOOD.
I FEEL MUCH BETTER NOW.
Ah
YOU'RE WELCOME...
SANO...?

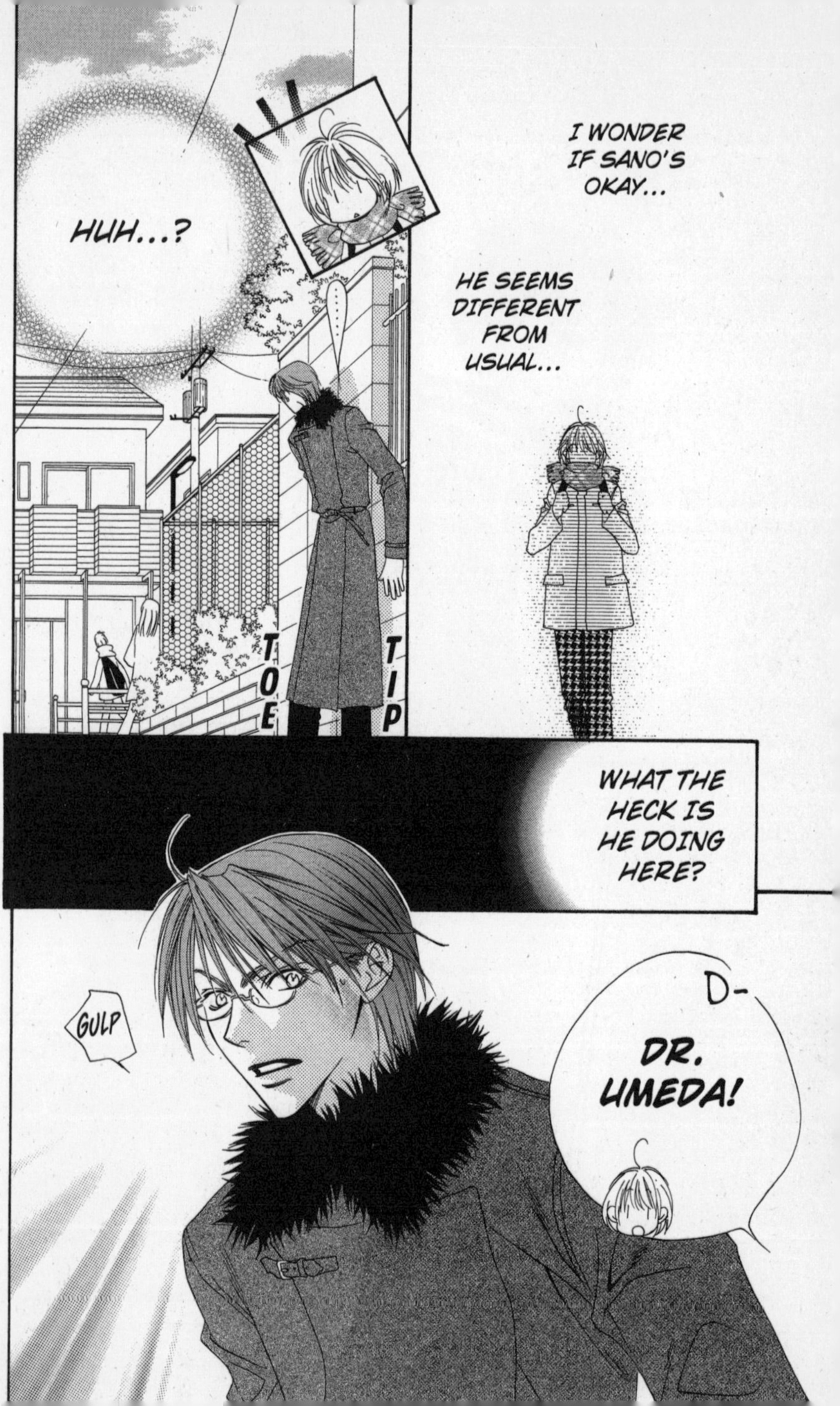
I WONDER IF SANO'S OKAY...
HE SEEMS DIFFERENT FROM USUAL...
HUH...?
TOE TIP
WHAT THE HECK IS HE DOING HERE?
D-
DR. UMEDA!
GULP

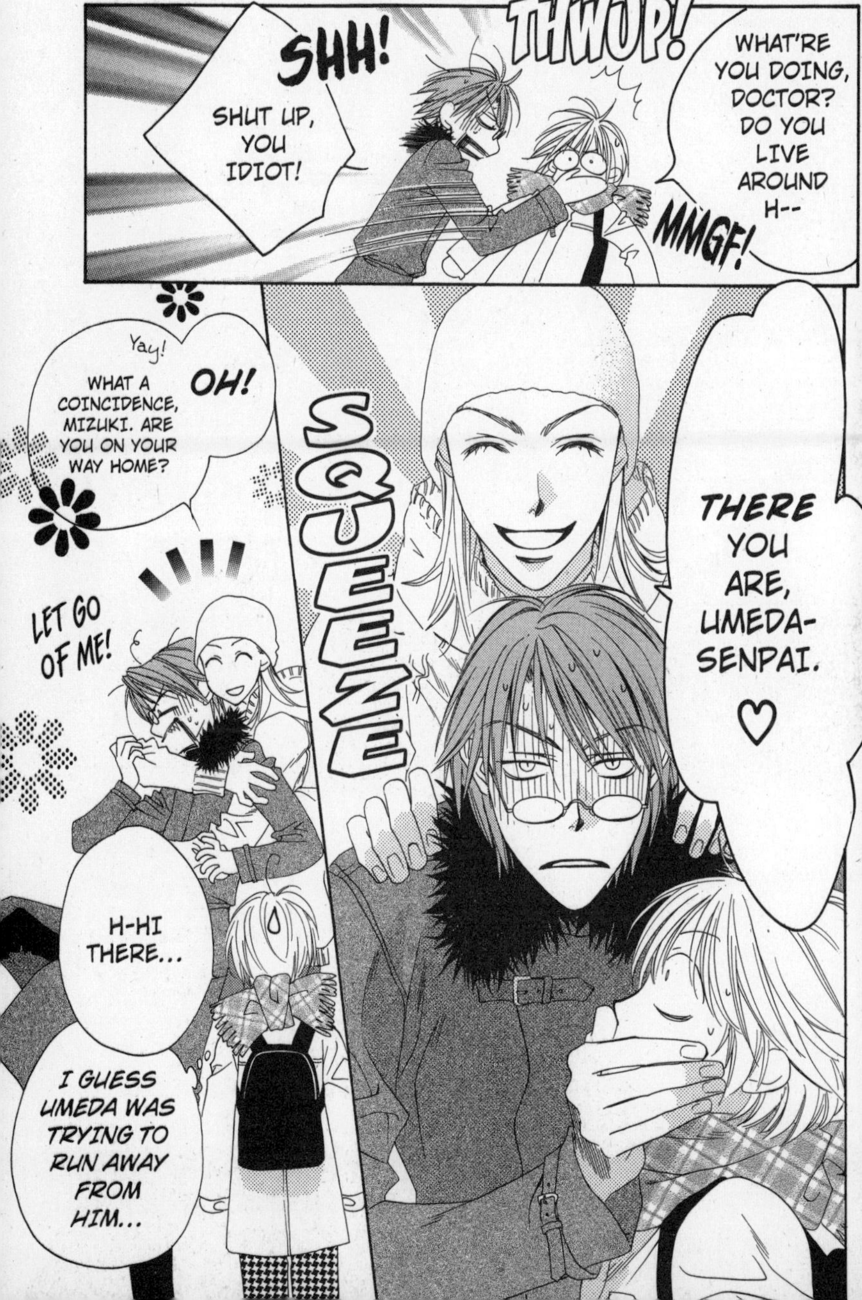
WHAT'RE YOU DOING, DOCTOR? DO YOU LIVE AROUND H--
MMGF!
THWUP!
SHH!
SHUT UP, YOU IDIOT!
THERE YOU ARE, UMEDA-SENPAI. ♥
SQUEEZE
OH!
Yay!
WHAT A COINCIDENCE, MIZUKI. ARE YOU ON YOUR WAY HOME?
LET GO OF ME!
H-HI THERE...
I GUESS UMEDA WAS TRYING TO RUN AWAY FROM HIM...

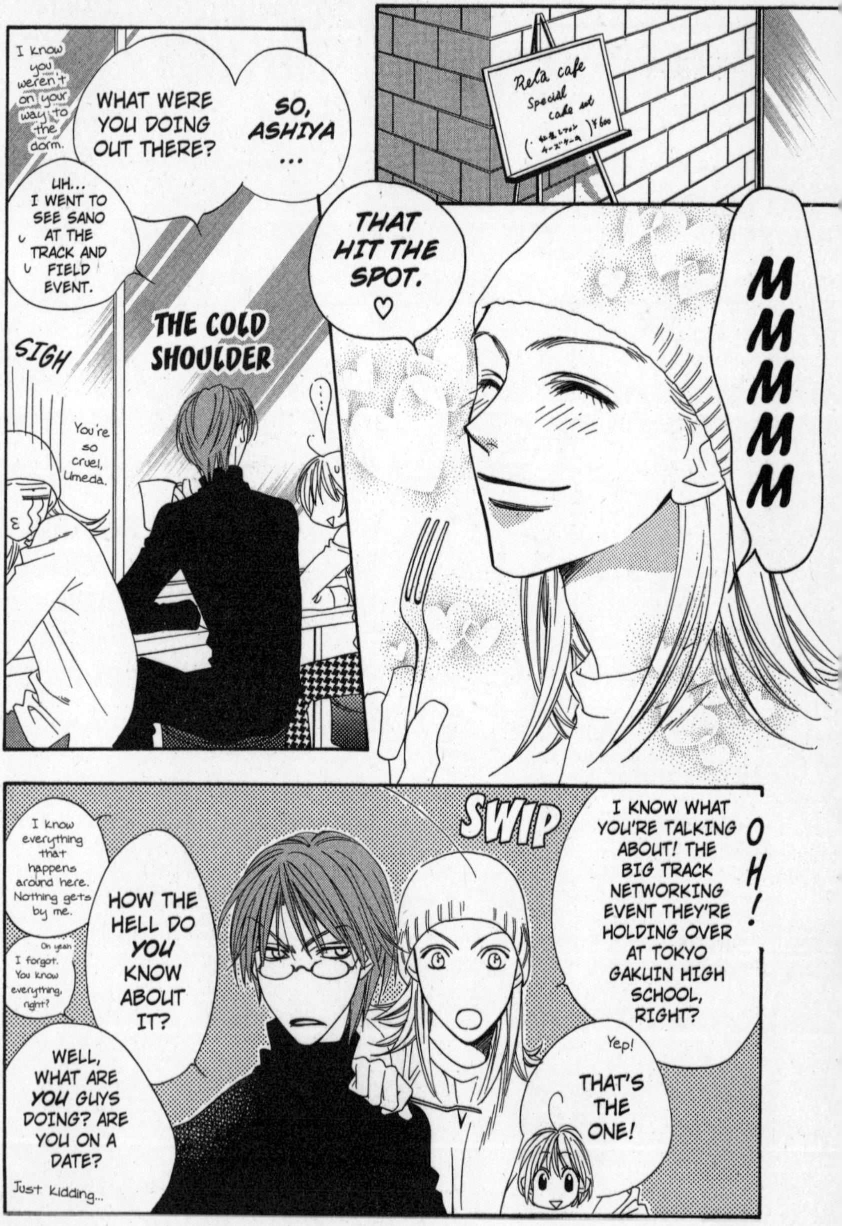
Rela cafe
Special cake set
¥600
MMMMM
THAT HIT THE SPOT. ♡
SO, ASHIYA...
WHAT WERE YOU DOING OUT THERE?
I know you weren't on your way to the dorm.
UH... I WENT TO SEE SANO AT THE TRACK AND FIELD EVENT.
THE COLD SHOULDER
SIGH
You're so cruel, Umeda.
OH!
I KNOW WHAT YOU'RE TALKING ABOUT! THE BIG TRACK NETWORKING EVENT THEY'RE HOLDING OVER AT TOKYO GAKUIN HIGH SCHOOL, RIGHT?
SWIP
Yep!
THAT'S THE ONE!
HOW THE HELL DO YOU KNOW ABOUT IT?
I know everything that happens around here. Nothing gets by me.
Oh yeah I forgot. You know everything, right?
WELL, WHAT ARE YOU GUYS DOING? ARE YOU ON A DATE?
Just kidding...

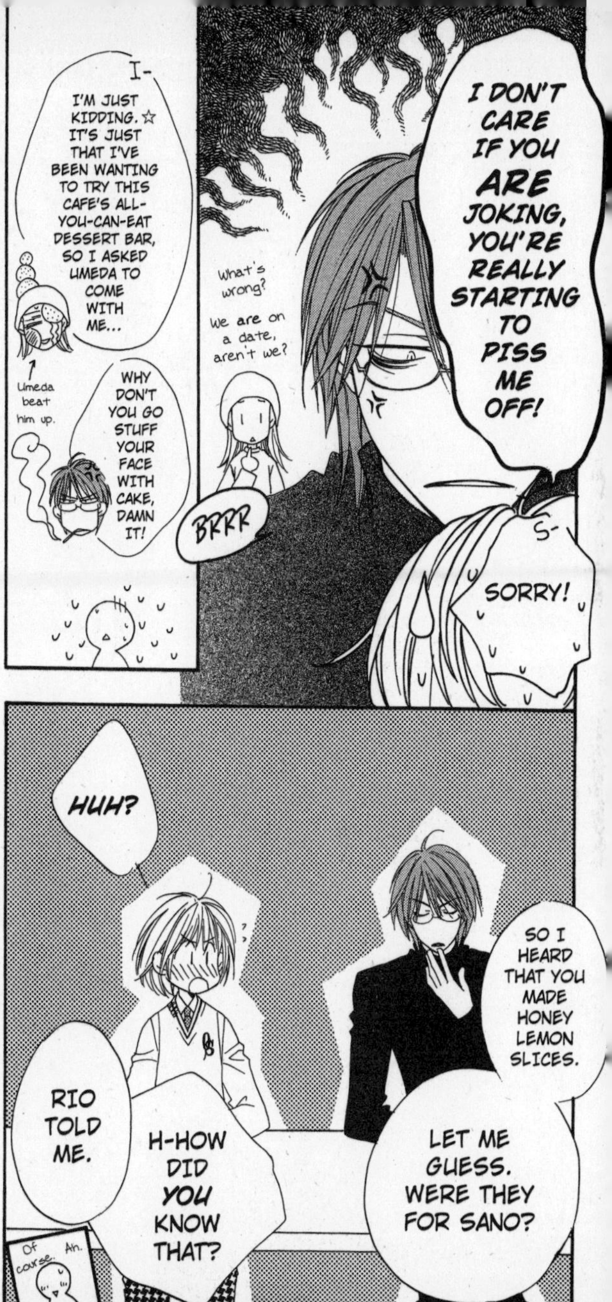
I DON'T CARE IF YOU ARE JOKING, YOU'RE REALLY STARTING TO PISS ME OFF!
BRRR
S-
SORRY!
I-
I'M JUST KIDDING. ☆ IT'S JUST THAT I'VE BEEN WANTING TO TRY THIS CAFE'S ALL-YOU-CAN-EAT DESSERT BAR, SO I ASKED UMEDA TO COME WITH ME...
What's wrong?
We are on a date, aren't we?
WHY DON'T YOU GO STUFF YOUR FACE WITH CAKE, DAMN IT!
Umeda beat him up.
SO I HEARD THAT YOU MADE HONEY LEMON SLICES.
HUH?
LET ME GUESS. WERE THEY FOR SANO?
H-HOW DID YOU KNOW THAT?
RIO TOLD ME.
Ah.
Of course.

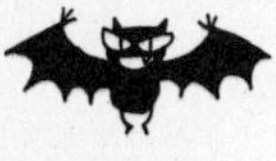

Kyogo Sekime

Birthday: October 14th
Grade: Second Year Japanese H.S. (equivalent of 11th grade in America)
Blood Type: B
Sign: Libra
Height: 178 cm (5'10")
Favorite Foods: Sushi, Yakitori, Pot Stickers
Favorite Celebrities: Ryoko Yonekura, Aya Matsuura
Favorite Colors: Navy Blue, Red, Beige
Favorite Subject: Math
Least Favorite Subject: History
Favorite Animal: Dog
Least Favorite Animal: Octopus
Major Worry: He doesn't have a girlfriend
Clubs and Affiliations: Track
Flower: Gladiolus

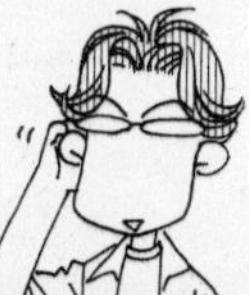

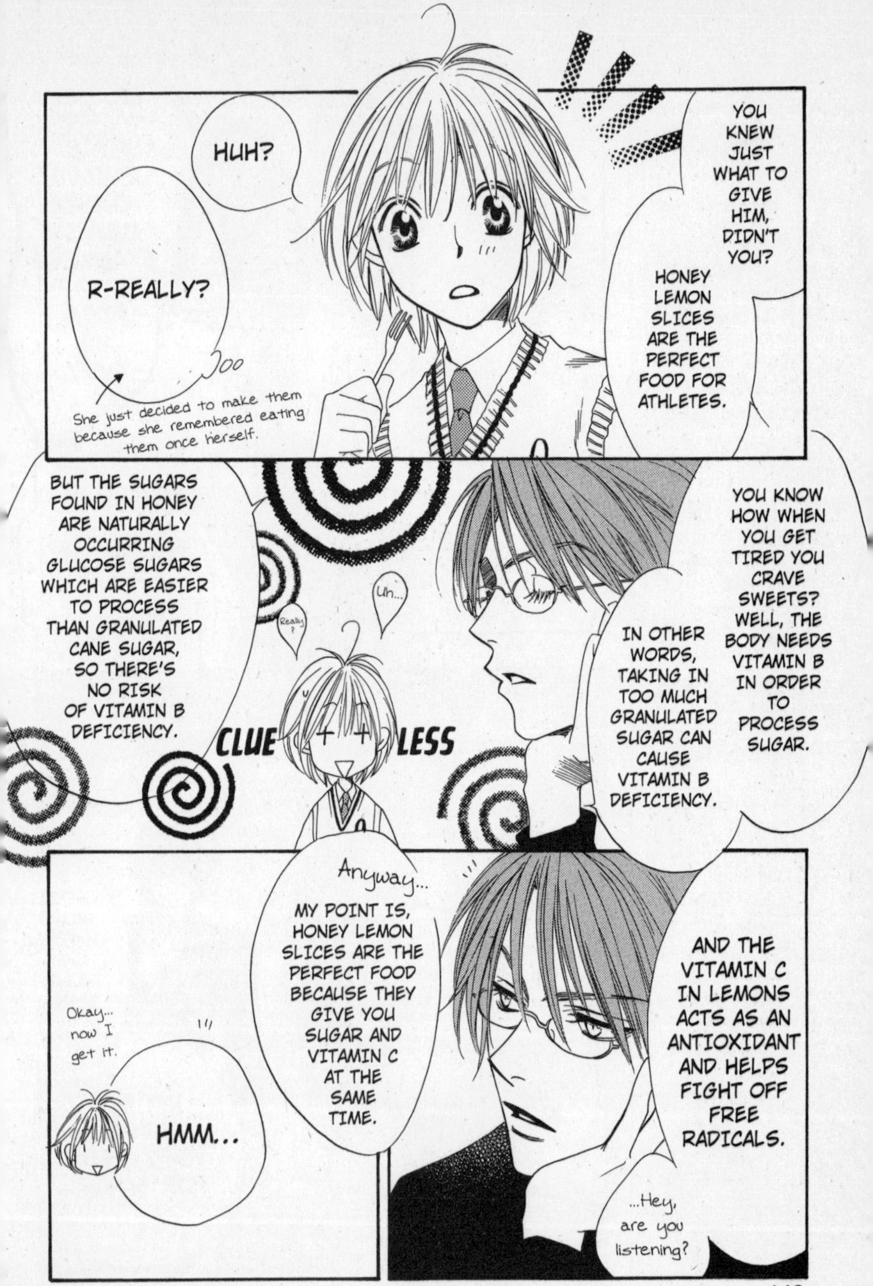
YOU KNEW JUST WHAT TO GIVE HIM, DIDN'T YOU?
HONEY LEMON SLICES ARE THE PERFECT FOOD FOR ATHLETES.
HUH?
R-REALLY?
She just decided to make them because she remembered eating them once herself.
YOU KNOW HOW WHEN YOU GET TIRED YOU CRAVE SWEETS? WELL, THE BODY NEEDS VITAMIN B IN ORDER TO PROCESS SUGAR.
IN OTHER WORDS, TAKING IN TOO MUCH GRANULATED SUGAR CAN CAUSE VITAMIN B DEFICIENCY.
Uh...
Really?
BUT THE SUGARS FOUND IN HONEY ARE NATURALLY OCCURRING GLUCOSE SUGARS WHICH ARE EASIER TO PROCESS THAN GRANULATED CANE SUGAR, SO THERE'S NO RISK OF VITAMIN B DEFICIENCY.
CLUELESS
AND THE VITAMIN C IN LEMONS ACTS AS AN ANTIOXIDANT AND HELPS FIGHT OFF FREE RADICALS.
Anyway...
MY POINT IS, HONEY LEMON SLICES ARE THE PERFECT FOOD BECAUSE THEY GIVE YOU SUGAR AND VITAMIN C AT THE SAME TIME.
...Hey, are you listening?
Okay... now I get it.
HMM...

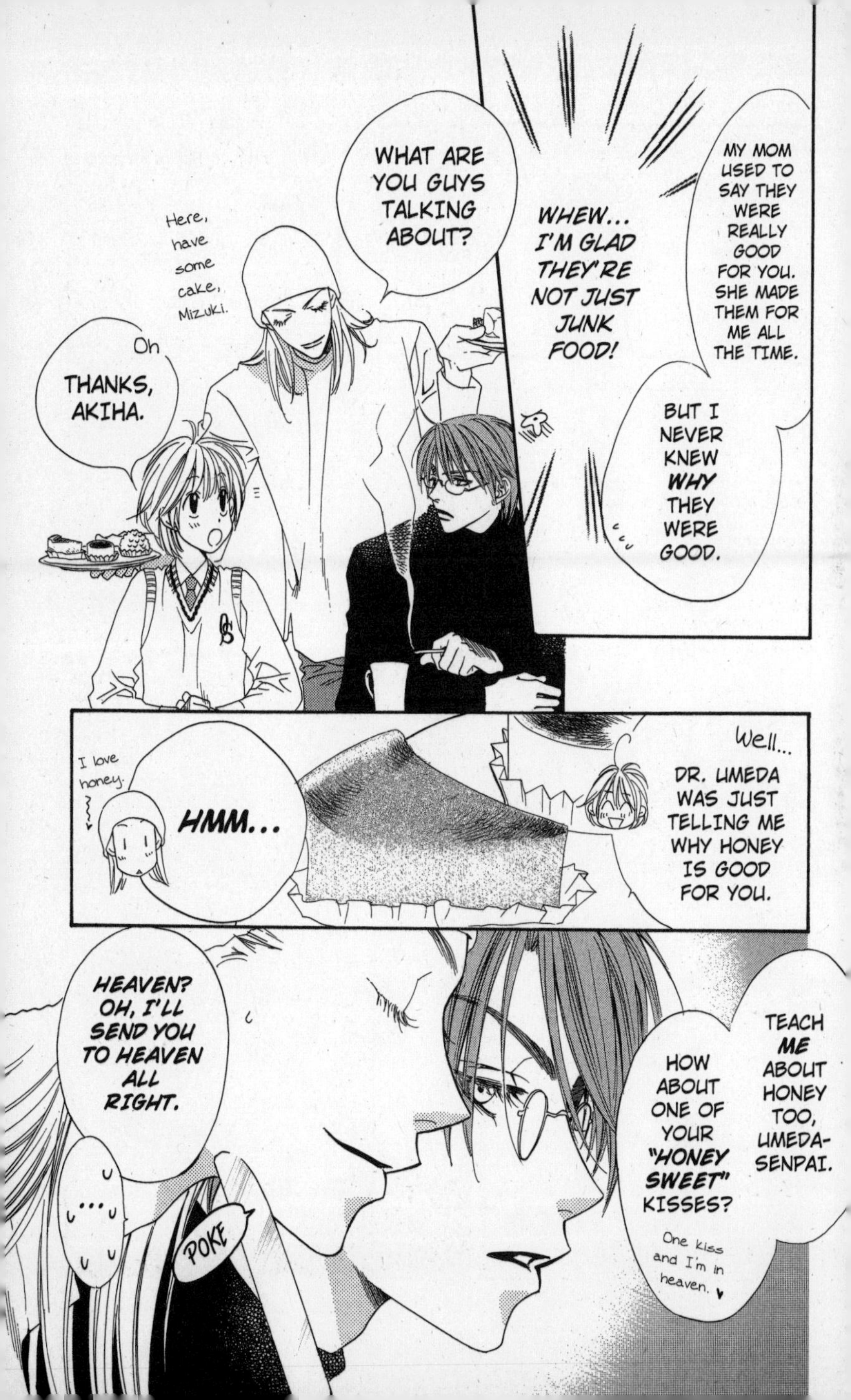
MY MOM USED TO SAY THEY WERE REALLY GOOD FOR YOU. SHE MADE THEM FOR ME ALL THE TIME.
BUT I NEVER KNEW WHY THEY WERE GOOD.
WHEW... I'M GLAD THEY'RE NOT JUST JUNK FOOD!
WHAT ARE YOU GUYS TALKING ABOUT?
Here, have some cake, Mizuki.
Oh
THANKS, AKIHA.
Well...
DR. UMEDA WAS JUST TELLING ME WHY HONEY IS GOOD FOR YOU.
HMM...
I love honey.
TEACH ME ABOUT HONEY TOO, UMEDA-SENPAI.
HOW ABOUT ONE OF YOUR "HONEY SWEET" KISSES?
One kiss and I'm in heaven.
HEAVEN? OH, I'LL SEND YOU TO HEAVEN ALL RIGHT.
...
POKE

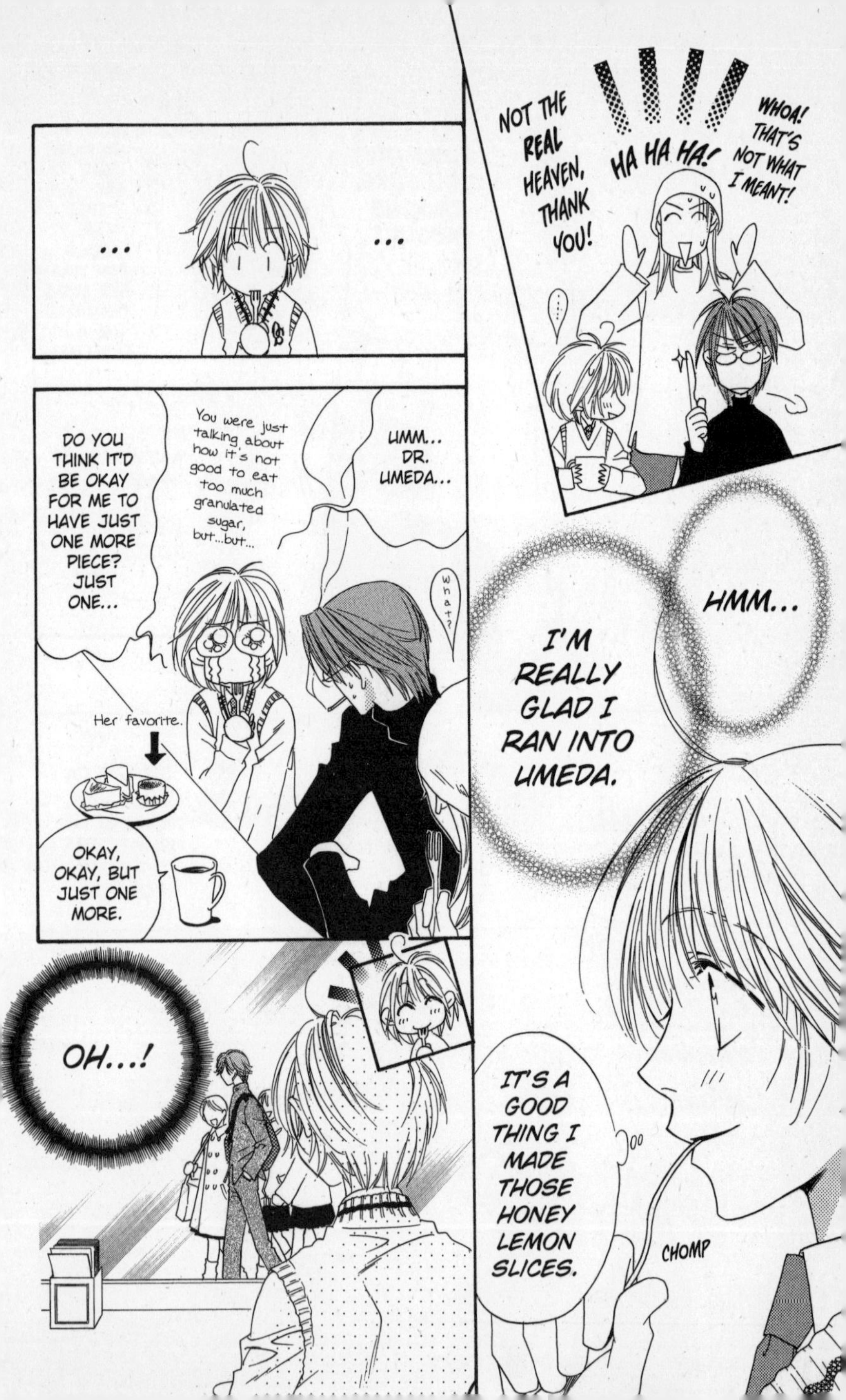

WHOA! THAT'S NOT WHAT I MEANT!
HA HA HA!
NOT THE REAL HEAVEN, THANK YOU!
...
...
...
UMM... DR. UMEDA...
what?
You were just talking about how it's not good to eat too much granulated sugar, but...but...
DO YOU THINK IT'D BE OKAY FOR ME TO HAVE JUST ONE MORE PIECE? JUST ONE...
Her favorite.
OKAY, OKAY, BUT JUST ONE MORE.
OH...!
HMM...
I'M REALLY GLAD I RAN INTO UMEDA.
IT'S A GOOD THING I MADE THOSE HONEY LEMON SLICES.
CHOMP

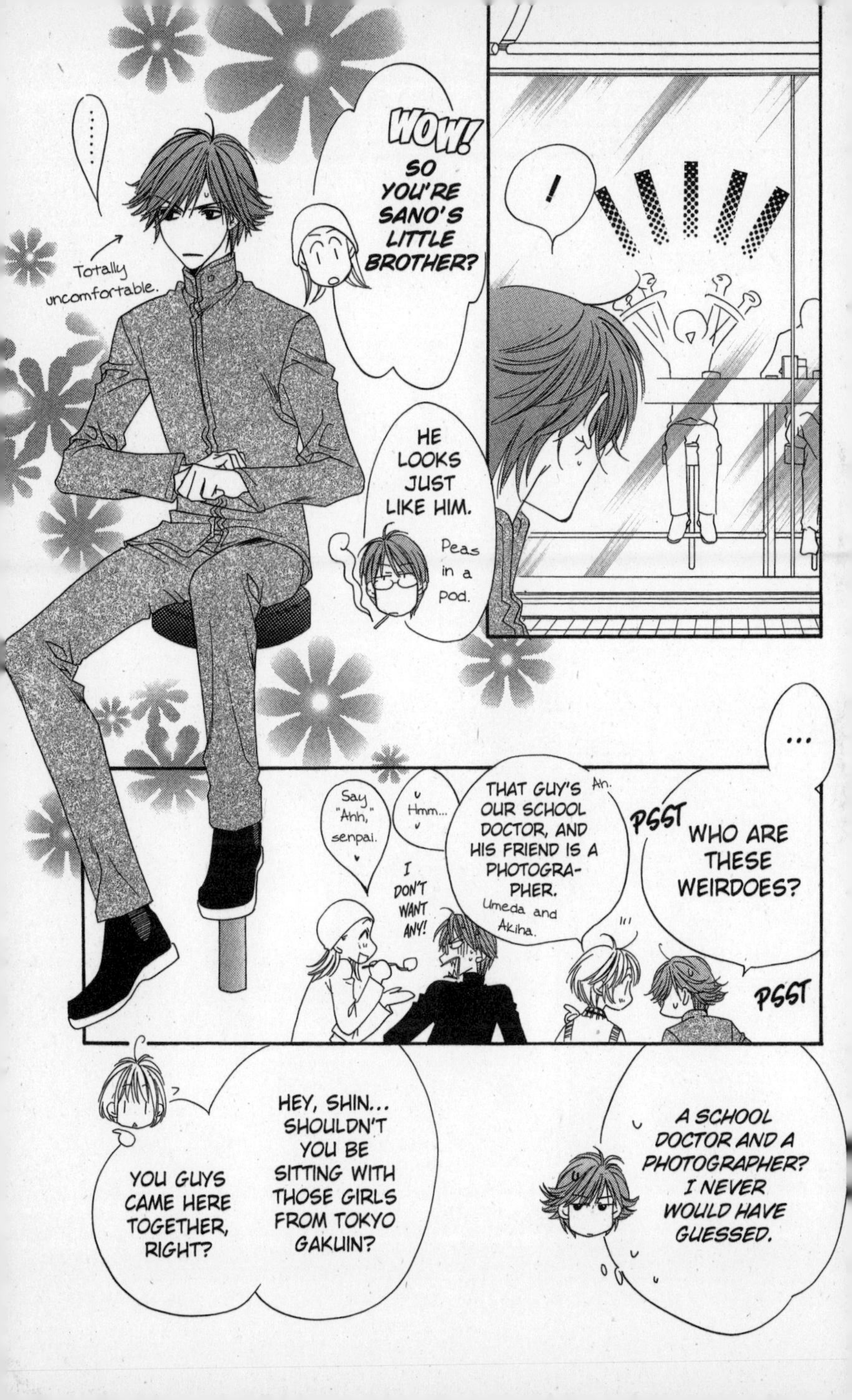
!
WOW! SO YOU'RE SANO'S LITTLE BROTHER?
...
Totally uncomfortable.
HE LOOKS JUST LIKE HIM.
Peas in a pod.
...
PSST
WHO ARE THESE WEIRDOES?
PSST
THAT GUY'S OUR SCHOOL DOCTOR, AND HIS FRIEND IS A PHOTOGRAPHER.
Umeda and Akiha.
Ah.
Hmm...
I DON'T WANT ANY!
Say "Ahh," senpai.
A SCHOOL DOCTOR AND A PHOTOGRAPHER? I NEVER WOULD HAVE GUESSED.
HEY, SHIN... SHOULDN'T YOU BE SITTING WITH THOSE GIRLS FROM TOKYO GAKUIN?
YOU GUYS CAME HERE TOGETHER, RIGHT?

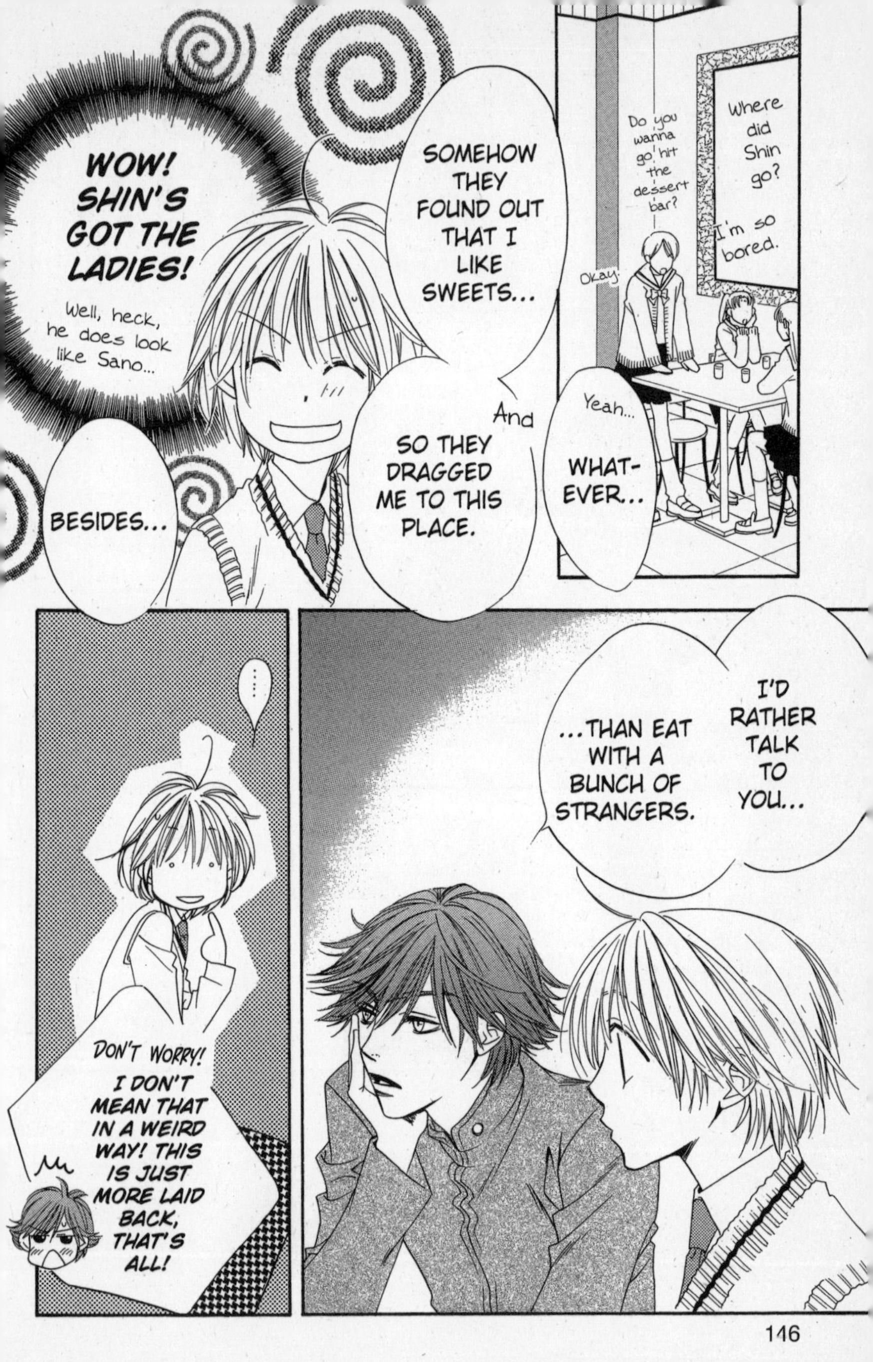
Where did Shin go?
I'm so bored.
Do you wanna go hit the dessert bar?
Okay.
Yeah... WHATEVER...
SOMEHOW THEY FOUND OUT THAT I LIKE SWEETS...
And SO THEY DRAGGED ME TO THIS PLACE.
BESIDES...
WOW! SHIN'S GOT THE LADIES!
Well, heck, he does look like Sano...
I'D RATHER TALK TO YOU...
...THAN EAT WITH A BUNCH OF STRANGERS.
...
DON'T WORRY! I DON'T MEAN THAT IN A WEIRD WAY! THIS IS JUST MORE LAID BACK, THAT'S ALL!

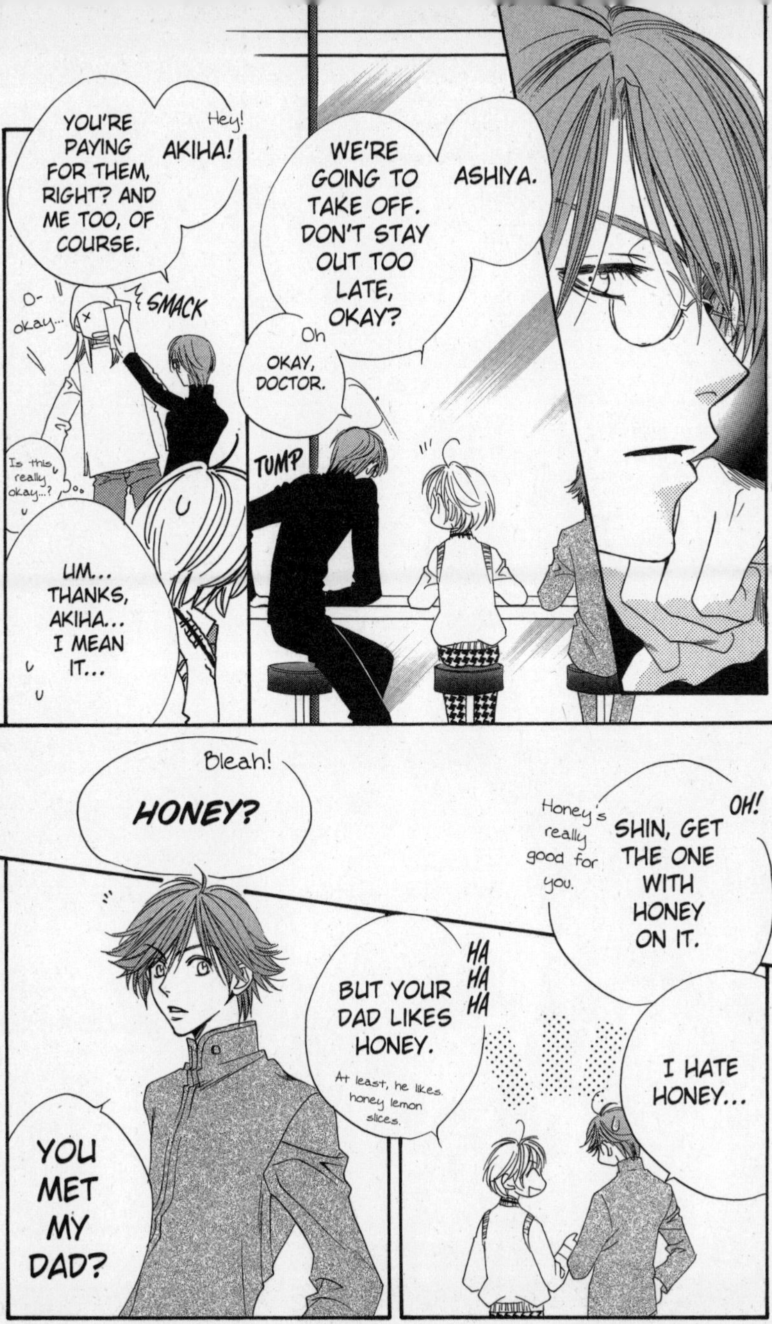
ASHIYA.
WE'RE GOING TO TAKE OFF. DON'T STAY OUT TOO LATE, OKAY?
Oh
OKAY, DOCTOR.
TUMP
Hey!
AKIHA!
YOU'RE PAYING FOR THEM, RIGHT? AND ME TOO, OF COURSE.
O- okay...
SMACK
Is this really okay...?
UM... THANKS, AKIHA... I MEAN IT...
OH!
SHIN, GET THE ONE WITH HONEY ON IT.
Honey's really good for you.
Bleah!
HONEY?
I HATE HONEY...
HA HA HA
BUT YOUR DAD LIKES HONEY.
At least, he likes honey lemon slices.
YOU MET MY DAD?

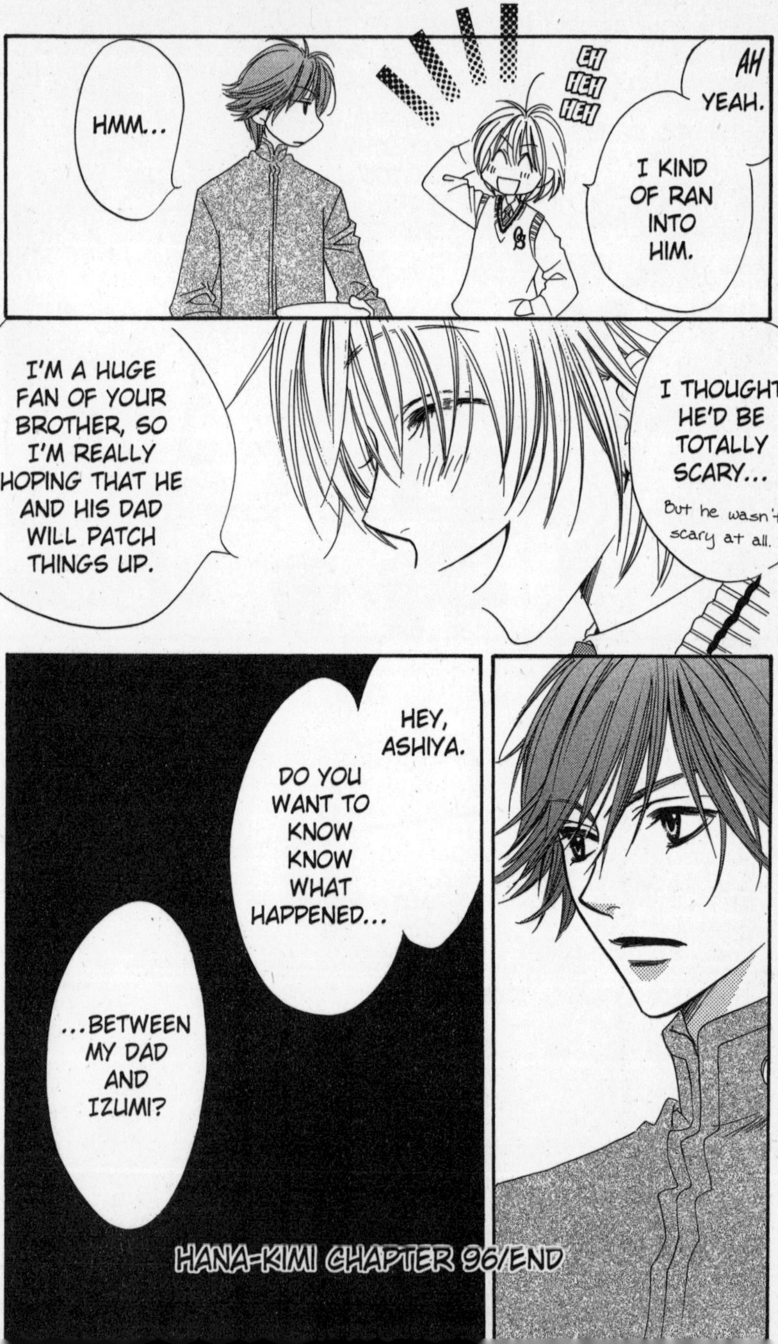
AH
YEAH.
I KIND OF RAN INTO HIM.
EH HEH HEH
HMM...
I THOUGHT HE'D BE TOTALLY SCARY...
But he wasn't scary at all.
I'M A HUGE FAN OF YOUR BROTHER, SO I'M REALLY HOPING THAT HE AND HIS DAD WILL PATCH THINGS UP.
HEY, ASHIYA.
DO YOU WANT TO KNOW KNOW WHAT HAPPENED...
...BETWEEN MY DAD AND IZUMI?
HANA-KIMI CHAPTER 96/END

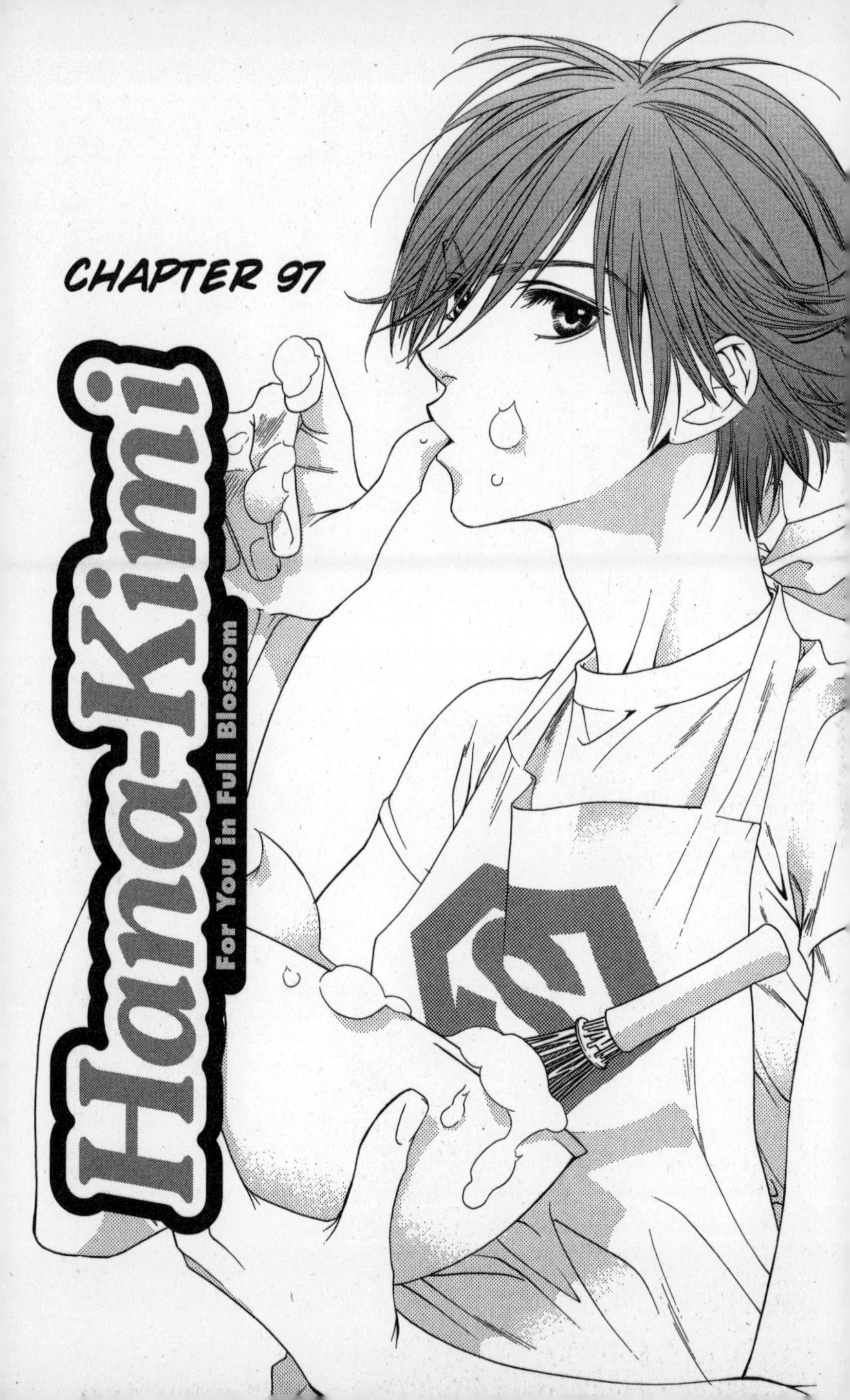
CHAPTER 97
Hana-Kimi
For You in Full Blossom

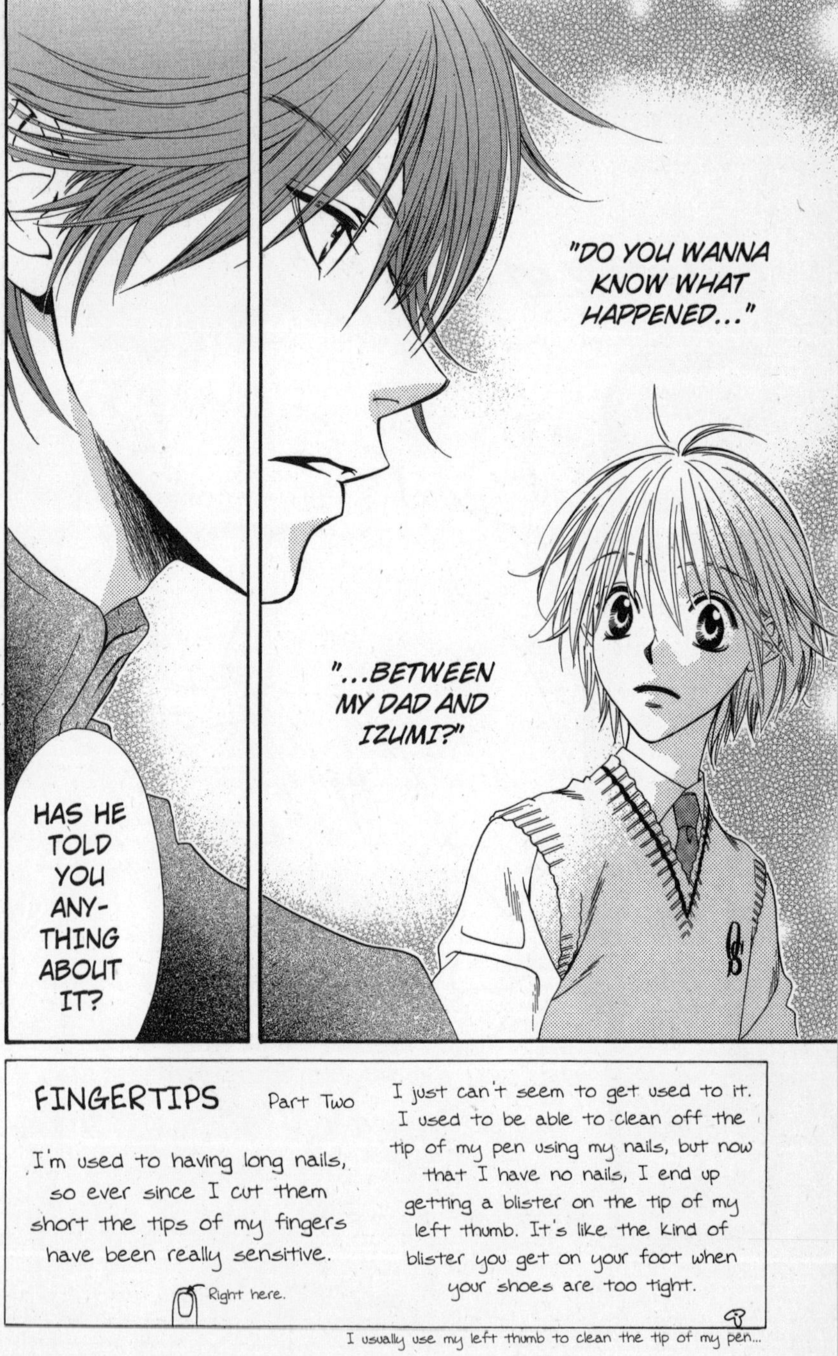
"DO YOU WANNA KNOW WHAT HAPPENED..."
"...BETWEEN MY DAD AND IZUMI?"
HAS HE TOLD YOU ANY-THING ABOUT IT?

FINGERTIPS Part Two

I'm used to having long nails, so ever since I cut them short the tips of my fingers have been really sensitive.

Right here.

I just can't seem to get used to it. I used to be able to clean off the tip of my pen using my nails, but now that I have no nails, I end up getting a blister on the tip of my left thumb. It's like the kind of blister you get on your foot when your shoes are too tight.

I usually use my left thumb to clean the tip of my pen...

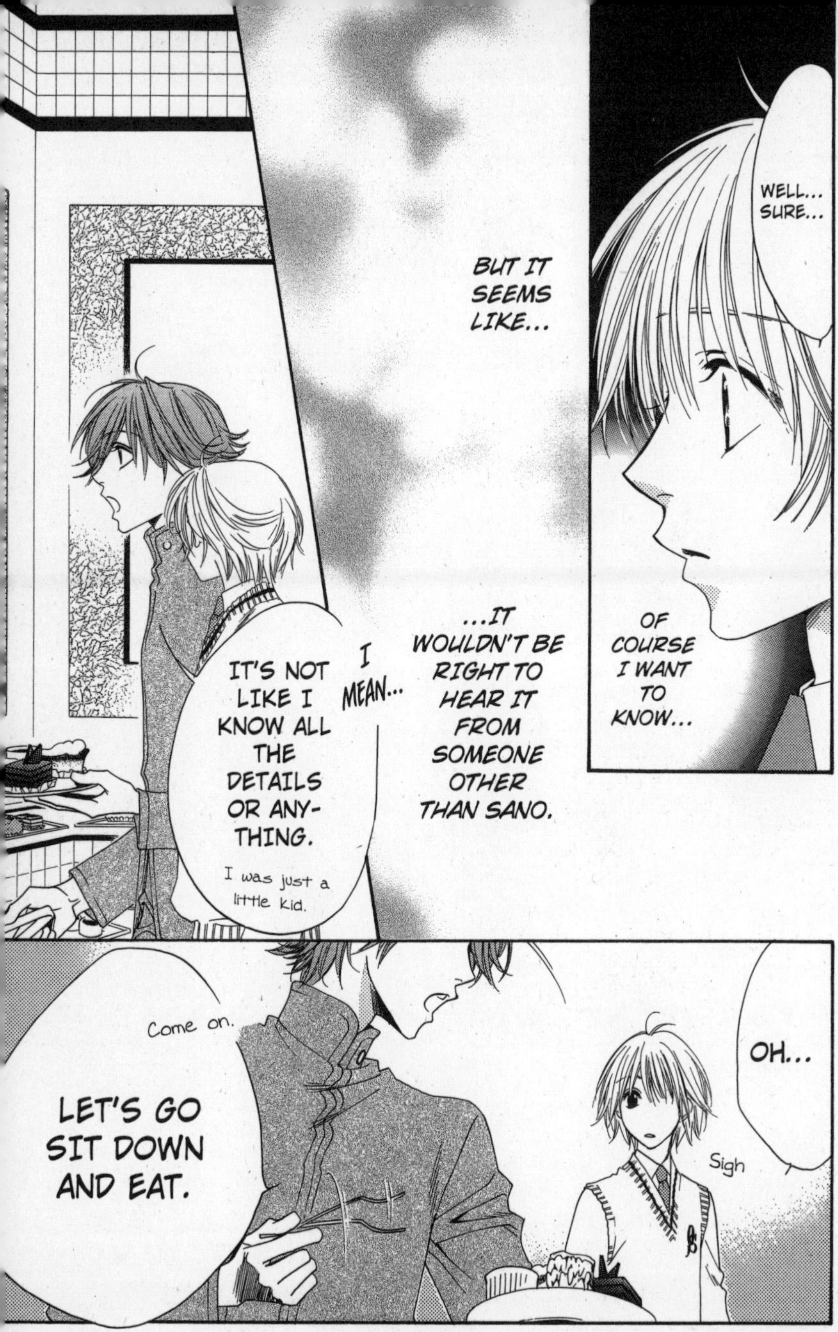
WELL... SURE...
OF COURSE I WANT TO KNOW...
BUT IT SEEMS LIKE...
...IT WOULDN'T BE RIGHT TO HEAR IT FROM SOMEONE OTHER THAN SANO.
I MEAN...
IT'S NOT LIKE I KNOW ALL THE DETAILS OR ANY-THING.
I was just a little kid.
OH...
Sigh
Come on.
LET'S GO SIT DOWN AND EAT.

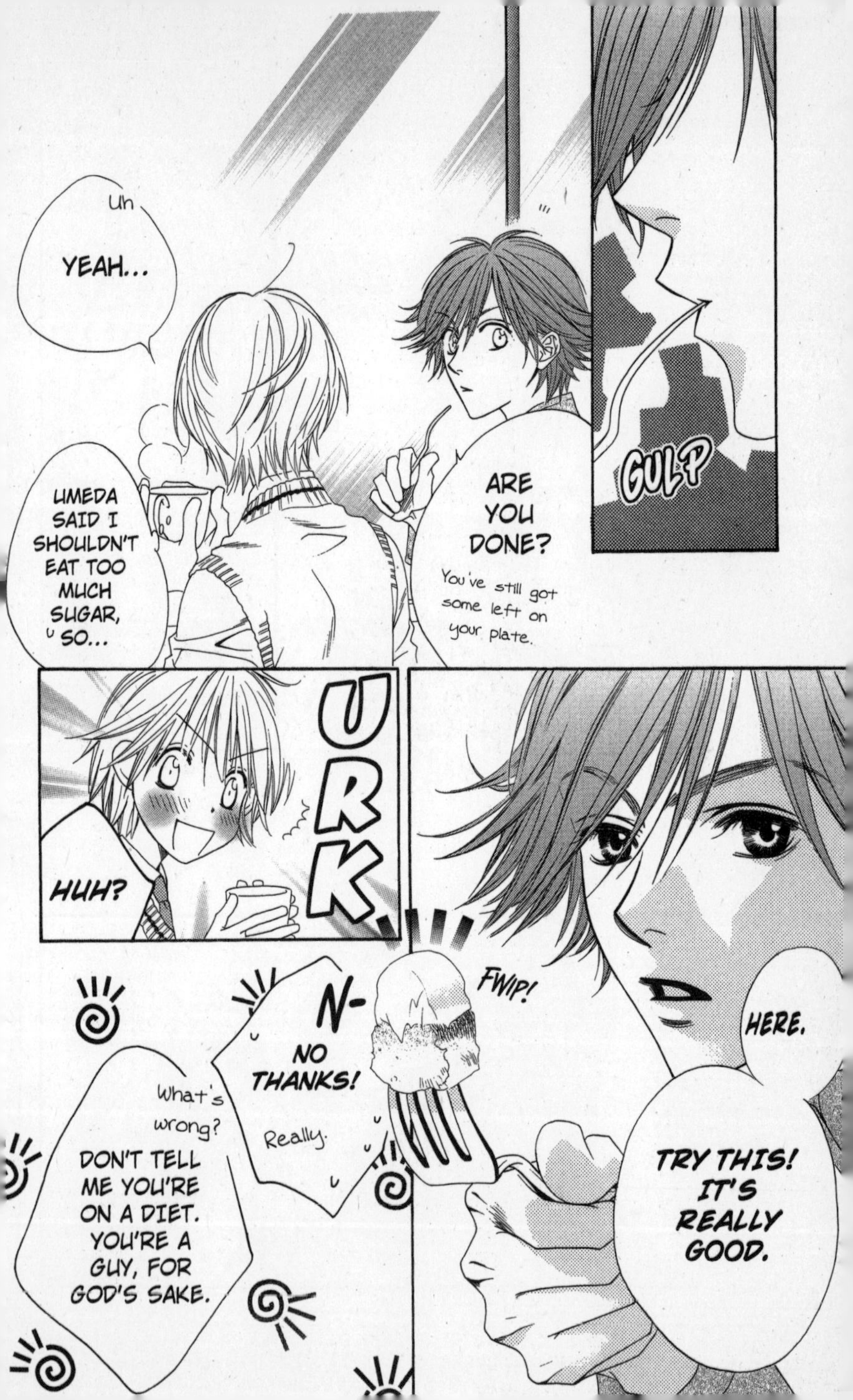
GULP
ARE YOU DONE?
You've still got some left on your plate.
Uh YEAH...
UMEDA SAID I SHOULDN'T EAT TOO MUCH SUGAR, SO...
HERE.
TRY THIS! IT'S REALLY GOOD.
URK
HUH?
FWIP!
N- NO THANKS!
Really.
What's wrong?
DON'T TELL ME YOU'RE ON A DIET. YOU'RE A GUY, FOR GOD'S SAKE.

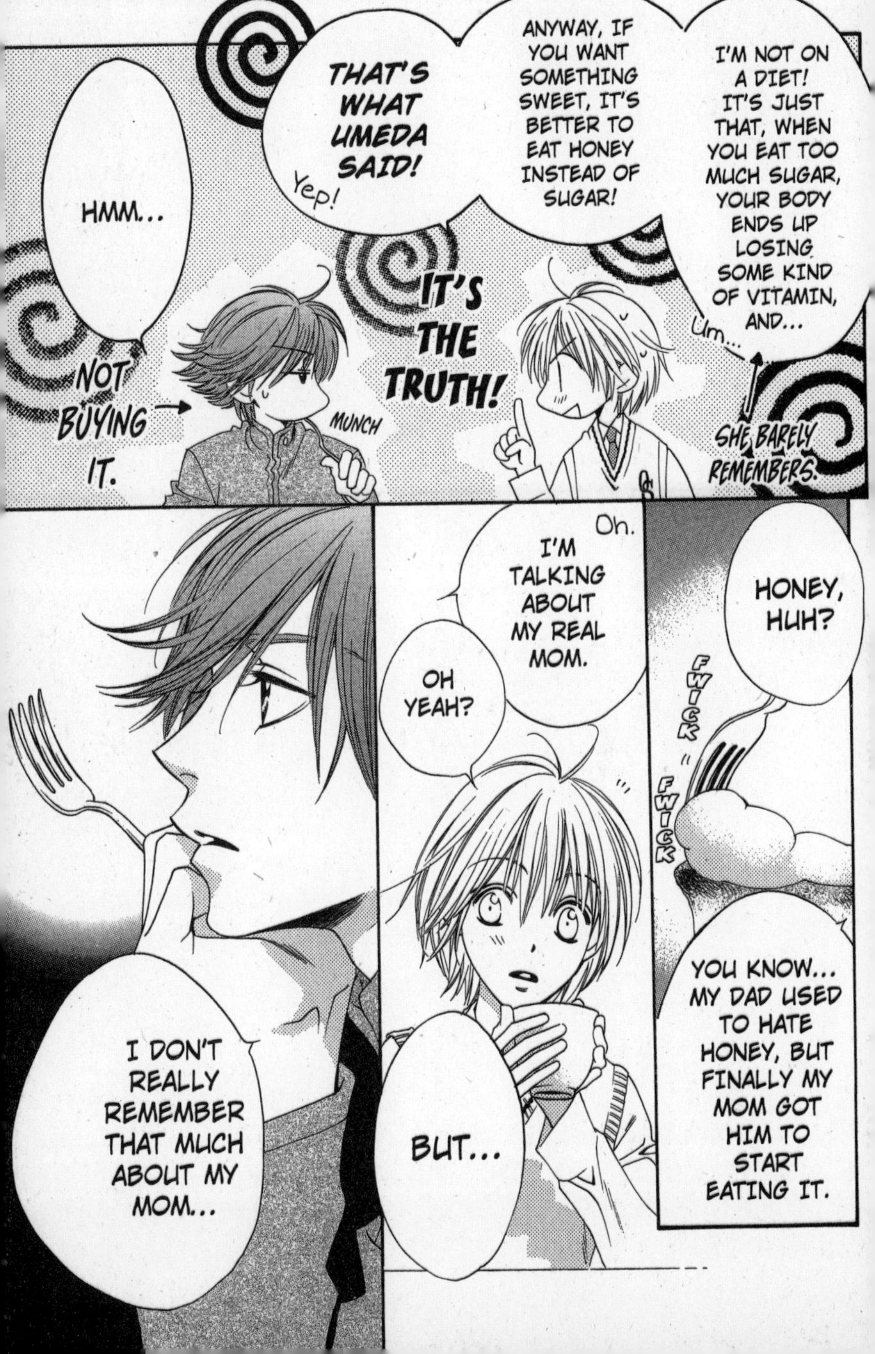
I'M NOT ON A DIET! IT'S JUST THAT, WHEN YOU EAT TOO MUCH SUGAR, YOUR BODY ENDS UP LOSING SOME KIND OF VITAMIN, AND...
Um...
SHE BARELY REMEMBERS.
ANYWAY, IF YOU WANT SOMETHING SWEET, IT'S BETTER TO EAT HONEY INSTEAD OF SUGAR!
THAT'S WHAT UMEDA SAID!
Yep!
IT'S THE TRUTH!
MUNCH
HMM...
NOT BUYING IT.
HONEY, HUH?
FWICK
FWICK
YOU KNOW... MY DAD USED TO HATE HONEY, BUT FINALLY MY MOM GOT HIM TO START EATING IT.
Oh.
I'M TALKING ABOUT MY REAL MOM.
OH YEAH?
BUT...
I DON'T REALLY REMEMBER THAT MUCH ABOUT MY MOM...

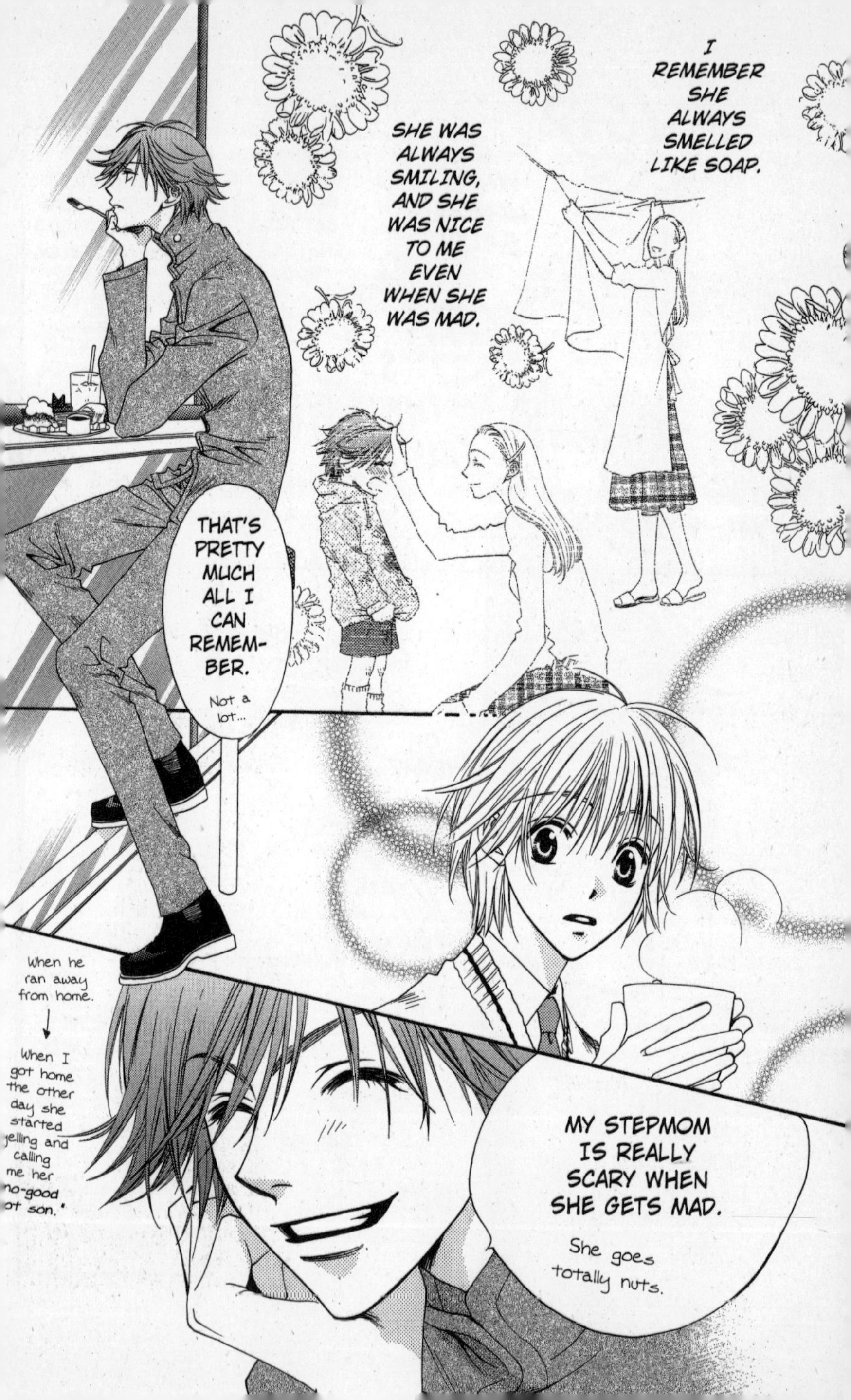

I REMEMBER SHE ALWAYS SMELLED LIKE SOAP.
SHE WAS ALWAYS SMILING, AND SHE WAS NICE TO ME EVEN WHEN SHE WAS MAD.
THAT'S PRETTY MUCH ALL I CAN REMEMBER.
Not a lot...
MY STEPMOM IS REALLY SCARY WHEN SHE GETS MAD.
She goes totally nuts.
When he ran away from home.
↓
When I got home the other day she started yelling and calling me her no-good
ot son."

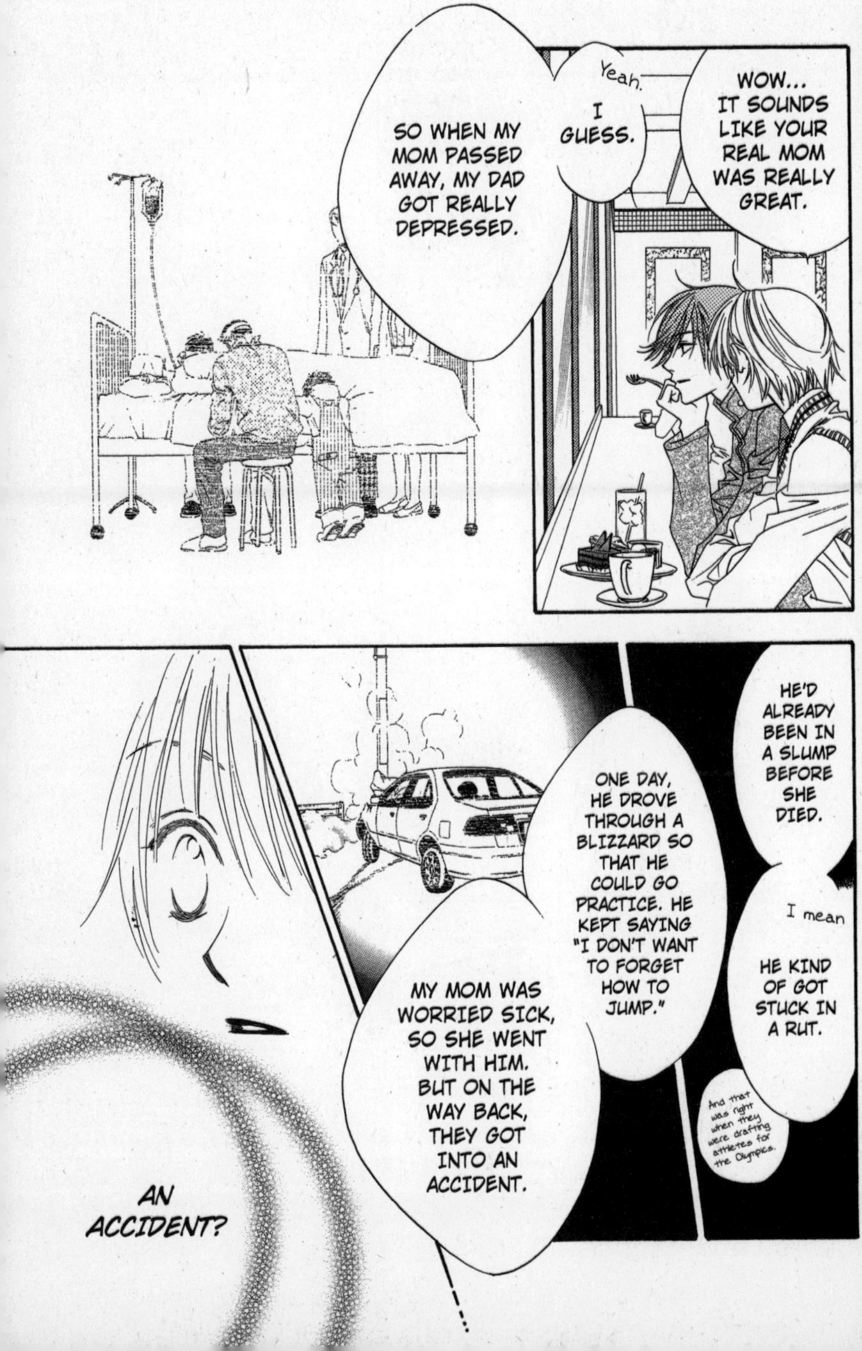
WOW... IT SOUNDS LIKE YOUR REAL MOM WAS REALLY GREAT.
Yeah.
I GUESS.
SO WHEN MY MOM PASSED AWAY, MY DAD GOT REALLY DEPRESSED.
HE'D ALREADY BEEN IN A SLUMP BEFORE SHE DIED.
I mean
HE KIND OF GOT STUCK IN A RUT.
And that was right when they were drafting athletes for the Olympics.
ONE DAY, HE DROVE THROUGH A BLIZZARD SO THAT HE COULD GO PRACTICE. HE KEPT SAYING "I DON'T WANT TO FORGET HOW TO JUMP."
MY MOM WAS WORRIED SICK, SO SHE WENT WITH HIM. BUT ON THE WAY BACK, THEY GOT INTO AN ACCIDENT.
AN ACCIDENT?

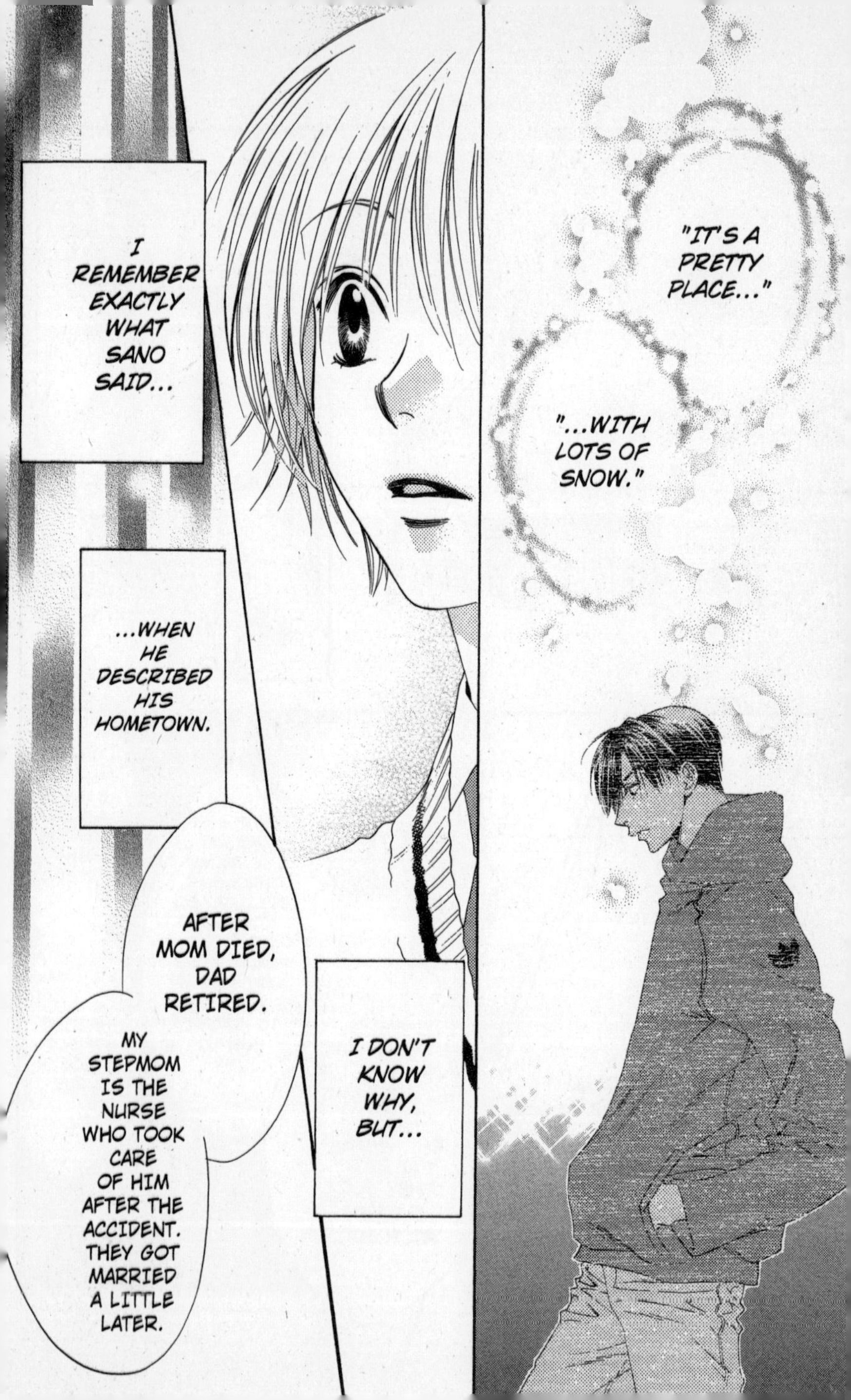
"IT'S A PRETTY PLACE..."
"...WITH LOTS OF SNOW."
I REMEMBER EXACTLY WHAT SANO SAID...
...WHEN HE DESCRIBED HIS HOMETOWN.
AFTER MOM DIED, DAD RETIRED.
MY STEPMOM IS THE NURSE WHO TOOK CARE OF HIM AFTER THE ACCIDENT. THEY GOT MARRIED A LITTLE LATER.
I DON'T KNOW WHY, BUT...

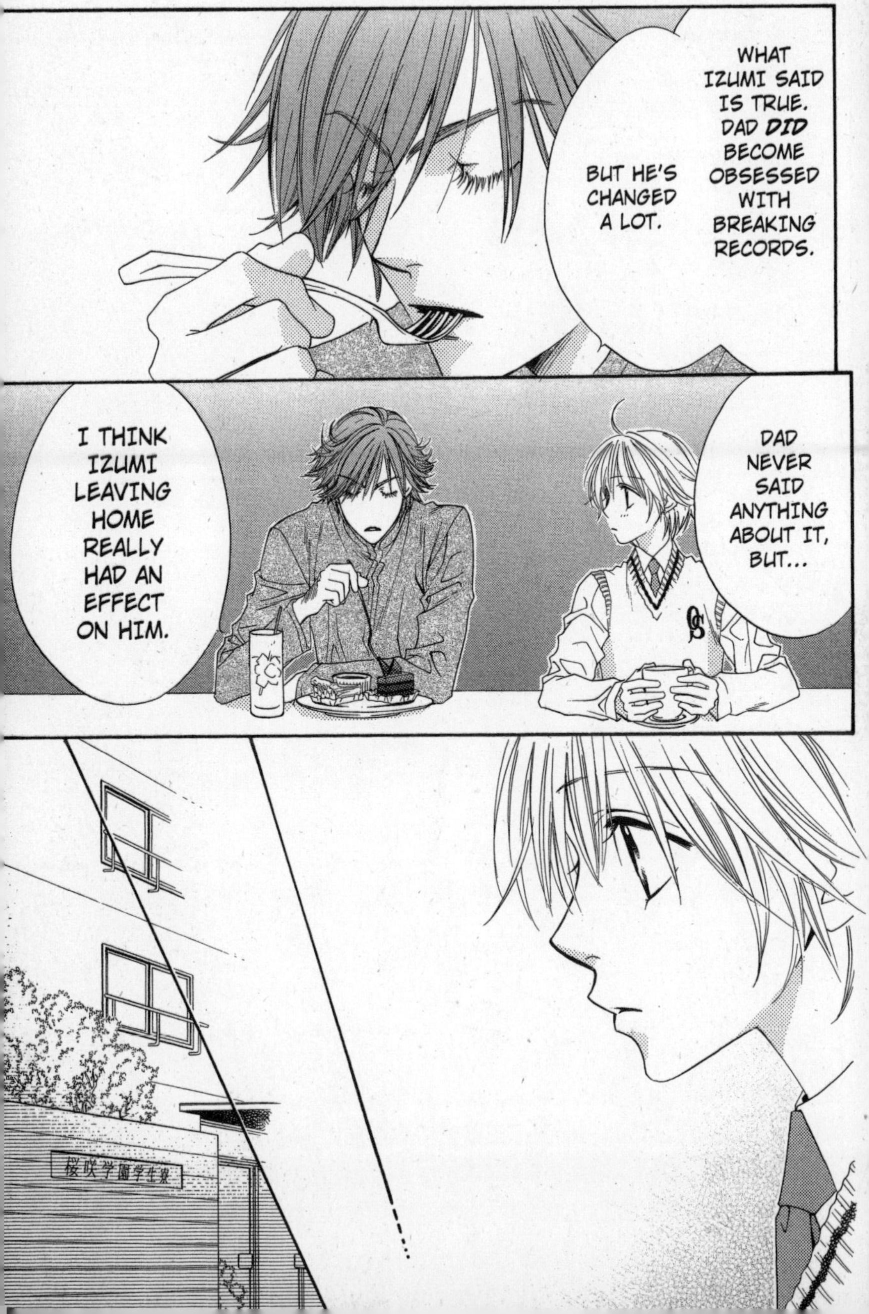
WHAT IZUMI SAID IS TRUE. DAD *DID* BECOME OBSESSED WITH BREAKING RECORDS.
BUT HE'S CHANGED A LOT.
DAD NEVER SAID ANYTHING ABOUT IT, BUT...
I THINK IZUMI LEAVING HOME REALLY HAD AN EFFECT ON HIM.
桜咲学園学生寮

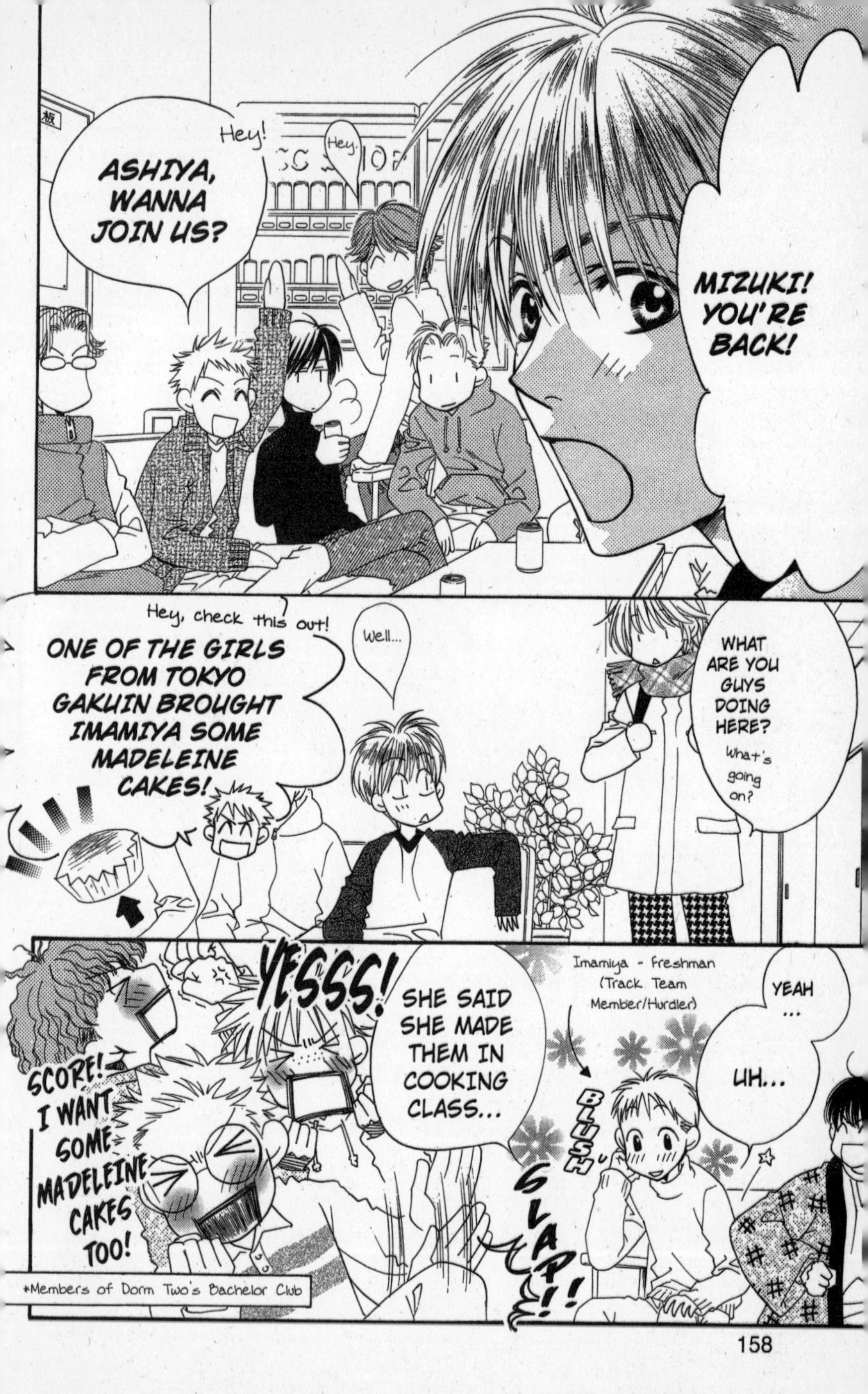
MIZUKI! YOU'RE BACK!
Hey.
Hey!
ASHIYA, WANNA JOIN US?
WHAT ARE YOU GUYS DOING HERE?
What's going on?
Well...
Hey, check this out!
ONE OF THE GIRLS FROM TOKYO GAKUIN BROUGHT IMAMIYA SOME MADELEINE CAKES!
YEAH...
UH...
Imamiya - Freshman (Track Team Member/Hurdler)
SHE SAID SHE MADE THEM IN COOKING CLASS...
BLUSH
YESSS!
SLAP!!
SCORE! I WANT SOME MADELEINE CAKES TOO!
*Members of Dorm Two's Bachelor Club

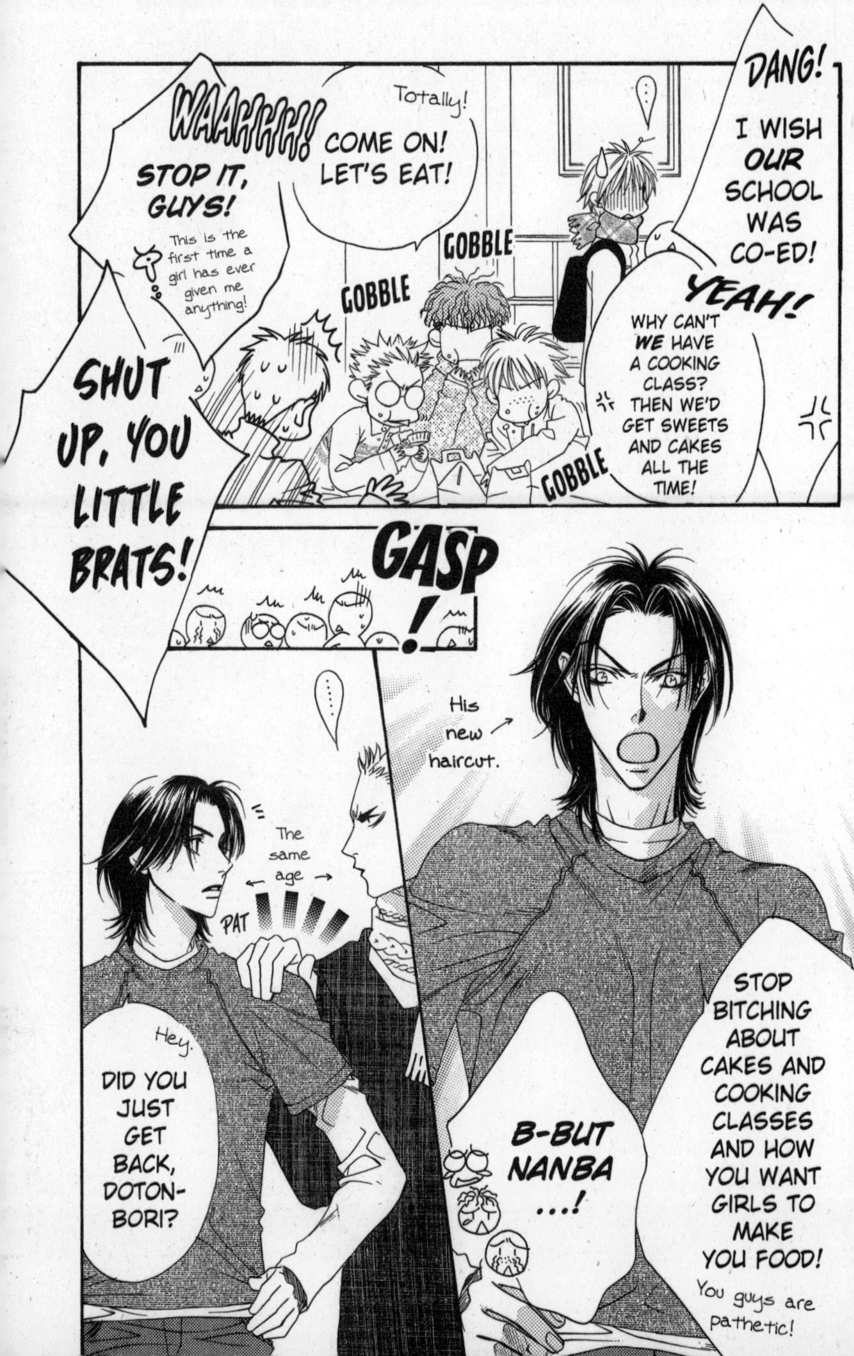
DANG!
I WISH OUR SCHOOL WAS CO-ED!
YEAH!
WHY CAN'T WE HAVE A COOKING CLASS? THEN WE'D GET SWEETS AND CAKES ALL THE TIME!
GOBBLE
GOBBLE
GOBBLE
Totally!
COME ON! LET'S EAT!
WAAHHH!
STOP IT, GUYS!
This is the first time a girl has ever given me anything!
SHUT UP, YOU LITTLE BRATS!
GASP!
His new haircut.
STOP BITCHING ABOUT CAKES AND COOKING CLASSES AND HOW YOU WANT GIRLS TO MAKE YOU FOOD!
You guys are pathetic!
B-BUT NANBA...!
The same age
PAT
Hey.
DID YOU JUST GET BACK, DOTON-BORI?

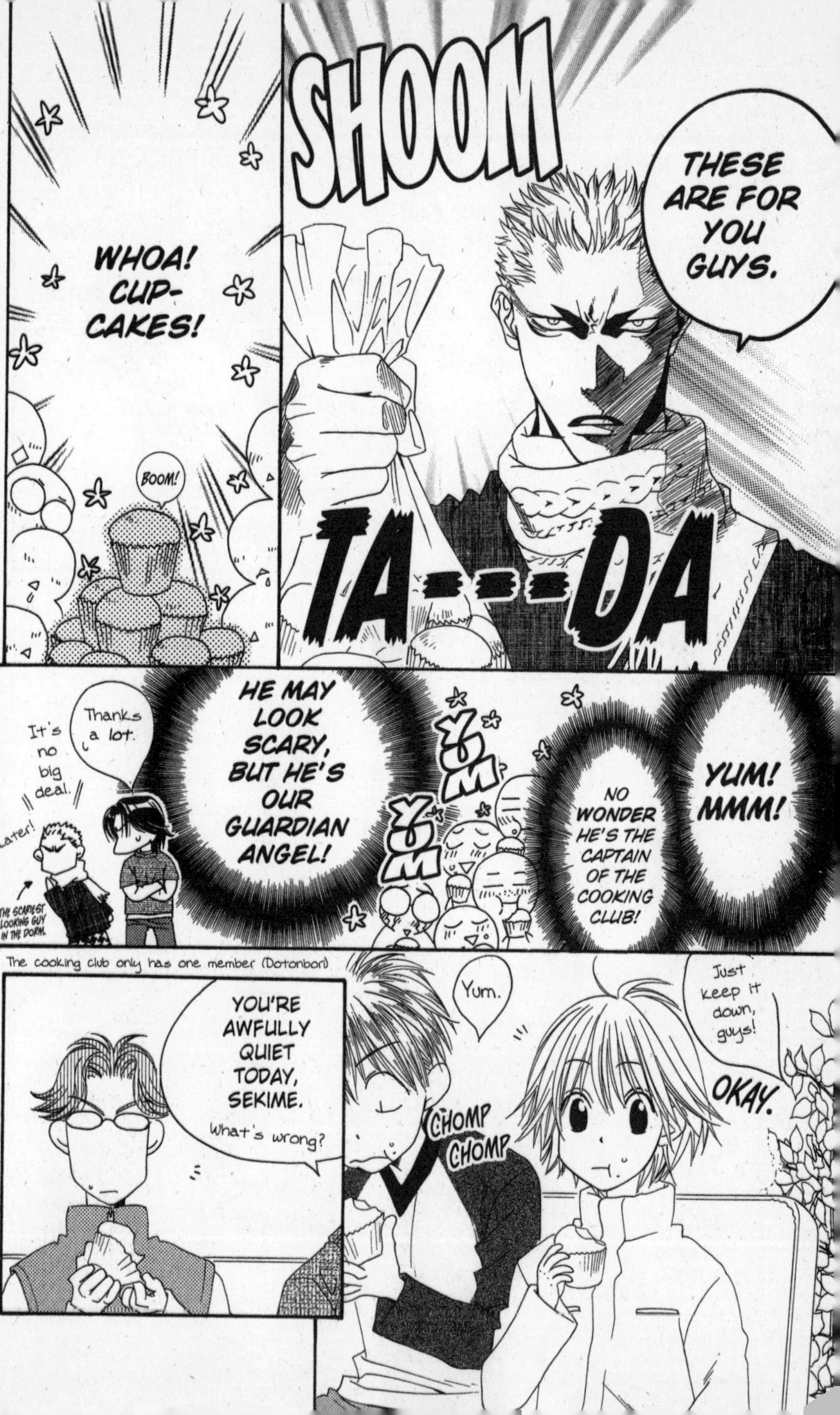
SHOOM
THESE ARE FOR YOU GUYS.
TA---DA
WHOA! CUP-CAKES!
BOOM!
YUM! MMM!
NO WONDER HE'S THE CAPTAIN OF THE COOKING CLUB!
YUM
YUM
HE MAY LOOK SCARY, BUT HE'S OUR GUARDIAN ANGEL!
Thanks a lot.
It's no big deal.
Later!
THE SCARIEST LOOKING GUY IN THE DORM.
The cooking club only has one member (Dotonbori)
Just keep it down, guys!
OKAY.
Yum.
CHOMP CHOMP
YOU'RE AWFULLY QUIET TODAY, SEKIME.
What's wrong?

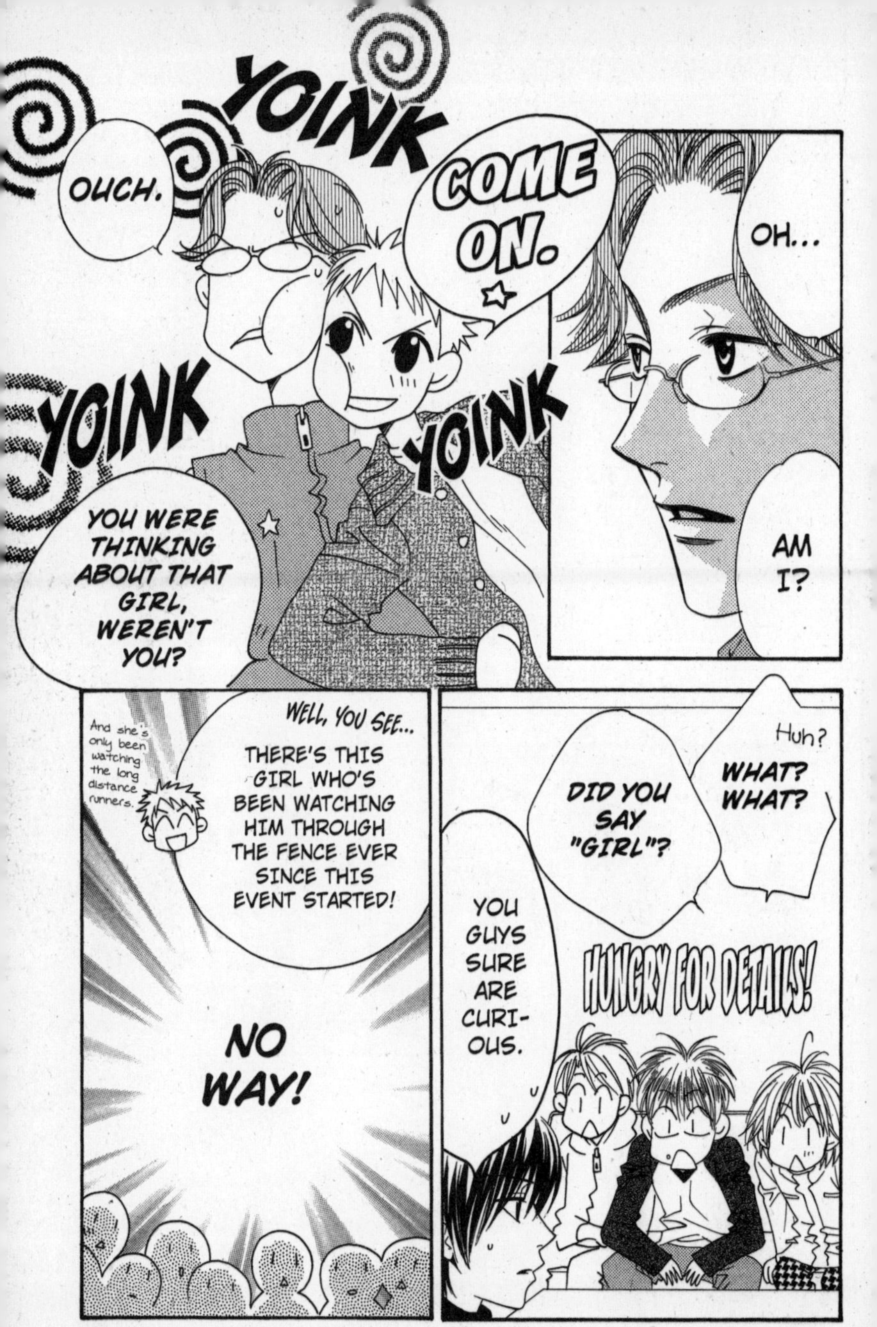
OH...
AM I?
YOINK
OUCH.
COME ON.
YOINK
YOINK
YOU WERE THINKING ABOUT THAT GIRL, WEREN'T YOU?
Huh?
WHAT? WHAT?
DID YOU SAY "GIRL"?
YOU GUYS SURE ARE CURI-OUS.
HUNGRY FOR DETAILS!
WELL, YOU SEE... THERE'S THIS GIRL WHO'S BEEN WATCHING HIM THROUGH THE FENCE EVER SINCE THIS EVENT STARTED!
And she's only been watching the long distance runners.
NO WAY!

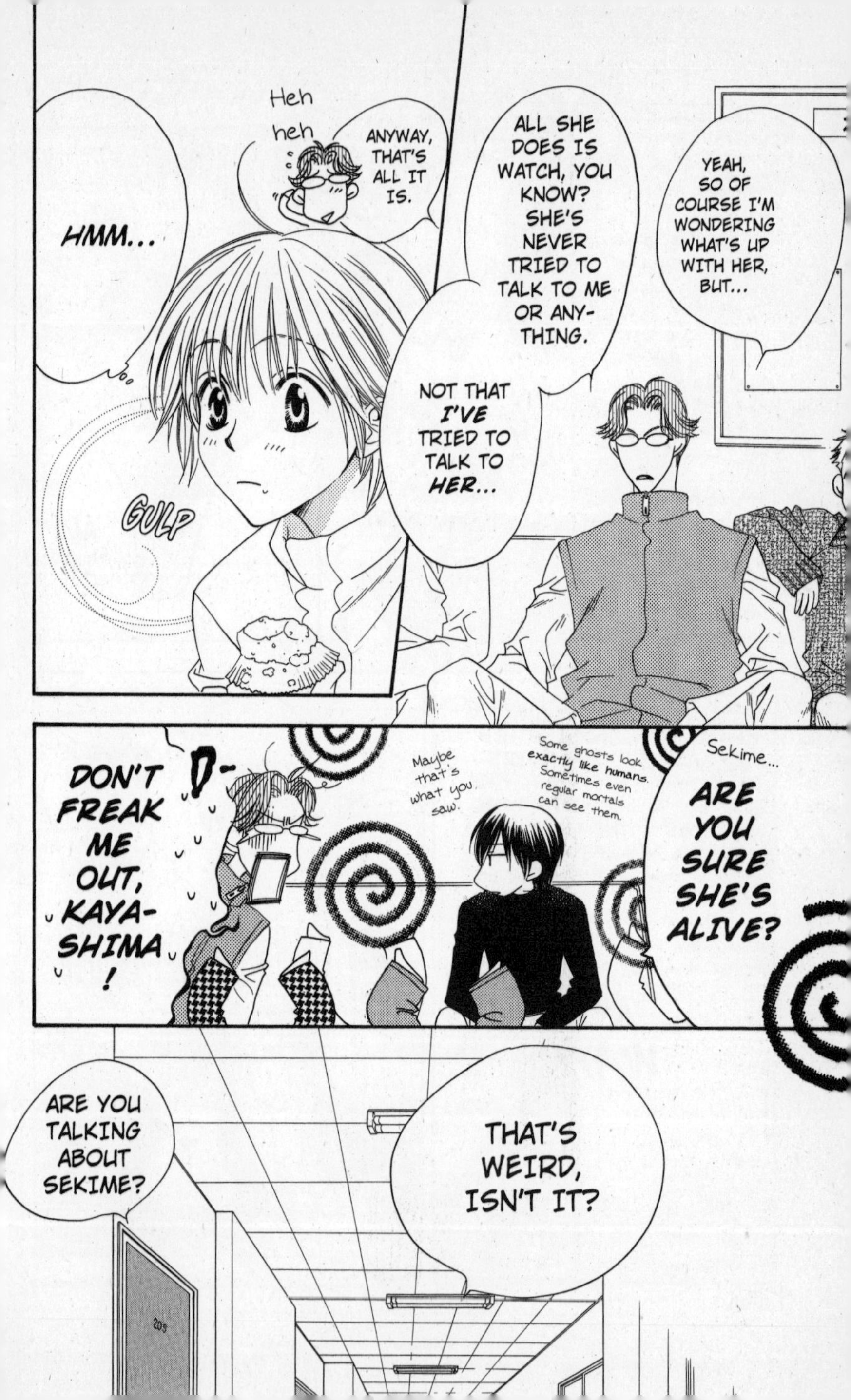
YEAH, SO OF COURSE I'M WONDERING WHAT'S UP WITH HER, BUT...
ALL SHE DOES IS WATCH, YOU KNOW? SHE'S NEVER TRIED TO TALK TO ME OR ANY-THING.
NOT THAT *I'VE* TRIED TO TALK TO *HER*...
ANYWAY, THAT'S ALL IT IS.
Heh heh
HMM...
GULP
Sekime...
ARE YOU SURE SHE'S ALIVE?
Some ghosts look exactly like humans. Sometimes even regular mortals can see them.
Maybe that's what you saw.
D-
DON'T FREAK ME OUT, KAYA-SHIMA!
THAT'S WEIRD, ISN'T IT?
ARE YOU TALKING ABOUT SEKIME?

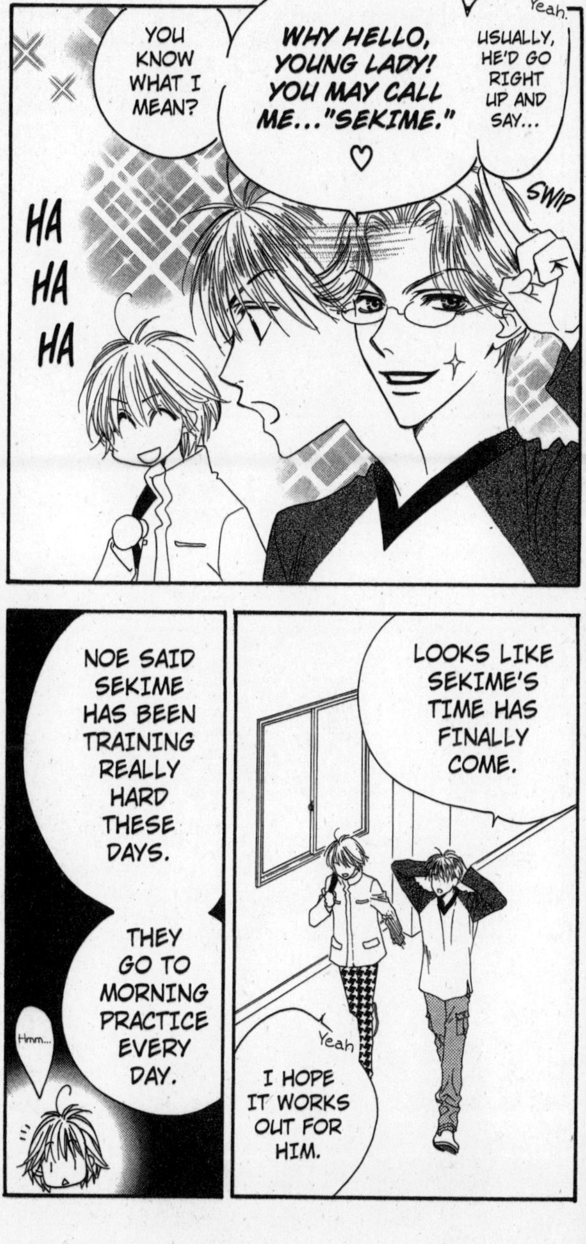
Yeah.
USUALLY, HE'D GO RIGHT UP AND SAY...
WHY HELLO, YOUNG LADY! YOU MAY CALL ME..."SEKIME." ♡
SWIP
YOU KNOW WHAT I MEAN?
HA HA HA
LOOKS LIKE SEKIME'S TIME HAS FINALLY COME.
Yeah
I HOPE IT WORKS OUT FOR HIM.
NOE SAID SEKIME HAS BEEN TRAINING REALLY HARD THESE DAYS.
THEY GO TO MORNING PRACTICE EVERY DAY.
Hmm...

✿

"SEE YOU LATER!"

Ever since Shin's first appearance a lot of people have been saying, "Shin is so cute!♥" That makes me so happy. (I wasn't expecting him to be so popular...) A lot of people sent in letters asking "Who is Shin's character modeled after?" but I didn't use anybody as a model. Most of the **Hana-Kimi** characters (there are a few exceptions) aren't really modeled after anybody. Sometimes, I'd pick a model after I created the character. I'd be like, "Hmm...this character kind of reminds me of this actor." But that really only happened early on, and my image of a character can change pretty rapidly. ☆

Okay, see you in book 13!

✿ February, 2002

Mizuki used to look like Kumiko Endo, but now they look nothing alike.

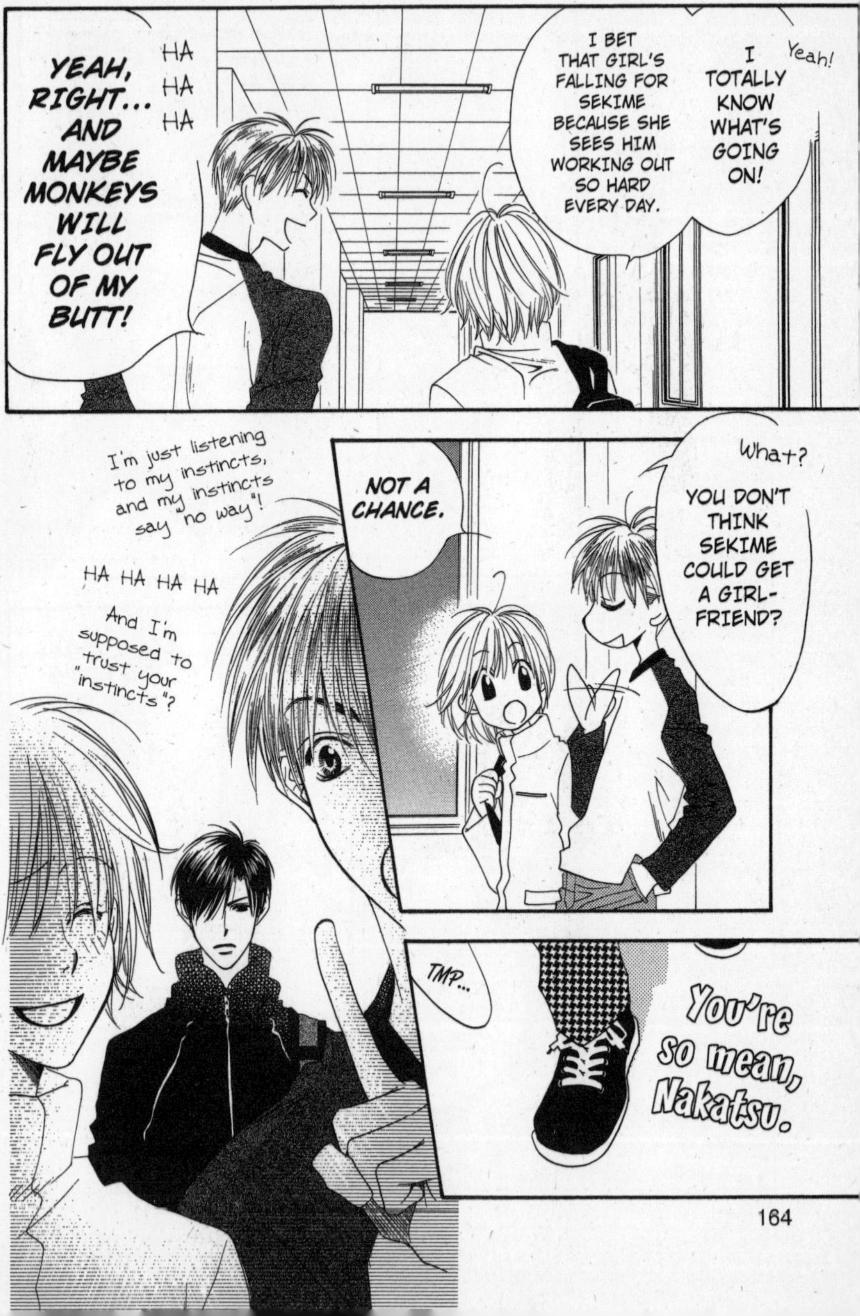
Yeah!
I TOTALLY KNOW WHAT'S GOING ON!
I BET THAT GIRL'S FALLING FOR SEKIME BECAUSE SHE SEES HIM WORKING OUT SO HARD EVERY DAY.
HA HA HA
YEAH, RIGHT... AND MAYBE MONKEYS WILL FLY OUT OF MY BUTT!
What?
YOU DON'T THINK SEKIME COULD GET A GIRL-FRIEND?
NOT A CHANCE.
TMP...
You're so mean, Nakatsu.
I'm just listening to my instincts, and my instincts say "no way"!
HA HA HA HA
And I'm supposed to trust your "instincts"?

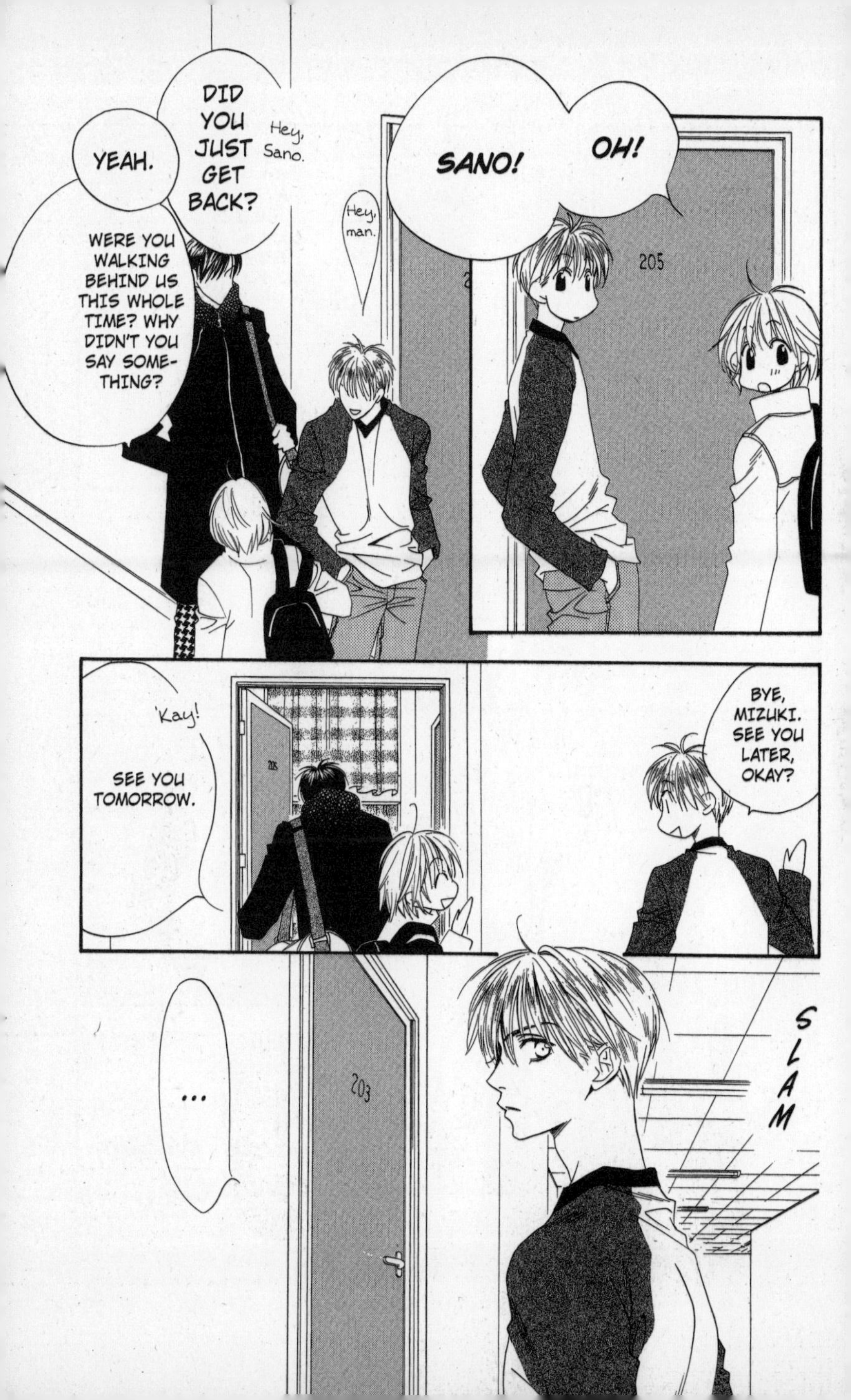
OH!
SANO!
Hey, man.
Hey, Sano.
DID YOU JUST GET BACK?
YEAH.
WERE YOU WALKING BEHIND US THIS WHOLE TIME? WHY DIDN'T YOU SAY SOME-THING?
BYE, MIZUKI. SEE YOU LATER, OKAY?
'Kay!
SEE YOU TOMORROW.
SLAM
...
205
203

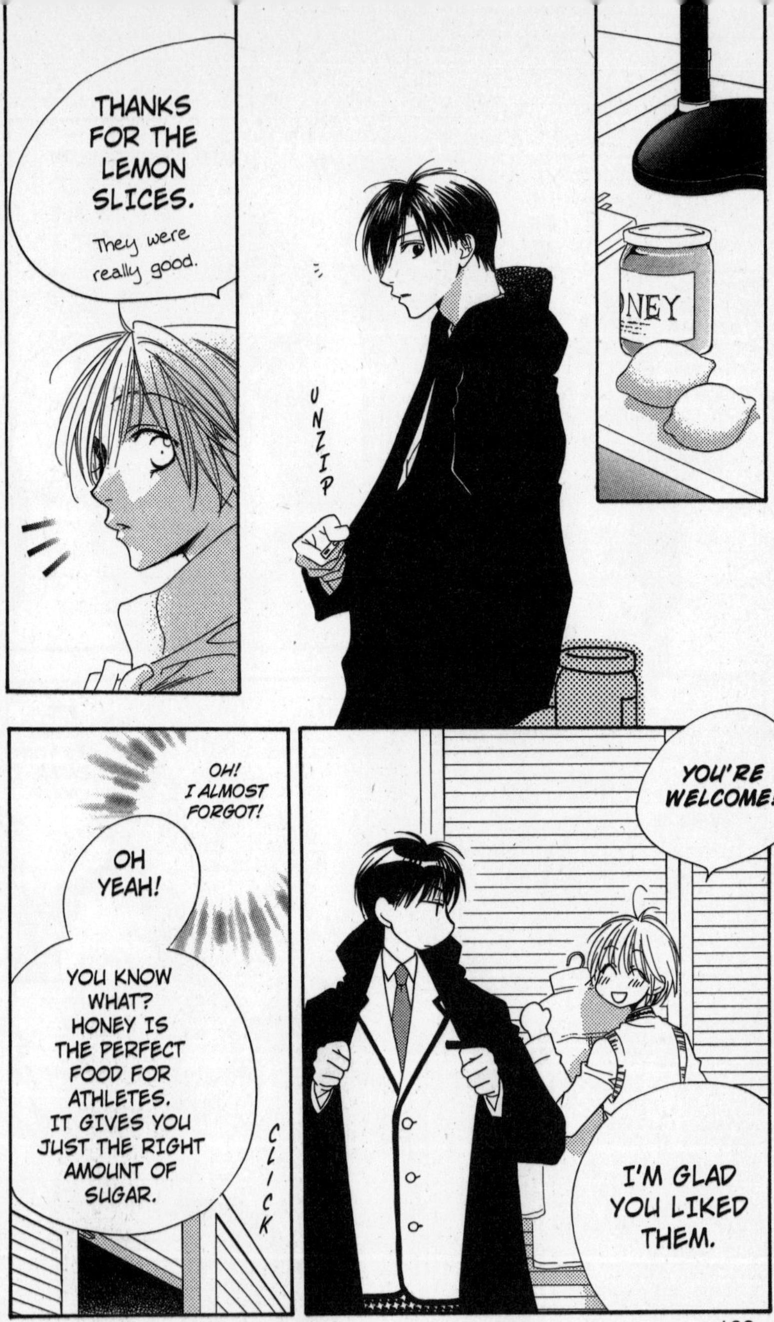
UNZIP
THANKS FOR THE LEMON SLICES.
They were really good.
YOU'RE WELCOME!
I'M GLAD YOU LIKED THEM.
CLICK
OH! I ALMOST FORGOT!
OH YEAH!
YOU KNOW WHAT? HONEY IS THE PERFECT FOOD FOR ATHLETES. IT GIVES YOU JUST THE RIGHT AMOUNT OF SUGAR.

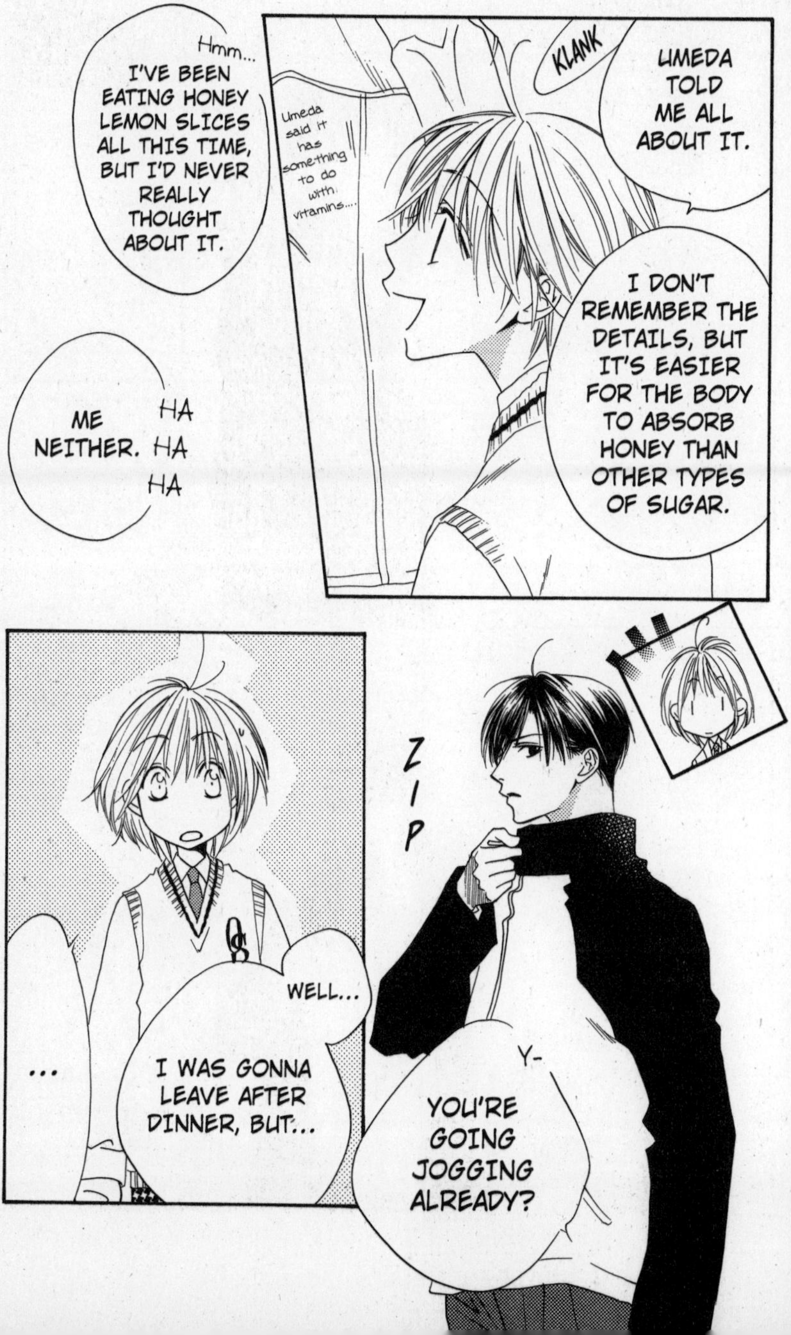
KLANK
UMEDA TOLD ME ALL ABOUT IT.
Umeda said it has something to do with vitamins...
I DON'T REMEMBER THE DETAILS, BUT IT'S EASIER FOR THE BODY TO ABSORB HONEY THAN OTHER TYPES OF SUGAR.
Hmm... I'VE BEEN EATING HONEY LEMON SLICES ALL THIS TIME, BUT I'D NEVER REALLY THOUGHT ABOUT IT.
ME NEITHER. HA HA HA
ZIP
Y- YOU'RE GOING JOGGING ALREADY?
WELL...
I WAS GONNA LEAVE AFTER DINNER, BUT...
...

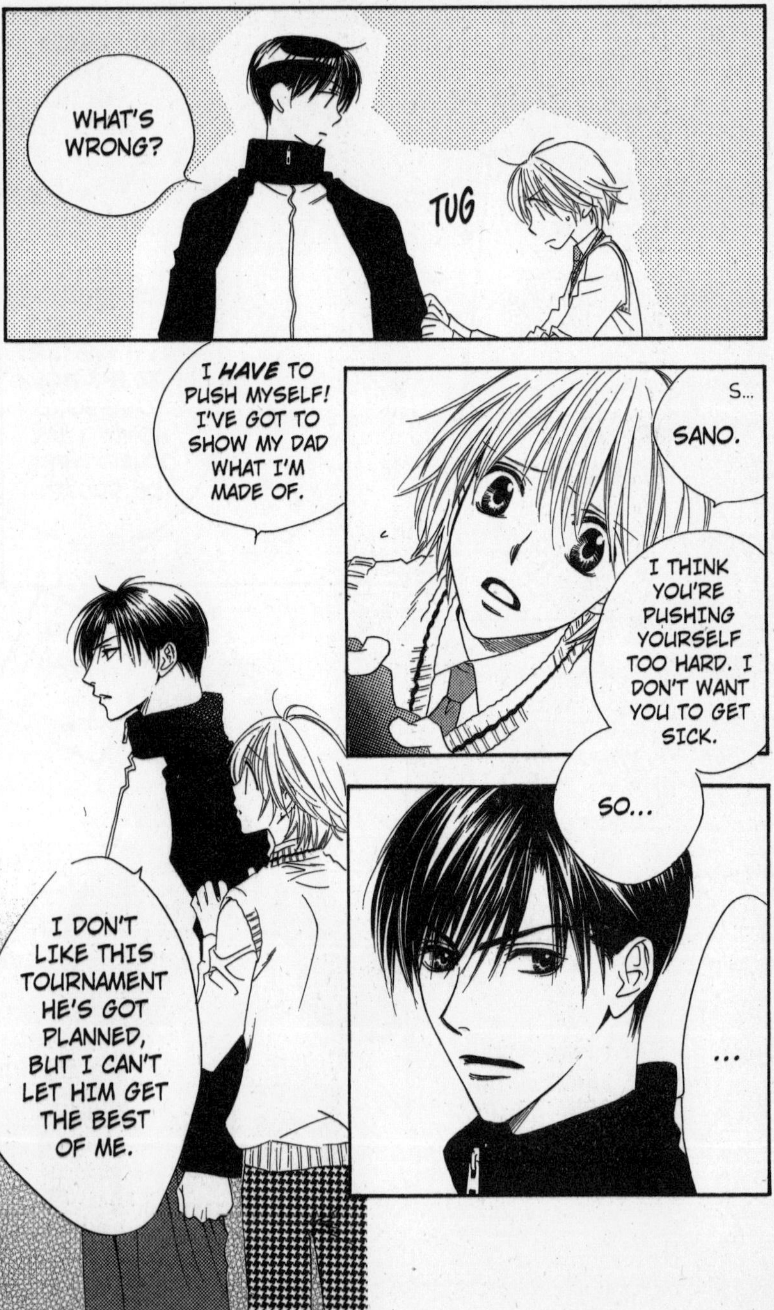
WHAT'S WRONG?
TUG
S...
SANO.
I THINK YOU'RE PUSHING YOURSELF TOO HARD. I DON'T WANT YOU TO GET SICK.
SO...
...
I HAVE TO PUSH MYSELF! I'VE GOT TO SHOW MY DAD WHAT I'M MADE OF.
I DON'T LIKE THIS TOURNAMENT HE'S GOT PLANNED, BUT I CAN'T LET HIM GET THE BEST OF ME.

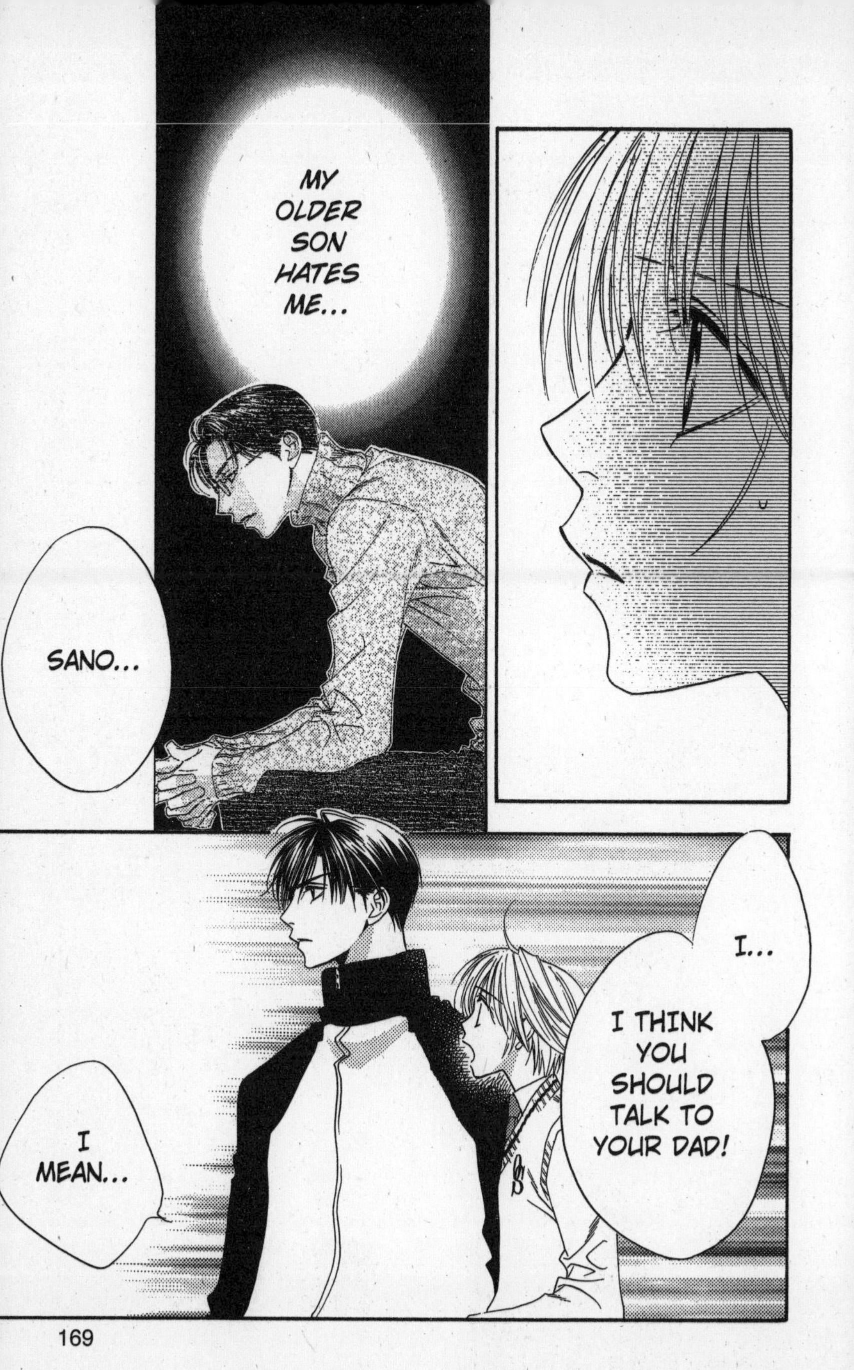
MY OLDER SON HATES ME...
SANO...
I...
I THINK YOU SHOULD TALK TO YOUR DAD!
I MEAN...

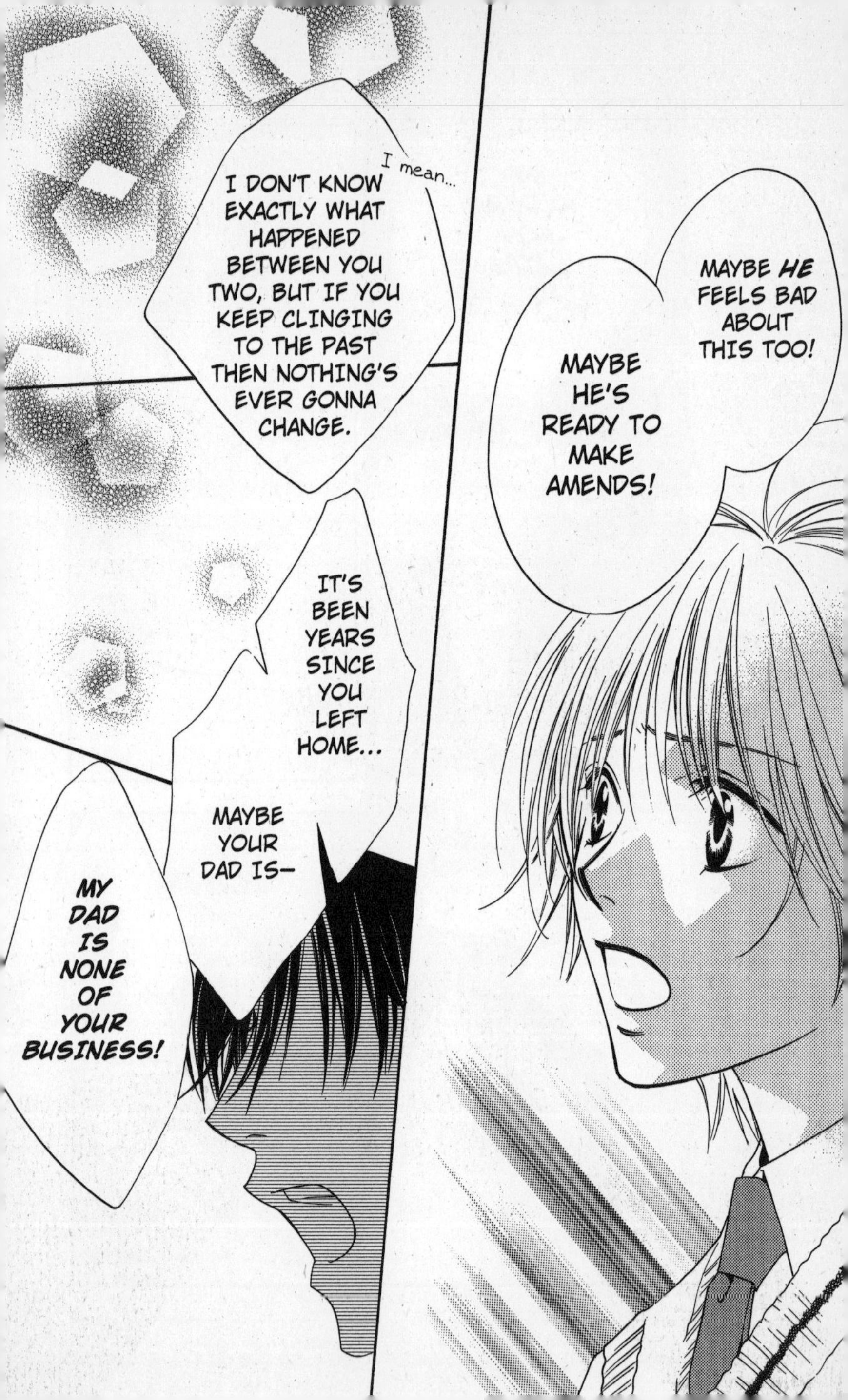
MAYBE *HE* FEELS BAD ABOUT THIS TOO!
MAYBE HE'S READY TO MAKE AMENDS!
I mean...
I DON'T KNOW EXACTLY WHAT HAPPENED BETWEEN YOU TWO, BUT IF YOU KEEP CLINGING TO THE PAST THEN NOTHING'S EVER GONNA CHANGE.
IT'S BEEN YEARS SINCE YOU LEFT HOME...
MAYBE YOUR DAD IS—
MY DAD IS NONE OF YOUR BUSINESS!

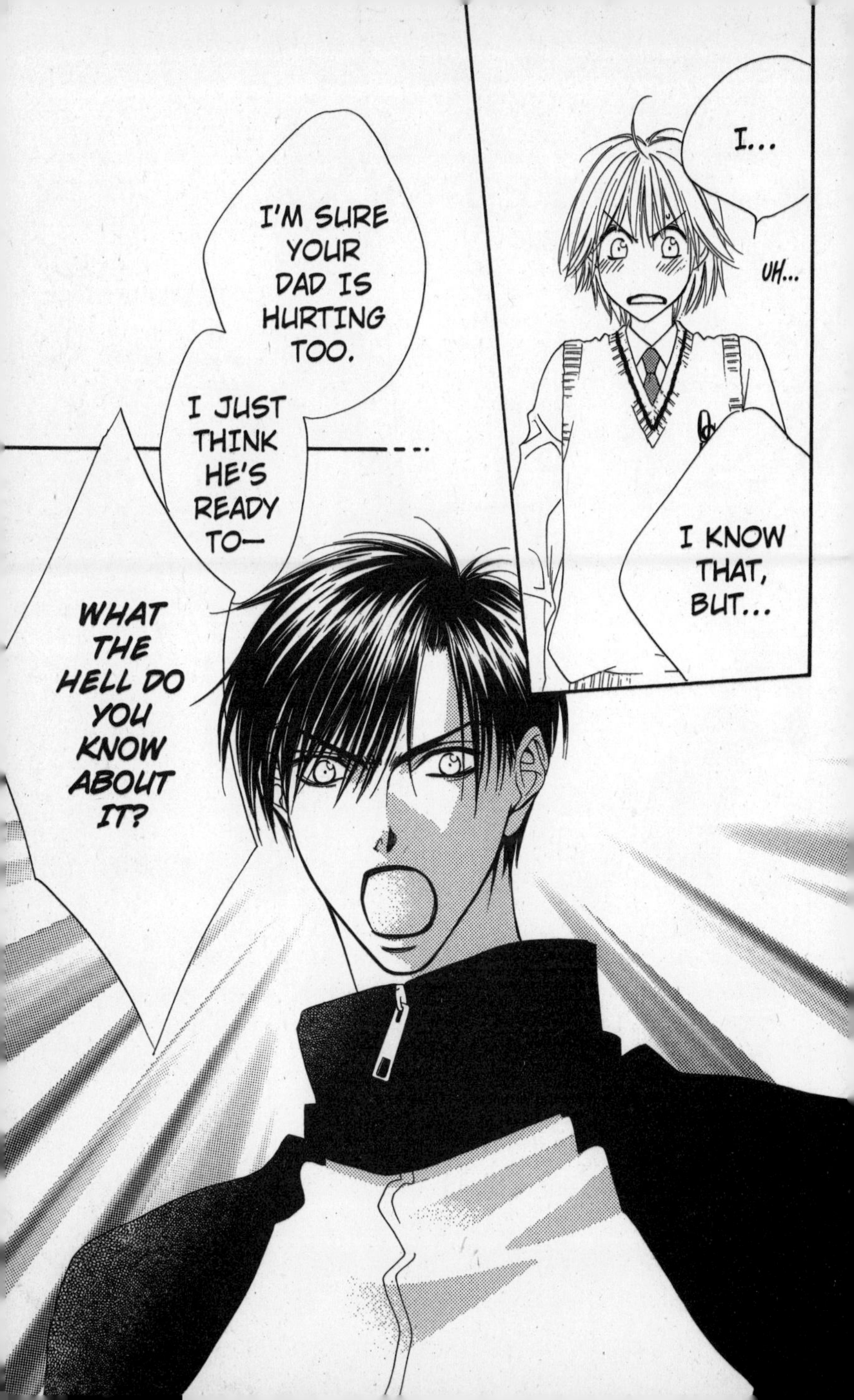
I...
UH...
I KNOW THAT, BUT...
I'M SURE YOUR DAD IS HURTING TOO.
I JUST THINK HE'S READY TO—
WHAT THE HELL DO YOU KNOW ABOUT IT?

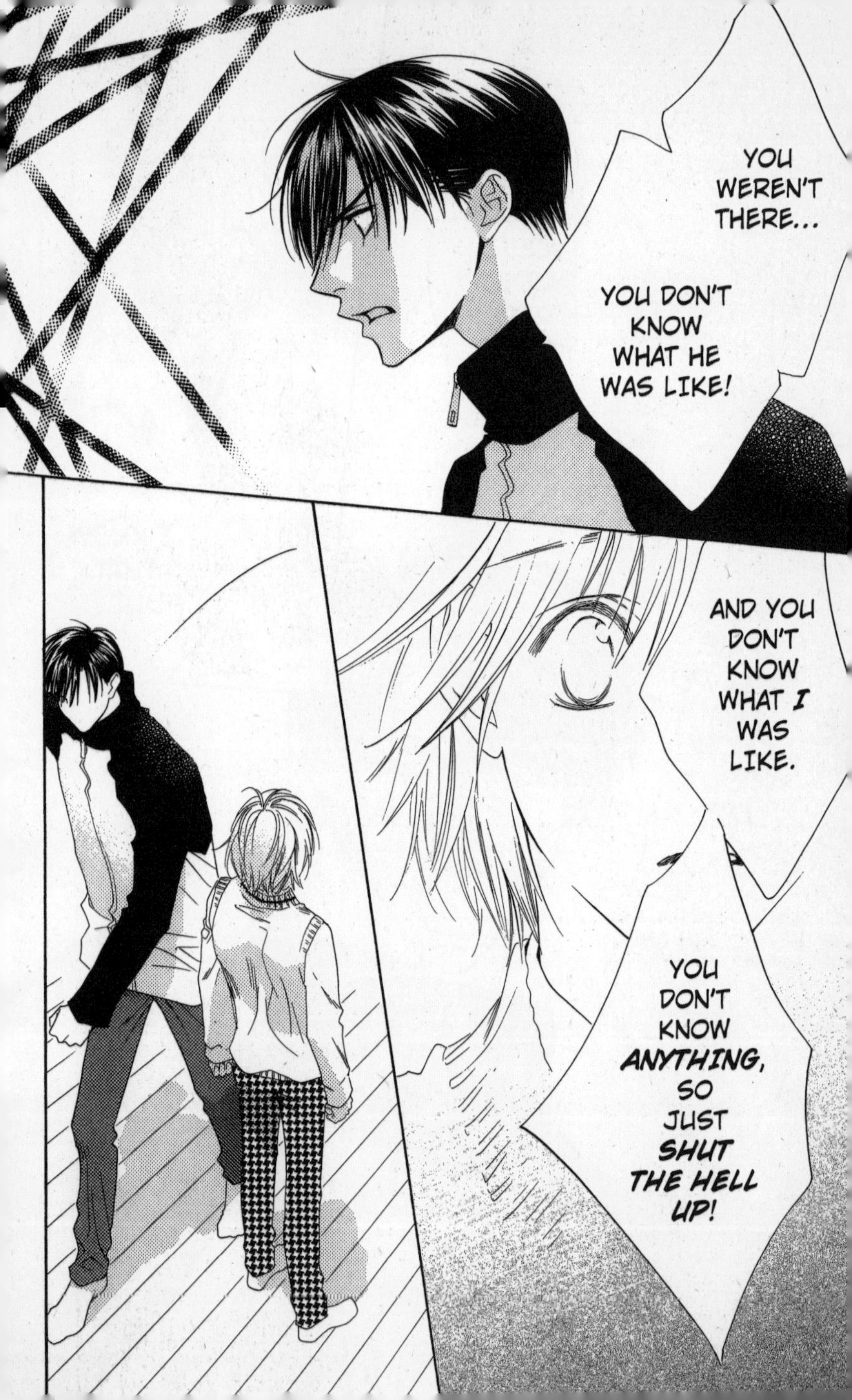
YOU WEREN'T THERE...
YOU DON'T KNOW WHAT HE WAS LIKE!
AND YOU DON'T KNOW WHAT *I* WAS LIKE.
YOU DON'T KNOW ***ANYTHING***, SO JUST ***SHUT THE HELL UP!***

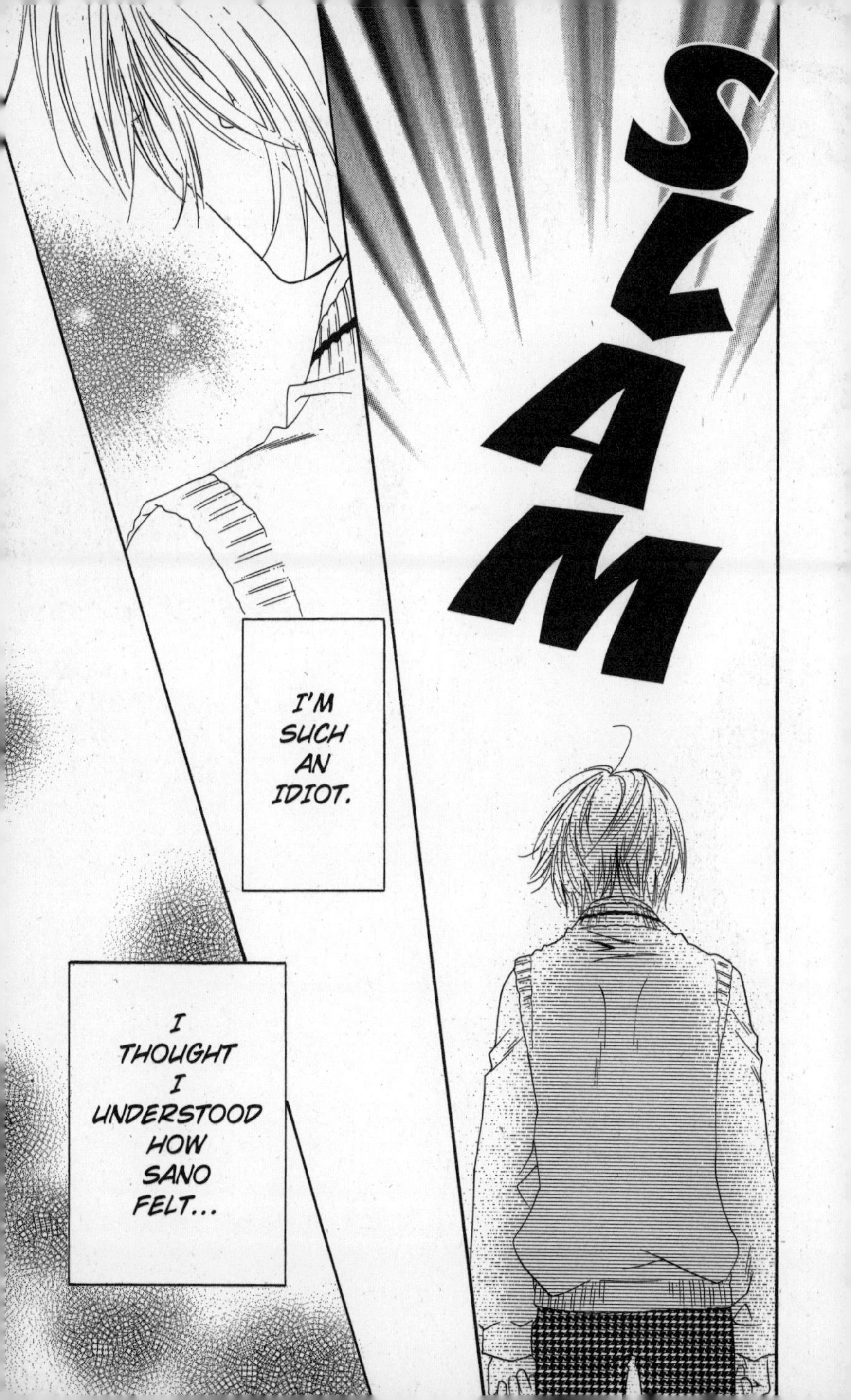
SLAM
I'M SUCH AN IDIOT.
I THOUGHT I UNDERSTOOD HOW SANO FELT...

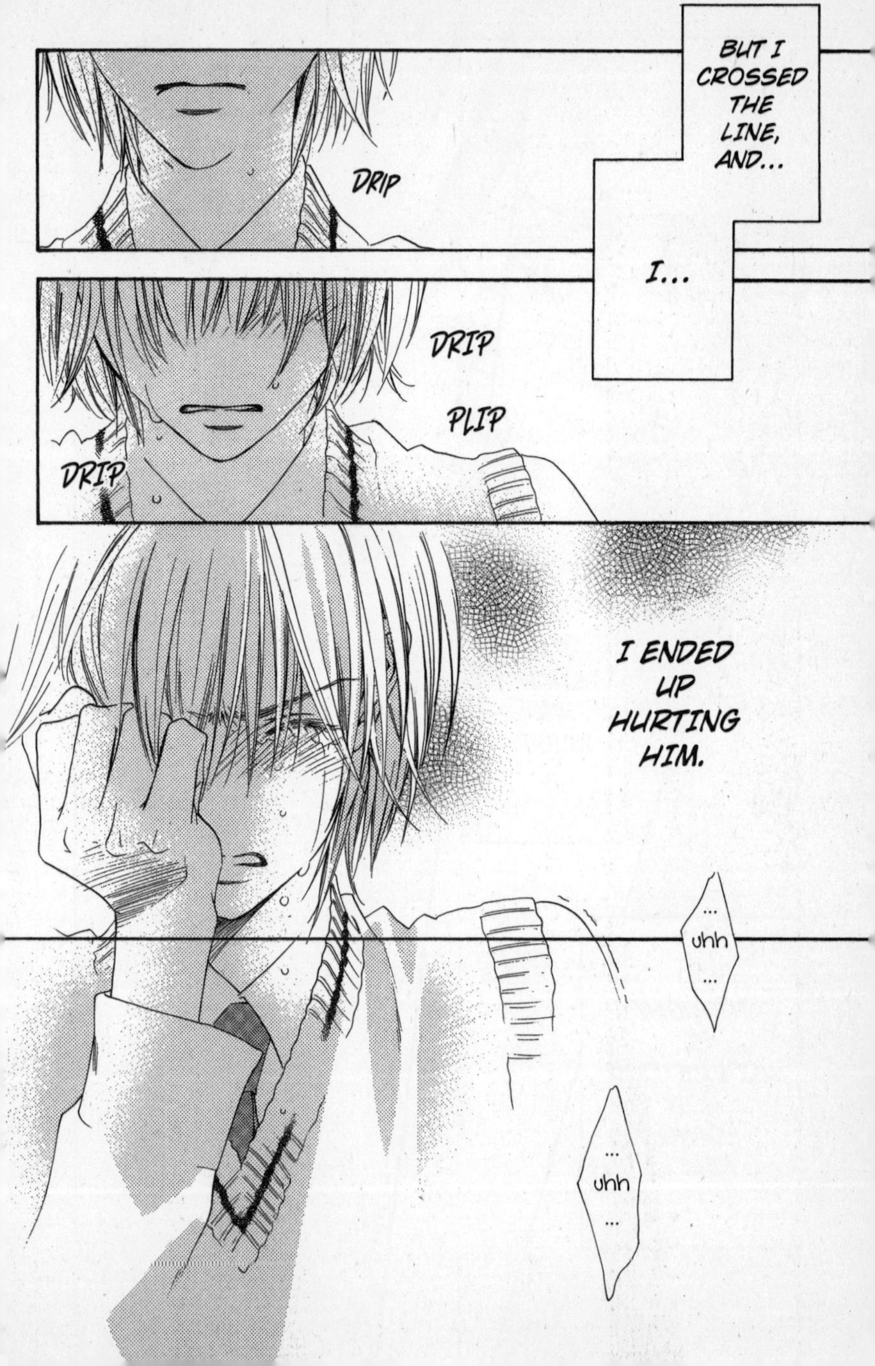
BUT I CROSSED THE LINE, AND...
DRIP
I...
DRIP
PLIP
DRIP
I ENDED UP HURTING HIM.
... uhh ...
... uhh ...

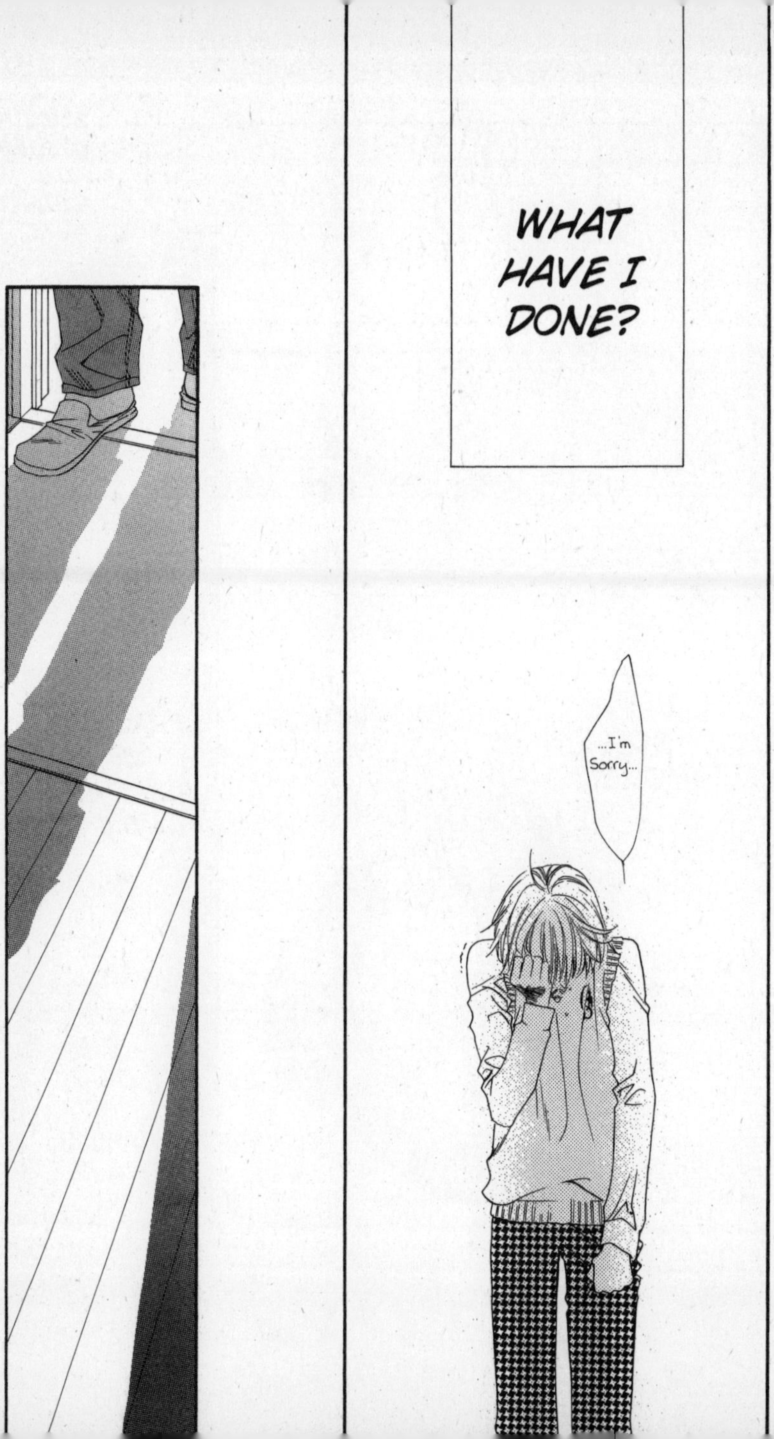
WHAT HAVE I DONE?
...I'm Sorry...

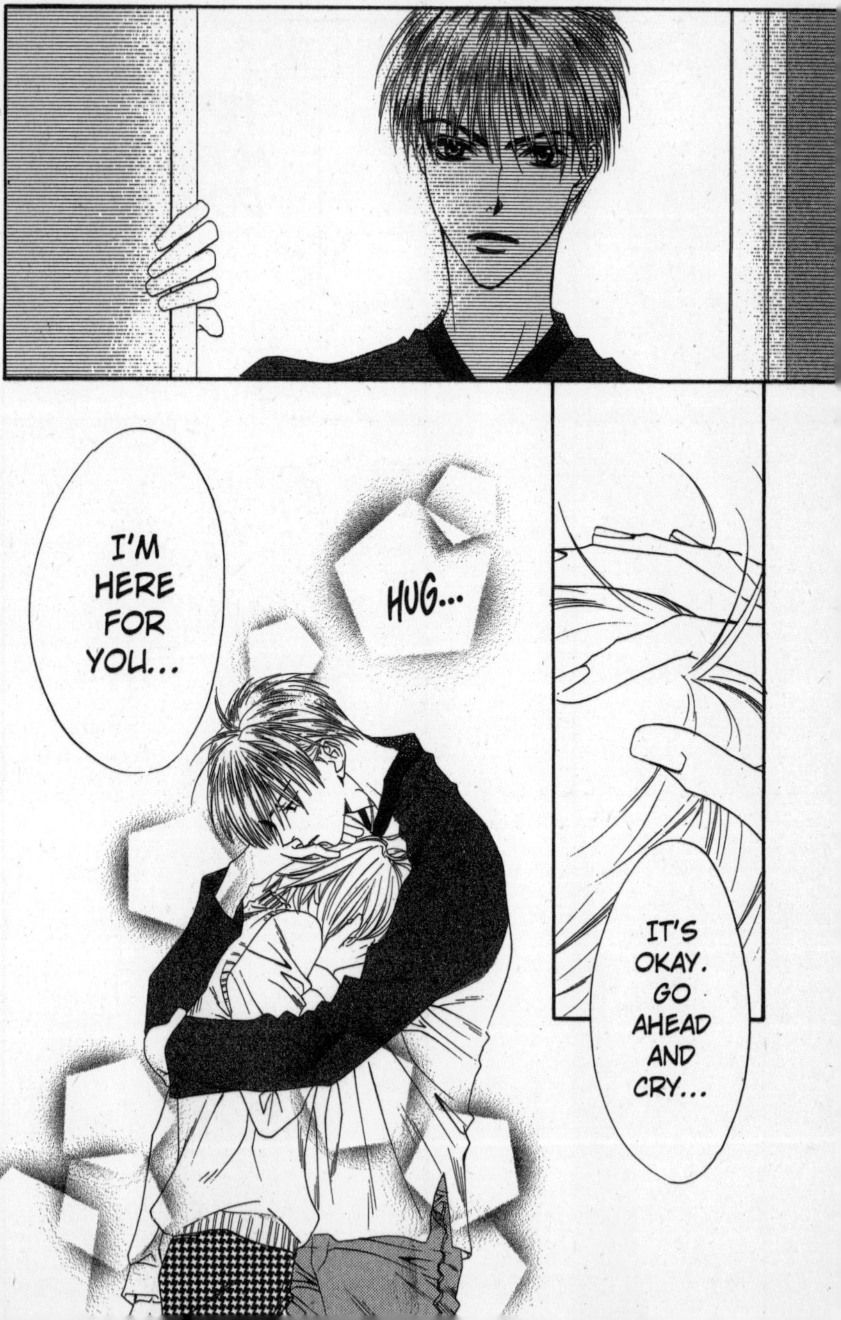
IT'S OKAY. GO AHEAD AND CRY...
HUG...
I'M HERE FOR YOU...

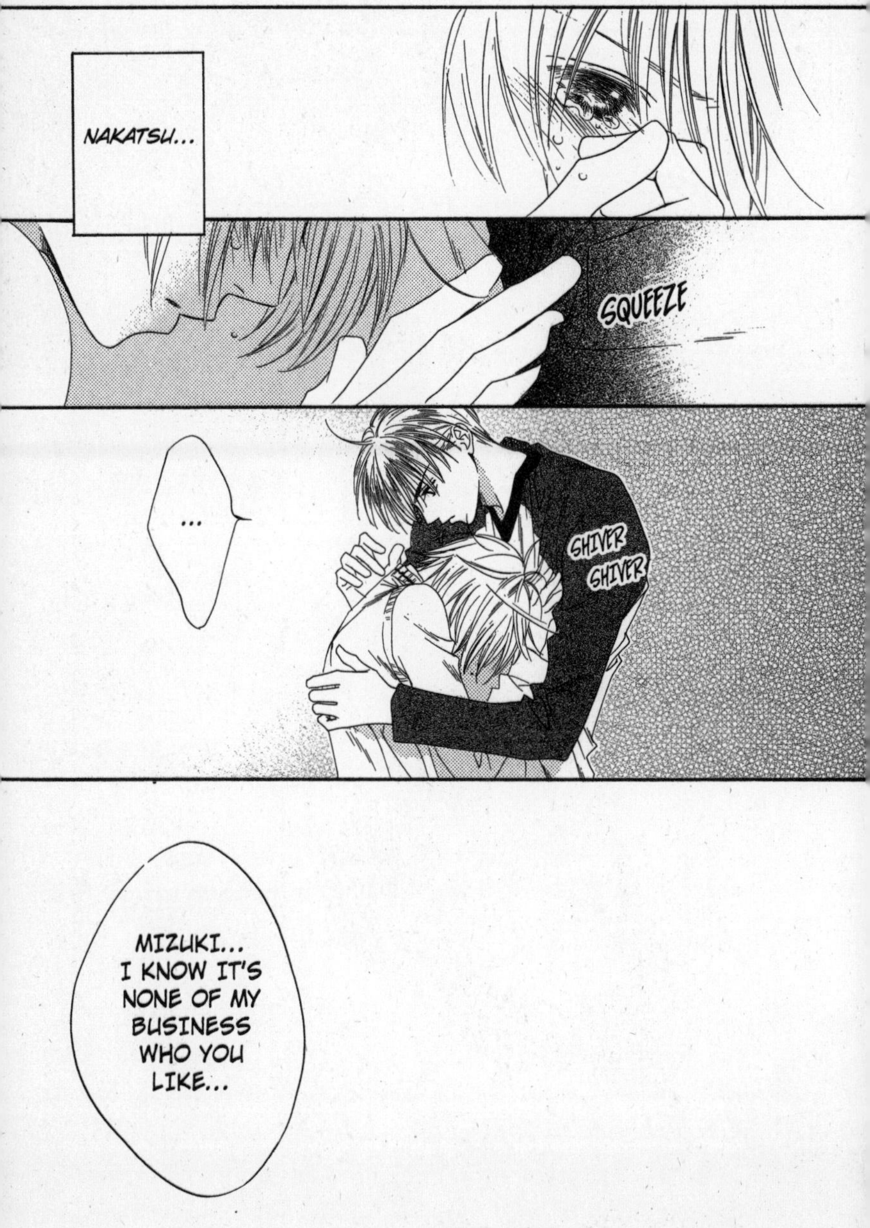
NAKATSU...
SQUEEZE
...
SHIVER SHIVER
MIZUKI... I KNOW IT'S NONE OF MY BUSINESS WHO YOU LIKE...

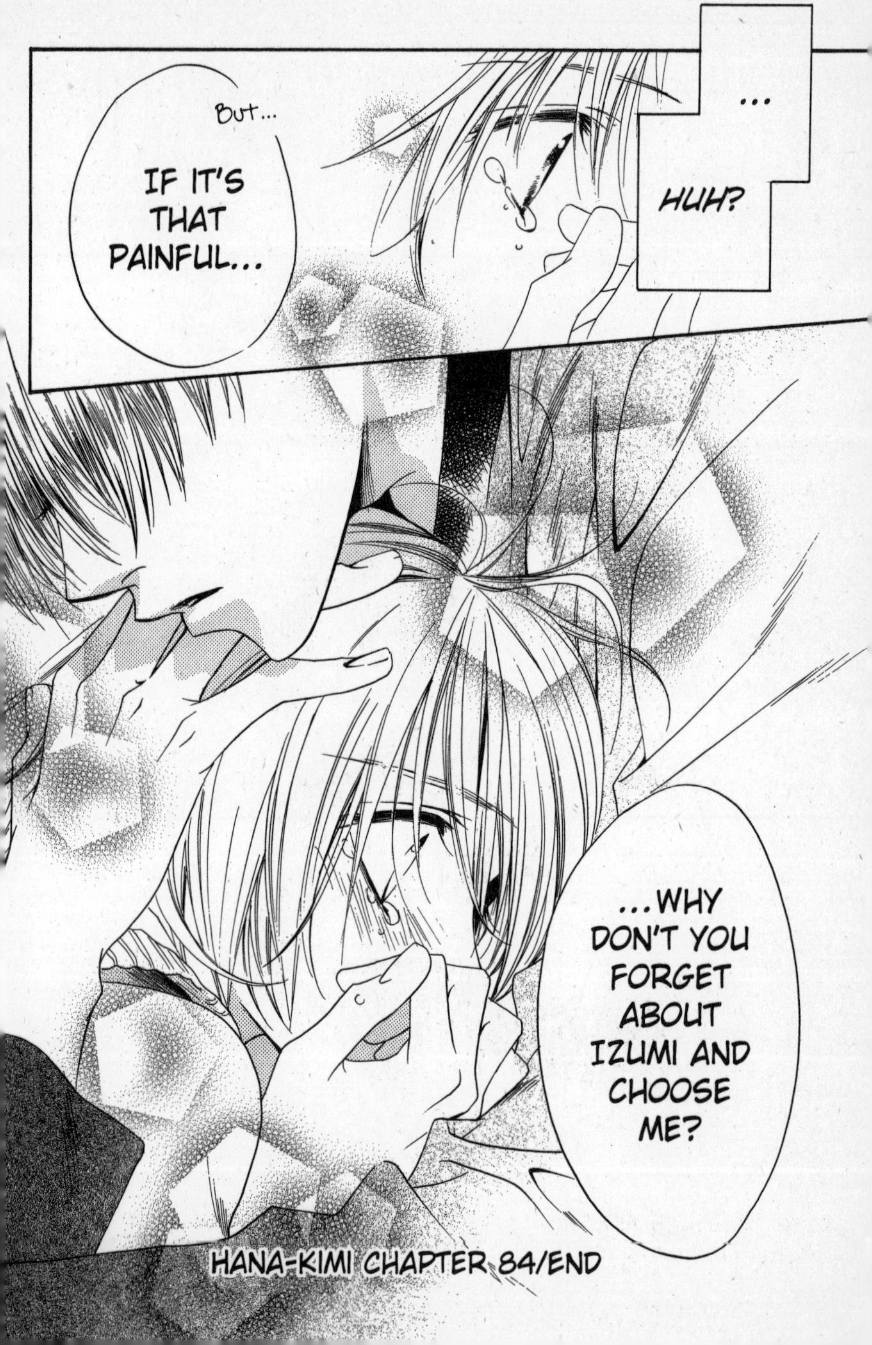
...
HUH?
But...
IF IT'S THAT PAINFUL...
...WHY DON'T YOU FORGET ABOUT IZUMI AND CHOOSE ME?
HANA-KIMI CHAPTER 84/END

← *BONUS PAGE*

BONUS PAGE FUN WITH SANO AND HIS FATHER

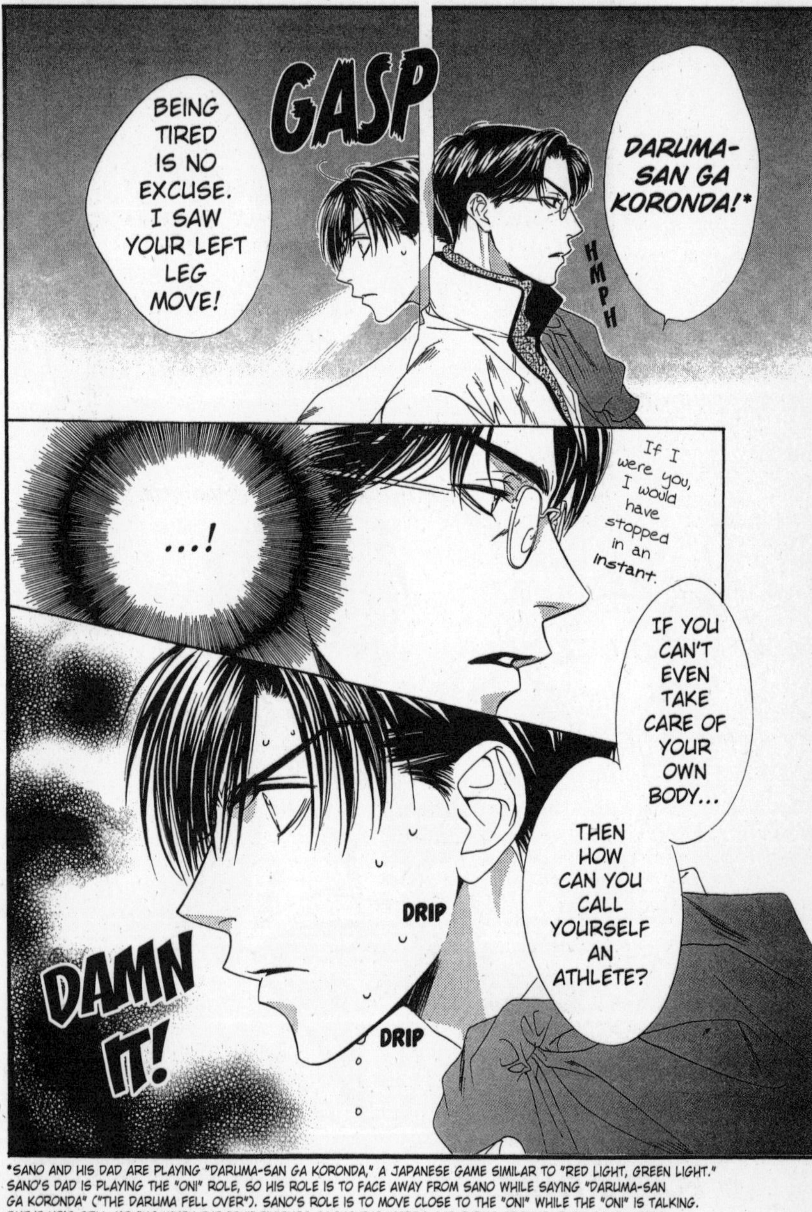
DARUMA-SAN GA KORONDA!*
HMPH
GASP
BEING TIRED IS NO EXCUSE. I SAW YOUR LEFT LEG MOVE!
If I were you, I would have stopped in an instant.
...!
IF YOU CAN'T EVEN TAKE CARE OF YOUR OWN BODY...
THEN HOW CAN YOU CALL YOURSELF AN ATHLETE?
DRIP
DRIP
DAMN IT!

Sorry, Sano fans...I just couldn't resist.

*SANO AND HIS DAD ARE PLAYING "DARUMA-SAN GA KORONDA," A JAPANESE GAME SIMILAR TO "RED LIGHT, GREEN LIGHT." SANO'S DAD IS PLAYING THE "ONI" ROLE, SO HIS ROLE IS TO FACE AWAY FROM SANO WHILE SAYING "DARUMA-SAN GA KORONDA" ("THE DARUMA FELL OVER"). SANO'S ROLE IS TO MOVE CLOSE TO THE "ONI" WHILE THE "ONI" IS TALKING. BUT IF HE'S STILL MOVING WHEN THE "ONI" FINISHES SAYING THE WORDS AND TURNS AROUND, THEN SANO LOSES.

ABOUT THE AUTHOR

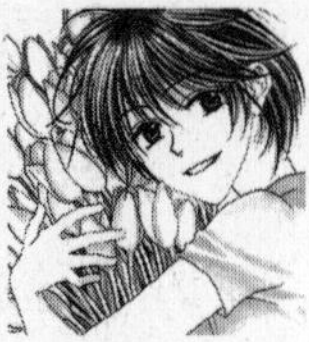

Hisaya Nakajo's manga series **Hanazakari no Kimitachi he** (For You in Full Blossom, casually known as **Hana-Kimi**) has been a hit since it first appeared in 1997 in the shôjo manga magazine **Hana to Yume** (Flowers and Dreams). In Japan, two **Hana-Kimi** art books and several "drama CDs" have been released. Her other manga series include **Missing Piece** (2 volumes) and **Yumemiru Happa** (The Dreaming Leaf, 1 volume).

Hisaya Nakajo's website:
www.wild-vanilla.com

IN THE NEXT VOLUME ...

Will the stress of the competition drive Mizuki away from Sano...or drive Nakatsu to desperation? Meanwhile, a schoolwide treasure hunt turns into a grudge match between Kayashima and his self-proclaimed rival, Modoru the ***onmyôji,*** a traditional Japanese occultist. Will psychic powers or black magic prevail? But Modoru has something else on his side: ***the power of cuteness!***

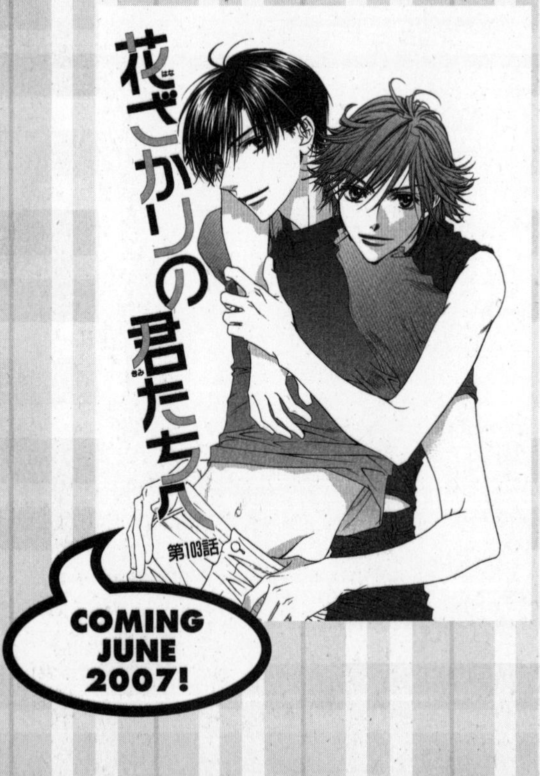
花ざかりの君たちへ
第103話
COMING JUNE 2007!

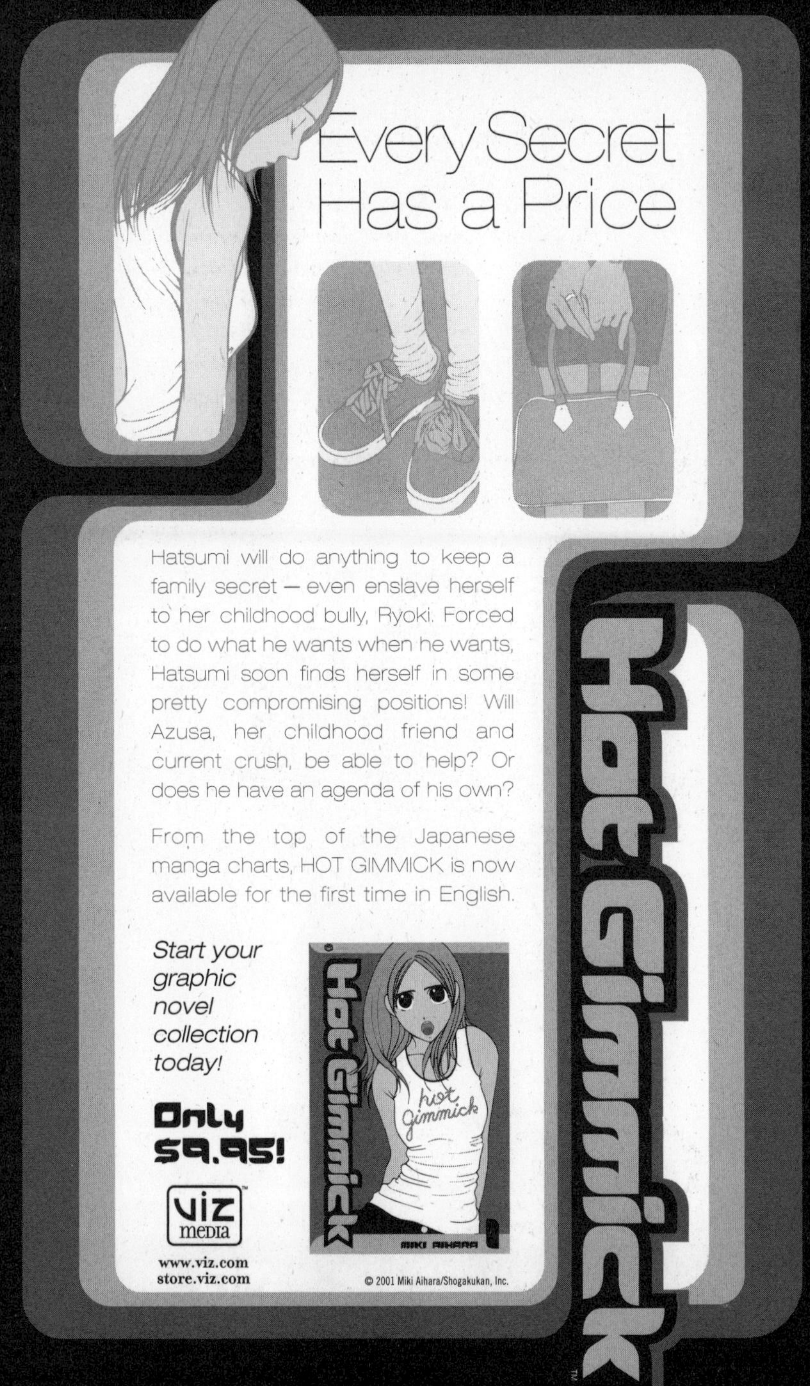
Every Secret Has a Price
Hatsumi will do anything to keep a family secret — even enslave herself to her childhood bully, Ryoki. Forced to do what he wants when he wants, Hatsumi soon finds herself in some pretty compromising positions! Will Azusa, her childhood friend and current crush, be able to help? Or does he have an agenda of his own?
From the top of the Japanese manga charts, HOT GIMMICK is now available for the first time in English.
Start your graphic novel collection today!
Only $9.95!
Hot Gimmick
hot gimmick
Miki Aihara
viz media
www.viz.com
store.viz.com
© 2001 Miki Aihara/Shogakukan, Inc.
Hot Gimmick™

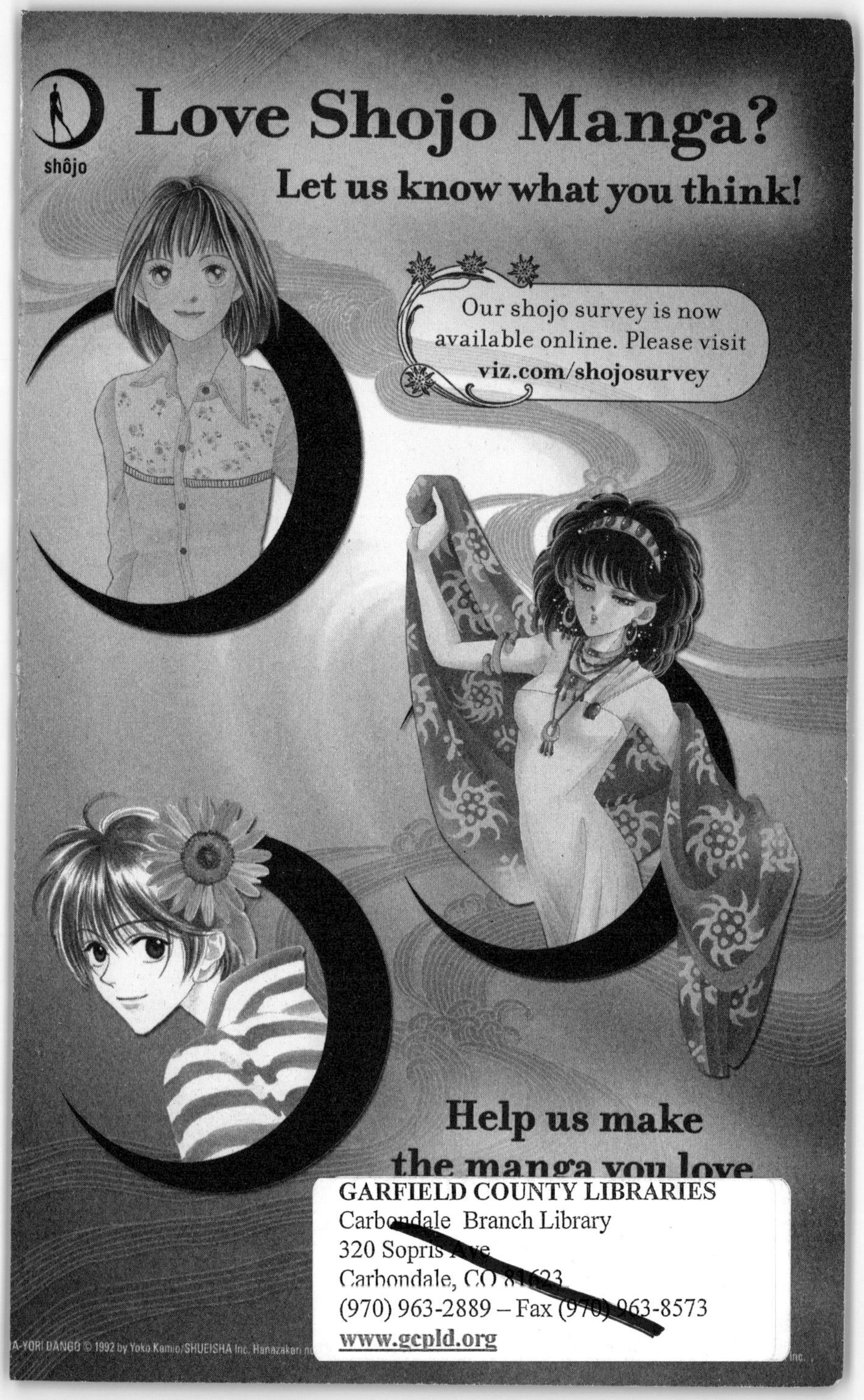
shôjo
Love Shojo Manga?
Let us know what you think!
Our shojo survey is now available online. Please visit viz.com/shojosurvey
Help us make the manga you love
A-YORI DANGO © 1992 by Yoko Kamio/SHUEISHA Inc. Hanazakari no
Inc.